# The Dynamics of Democratization

# The Dynamics
# of Democratization

*Dictatorship, Development,
and Diffusion*

Edited by Nathan J. Brown

The Johns Hopkins University Press
*Baltimore*

The Johns Hopkins University Press
2715 North Charles Street
Baltimore, Maryland 21218-4363
www.press.jhu.edu

Library of Congress Cataloging-in-Publication Data

The dynamics of democratization : dictatorship, development,
and diffusion / edited by Nathan J. Brown.
      p. cm.
   Includes bibliographical references and index.
   ISBN-13: 978-1-4214-0008-2 (hardcover : alk. paper)
   ISBN-13: 978-1-4214-0009-9 (pbk. : alk. paper)
   ISBN-10: 1-4214-0008-1 (hardcover : alk. paper)
   ISBN-10: 1-4214-0009-X (pbk. : alk. paper)
      1. Democratization—Developing countries.   2. Democracy—
Developing countries.   3. Dictatorship—Developing
countries.   4. Economic development—Political aspects—
Developing countries.   5. Developing countries—Politics and
government.   I. Brown, Nathan J.
   JF60.D96 2011
   321.809172'4—dc22      2010043800

A catalog record for this book is available from the British
Library.

*Special discounts are available for bulk purchases of this book. For
more information, please contact Special Sales at 410-516-6936 or
specialsales@press.jhu.edu.*

The Johns Hopkins University Press uses environmentally
friendly book materials, including recycled text paper that is
composed of at least 30 percent post-consumer waste,
whenever possible. All of our book papers are acid-free, and our
jackets and covers are printed on paper with recycled content.

# Contents

# Preface

The authors of the essays in this volume do two things at the same time: reflect on what we know about democratization and suggest where scholars should be directing their attention in the future. By casting their arguments broadly and writing in more general terms, they also hope to inform readers who are not full-time scholars of democratization.

The idea for the book grew out of a series of conferences and events held over the past three years at George Washington University's Elliott School of International Affairs on the "Future of Democracy." Scholars, students, activists, and policy makers met and presented, deliberated, and argued over democracy and the global prospects for democratization. We noted over time that while interest in the subject was deep on many levels—public interest, policy debates, and academic research—the insights gained from decades of scholarship did not always present themselves in accessible form. There was clearly sufficient research and wisdom to justify a stocktaking project rather than just a simple review of academic literature, which would make for dry and unrewarding reading.

We therefore gathered together a group of leading scholars and asked them not only to distill what they and their colleagues had learned but also to examine what we did not know; we encouraged them to use the lacunae they uncovered to push our understandings forward.

The contributors to this volume gathered in two workshops, one at the beginning of the project (where we were joined by Marc Lichbach of the University of Maryland, who greatly enriched our discussions) and one when the contributions had been nearly completed (where we were joined by Sheri Berman of Barnard College and Cynthia McClintock of George Washington University, who offered a number of useful, broad, and specific suggestions).

Throughout we enjoyed the unstinting support of Michael Brown (the dean of the Elliott School) and Kristin Lord (the associate dean, who actively helped shape the project in its formative stages). The Cumming family, close friends of the Elliott School, provided great financial support to the initiative. Craig Kauffman, a doctoral student at George Washington, worked on behalf of the book on all levels—his contributions to the introduction and conclusion were sufficiently substantial that they bear his name as co-author; he also helped with logistical, research, and editing support. When Craig left the country to pursue his own research, Jordan Steckler saw the project through to completion.

The Johns Hopkins University Press has been faithful and steady in its support for the volume since we had our initial discussions about the possibility of publication. We were fortunate to work with a very skillful editor at the Press, Henry Tom. With his death, the scholarly world has lost a talented and accomplished figure. We are honored that this book joins so many others in serving as a standing and permanent tribute to his memory.

# The Dynamics of Democratization

# Introduction

## *Nathan J. Brown and Craig M. Kauffman*

Over the past two decades, political scientists have become more fascinated by democracy and democratization, moving it to the center of scholarly agendas. And they have not been alone. Democratization has become a central concern of policy makers (albeit with uncertain results at best).

Indeed, democratization is one of the rare topics that have captured the interest of academics, activists, and policy makers alike. This is due in large part to the explosive spread of democracy around the world over the past thirty-five years, which has radically transformed the international political landscape from one in which democracies were the exception to one in which they are closer to the rule. The interest in democratization also reflects the strengthening of international norms casting democracy as the best available political system and associating it with many positive attributes, from human rights to economic prosperity to security. Democracy promotion received a boost after U.S. policy makers explicitly made democratization a national security issue after the September 11, 2001, terrorist attacks.

Our interest has grown. But have we learned anything?

## The Questions

In this book, we present a variety of views on what causes democratization and what democratization can deliver. While the analysis and tools vary, taken as a whole, the authors pose three questions and deliver three clear (if quite nuanced) answers:

*1. What causes a democracy to emerge and then maintains it?* Here our collective wisdom suggests not a single answer but instead a new set of places to look. In particular, we need to broaden not only our historical but also our geographic focus, making far better use of a wide variety of successful demo-cratizations, unsuccessful ones, and ways in which democratic mechanisms sit quite comfortably in nondemocratic settings. And we must develop explana-tions that account for both continuity and change, overcoming the tendency to emphasize one or the other. When we do so, we emerge with a set of surpris-ing findings about which institutions matter (our authors find, for instance, that the military is sometimes less of a factor and parliaments more of one than we have been led to expect). But we also develop a far greater apprecia-tion not only of the way in which various democratic and authoritarian forms slide into each other but also of the need to integrate our understanding of both forms of government and the way they are combined. Further inquiry into democratization cannot proceed far without a more sophisticated under-standing of authoritarianism.

*2. Does democracy make things better?* Most if not all of the authors would probably answer yes. But they also insist on asking the question if making things better (particularly in the economic realm) makes things easier for democracy. And of equal interest are the specifications our authors would at-tach to this very general answer. Thus, a more useful—if at first glance almost evasive answer—would probably be: "On balance, and over the long term, de-mocracy probably has some beneficial effects. But it is effect as well as cause: democracy is often rendered more stable by developments in the economic sphere." One section of the book explores these specifications and qualifica-tions, because that is where our most helpful contribution lies.

*3. Can democracy be promoted?* International action can shape the possibili-ties for democratization and the path that democratic development takes. But it does so in some varied, unanticipated, and sometimes long-term ways that will likely frustrate conscious democracy promotion policies.

## How Scholars Study Democratization

In the social sciences, we rarely expect broad, general, and definitive answers, but we do expect better-informed questions, more sophisticated ways of an-swering them, and steadily refined (if generally tentative and qualified) con-clusions. Are we getting better at studying democratization?

We certainly try more. Scholars never ignored democratization, but for an extended period—in which democratic government seemed more the excep-tion than the rule—it was rarely at the center of research agendas. Events in the 1980s and 1990s (Samuel Huntington's "third wave")[1] sucked academics into studying what was occurring. Scholarly interest has therefore grown partly as a reaction to a changing world.

Early scholarship on the third wave focused on the moment of transition itself, for understandable reasons. The breakdown of authoritarian regimes and the emergence of an embryonic democratic order—whether in Greece, Argentina, Poland, Russia, Spain, or South Korea—constituted a dramatic story. And much of it was unexpected. As interest deepened, however, scholars have widened their focus considerably. They now debate how authoritarian regimes give way to more democratic ones, how democracy is consolidated, how democracies are structured and how they perform, the relationship between democracy and economic growth, and why democratic mechanisms often seem to coexist with authoritarian ones.

Of course, democracy is not solely of scholarly interest. Understanding democracy and its complex evolution has important implications for policy and politics worldwide. Democracy and democracy promotion not only have taken center stage in policy debates; they have also absorbed the energies of countless activists throughout the world. Even countries that have completed democratic transitions are now wrestling with how democratic government can endure and how it can perform and deliver on its promise of more responsive and accountable governance.

As we claim, social science in general and comparative politics specifically move forward less by the steady accretion of bits of knowledge and more by the ability to ask new and better questions and to answer them in new and better ways. Scholars generally embrace this way of proceeding, but students and policy makers are sometimes frustrated by our inability to develop clear and definitive answers to the questions we pose. We acknowledge, but do not apologize for, our proclivity to debate much more than we can resolve.

In this collection, we write as part of the scholarly tradition, as people who have learned from, contributed to, and seek to shape the way that the academy understands democratization. We are not policy makers (though many of us have advised those who do make policy). But while we are scholars, we are not using this volume as an opportunity to present the latest findings of our very specific research. In some cases, very recent and specific research is included, and in all cases our own research has deeply informed our views. But we have written this volume to present what we think we collectively are learning—and to do so not simply by summarizing the views of others but by assessing what has come before us and shoving future scholarly inquiry in the direction we think is most appropriate.

We are thus presenting a hybrid between a review of the field and cutting-edge research. We hope this compilation will be useful to our colleagues in the academy; to new students of the subject, who will learn not only what but also how the academy contributes to efforts at understanding political change; and, finally, to those who make policy.

The book is both backward looking (toward past work) and forward looking (on where we should focus on efforts)—with an emphasis on the latter. And in the conclusion, we consider the general lessons that we are able to draw. We will examine as well whether those lessons—framed as they inevitably are in the qualified, querying, and querulous ways of scholars—provide any help to those whose interests are more applied and practical.

The rest of this introductory chapter, however, tilts the balance in the opposite direction—we are beginning this volume by looking a bit backward. We reflect on the record of scholarship, especially on the early reactions to the third wave because those reactions have set the agenda for much subsequent scholarship on democratization. Specifically, we seek to answer five questions:

1. How did political scientists approach democratization before the third wave?
2. How did the third wave change the scholarly agenda?
3. What have we come to realize that the initial agenda led us to overlook at first?
4. Did that agenda lead us in the right direction?
5. What did that agenda stress that later turned out to be less important?

## How Political Scientists Used to Think about Democratization

The study of democracy is as old as the study of politics—indeed, many of our most basic terms and concepts about politics come from an ancient tradition of normative and empirical inquiry in which democracy was considered a possible political form (though often not a stable or just one). Partly because democracy was seen as unstable, writers on democracy beginning with Aristotle have been concerned with democratization (how democracies are born) and even more with how democracies fail or degenerate.

The modern study of democratization has shown far more normative sympathy with its subject and also has been far more inclined to see democracy as potentially quite stable. Given the greater faith in democratic stability, the interest in transitions to and away from democracy often drew less attention. And the level of interest in democracy has varied greatly.

For if democracy is a perennial concern, it has not always been central. And democratization—studying how political systems become democratic—has excited, at best, episodic attention. While in the modern era democracy has generally been seen as the most appropriate form of government for developed societies, there has often been a recognition that, even in such societies, other political forms had emerged and shown (especially during the Cold War) apparent health and viability. As for the developing world, democracy was generally viewed as associated with higher levels of development and therefore something that might emerge only over the very long term.

Indeed, scholarship preceding the third wave, while it showed significant variation in approach and method, generally displayed two common features. First, it tended to explain democratization by reference to long-term factors and impersonal forces—the size of the middle class, political culture, the level of economic development, or the class structure. Democracy was seen as something that emerged rather than something that was created, and it emerged over decades or even centuries. Democracy was sometimes portrayed as possessing specific prerequisites or the outcome of complex social evolution rather than as a political system that could be purposively designed at any time.[2]

Second, democratization was connected not just to long-term social factors but, most commonly, to those with an economic aspect. For example, both modernization theory and dependency theory (adopted by some in the academy in conscious rebellion against modernization theory) linked democratization with political economy, albeit in very different ways—modernization theory quite loosely by positing a relationship between level of development and democracy, and dependency theory somewhat more tightly by arguing that emerging patterns in what had been viewed as the "developing world" were undermining both prosperity and democracy. And, indeed, some of the most innovative work in the 1970s and early 1980s used patterns of economic change and political economy to explain the new forms of authoritarianism that were emerging.

To be sure, there were some whose approach did not display these features. Most presciently perhaps (at least in terms of anticipating subsequent scholarship) was Dankwart Rustow's argument that democracy had no specific prerequisites, other than a sense of national unity to clearly set the boundaries of the political community; and that it was most likely when rival elites could not dominate each other but had to invent a set of rules for sharing (and ultimately alternating) in power.[3] Rustow's more focused and voluntaristic approach was revived at the beginning of the third wave and has remained influential.

## The Beginnings of a Research Agenda

Political scientists who had explained the rise of authoritarianism in southern Europe and South America were taken by surprise by the collapse of authoritarianism, beginning in the mid-1970s. Many were not merely surprised but also delighted—the nationalistic, repressive, right-leaning, and occasionally bellicose authoritarian regimes of Greece, Spain, Argentina, and Chile were mourned by few scholars. A strong normative interest in democratization— never completely absent but often seen as naive and even ethnocentric before the third wave—came to characterize the study of democratization, a feature it has not shed.

When scholars reached for an explanation of what seemed at first to be a regional trend rather than a global wave, they tended to leave behind the focus on political economy and deep structure that had characterized their study of authoritarianism. Partly this was because they were examining changes as they were occurring—and outcomes still seemed quite uncertain. Indeed, they were more likely to talk first about the "breakdown of authoritarianism" and then "transitions" than voice a confident expectation of "democratization."

But mild surprise turned to total astonishment as the uncertain transitions in southern Europe and South America were followed by the collapse of communist rule in central and eastern Europe. Accompanying these changes was a series of democratic breakthroughs in East Asia as well as some in sub-Saharan Africa. Something quite general—a global wave of democratization— seemed to call for new approaches and understandings.

And yet the widening wave largely deepened the scholarly trends that had already emerged. First, the normative interest in democratic outcomes continued— few were interested in questioning prevailing feelings that something quite positive was occurring. If academics did not subscribe to the messianic euphoria that seeped into politicians' speeches and newspaper columns, few denied that they were rooting for democratic outcomes.

Second, the global nature of the wave deepened the turn away from attempts to search for preconditions and prerequisites. The idea that democracy was possible only under restrictive conditions seemed at odds not only with the burgeoning global interest in building democracy but with the normative preferences of scholars for democratic governance. Similarly, the realization that democracy could break out in unexpected places accentuated a tendency against the search for long-term processes and toward shorter-term and conjunctural factors.

Third, the fact that scholars were studying events as they happened tilted the balance toward explaining processes and away from predicting outcomes. In other words, there was far more confidence analyzing the "transition" away from authoritarianism than the "consolidation" of a stable democracy. This in turn augmented the shift of focus to human agency, deliberate actions, and tactical choices: democratization came to be studied as the result of conscious decisions made by political leaders.

It is probably fair to describe this emerging set of features as a "transition paradigm," even though those held responsible for developing it—both inside and outside the academy—have disavowed some of these key elements (especially the implicit optimism).[4] But it should also be noted that there were attempts at correctives and modifications from the very beginning. The turn away from analyzing democratization in terms of structural factors and long-term processes, for instance, did not result in a full repudiation of any interest in the connection between political economy and democracy. Indeed, especially when attention turned from transition to consolidation, the relationship between economic performance and democratic stability loomed large.

Similarly, the focus on leaders and tactical choices left some uncomfortable—democratization seemed to rely to a remarkably small extent on the demos. Correction took two forms. First, some insisted that the role of popular participation in democratic transitions should not be discounted and that it was impossible to write the history of transitions simply by focusing on the shrewd and restrained tactics of moderate leaders.[5] Second, *civil society,* a term at the margins of scholarly discourse in the 1970s into the 1980s, became a central concern for scholars of democracy, though the term displayed some markedly different meanings.[6]

## What That Agenda Missed—But We Have Learned Since

The transition paradigm was influential indeed, but it was not really more than a set of empirically generated insights. And as scholarly debates continued, some of its blind spots became clear. The nuances of many scholarly debates often got lost when arguments entered the policy arena, however, so that scholarly refinements and reversals did not immediately enter broader policy discussions. We list here five important correctives that developed in scholarly writings about democratization over time.

*1. Structural conditions may not be determinative, but they should not be ignored.* The "no preconditions," "anyone can do it" thrust of the "transition paradigm" led policy makers to hope that the only requirement for "democratization was a decision by the country's political elites to move toward democracy and an ability on the part of those elites to fend off the contrary actions of remaining anti-democratic forces."[7] No scholar ever claimed that democratization was solely an act of will by a political elite. But the initial work focused on elite choices and strategies. And because they tended to study successful cases and dramatic moments of authoritarian collapse, a short-term voluntaristic bias crept in.

But subsequent research has undermined this voluntaristic view of the transition paradigm. While the choices of elites certainly matter, they are shaped by myriad contextual factors. Recent work focuses on the complex interaction of elites and institutions, the role of popular mobilization, and the interaction of economic and political structures and policy choices, among many other factors.

Examples of political change in less happy places such as Bosnia, Iraq, and Afghanistan have led scholars to reemphasize the importance of structural conditions in determining the success of democratization processes. These cases, along with many other transitional democracies left unconsolidated as the third wave receded, renewed arguments for a focus on structural factors and preexisting conditions, such as social cohesion, democratic values, and sufficiently strong and well-designed political institutions, not to mention physical and economic security. There is no consensus on which conditions are most important, or how necessary they are for success, and their exact role in promoting democracy is not well understood. However, there is an increasing recognition that getting elites to agree to pursue democracy is only part of the story. The long, arduous task of sustaining and deepening democracy is much more difficult and more related to structural conditions. It may not make sense to talk of absolute preconditions to democracy, but economic factors and history cannot be ignored.

*2. There is no single path to democratization.* No scholar ever claimed—or would claim—that there is a single path to democratization. But early research tended to look for general patterns that cut across cases, and therefore scholars were a bit slow to develop approaches to understanding various processes of change. As they began to do so, they also reviewed their understandings of earlier cases of democratization. One lesson learned is that democratization is not as easy as perhaps once thought. It is often a long and conflictual process that does not proceed in a linear fashion.[8] A second effect was that the early emphasis on the development of elite "pacts"—an important element in some transitions—gave way to a more variegated understanding of possible sequences.

*3. Transitions should not be viewed as abrupt.* By focusing on the drama of authoritarian collapse, there was an implicit bias in early studies of the third wave toward sudden change. But this was combined with a fear that overly radical demands from the opposition would disrupt the process. According to the early approach, there is a point where the existence of the authoritarian regime is directly challenged. The right choices by moderate leaders could lead to a bargaining process that could fairly quickly establish the rules of the new regime.

However, subsequent research tended to take a slightly longer-range view. While scholars rarely spoke in centuries (as they had in the 1960s and 1970s), they did begin to speak in decades. And they enlarged the scope of cases to include countries such as Bangladesh, Indonesia, Kenya, and Mexico, where democratization proceeded gradually without an abrupt challenge to the incumbent regime. Instead of a fissure among authoritarian elites leading to a renegotiation of the rules of the game, the change occurred through continuous and prolonged struggles between incumbents and opposition over the formal institutional playing field.[9]

This longer-range focus engendered its own problems. If some transitions are understood as protracted processes, it becomes more difficult to differentiate "protracted transitions" from stable "hybrid regimes." We can recognize a protracted transition only in hindsight after the country successfully completes the transition, and this problem is at the heart of the current debate over how to understand hybrid regimes.

*4. Democratization is not solely a domestic process.* The bias against international factors at the beginning of the third wave was largely unconscious. But for the most part, scholars were interested primarily, and sometimes exclusively, in domestic processes.[10]

But as new democracies continued to emerge in rapid succession, it became increasingly clear that there must be some international forces behind the various "waves" of democracy. Certainly there is increasingly normative force behind democracy, propelled by the world's most powerful states and institutions. Access to financial resources, international legitimacy, and membership in international organizations such as the European Union are often conditioned on democratic qualities. In addition, various actors from governments to transnational nongovernmental organizations to leaders of previously successful democratization movements are directly involved in all stages of the democratization process. International attempts to promote democracy involve a diverse range of policies and programs, such as funding of opposition groups and civil society movements, sanctioning democratic backtrackers, funding and monitoring elections, and providing technical and financial assistance for the strengthening of key institutions such as political parties and the judiciary.

Only recently have academics begun to study the effect of various international factors in a rigorous and systematic manner, with a particular focus on democracy-promotion efforts. In part, this new emphasis reflects the fact that democracy has moved to the center of the foreign policy discourse among Western powers. This was particularly true after the September 11 terrorist attacks when democracy promotion became linked to security.

Initial academic studies of democracy assistance programs suggest they are more effective at weakening authoritarian regimes than in actually promoting democratization per se or giving added momentum to a consolidation process already under way.[11] In part, this is because of the preoccupation with short-term projects and short time horizons, which are ill suited to the long-term process of building a stable democracy. Another problem, however, is the cross-pressures and often deep ambivalence of the democracy promoters themselves.

Scholars have recently begun to turn their attention to international actors other than the Western governmental actors with democracy-promotion missions. The role of activists, learning across borders, and international organizations are beginning to draw attention. The story of democratization will remain one with a significant domestic component, but it is no longer one in which international factors are overlooked.

5. *Some aspects of the relationship between democracy and economics turned out to be less significant.* The early writings on the third wave did show great interest in the relationship between economics and politics, but they tended to focus on two questions that now seem dated. First, what was the relationship between democratization and socialism? Some of the scholars most active in the early scholarship had strong sympathies with demands for social and economic equality, seeing it as a natural extension of the political equality associated with democracy. And there is therefore a sense of regret in some early works, as many of these scholars came to feel that pressing for radical social and economic transformation would disrupt and even reverse the transition process. Socialism had to be postponed.

Second, what was the relationship between democratization and rapid economic liberalization? Did such rapid economic reform require authoritarian government (or perhaps lead to conditions that encouraged authoritarianism to emerge or sustain itself)? Or was a dispersal of political and economic power through a combination of democratic and market mechanisms mutually reinforcing?

These questions were pressing indeed in the late 1980s and early 1990s. But scholars now have focused on democracy over the long haul—not simply its relationship to short-term policy questions.

## What We Have to Keep Relearning

While the early third wave scholarship had blind spots and biases that had to be corrected by subsequent scholarship, in other areas it was more prescient. Indeed, in some areas we have continued to find ourselves reinventing the wheel by discovering again insights that were made clear by the first scholars who began work on the third wave. The optimism, short-term focus, and normative inclinations of the early writings led many to overlook three critical insights that subsequent authors often find themselves uncovering afresh.

1. *Authoritarian regimes can remain robust in the face of pressures to democratize.* In the early 1990s, at the height of the third wave, there was a tendency to view authoritarian regimes as quite vulnerable. There was a sense of optimism among scholars and policy makers alike that transnational pressures and transformations in the world economy and technology were forcing

authoritarian regimes to open up. In their seminal work, O'Donnell and Schmitter had recognized that authoritarian regimes faced a more difficult time legitimizing their rule in the face of international norms favoring democracy.[12] However, they also stressed that democratization could not occur when the authoritarian regime remained united. Their characterization of democratization depicts a fragile process that faces serious obstacles, where under certain conditions authoritarian regimes could forestall democratization indefinitely. Their view was more pessimistic than the dominant outlook in the early 1990s, but has proved to be largely correct. Since 2000, with a recognition that the third wave has crested, the research on transitions has moved back to focusing on the resiliency of authoritarianism. This reflects a shift in general attitudes among scholars regarding the vulnerability of authoritarian regimes. While the third wave certainly showed that authoritarianism could be undermined anywhere, the persistence of authoritarian tendencies in many regions, including many "third wave" countries, suggests that authoritarianism is more robust that commonly thought in the 1990s.

*2. Democratization is a matter of degree.* Scholars have continually had to relearn that democracy is often better understood in relative terms rather than as a political system that is absolutely present or absent. This should not have been necessary. Again, in their seminal work, O'Donnell and Schmitter argue that democratization should be understood as a matter of degree and note that it can vary along two dimensions: the conditions that restrict political competition and electoral choice; and the development of "decisional mechanisms" that circumvent accountability to popularly elected representatives by placing certain issues out of their reach (e.g., autonomous agencies, corporatist assemblies). In some ways, this simply reinvented Robert Dahl's earlier two-dimensional definition of "polyarchy," in which regimes differed by their degree to which they allowed contestation for political power and the extent to which they opened up political participation.[13]

Such scholars were acknowledging the existence of a "gray zone"—or even a series of zones—between authoritarianism and democracy. More explicitly, Lucian Pye also recognized the problem of what came to be known as "hybrid regimes" in his 1990 presidential address to the American Political Science Association. While the theme of the address was the crisis of authoritarianism, he predicted that "in the wake of the crisis of authoritarianism we can expect a wide variety of systems that will become part authoritarian and part free and that will fall far short of any reasonable definitions of democracy" and "which do not conform to our classical typologies." He called for "richer typologies [that] should identify types of systems that represent varying states of equilibrium along the continuum from authoritarian to democratic."[14]

*3. The legacy of the authoritarian period shapes the transition process.* While not often mentioned in the conventional transition story, O'Donnell and Schmitter recognized from the beginning that the nature of the authoritarian period shapes the transition process that follows. In particular, they were concerned with the extent to which authoritarian regimes "destroyed previous [representative] institutions and practices without replacing them with alternative forms of representation, decision-making, or policy implementation."[15] For example, they argued that if the longevity or ruthlessness of regimes eradicated national political institutions and local autonomies, the transition would occur as a blank slate (e.g., Portugal). In authoritarian regimes of shorter duration, the structures and personnel inherited from previous democracies show a surprising capacity for revival (e.g., Brazil and Peru).

Subsequent scholars have rediscovered this insight and attempted to inject a greater measure of precision and rigor into understanding just how authoritarian legacies matter. For instance, some have focused on institutional arrangements, because they shape elite incentives and the ability to overcome collective action and coordination dilemmas.[16]

## The Questions Again

We come back then to the questions of this book:

*1. What causes a democracy to emerge and then maintains it?* In the first section of the book, we examine democracy and ask where it comes from and why it succeeds, but we also advance some further questions. Given the widespread adoption of democratic mechanisms, how do we know when democracy has really emerged? How do we approach political systems that seem to blend democratic and nondemocratic elements?

*2. Does democracy make things better?* Scholars often study democracy not merely because it is there but because they like it. Does it perform better? Or does it need policy success in order to survive? In this book's second section, we focus specifically on the relationship between economic development and democracy—a traditional subject of interest—to see what we have learned and should be learning.

*3. Can democracy be promoted?* It is clear that the international context makes some difference in the emergence of democracy. But how? What sort of mechanisms foster democracy? And is democracy something that spreads not merely passively but also actively—that is, does a policy of "democracy promotion" show any promise?

NOTES

1. Samuel P. Huntington, *The Third Wave: Democratization in the Late Twentieth Century* (Norman: University of Oklahoma Press, 1991).

2. Seymour Martin Lipset, "Some Social Requisites of Democracy: Economic Development and Political Legitimacy," *American Political Science Review* 53, no. 1 (1959): 69–105; Barrington Moore Jr., *Social Origins of Dictatorship and Democracy: Lord and Peasant in the Making of the Modern World* (Boston: Beacon Press, 1966).

3. Dankwart A. Rustow, "Transitions to Democracy: Toward a Dynamic Model," *Comparative Politics* 2 (April 1970): 337–63.

4. Thomas Carothers, "The End of the Transition Paradigm," *Journal of Democracy* 13, no. 1 (January 2002): 5–21. For the debate surrounding the "End of the Transition Paradigm," see the special issue devoted to "Debating the Transition Paradigm" in the *Journal of Democracy* 13, no. 3 (July 2002).

5. Nancy Bermeo, *Ordinary People in Extraordinary Times: The Citizenry and the Breakdown of Democracy* (Princeton: Princeton University Press, 2003).

6. Particularly influential was Robert Putnam, *Making Democracy Work: Civic Traditions in Modern Italy* (Princeton: Princeton University Press, 1993). On the variable meanings, see Michael W. Foley and Bob Edwards, "The Paradox of Civil Society," *Journal of Democracy* 7, no. 3 (July 1996): 38–52.

7. Carothers, "The End of the Transition Paradigm," p. 7. See also Carrie Manning, "Political Elites and Democratic State-Building Efforts in Bosnia and Iraq," *Democratization* 13, no. 5 (December 2006): 724–38.

8. Sheri Berman, "How Democracies Emerge: Lessons from Europe," *Journal of Democracy* 18, no. 1 (January 2007): 28–41.

9. Todd Eisenstadt, "Eddies in the Third Wave: Protracted Transitions and Theories of Democratization," *Democratization* 7, no. 3 (Autumn 2000): 3–24.

10. Occasionally a scholar would be explicit: "International actors play an 'indirect and usually marginal role' in the democratization process"; Philippe C. Schmitter, "An Introduction to Southern European Transitions," in Guillermo O'Donnell, Philippe C. Schmitter, and Laurence Whitehead, eds., *Transitions from Authoritarian Rule: Southern Europe* (Baltimore: Johns Hopkins University Press, 1986), p. 5.

11. James M. Scott and Carie A. Steele, "Assisting Democrats or Resisting Dictators? The Nature and Impact of Democracy Support by the United States National Endowment for Democracy, 1990–99," *Democratization* 12, no. 4 (August 2005): 439–60.

12. Guillermo O'Donnell and Philippe C. Schmitter, *Transitions from Authoritarian Rule: Tentative Conclusions about Uncertain Democracies* (Baltimore: Johns Hopkins University Press, 1986).

13. Robert A. Dahl, *Polyarchy* (New Haven: Yale University Press, 1971).

14. Lucian W. Pye, "Political Science and the Crisis of Authoritarianism," *American Political Science Review* 84, no. 1 (March1990): 13.

15. O'Donnell and Schmitter, *Transitions from Authoritarian Rule*, p. 22.

16. Perhaps most notable here is the work of Barbara Geddes. See, for example, her unpublished manuscript, "Authoritarian Breakdown," January 2004, http://weber.ucsd.edu/~jlbroz/PElunch/Geddes%20authn_breakdown.pdf, and "Party Creation as an Autocratic Survival Strategy," paper presented at the Conference on Dictators, Princeton University, April 2008.

# Part I. Democracy and Dictatorship

## INTRODUCTION

Comparative scholarship on democratization over the past century has often been perceptive and sometimes even prescient, but it has understandably been far stronger at analyzing what has already taken place rather than producing sound expectations for the future. Taken as a whole, however, far more striking than its record of accuracy has been the manic swings in tone. Not only has the mood of scholars swung from one decade to the next, but the centrality of democratization as a concern has varied greatly. The result is that democracy has been viewed (implicitly at least) as both an oddity and an almost natural political condition; dictatorship has been seen as both the norm, barely in need of an explanation, and the exception. Three decades ago, scholars had a rich vocabulary to describe the varieties of authoritarianism;[1] today it is gradations of democracy that draw the efforts of the concept mongers.[2]

In the 1960s a general optimism prevailed in comparative politics under the sway of modernization theory. Because it assumed that there was a process of "modernization" that linked various kinds of social, technological, economic, and political changes and that some variation of a process that had begun in western Europe was now replicating itself in other areas of the world, modernization theory was based on a cheery world view. But for all its optimistic spirit, modernization theory treated democratization with some diffidence. First, modernization theorists always acknowledged that, for all that it offered, modernity could take some problematic forms and force hard choices, at least over the short to medium term. And democracy was generally not a priority. Second, a focus on long-term developments suggested that even if democracy was a replicable and quintessentially modern form of government, it may not arise any time soon. Third, while modernization theorists were very much concerned with politics, they tended to show much less interest in the form the political system might take (and, indeed, modernization theory itself was based partly on the claim that previous generations of scholars had focused far too much on formal procedures). Instead, they focused on broad processes and phenomena, such as political mobilization and integration. Thus, modernization theory's general long-term optimism translated not into an assumption that most societies would democratize soon but instead into an indifference toward the subject and an acceptance that other political forms (such as a single-party state) might serve developmental ends, at least for a considerable period.

A sharp swing against modernization theory set in during the 1970s—but one that placed dictatorship (or authoritarianism) at the center of the research agenda rather than democracy. Rebelling against the idea that there was a coherent process of "modernization" and that there was a continuum of development, scholars focused on how patterns of development could lead to very different outcomes.[3] Dependency theory, perhaps the most pessimistic of the newer approaches, found the non-Western world moving not only toward various distorted economic outcomes but also toward new and deeply entrenched forms of dictatorship.[4] In short, form of government had moved back onto the research agenda but not in a happy way: it was authoritarianism that needed—and received—an explanation.

Thus, by the early 1980s most comparativists had followed approaches that led them to an inclination against deep interest in democratization—democracy seemed to be a historically unusual form of government, and there was a stronger wish to explain what political systems were rather than what they were not. As indicated in the introduction, there were certainly scholars who fell outside of this consensus.

But even such mildly dissident voices did not prepare the ground for the changes in southern Europe, Latin America, and the former Soviet bloc. A "third wave" of democracy was at hand.

In reaction, the disciplinary mood changed dramatically during the 1980s and 1990s as various kinds of authoritarian regimes broke down, most often giving way to democracies of a sort—even in places that were considered highly unlikely candidates for democratization. Authoritarian regimes came to be viewed as much more vulnerable than previously thought. There was a sense of optimism among scholars and even more among policy makers that transnational pressures and domestic transformations and technology were forcing authoritarian regimes to open up.

Yet attitudes shifted once again in the 2000s, when it became apparent that the third wave was receding and authoritarianism proved much more durable than expected. Given that democratic transitions had occurred in so many unexpected places, scholarly interest grew in attempting to explain the persistence of authoritarianism in places such as the Middle East and China. And scholars became more interested not simply in the transition between authoritarianism and democracy but also in combinations, hybrids, and gradations between the two.

As might be expected, the focus of democratization studies also shifted according to the various stages of the third wave. During the initial period of the 1970s and 1980s, "transitologists" investigated the conditions and modes of transition from dictatorship to democracy. As the wave peaked in the 1990s, "consolidologists" tried to understand the causes and conditions under which young democracies consolidated and matured. By the 2000s, most third wave democracies were more than a decade old, and scholars naturally turned to the question of how well democracy was working in various cases, and what constitutes a "good" versus "bad" democracy. Perhaps inevitably, the question of how to categorize regimes that do not fit ideal types of democracy or authoritarian regimes became the predominant trend in the democratization literature.

It is now generally acknowledged that the third wave of democracy has receded. But rather than leading to the consolidation of liberal democracies, the third wave has resulted in the rise of hybrid regimes that share elements of both democracy and dictatorship. This empirical reality contradicts a hidden assumption implicit in some of the literature on transition and consolidation, which is that countries will inevitably take one of two paths— either toward a consolidated liberal democracy or back into authoritarianism. This reality is what distinguishes the third wave from previous waves and has forced academics to rethink their understanding of the democratization process, standard conceptions of regime types, and definitions of democracy.

Thus, these two trends—the persistence of authoritarian regimes in certain regions, and the development of hybrid regimes—have driven renewed interest in the relationship between democracy and dictatorship. If we look back, it appears that much of the third wave was propelled and shaped by the failure of authoritarianism rather than the success of democracy. As a result, many third wave countries are characterized by ambivalent attitudes toward democracy. Polls in many parts of the world show that democracy has not lived up to the expectations many had placed on it, yet political alternatives to democracy have also lost much of their appeal. Empirically, we can say that democracy is more prevalent than ever before. It is also notable that so few third wave democracies have reverted to pure authoritarianism, as so frequently happened when the first and second waves receded. The problem, however, is that the majority of third wave countries have not achieved a relatively well-functioning democracy or do not seem to be moving in that direction.[5]

How to deal with these countries in the "gray zone" between naked authoritarianism and liberal democracy has become a top focus of the democratization literature in the past few years. Questions have arisen over how to classify these regimes. For example, should they be categorized as regimes in transition toward either democracy or dictatorship or as stable and distinct regime types? Do these regimes exhibit common structural and functional characteristics that could help us categorize them as new regime types, and if so, what are they? How do we explain the emergence and persistence of these new regime types?

The issue of hybrid regimes also taps into long-standing debates over the definition of democracy. Even if we define hybrid regimes on their own terms rather than on what they are not, they are still relevant to debates over definitions of democracy because they are, by definition, partly democratic. Many of the institutions and characteristics of democracy exist in these regimes, yet they do not function as democracies should. This inevitably raises questions regarding the criteria of democratic quality. What is a "good" democracy, and how can it be clearly distinguished from a "bad" or "defective" democracy? Another way to conceive of this problem is to ask if hybrid regimes are a distinct regime type and where the boundaries of democracy and authoritarianism end and the boundaries of these new regime types begin. Because of the tremendous diversity among hybrid regimes and the uncertainty of what values should be considered as characteristic of democracy, these questions cannot be answered empirically.

Taken as a whole, the chapters in this section focus on continuity more than change. But they do not assume such continuity; indeed, they seek to explore and explain it: Why do democratic regimes persist? Why do authoritarian ones? And what about regimes that combine elements of both?

Kathleen Bruhn's essay focuses on three decades of writings on Latin America. She reminds us that, for all the optimism of the democratization literature in general, it began with a gloomier outlook: those who studied the region a quarter century ago were convinced that democracy was fragile and faced stern obstacles. The first scholarly reaction to what was soon termed the third wave was that it represented a short-term and cyclical phenomenon. Bruhn focuses on three expected barriers to democratic consolidation—the military, economic liberalization, and flaws in institutional design—and shows why the initial fears of the scholars were not borne out.

By contrast, Bruce Dickson starts with a political system that has remained wholly authoritarian in China. Expectations for systemic political change in China have not been met; instead the authoritarian order there has shown itself to be fairly able to adapt. It remains repressive to be sure, but it has also developed a set of other tools that have allowed it to maintain its authority—and even, Dickson claims, surprising legitimacy—and shows remarkable resilience. Dickson focuses particular attention on the roles and strategies of the Chinese Communist Party, an organization that he describes as having abandoned its Marxism but not its Leninism.

Both Dickson and Bruhn might be said to incorporate a significant role for agency—how various political actors have built the system and fended off challenges. Steven Fish prefers to focus on structures, especially parliaments. While placing less emphasis on their design or their function, he considers the implications of parliamentary strength (and weakness) for democratic persistence. Fish develops a surprising argument—stronger parliaments (measured not by some abstract reading of constitutional texts but by a careful consideration of actual authority) make for stabler democracies. The finding may be far more surprising for scholars (who have debated questions of institutional design for generations) than for the hundreds of millions living under authoritarian systems who see formal parliamentary bodies so dominated by executives that paper democratic procedures have little role in actual politics.

Henry Hale and Nathan Brown consider the vast array of regimes that do not seem to fall fully within democratic or nondemocratic categories. They agree on some fundamental observations: some of these regimes are remarkably stable; we know much more about what such regimes are not like than what they are like; and political science has had conceptual difficulties approaching them—at least with any coherence. Hale works to lead the way forward largely empirically by exploring what we do know about such regimes—where they come from and what they do. Brown, by contrast, focuses on the conceptual issues, seeking to show why our theorizing has run into trouble and how to respond.

## NOTES

1. For a review of the literature on different forms of authoritarianism, see Juan Linz, *Totalitarian and Authoritarian Regimes* (Boulder, CO: Lynne Rienner Publishers, 2000).

2. See, for example, David Collier and Steven Levitsky, "Democracy 'With Adjectives': Conceptual Innovation in Comparative Research," *World Politics* 49, no. 3 (1997): 430–51; Larry Diamond, "Elections without Democracy: Thinking about Hybrid Regimes," *Journal of Democracy* 13 (April 2002): 21–35.

3. See, for example, Barrington Moore Jr., *Social Origins of Dictatorship and Democracy: Lord and Peasant in the Making of the Modern World* (Boston: Beacon Press, 1966); Samuel P. Huntington, *Political Order in Changing Societies* (New Haven: Yale University Press, 1968); and Guillermo O'Donnell, *Modernization and Bureaucratic-Authoritarianism: Studies in South American Politics* (Berkeley: Institute of International Studies, University of California, 1973).

4. Fernando Enrique Cardozo and Enzo Faletto, *Dependency and Development in Latin America* (Berkeley: University of California Press 1979); J. Samuel Valenzuela and Arturo Valenzuela, "Modernization and Dependency: Alternative Perspectives in the Study of Latin American Underdevelopment," *Comparative Politics* 10, no. 4 (July 1978): 543–57.

5. Larry Diamond, *Developing Democracy: Toward Consolidation* (Baltimore: Johns Hopkins University Press, 1999); Aurel Croissant and Wolfgang Merkel, "Introduction: Democratization in the Early Twenty-first Century," *Democratization* 11, no. 5 (December 2004): 1–9.

# CHAPTER 1

# Hybrid Regimes

## When Democracy and Autocracy Mix

*Henry E. Hale*

Some regimes just do not fit comfortably into the categories of either democracy or authoritarianism. For example, today's Malaysia allows opposition parties to compete in regularly held elections, which autocracies generally do not do, but gives progovernment candidates far greater advantage in these contests than is allowed by most countries we would call true democracies. South Africa before 1994, as a different kind of example, was highly democratic for its small Afrikaner population, but brutally authoritarian as far as the majority black population was concerned. Polities such as these, which seem to combine democratic and autocratic elements in significant measure, have increasingly become known as hybrid regimes.

Political science has not yet settled on an approach to understanding such systems. The dominant tendency has been to study these countries primarily through the lenses of what they are not, treating them as defective democracies, weak autocracies, or unstable countries in a potentially long process of "transition" to democracy or "backsliding" to autocracy. The chief goal of research has been less to understand how these regimes actually function and more to evaluate their prospects for becoming more democratic.

Hybrid regimes deserve to be studied in their own right, not only through the lenses of what they are not (autocracy or democracy). In support of such an approach, this chapter makes four central points. First, there are a large number of such systems, found by some measures in as many as a third of all countries. Second, many hybrid regimes are too long-lived to be considered transitory. Third, there is evidence that hybrid regimes have distinct effects on everything from international conflict to the economy. Fourth, there exist plausible logics that explain why such regimes should be numerous, enduring, and distinctive in their effects. Most previous works arguing for the importance of hybrid regimes have focused primarily on making the first two points. But it is the last two that raise the most interesting and important questions for research and that ultimately make the strongest case for treating hybrid regimes as a category of their own.

## Hybrid Regimes as What They Are Not

Until recently, the most prominent social science research on political regimes tended to focus on either democracy or autocracy. Classic works on democracy sought to elaborate preconditions for its emergence and successful operation, highlighting the importance of social structure, values, culture, history, and patterns of elite interaction.[1] A parallel literature examined the dynamics of authoritarian—including totalitarian—systems.[2] Some works ambitiously sought to explain the dynamics and origins of both.[3] True, many scholars simultaneously noted that countries frequently did not fit the ideal-type concepts that usually were the reference points for these studies. For example, Dahl's famous concept of *polyarchy*—a political system characterized by high levels of contestation and participation—was developed in answer to the observation that even those states that were widely regarded as democracies generally did not (and possibly could not) fully live up to democratic ideals.[4]

By the late 1980s, scholars had begun to pay more attention to countries that were distinctly in between democracy and autocracy. The dominant way in which such "in-between" regimes came to be studied was as cases of countries "in transition," with transition itself becoming a major research focus by the early 2000s.[5] This "transitology" tradition generated groundbreaking efforts to conceptualize politics in countries that were not democracies but were also not pure autocracies. The first significant effort to coin a term for these regimes, an important step in their conceptualization, came from O'Donnell and Schmitter's seminal work on transitions: *dictablandas* were systems whose autocrats had decided to liberalize but only partially, whereas *democraduras* were democracies without full measures of liberty.[6] They argued that the former were highly unstable, though the latter could endure for some time before legitimacy crises were likely to generate splits among elites and lead to eventual democratization. These terms did not stick, with most such regimes becoming more commonly known among transitologists as "unconsolidated democracies."[7] In this way, they were understood not so much for what they were but with primary reference to what they were becoming or failing to become.

Another advance was made by a related series of works that still treated the in-between countries as transitional but focused on distinct points in the transition. As such, they were studied as substandard types of democracy—for example, "delegative democracy,"[8] "illiberal democracy,"[9] "managed democracy,"[10] "directed democracy,"[11] or other forms of "democracy with adjectives."[12] The underlying idea of most such studies, though, was that these systems were nevertheless nascent democracies, thereby focusing debate on the kind of "obstacles" they faced in either stabilizing or deepening their democratic content.

Over the past decade, a different set of scholars began to object to the notion that democracy should be the point of reference in studying such regimes. In a 2002 issue of the *Journal of Democracy*, Carothers argued that many of the regimes usually treated as "transitional" had in fact proved highly durable without moving discernibly toward democracy or autocracy.[13] The next issue featured a set of articles calling attention to the need to consider "hybrid regimes" as a distinct and potentially durable regime type.[14] This move had roots in certain earlier prominent work on regime "hybridity" in Latin America, Africa, and the former Soviet Union.[15] The most prominent of these new works sought primarily to reorient the point of analytical reference from democracy to autocracy. While they recognized that hybrid regimes did contain certain democratic features, they generally argued that the conceptual tools for understanding autocracy were better suited for understanding hybrid regimes than were those usually used to understand democracy. This is reflected in the new labels applied to the same set of systems, including "competitive authoritarianism,"[16] "electoral authoritarianism,"[17] and "semiauthoritarianism."[18] Even so, much of this work has focused on when these systems break down, permitting breakthroughs to democracy.[19]

Is there any scholarly value to be had from going a step further, treating hybrid regimes as a truly distinct category that deserves conceptual tools of its own regardless of whether we are ultimately interested in democratization or autocratization? The rest of this chapter makes such a case in four parts.

## Hybrid Regimes as a Large Share of the World's Political Systems

By almost all indicators, a very large share of the world's countries belong somewhere between the categories of full democracy and full autocracy. Let us for the moment set aside debates over definitions and look at what the most prominent efforts to categorize the world's political systems have found. Freedom House's "Freedom in the World" project, which considers political rights and civil liberties, breaks all countries' political systems down into the categories of "free," "partly free," and "not free" on the basis of detailed reports by country specialists. As table 1.1 indicates, ever since the project began in the 1970s, roughly one-quarter to one-third of all countries are classified as "partly free" each year. At the start of 2010, fifty-eight countries (30% of the total) were hybrid by this measure.

Other prominent indices concur that a large share of the world's regimes are hybrids. The Economist Intelligence Unit's "Index of Democracy," which

*Table 1.1.*    Percentage of Countries with Hybrid Regimes
by Different Measures

| Criterion | Percentage |
|---|---|
| Freedom House "partly free" 1978 | 35 |
| Freedom House "partly free" 1988 | 23 |
| Freedom House "partly free" 1998 | 28 |
| Freedom House "partly free" 2008 | 32 |
| Economist Intelligence Unit "hybrid regime" 2006 | 18 |
| Economist Intelligence Unit "hybrid regime" 2008 | 22 |
| Polity IV "anocracy" 2007 | 25 |
| Political Atlas of Modernity IFDI 2005 | 33 |

*Sources:* Freedom House, www.freedomhouse.org/uploads/fiw09/FIW09_Tables&GraphsForWeb.pdf, accessed April 20, 2009; Laza Kekic, "The Economist Intelligence Unit's Index of Democracy," *Economist Intelligence Unit,* 2006, /www.economist.com/media/pdf/Democracy_Index_2007_v3.pdf, accessed April 20, 2009; "The Economist Intelligence Unit's Index of Democracy 2008," *Economist Intelligence Unit,* http://a330.g.akamai.net/7/330/25828/20081021185552/graphics.eiu.com/PDF/Democracy%20Index%202008.pdf, accessed April 20, 2009; Monty G. Marshall, *Polity IV Project: Political Regime Characteristics and Transitions 1800–2007,* www.systemicpeace.org/polity/polity4.htm, accessed April 20, 2009; A. Yu. Mel'vil', ed., *Politicheskii atlas sovremennosti: Opyt mnogomernogo statisticheskogo analiza politicheskikh sistem sovremennykh gosudarstv* (Moscow: MGIMO-Universitet, 2007): 174–75.

gives the quality of governance more emphasis than does Freedom House in defining democracy, classifies about a fifth of all countries as hybrid regimes for each of the two years the study was conducted, 2006 and 2008. Another 32 percent in 2006 and 29 percent in 2008 were categorized as "flawed democracies," which might also be considered hybrid by some definitions. A third prominent data source is the Polity IV Project, which rates countries on broad measures of authoritarian and democratic characteristics. Countries that display "mixed" democratic and authoritarian traits or "incoherent" regime types are dubbed "anocracies." According to the criteria that Polity IV supplies as of 2007, about a quarter of all countries with a population greater than 500,000 are anocracies. Even if we turn to the Political Atlas of Modernity's Institutional Foundations of Democracy Index (IFDI), which was created by Russian scholars as an alternative to what they see as the pro-American "bias" of organizations such as Freedom House, we see a highly similar picture. About 33 percent of all UN member states (plus Taiwan) fall between scores of 4 and 6 on the IFDI's 10-point scale as of 2005.

Moreover, some of the world's most important countries are or have been governed by hybrid regimes, including countries as populous, rich, or geopolitically significant as Russia, Nigeria, Venezuela, Egypt, and Malaysia. Historically, hybrid regimes have occurred even in major western European countries, including France and Germany.[20]

## Hybrid Regimes as (Often) Long-Lived and Stable Political Systems

Not only are hybrid regimes plentiful, but many have been stable for significant periods of time, as is clear from a more detailed examination of all world countries. Here we rely primarily on the two data collection efforts that have sought to characterize political systems in almost every country on a yearly basis, the Freedom House project (coverage starting 1972) and the Polity IV project (which evaluates political systems back to 1800). The results provide additional grounds for studying hybrid regimes as an important regime type in their own right.

Table 1.2 shows that of regimes that are currently hybrid, that is, those classified as "anocracies" by Polity IV and "partly free" by Freedom House according to recent reports, more than half have been in this category for at

*Table 1.2.*    Age of Currently Existing Hybrid Regimes (%)

| Longevity | Polity IV's Anocracies | Freedom House's Partly Free |
|---|---|---|
| < 5 years | 26 | 21 |
| 5–9 years | 21 | 18 |
| 10–19 years | 46 | 42 |
| ≥ 20 years | 8 | 19 |

*Note:* As of 2007 for Polity IV and 2008 for Freedom House. Percentage totals may exceed 100 due to rounding.

*Table 1.3.*    Longevity of Hybrid Regimes (%)

| Longevity | Polity IV's Anocracies, 1800–2007 | | Freedom House's Partly Free, 1972–2008 | |
|---|---|---|---|---|
| | Total | Still Hybrid | Total | Still Hybrid |
| < 5 years | 31 | 4 | 46 | 5 |
| 5–9 years | 23 | 3 | 21 | 4 |
| 10–19 years | 23 | 6 | 25 | 10 |
| ≥ 20 years | 24 | 1 | 8 | 5 |

least ten years. Only about a quarter of currently hybrid regimes are new arrivals within the previous five years.

Of course, to understand their degree of longevity, we also need to consider hybrid regimes that have ceased to be hybrid. These data, as indicated in table 1.3, confirm that a significant number of hybrid regimes are transitory: 31 percent of all such regimes reported by Polity IV have lasted less than five years, as have 46 percent of such regimes as categorized by Freedom House. Nevertheless, table 1.3 also shows that historically there have been significant numbers of long-lived hybrid regimes. According to Polity IV, 47 percent of all hybrid regimes have lasted for at least ten years, with about half of that set surviving for at least twenty years. Examples of such enduring hybrid regimes include Singapore (1965 to the present), Mexico (1977–97), South Africa (1910–92), Malaysia (1969 to the present), and Germany (1871–1918).

These figures underestimate longevity for regimes that are still in existence and may yet prove to last much longer. The degree of underestimation, however, is not dramatic; for example, if 31 percent of all hybrid regimes survived for less than five years according to Polity IV, only 4 percent have been in existence for less than five years but are still hybrid. Thus, even if those 4 percent all eventually lasted more than five years, that still means that 27 percent of

*Table 1.4.* Stability of Hybrid Regimes, 1800–2007
(Polity IV's Anocracies)

| Length of Time without Any Significant Political System Change | Percentage of All Hybrid Regimes |
| --- | --- |
| <5 years | 46 |
| 5–9 years | 25 |
| 10–19 years | 18 |
| ≥20 years | 11 |

all hybrid regimes existing between 1800 and 2007 changed into something else less than five years after appearing. A similar calculation shows that only 37 percent of all hybrid regimes documented by Polity IV between 1800 and 2007 have a chance of lasting twenty years or more (i.e., the twenty-four that already passed the 20-year mark plus the thirteen that are still in existence and could yet reach it). Nevertheless, the conclusion that nearly half (47 %) of all world hybrid regimes by Polity IV's measure and a third (33 %) according to Freedom House have lasted at least ten years is a conservative one. Because a decade is a significant period of time for a regime to endure, it would seem to be important to understand any dynamics that might be peculiar to such states of hybridity.

The Polity IV dataset lets us go one step further in concluding that many hybrid regimes are reasonably stable. The figures in table 1.3 reflect the length of time that a regime stays broadly within the hybrid category, but it may be the case that hybrid regimes are constantly changing within the category, demonstrating a state of flux that indicates we are not dealing with anything worthy of the term "regime." Table 1.4 addresses this issue by breaking hybrid regimes down according to how long they went without any significant change in their political systems, regardless of whether the change left them in the hybrid category. While we do see that just under half changed their political systems within their first five years of existence, we also find that 29 percent remained virtually unchanged for at least ten years. Of course, frequent changes in political system do not necessarily reflect instability if the changes are somehow predictable or part of the broader, underlying hybrid system that is itself quite durable.

How hybrid regimes end also tells us something about their nature. Polity IV provides the most detailed breakdown and most historically comprehensive data, summarized in table 1.5. A significant share (14% of the total since

*Table 1.5.*   How Hybrid Regimes End, 1800–2007, Percentage by Longevity
(Polity IV's Anocracies)

| Longevity | Democracy | Autocracy | Hybrid Now | Foreign Interruption | Anarchy | Negotiations/Other |
|---|---|---|---|---|---|---|
| <5 years | 18 | 38 | 11 | 3 | 9 | 20 |
| 5–9 years | 19 | 30 | 13 | 6 | 3 | 30 |
| 10–19 years | 20 | 23 | 28 | 12 | 2 | 15 |
| ≥20 years | 22 | 29 | 4 | 13 | 3 | 28 |
| All | 20 | 31 | 14 | 8 | 5 | 23 |

*Table 1.6.*   How Hybrid Regimes End, 1972–2008, Percentage by
Longevity (Freedom House's Partly Free)

| Longevity | Democracy | Autocracy | Hybrid Now | Uncoded |
|---|---|---|---|---|
| <5 years | 33 | 55 | 11 | 1 |
| 5–9 years | 38 | 33 | 21 | 8 |
| 10–19 years | 30 | 29 | 41 | 0 |
| ≥20 years | 19 | 24 | 57 | 0 |
| Total | 32 | 41 | 25 | 2 |

1800) remains hybrid today. Moreover, we observe that some did not appear to end of their own accord: for hybrid regimes that survived their first ten years of existence, 12–13 percent were undone by events that were plausibly exogenous, such as foreign occupation. Regardless of longevity, though, about a fifth of all hybrid regimes eventually switched to democracy, while around a quarter to a third became authoritarian, with about 5 percent descending into anarchy and another quarter entering an indeterminate but deliberate process of negotiated regime change. The less detailed coding supplied by Freedom House, whose data are summarized in table 1.6, reveals a similar picture. Hybrid regimes tend to break slightly more frequently toward authoritarianism than to democracy, and hybrid regimes that survived their first five to ten years are significantly more likely to be hybrid today.[21]

Polity IV and Freedom House data indicate that "hybrid regime" is not merely a transitory or artificially conceived category. The number of hybrid regimes that last a long time is far from trivial, and those that do survive their first few years of existence often become reasonably stable. While some hybrid regimes frequently adjust their political systems while remaining hybrid, others display high degrees of institutional stasis. They are not simply, universally, or quickly turning into either autocracies or democracies, and when they do go into transition, they can go in either direction or into a state of indeterminate regime type. The results would argue against studying hybrid regimes only through the conceptual prisms of either democratization or autocratization. Further work should be done to study hybrid regimes on their own terms.

## Prima Facie Evidence That Hybrid Regimes May Have Distinct Effects

There is good reason to believe that hybrid regimes may also generate distinct and important effects. Some of these effects are what we might expect. Hybrid regimes produce some of the advantages of democracy or some of the problems of autocracy, but not in full measure. For example, studies of subnational elections in Russia and national-level elections in Africa have found that even imperfect elections tend to give ordinary people some power: less than in true democracies, but more than in full-fledged authoritarian regimes. Thus, Konitzer concludes that when gubernatorial elections existed in Putin's Russia, the least popular incumbents tended to lose office despite the regime's attempts to manipulate outcomes, and Lindbergh reveals that African elections held even under repressive conditions have systematically given people and elites experience that can force more democratic outcomes in subsequent elections.[22] Government responsiveness and accountability are very important to ordinary citizens, and hybrid regimes seem to display levels of responsiveness and accountability that are different from levels typical of authoritarianism or democracy.

Not all effects attributed to hybrid regimes can be reduced to some kind of average of the effects of democracy and authoritarianism, however. In some spheres, hybridity appears to create something entirely outside the range of what democracies and autocracies produce. States lying in the middle of the democracy-autocracy continuum, for example, are significantly more prone than either democracies or autocracies to state failure and political instability more generally.[23] Thus, even though many hybrid regimes demonstrate significant durability, as in Singapore, others, such as the one in Sierra Leone in the mid-1990s, have descended relatively quickly into anarchy and may be more likely to do so than either democracies or autocracies.

Other indications that hybrid regimes are more than the sum of their parts can be found in various policy realms. In their worldwide study, for example,

Mansfield and Snyder report that countries between democracy and autocracy tend to display more warlike behavior than do either full democracies or full autocracies.[24] While the authors attribute this behavior to transition (democratization), it is conceivable that such foreign policy aggressiveness might also be understood as an effect of hybridity that would occur regardless of whether the regime was moving toward democracy. In another study, Kenyon and Naoi examine surveys of business representatives in postcommunist countries and find that the relationship between business confidence and regime type is U-shaped: hybrid regimes display systematically lower levels of business confidence than either democracies or autocracies.[25] Other research concludes that these in-between systems tend to face greater ecological problems.[26]

If upheld by further research, such findings that hybridity may be more than the sum of its parts would make the strongest case for considering hybrid regimes as a distinct category in our research into political systems. A great deal remains to be done before we can have such confidence, however. For one thing, there remain problems with indicators. Vreeland, for example, has observed that the Polity project treats factionalized and violent political competition within a country as an indicator that it is neither fully democratic nor fully autocratic. Thus, while some scholars have relied on Polity datasets to argue that hybrid regimes ("anocracies") cause more violent domestic political competition and civil war than do democracies or autocracies, Vreeland's analysis shows that this is borne out only by definition. When the dataset is adjusted to avoid this circular reasoning, no clear relationship between hybridity and civil war remains.[27] Researchers must be careful to understand how the data one uses to explore hybridity's effects are constructed.

Researchers must also be careful to avoid other problems of spurious or even reverse causality. For example, if one finds that hybrid regimes tend to exist in countries that have bad relations with their neighbors, this could mean one of three things: that hybrid regimes tend to generate hostile policies toward neighbors; that hostile relations with neighbors tend to produce hybrid regimes; or that some other underlying factor causes both regime hybridity and hostile attitudes toward one's neighbors. The possibility of important third factors also calls attention to the need to include the right set of control variables in our studies. Analysts must also be careful to consider issues of time: regime hybridity may not produce its most important effects instantaneously, just as the legacies of an old regime can continue to impact politics long after a new one has replaced it.[28]

The point of this section is not to resolve such issues but to make the simple case that these issues need to be resolved. The studies cited in the first few paragraphs all represent careful analyses finding that hybrid regimes impact important political outcomes in ways autocracies and democracies do not. Given how numerous hybrid regimes are, and how enduring some of them are, scholars would do well to explore more systematically what the effects of regime hybridity are.

## A Plausible Logic of Hybridity to Explain Regime Longevity and Effects

Conceptualizing regime hybridity is a challenge because there are potentially infinite ways that different autocratic and democratic elements might be combined, as is reflected in the different definitions of the in-between regimes adopted by institutions such as Freedom House, Polity IV, and the Economist Intelligence Unit. Presented here is an effort to depict only one of many possible logics of hybrid regimes with the very limited (but important) goal of demonstrating the plausibility of the notion that there is something about hybridity itself that is sustainable as a regime and that can have important effects that are linked to hybridity itself.

For this limited purpose, it is useful to start with a classic conceptual scheme that has come to underlie much of our thinking about democracy and autocracy. Dahl's concept of *polyarchy* distills the practical essence of democracy to two dimensions: high levels of mass *participation* (or "inclusiveness," the share of individuals allowed to take part in politics) and high degrees of *contestation* (or what he also calls the extent of "liberalization" or "opportunities for political oppositions").[29] Figure 1.1 adapts and expands on a figure Dahl presented in his book. Dahl also notes that these dimensions supply two categories of what he calls "hegemony," which reflects opportunities for opposition politics so scant that one could not say they have any meaningful democratic content. Both "inclusive hegemony" and "closed hegemony," as well as everything else below the horizontal dotted line in the figure, are what we would typically call autocracy or authoritarianism.

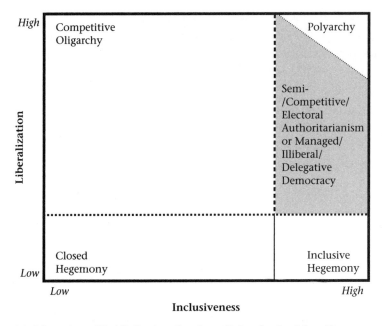

*Figure 1.1.* Adaptation of Dahl's Regime Typology (*Polyarchy*, fig. 1.2, p. 7)

Every space that is neither "hegemony" nor "polyarchy" on Figure 1.1 represents some kind of hybrid regime. Dahl himself gave a distinct label to only one set of hybrid regimes: "competitive oligarchies," regimes at the upper left corner of the figure that feature strong opportunities to oppose the regime but only among a small part of the population (as in the South African example given in the introduction). Beyond this, it is striking that Dahl's scheme actually left the vast majority of his regime quadrant's space—all but the four corner areas—blank and unnamed, despite noting that "perhaps the preponderant number of national regimes in the world today would fall into the mid-area."[30] When referring to them, he called them only "near-polyarchies," "near-closed hegemonies," and so on.[31] But this middle area, above the threshold at which a system is at least somewhat competitive and beyond the line that makes a system inclusive, refers to precisely those regimes that have gained the most attention of late as semi-/competitive/electoral authoritarianism or managed/illiberal/delegative democracy. That is, this particular "mid-area" includes political systems such as the Malaysian one described in the opening paragraphs, where the opposition does have at least some opportunity to contest elections (hence placing the system above the horizontal dotted line defining a hegemony/dictatorship) but where the incumbents systematically weight the outcome in favor of their supporters in ways that seriously compromise democratic principles.[32] We might therefore usefully break hybrid regimes into two categories, competitive oligarchies[33] and the category that includes systems variously referred to as semi-/competitive/electoral authoritarianism or managed/illiberal/delegative democracy (a category that I, in order to preserve neutrality in the terminological debate, refer to here with the demonstratively awkward acronym SCEAOMIDD).

There is reason to suppose that closed hegemonies may well be a dying breed. Spreading global norms of ethnic equality, among other things, have seriously undermined the legitimacy of regimes that explicitly and systematically exclude large segments of their adult populations from political life on an ascriptive basis. The downfall of South Africa's apartheid system under withering international and domestic pressure is one illustration of the difficulty that such regimes now face. Another is the near elimination of gender- and land-based restrictions on the franchise that once existed in the United States and many other countries. We therefore focus here primarily on the other broad category of hybrid regime, the SCEAOMIDD systems, which are in widespread existence today.

What is distinctive about SCEAOMIDD systems, according to Dahl's conceptual scheme, is that real political contestation takes place but is not fair. More precisely, at least some of the most important national political decision makers are chosen through regularly scheduled elections that feature the near-universal adult franchise and that are contested by at least two (sets of) candidates with substantially distinct interests or positions, but where state authorities and their collaborators significantly and systematically, through formal or informal coercive or corrupt methods, hinder the ability of opposition candidates to gain public support and/or to convert this support into officially recognized votes.[34] This specification distinguishes SCEAOMIDD regimes from fully authoritarian (hegemonic) systems, where no significant elections are contested by political forces independent of the rulers. It also differentiates them from democracies (polyarchies), which have experienced the effective removal of most systematic state coercion and corruption from the electoral process. What is hybrid, then, is not just a vague confluence of authoritarian and democratic elements, but the combination of significantly contested elections with state political coercion and corruption. Naturally, these regimes can vary cross-sectionally and intertemporally in the balance of contestation and coercion/corruption they involve and in the form that the elements of contestation and coercion/corruption take.

Research has uncovered myriad coercive or corrupt methods that incumbent SCEAOMIDD authorities use to defeat their opponents. Many fall into the following categories:

1.  *Media manipulation.* Where the state owns mass media, it can directly bias content in favor of pro-incumbent candidates and policies. Where media are privately owned, owners can be pressured in a variety of ways to toe the authorities' line. Television is of paramount importance if most people have access to it because it tends to be the most influential on political views.[35]

2.  *Coercing or buying votes.* Authorities frequently promise material rewards or threaten denial of basic services to communities in order to get them to vote in the "right" way.[36] This can be particularly effective when it comes to public-sector employees. Hybrid regime rulers can also promise more severe punishments for an "incorrect" ballot by jailing protesters and hinting that they will be able to find out who voted for whom.[37] Sometimes direct forms of vote buying are employed, such as systems whereby people are paid after proving they voted the right way by presenting a mobile phone picture of their ballot, or a "carousel" whereby one individual is given a premarked pro-regime ballot to cast in place of his or her own ballot, which must be brought to the organizer unmarked so that it can be marked for the authorities and given to the next person in the carousel.

3.  *Supporting informal groups to attack opposition.* Rulers have been reported to support (or even create) loyal nonstate organizations that serve the purpose of attacking opposition representatives or hindering their activities.[38]

4.  *Manipulation of the choice set.* Some SCEAOMIDD authorities have become masters at creating fake opposition movements, sets of politicians or parties that criticize the government publicly but that are really supported by the incumbent regime as a way of channeling or diverting opposition votes. Authorities can also selectively disqualify, ban,

or disadvantage certain opposition parties or candidates in an attempt to manipulate the choices voters face.[39]

5. *Pressuring, co-opting, or blackmailing elites.* Incumbent officials frequently deny licenses or audit disloyal businesses and privilege the loyal ones; pressure, fire, or subvert regional leaders, bureaucrats, or officials in state enterprises or institutions who do not produce sufficient voting for the regime; or simply prosecute, blackmail, or pay off potential backers of the opposition.[40]

6. *Selective prosecution.* Incumbents have also been found to adopt an elaborate set of laws governing important political processes that are almost impossible to follow fully in practice and that are often designed intentionally to maximize the discretion of courts and prosecutors. When almost everyone can be found guilty, the authorities gain the power to prosecute or disqualify almost anyone they want, at the same time ensuring that friendly parties, candidates, or individuals can get away with illegal activities that give them electoral advantage.[41]

7. *Falsification.* Sometimes elections are simply stolen, though rarely wholesale and mostly as a last resort because SCEAOMIDD authorities' dominance tends to rest more on the other methods listed here. Fraud can consist of the manipulation of voter rolls, false ballots, biased criteria for ruling on questionable ballots, or fabricated counts.[42]

The most important point here is that the application of these techniques *when at least some true opposition is allowed to compete* (i.e., the *interaction* between the democratic and autocratic elements that make a regime hybrid) can produce cumulative effects that are typical of neither full democracies nor full autocracies, that are not necessarily short-lived, and that might plausibly be associated with the kind of unique outcomes discussed in the previous section. A brief discussion is enough to make the point. Let us first show how the presence of at least some genuine opposition can alter the impact of each coercive/corrupt element before turning to the bigger picture.

1. *Media manipulation.* People are not infinitely manipulable through media, and it often happens that criticism by mistrusted official media can enhance the popularity of opposition figures.[43]

2. *Coercing or buying votes.* Individuals sometimes are so committed (or so deeply opposed) to a candidate or party that they cannot be bought off. In such cases, attempts at intimidation or vote buying not only fail but can backfire. This is especially true because in SCEAOMIDD systems people do not actually have to go out into the streets to have an impact: they also have the option of simply casting an opposition ballot; a relatively safe act that can have massive effects when done in large numbers (see point 7 below on election fraud). While authorities frequently find clever ways to monitor voters in vote-buying schemes, voters are often just as clever in finding ways to take the money and vote as they please.

3. *Supporting informal groups to attack opposition.* While such groups can intimidate, they can also inspire hatred for the incumbent authorities, contributing to their unpopularity and emboldening committed opposition forces when they get a chance to strike back.

4. *Manipulation of the choice set.* Even "puppets" of the regime or regime-created "virtual" parties can take on lives of their own. The stronger opposition sentiment is in a country, the greater incentive the puppets have to become a real opposition and grab their own strings. Indeed, puppets may be using the regime to gain resources for their own political agendas as much as they are being used.

5. *Pressuring, co-opting, or blackmailing elites.* The effectiveness of these tactics depends on whether the elites believe the incumbent authorities will still be in power *after* the elections to follow through on the threatened punishments or promised rewards.[44] And because the authorities depend on elites to mete out punishments and dole out rewards—including those who officially count the votes, police the streets, transfer the funds, and rule on disputes—elite calculations about the authorities' longevity are also likely to depend on what they think other elites are thinking. Given that the other coercive/corrupt mechanisms discussed here can break down or backfire when the opposition enjoys popular support, public opinion is likely to strongly influence elite calculations as to the likelihood a given SCEAOMIDD leader will be able to win an election and as to whether it is in their interests to "defect" or to hedge their bets by covertly supporting opposition candidates as well.

6.  *Selective prosecution.* Because selective prosecution hinges on discretion in applying the law, the elites wielding this discretion on behalf of ruling authorities (including court justices) are also subject to the same pressures facing the other elites discussed in point 4. Moreover, where the outcome of an electoral struggle is uncertain, judges may perceive they have the power to tip the scales with their ruling, especially when they are ruling on the final results of an election. That is, they may see that they themselves can decide which political force will be in a position to do the rewarding and punishing after the election. In such cases, they can behave quite independently, with or without the guidance of the law.

7.  *Falsification.* The greater and more obvious is mass support for the opposition, the riskier and costlier is falsification for incumbents and the safer is street protest for the opposition. Tucker explains why: elections constitute a kind of "focal point" that can facilitate mass protest outside the polling place, protest that itself becomes another channel for mass influence on SCEAOMIDD outcomes. That is, elections in which an opposition candidate is "obviously" the victim of fraud provide a precise time when individuals willing to challenge the incumbents understand that like-minded individuals are also likely to go out and challenge the incumbents. This solves an important coordination problem (deciding on a single time to protest) and creates some expectation of "safety in numbers" that can facilitate mass opposition mobilization when it would not otherwise occur.[45]

All together, these dynamics—the interaction of the democratic and autocratic elements that make a SCEAOMIDD regime hybrid—produce a certain subset of regime behaviors that are not typical of democracies or autocracies but that deserve deeper scholarly exploration in their own right. We see that public opinion matters greatly in SCEAOMIDD systems, even producing a certain form of accountability. This accountability is simply realized through a dissolution of elite unity rather than through—as in democracies—an honest count of votes won in a reasonably free and fair campaign. The postelection protest against unpopular incumbents, therefore, can be an integral part of the SCEAOMIDD accountability mechanism. Examples range from the postcommunist colored revolutions (Serbia 2000, Georgia 2003, Ukraine 2004, Kyrgyzstan

2005) to the Iranian uprising of 2009 to the postelection protests that forced incumbents to share power with oppositions in Kenya in 2007 and Zimbabwe in 2008. This helps account for the "instability" researchers have found is associated with SCEAOMIDD systems. But to the extent that such protests are regular and reasonably predictable (possibly even cyclic), we must be careful not to equate their appearance with a lack of regime institutionalization. It is instead *reflective* of a *certain kind* of regime institutionalization—just not democratic or autocratic institutionalization, and an institutionalization in which informal rules and procedures are often more prominent than formal ones.[46]

This simple perspective also helps us understand some of the other findings as to hybrid regime effects that were discussed earlier. If hybrid regimes are associated with greater propensities for war, it could be that the threat of war can be useful to unpopular authorities as a way to preserve elite unity (through a rally-round-the-flag effect) in the face of a more popular opposition. If SCEAOMIDD systems display lower levels of business confidence, this could be because the authorities systematically politicize business at the same time that (or perhaps because) they are more vulnerable to disorderly ouster, ouster that for business could mean the collapse of previous deals or the loss of investments.

## Conclusion

Overall, political science and policy making are both likely to benefit from a research program that, while not denying the importance of continuing to study democratization, focuses on hybrid regimes for what they are, comparing them not only to democracies and autocracies but to each other and with respect to outcomes other than just whether in the end they become democracies or autocracies.[47] For one thing, we have found that there are numerous hybrid regimes. Moreover, once they appear, they often last quite a while. According to one measure, almost half (47%) since 1800 have lasted at least ten years, and surely that is enough time for the dynamics of such systems to matter and be worth studying. And there is at least prima facie evidence that these dynamics are distinct: studies have found that hybrid regimes display more warlike foreign policy behavior, lower business confidence, greater environmental problems, and more frequent formal institutional disruption than either democracies or autocracies—findings that resonate with what one might expect from the interaction of democratic and autocratic elements in a polity. Because some of the world's most influential countries are classified by some definitions as hybrid regimes—such as Russia, Egypt, Nigeria, and Venezuela—we would seem to ignore a theoretical understanding of their nature at our own peril.

The purpose of this chapter is not to present these claims as definitive. Too little research has been devoted to hybrid regimes as a distinct category, with the vast bulk of research treating them essentially as regimes in transition to something else or as transitory states of being that are not worthy of deep or systematic theoretical inquiry in their own right. It may yet be that the latter claims are right, though the preliminary evidence presented here strongly suggests otherwise. The main argument of this chapter, therefore, is that there are sufficient grounds for putting hybrid regimes at the center of a research agenda of their own.

NOTES

The author gratefully acknowledges helpful feedback from Nathan Brown, Sheri Berman, and other participants in two workshops dedicated to this volume at The George Washington University's Elliott School of International Affairs in Washington, DC. He is also grateful for the research assistance of Craig Kaufman and Marketa Jenesova and for support provided to the author as a Title VIII Research Scholar at the Woodrow Wilson International Center for Scholars' Kennan Institute during 2009. The views expressed here, of course, are solely those of the author and not those of the U.S. government or any institution.

1. Gabriel A. Almond and Sidney Verba, *The Civic Culture* (Princeton: Princeton University Press, 1963); Samuel P. Huntington, *The Third Wave: Democratization in the Late Twentieth Century* (Norman: University of Oklahoma, 1991); Seymour Martin Lipset, *Political Man* (Garden City, NY: Doubleday, 1960); Adam Przeworski, *Democracy and the Market* (New York: Cambridge University Press, 1991); Robert Putnam, *Making Democracy Work* (Princeton: Princeton University Press, 1993); Dankwart Rustow, "Transitions to Democracy: Towards a Dynamic Model," *Comparative Politics* 2 (1970): 337–63.

2. Houchang E. Chehabi and Juan J. Linz, *Sultanistic Regimes* (Baltimore: Johns Hopkins University Press, 1998); David Collier, ed., *The New Authoritarianism in Latin America* (Princeton: Princeton University Press, 1979); Carl J. Friedrich and Zbigniew K. Brzezinski, *Totalitarian Dictatorship and Autocracy* (Cambridge, MA: Harvard University Press, 1956); Juan J. Linz, *Totalitarian and Authoritarian Regimes* (Boulder, CO: Westview Press, 2000).

3. Daron Acemoglu and James Robinson, *The Economic Origins of Dictatorship and Democracy* (Cambridge: Cambridge University Press, 2007); Juan J. Linz and Alfred Stepan, "Political Crafting of Democratic Consolidation or Destruction: European and South American Comparisons," in Robert A. Pastor, ed., *Democracy in the Americas:*

*Stopping the Pendulum* (New York: Holmes & Meier, 1989), pp. 41–61; Barrington Moore Jr., *Social Origins of Dictatorship and Democracy* (Boston: Beacon Press, 1966).

4. Robert A. Dahl, *Polyarchy* (New Haven: Yale University Press, 1971).

5. Nancy Bermeo, "Democracy in Europe," *Daedalus* 123 (Spring 1994): 159–78; Larry Diamond, *Developing Democracy* (Baltimore: Johns Hopkins University Press, 1999); Giuseppe Di Palma, *To Craft Democracies: An Essay on Democratic Transitions* (Berkeley: University of California Press, 1990); M. Steven Fish, *Democracy from Scratch* (Princeton: Princeton University Press, 1995); Terry Lynn Karl and Philippe Schmitter, "Modes of Transition in Southern and Eastern Europe, Southern and Central America," *International Social Science Journal* 128 (May 1991): 269–84; Michael McFaul, *Russia's Unfinished Revolution* (Ithaca: Cornell University Press, 2001).

6. Guillermo O'Donnell and Philippe C. Schmitter, *Transitions from Authoritarian Rule: Tentative Conclusions about Uncertain Democracies* (Baltimore: Johns Hopkins University Press, 1986): 41–44.

7. Valerie J. Bunce, "Rethinking Recent Democratization: Lessons from the Post-Communist Experience," *World Politics* 55 (January 2003): 167–92; Stephen E. Hanson, "Defining Democratic Consolidation," in Richard D. Anderson Jr., M. Steven Fish, Stephen E. Hanson, and Philip G. Roeder, *Postcommunism and the Theory of Democracy* (Princeton: Princeton University Press, 2001); Juan J. Linz and Alfred Stepan, *Problems of Democratic Transition and Consolidation: Southern Europe, South America, and Post-Communist Europe* (Baltimore: Johns Hopkins University Press, 1996); Geraldo L. Munck, "The Regime Question: Theory Building in Democracy Studies," *World Politics* 54 (October 2001): 119–44; Andreas Schedler "What Is Democratic Consolidation?" *Journal of Democracy* 9 (April 1998): 91–107.

8. Guillermo O'Donnell, "Delegative Democracy," *Journal of Democracy* 5 (January 1994): 55–69.

9. Fareed Zakaria, "The Rise of Illiberal Democracy," *Foreign Affairs* 76 (November–December 1997): 22–43.

10. Timothy J. Colton and Michael McFaul, *Popular Choice and Managed Democracy: The Russian Elections of 1999 and 2000* (Washington, DC: Brookings Institution Press, 2003).

11. John Ssenkumba, "The Dilemmas of Directed Democracy: Neutralizing Opposition: Politics under the National Resistance Movement (NRM) [Uganda]," *East African Journal of Peace & Human Rights* 3, no. 2 (1996): 240–61.

12. David Collier and Steven Levitsky, "Democracy with Adjectives: Conceptual Innovation in Comparative Research," *World Politics* 49 (April 1997): 430–51.

13. Thomas Carothers, "The End of the Transition Paradigm," *Journal of Democracy* 13 (January 2002): 5–21.

14. Larry Diamond, "Thinking about Hybrid Regimes," *Journal of Democracy* 13 (April 2002): 21–35; Steven Levitsky and Lucan A. Way, "The Rise of Competitive Authoritarianism," *Journal of Democracy* 13 (April 2002): 51–65; Andreas Schedler, "The Menu of Manipulation," *Journal of Democracy* 13 (April 2002): 36–50; Nicolas Van de Walle, "Africa's Range of Regimes," *Journal of Democracy* 13 (April 2002): 66–80.

15. Respectively: Terry Lynn Karl, "The Hybrid Regimes of Central America," *Journal of Democracy* 6 (July 1995): 72–87; Jeffrey Herbst, "Political Liberalization in Africa after Ten Years," *Comparative Politics* 33 (April): 357–75; and Vladimir Gel'man, "Regime

Transition, Uncertainty and the Prospects for Redemocratisation," *Europe-Asia Studies* 51 (1999): 939–56.

16. Levitsky and Way, "The Rise of Competitive Authoritarianism"; Lucan A. Way, "Authoritarian State-Building and the Sources of Regime Competitiveness in the Fourth Wave: The Cases of Belarus, Moldova, Russia, and Ukraine," *World Politics* 57 (January 2005): 231–61.

17. Beatriz Magaloni, *Voting for Autocracy: Hegemonic Party Survival and Its Demise in Mexico* (New York: Cambridge University Press, 2006); Andreas Schedler, ed., *Electoral Authoritarianism: The Dynamics of Unfree Competition* (Boulder, CO: Lynne Rienner, 2006).

18. Marina Ottaway, *Democracy Challenged: The Rise of Semi-authoritarianism* (Washington, DC: Carnegie Endowment for International Peace, 2003).

19. Recent examples include Jason Brownlee, "Portents of Pluralism: How Hybrid Regimes Affect Democratic Transitions," *American Journal of Political Science* 53 (July 2009): 515–32; Valerie J. Bunce, and Sharon L. Wolchik, "Defeating Dictators: Electoral Change and Stability in Competitive Authoritarian Regimes," *World Politics* 62 (January 2010): 43–86; Steven Levitsky and Lucan A. Way, *Competitive Authoritarianism: Hybrid Regimes after the Cold War* (New York: Cambridge University Press, 2010).

20. See Giovanni Capoccia and Daniel Ziblatt, "The Historical Turn in Democratization Studies: A New Research Agenda for Europe and Beyond," *Comparative Political Studies* 43 (August–September 2010): 931–68.

21. In comparing the Freedom House and Polity IV data here, remember that because Polity IV records countries starting in 1800, relatively few instances of hybrid regimes are likely to survive to the present, unlike Freedom House, where the coding started with 1972.

22. Andrew Konitzer, *Voting for Russia's Governors* (Baltimore: Johns Hopkins University Press, 2005); Staffan I. Lindberg, *Democracy and Elections in Africa* (Baltimore: Johns Hopkins University Press, 2006).

23. Jack A. Goldstone, Robert H. Bates, David L. Epstein, Ted Robert Gurr, Michael B. Lustik, Monty G. Marshall, Jay Ulfelder, and Mark Woodward, "A Global Model for Forecasting Political Instability," *American Journal of Political Science* 54 (January 2010): 190–208; Jack A. Goldstone, Ted Robert Gurr, Barbara Harff, Marc A. Levy, Monty G. Marshall, Robert H. Bates, David L. Epstein, Colin H. Kahl, Pamela T. Surko, John C. Ulfelder Jr., and Alan N. Unger, *State Failure Task Force Report: Phase III Findings* (MacLean, VA: Science Applications International Corporation, September 30, 2000), http://globalpolicy.gmu.edu/pitf/SFTF%20Phase%20III%20Report%20Final.pdf, accessed January 12, 2007.

24. Edward Mansfield and Jack Snyder, *Electing to Fight: Why Emerging Democracies Go to War* (Cambridge, MA: MIT Press, 2005).

25. Thomas Kenyon and Megumi Naoi, "Policy Uncertainty in Hybrid Regimes: Evidence from Firm-Level Surveys," *Comparative Political Studies* 43 (April 2010): 486–510.

26. David L. Epstein, Robert Bates, Jack Goldstone, Ida Kristensen, and Sharyn O'Halloran, "Democratic Transitions," *American Journal of Political Science* 50 (July 2006): 551.

27. James Raymond Vreeland, "The Effect of Political Regime on Civil War: Unpacking Anocracy," *Journal of Conflict Resolution* 52, no. 3 (2008): 401–25.

28. Keith Darden and Anna Grzymala-Busse, "The Great Divide: Literacy, Nationalism, and the Communist Collapse," *World Politics* 59 (October 2006): 83–115.

29. Dahl, *Polyarchy*, pp. 7, 232.

30. Ibid., p. 8.

31. This reflected Dahl's focus on transition (*Polyarchy*, p. 1), on understanding why and how regimes can move toward the one corner area of primary interest, polyarchy, rather than on identifying specific logics common to the "mid-area."

32. On Malaysia, see Dan Slater, *Ordering Power: Contentious Politics and Authoritarian Leviathans in Southeast Asia* (New York: Cambridge University Press, 2010).

33. Here understood (somewhat more broadly than Dahl understands them) as any regime combining significant contestation with any level of political exclusion (denial of participation) that would disqualify a regime from being considered a polyarchy. Thus, we do not limit competitive oligarchies to the very upper-left corner of the regime space.

34. Some of the language modifies Huntington's definition of democracy in *The Third Wave*, 7.

35. Schedler, "The Menu of Manipulation"; Andrew Wilson, *Virtual Politics: Faking Democracy in the Post-Soviet World* (New Haven: Yale University Press, 2005).

36. Paul D'Anieri, "Explaining the Success and Failure of Postcommunist Revolutions," *Communist and Post-Communist Studies* 39 (September 2006): 331–50; Schedler, "The Menu of Manipulation."

37. Javier Corrales, "Venezuela: Petro-politics and the Promotion of Disorder," in Christopher Walker, ed., *Undermining Democracy: 21st Century Authoritarians* (Washington, DC: Freedom House, June 2009), pp. 65–80; report available at www.underminingdemocracy.org/files/UnderminingDemocracy_Full.pdf, accessed April 25, 2010.

38. Ibid.

39. Schedler, "The Menu of Manipulation"; Wilson, *Virtual Politics*.

40. Keith Darden, "Blackmail as a Tool of State Domination: Ukraine under Kuchma," *East European Constitutional Review* 10 (Spring–Summer 2001): 67–71; Keith Darden, "The Integrity of Corrupt States: Graft as an Informal State Institution," *Politics & Society* 36, no. 1 (2008): 35–59; Schedler, "The Menu of Manipulation."

41. Corrales, "Venezuela: Petro-politics and the Promotion of Disorder"; Steven Levitsky and Lucan A. Way, "Why Democracy Needs a Level Playing Field," *Journal of Democracy* 21 (January 2010): 57–68.

42. Corrales, "Venezuela: Petro-politics and the Promotion of Disorder"; Mikhail Myagkov, Peter C. Ordeshook, and Dmitri Shakin, "Fraud or Fairytales: Russia and Ukraine's Electoral Experience," *Post-Soviet Affairs* 21 (April–June 2005): 91–131; Schedler, "The Menu of Manipulation"; Mark R. Thompson and Philipp Kuntz, "After Defeat: When Do Rulers Steal Elections?" in Schedler, *Electoral Authoritarianism*, pp. 113–28.

43. Denis McQuail, *Mass Communication Theory: An Introduction*, 2nd ed. (London: Sage, 1987).

44. Susan C. Stokes, "Perverse Accountability: A Formal Model of Machine Politics with Evidence from Argentina," *American Political Science Review* 99 (August 2005): 315–25; Henry E. Hale, "Regime Cycles: Democracy, Autocracy, and Revolution in Post-Soviet Eurasia," *World Politics* 58, no. 1 (October 2005): 133–65.

45. Joshua A. Tucker, "Enough! Electoral Fraud, Collective Action Problems, and the '2nd Wave' of Post-Communist Democratic Revolutions," *Perspectives on Politics* 53, no. 5 (2007): 537–53.

46. On the distinction between formal and informal institutions, see Steven Levitsky and Gretchen Helmke, *Informal Institutions and Democracy: Lessons from Latin America* (Baltimore: Johns Hopkins University Press, 2006).

47. See also Marc Morje Howard and Philip G. Roessler, "Liberalizing Electoral Outcomes in Competitive Authoritarian Regimes," *American Journal of Political Science* 50 (April 2006): 365.

# CHAPTER 2

# Dictatorship and Democracy through the Prism of Arab Elections

## *Nathan J. Brown*

In 2006 opposition deputies in Kuwait's parliament pressed so forcefully for electoral reform that the country's amir dissolved the body and called for new elections. When Kuwaitis went to the polls, they delivered a stunning victory to the opposition—stunning not only because the opposition had won but also because it was not clear what it had won. While Kuwaitis marveled that "the opposition is now the majority," they highlighted the irony of the result—in normal circumstances in a democracy, when the opposition becomes the majority, it ceases being in opposition and begins governing. That did not happen in Kuwait. The opposition won some concessions, and some of its members won a smattering of cabinet seats. But the fundamental shape of the policy and politics remained unchanged.

The Kuwaiti elections of 2006 were extremely unusual for the Arab world in their result. (They were unusual in one other respect as well—formal political parties are not recognized by law making it a bit unclear at times who is in the government and who is in the opposition.) But in one way they starkly illustrated the general pattern of Arab elections in recent years—the opposition can run, but it cannot win. Political systems have been carefully designed to ensure that opposition parties remain precisely that—opposition parties.

In this chapter, I argue that the critical difference between fully authoritarian, semiauthoritarian, and democratic regimes lies in what the opposition is allowed to do. Specifically, is the opposition allowed to operate, and is it allowed to take power? Focusing on the combination of dull, predictable outcomes and constantly shifting rules can help us think a bit more clearly about democracy, authoritarianism, the space between them, and the transition among categories.

## Introduction: The Interesting Case of the Boring Elections

Judging by the suspense they engender, Arab elections would seem to be worthy at most of a passing mention in a book on democratization and not a very polite one at that. While the rules by which they are governed vary greatly—and are often redesigned each time they are held—with the rarest of exceptions it is only the margin of victory for the governing party that lies in doubt. But this chapter is based on an audacious claim—that these two features of Arab elections—the increasing unpredictability of their rules but the dull predictability of their results—allows us to clarify three issues that have led to confusion among students of democracy and democratization.

First, the very idea of elections would seem to be based on the principle that the people rule themselves. The obvious purpose of elections is to allow people to express their preferences. Yet elections are widely used in nondemocratic settings where the people clearly do not rule. Why?

Second, the realization that not every society is a democracy waiting to break out has led to an increased interest in nondemocratic systems—and especially in regimes that fall between pure authoritarianism and stable democratic systems. But our vocabulary has burgeoned without any increase in clarity (or even terminological standardization): we have learned about "hybrid" regimes, "semiauthoritarianism," "electoral authoritarianism," and assorted political regimes that populate a vast "gray area." Those who focus on such concepts often show deep ambivalence about what they wish to understand.[1] While they insist that the regimes they study are stable, not merely transitional or in-between phases, they cannot resist focusing on the seams among categories and studying how regimes move from one category to another. It is not clear whether it is the stability of such regimes or their evolution that should draw more of our attention. We clearly need more clarity as well as a way to account for both stability and transformation.

Third, the frequently repeated cliché about the relationship between elections and democracy—that "democracy is more than elections"—creates deep problems for the analyst the more it becomes accepted. While it captures the reality of nondemocratic elections, the cliché threatens to discard the shred of conceptual clarity still contained in the word "democracy." The claim that democracy is more than elections is generally followed by associating it with a shopping list of fashionable procedures and laudatory values from speech guarantees to property rights to tolerance. If democracy is quite literally to be defined by everything in politics that is deemed good, it is clear why we like it so much. But how is any analytical content left in the term? How can such a shopping list help us distinguish what is a democracy and what is not? The threat of conceptual imprecision is not merely one for academics; terminological elasticity also allows deeply authoritarian regimes to pose as democratic. As a recent Freedom House report noted, "Leading authoritarian regimes are working to reshape the public understanding of democracy. A redefined and heavily distorted version of the concept is communicated to domestic audiences through state-dominated media."[2]

In this chapter, we use Arab elections and their changing nature because the Arab world is a particularly fertile field in which to explore our three areas of inquiry. First, it is rich with the nondemocratic elections we seek to understand. Second, it is rich as well with varieties of authoritarian and hybrid regimes. Indeed, scholars of the Arab world agree that authoritarianism is widespread throughout the region, but they also hasten to add adjectives, describing Arab authoritarianism in various countries as "upgraded," "liberalized," or adulterated in some way.[3] Third, it will help us learn something about the region we have chosen for special focus: the more conceptually precise definition of democracy we develop can help us engage in some very modest predictions about the likely flashpoints of Arab politics in coming years.

We begin with the broadest puzzle: why are voters asked to express their preferences through voting when their votes do not matter? Our answer leads us to recast the question to ask not why elections are held but how they are used, and doing so helps illuminate the increasingly used but ill-defined distinction between semiauthoritarian and fully authoritarian regimes. By using elections as a tool for understanding the distinctions among categories, we can learn something about the essence of the categories and something about elections as well.

## Motivations for Nondemocratic Elections

Let us start not with a shopping list of good things but with a far more precise definition of democracy introduced by Adam Przeworski—that it is a political system in which parties lose elections.[4] Less concisely, Przeworski means to suggest that democracy exists if there is no political party that can be assured victory. If there exists a party that must always win, the system is not democratic. (If one party always wins in fact, but it is not clear that the system is rigged to prevent other results, then we do not know whether the system is democratic or not.) This definition was consciously designed to return the relationship of democracy with liberal values and practices back to the realm of research, preventing the imposition of association of democracy with good things by conceptual and definitional fiat. In this regard, the definition appears to recover democracy's original and core meaning—rule by the people— stripping it of all the normative and institutional baggage it has acquired, especially over the past century (though later we will explore how Przeworski's definition is actually neither so bare nor so classical as it initially appears).

According to this definition, elections are a necessary but not sufficient condition for democracy—that is, for democracy to exist, all parties entering elections must be able to lose. Thus, our question regarding nondemocratic elections becomes, Why are elections held if there is a party that is guaranteed victory? The question is of widespread relevance. Elections are close to ubiquitous in extant political systems, but democracy is not. This anomaly is particularly acute in the Arab world. No Arab political system is democratic, but all have elections. And elections are being held more often.

Some Arab electoral systems, to be sure, are formally and explicitly restricted in their reach. In the family monarchies of the Arabian Peninsula, the identity of the ruler and the most sensitive positions in the kingdom are determined behind closed doors by members of the ruling family. In Saudi Arabia, elections are restricted to local government; in other states, national elections exist but are fairly new. In the United Arab Emirates, the government selects certain citizens to vote—an odd reversal of the democratic norm in which it is the voters who select the rulers. And in all countries, regimes are only slightly more bashful than in the Emirates—throughout the region, electoral rules are crafted and recrafted in order to guide the people's will into very specific outcomes.

Yet for all these restrictions, elections remain far more remarkable for their presence than their absence. They are hardly new, having been introduced in the Arab world in the nineteenth century. Elections are generally held regularly, their use is gradually spreading, and the right to participate has widened as well so that in almost all countries all adult citizens may vote. Every regime in the Arab world has strong authoritarian features but almost every one also has elections. Why? In this regard, three reasons are generally adduced.

The first motivation is legitimation. While often exaggerated, this motivation can be important. Rigged elections fool few people, but they can still serve an important function for regimes by making them appear inevitable. In this respect, ritualistic victory by rulers serves more to frustrate would-be opponents rather than win them over. Elections can show that even formally democratic challenges are futile.[5]

Second, elections have been observed to be part of the construction of patronage networks.[6] One scholar of authoritarianism in the Arab world claims that, while "there is a significant amount of competition in authoritarian elections," the competition is "over access to state resources" in which deputies are elected not on the basis of program, ideology, or legislative record but simply according to their ability to pass benefits on to constituents.[7] Such usage is hardly restricted to the republics with their dominant party machines—though such regimes (including those in Egypt, Syria, Palestine, and Yemen) have used them with abandon—but is extended to monarchies as well. Indeed, monarchies intervene in elections often through favoring specific individuals (or, on rare occasions, parties) deemed friendly or supportive. In Kuwait, the ruling family even brought new elements of the society into the political system from outlying districts in order to have a supportive parliament; it did so through the provision of benefits, services, and access to selected tribal leaders and pliant candidates.[8] Bahrain now appears to be following a similar path of generous grants of citizenship to formerly excluded groups in order to make elections safe for the monarchy.

Third, elections can serve to signal and reinforce major policy initiatives and ideological reorientations. When Egypt adopted socialism in the early 1960s and then turned away from it in the 1970s, and when it moved to give Islamic coloration to its political system in the 1970s and then turned away from that three decades later, ritualistic and essentially uncontested referenda about constitutional texts consecrated these shifts. Such elections are opportunities for senior leaders to pound in a message about policy and ideology—and bring officialdom into active support of new themes and policy directions.

What is notable about all these uses for elections is that they attenuate the tie between elections and regime type. These purposes might be useful to any political system.[9] They require little in the way of free speech, pluralist political party systems (or even individual parties), neutral electoral administration, or procedural fairness. (Some, but not all, of the legitimating functions of elections might be assisted by recognizable freedoms and fairness, but no Arab regime has been willing to pay the full price to obtain international or domestic legitimacy through undeniably free and fair elections.)

It is thus not hard to understand why elections are widespread—they provide some benefits and can be designed to minimize costs by shutting out political opposition completely. And we can understand as well why elections persist—once brought into being, such elections rarely provoke an urge to abolish them even if there is a radical change in the regime. Elections can be mildly useful to any regime. What varies is how elections are used—and therefore how they are held.

## Semiauthoritarian Elections

To understand what kind of elections regimes might hold, we must consider regime type, because different regimes favor different kinds of elections. In so doing, we discover that we can return some analytical clarity to terms such as authoritarianism and democracy.

### *The Prominence of Semiauthoritarianism*

Not all Arab regimes are fully authoritarian. Most have come to allow for some pluralism in party organization and a degree of free expression—always within harsh if constantly shifting limits. Generally, party pluralism is central to this loosening—political parties are allowed to operate within certain bounds. They may compete in elections, but they cannot challenge the policies, preferences, and identities of the ultimate holders of power. The reason for the emergence of such regimes is beyond our focus in this essay; for now we seek only to understand how they use the elections they have inherited, generally from fully authoritarian predecessors.

Our effort to understand why elections are held is, in a real sense, an odd task: It is a question rarely posed by the people who hold elections, run in them, or even those who vote. In fact, the question almost presumes a conscious decision to hold elections. But while elections have generally been introduced at a specific time by conscious decision, that time was long ago in most countries. By now elections are routine. There are a few countries that have avoided them or still use them only in an episodic fashion. But most have them regularly, at a time mandated by the constitution. In that sense, there is no decision to hold elections; balloting is simply a part of the political landscape.

The questions that regimes (and oppositions) ask involve not whether to hold elections but how to hold them—and how to use them. And that leads us to a remarkable feature of Arab elections: it is only a slight exaggeration to say that the fact of elections seems written in stone but that the rules governing them are written on water.

The situation is not as unusual as might initially appear. Students of politics have noted in recent years how widespread some democratic mechanisms are—most notably multiparty or multicandidate elections—in political systems that are not democratic.[10] Scholars have reacted by setting to work in seeking to understand the emergence and persistence of "hybrid," "semiauthoritarian," or "liberalized autocratic" regimes. Such writings help illuminate the way, but they have blind spots. Most particularly, writings on semiauthoritarianism have not overcome the very democratic teleology they are generally reacting against. Scholars writing on authoritarianism, democracy, and transitions in the 1980s and 1990s rarely sought to mask their championing of democratic outcomes, thus mixing scholarship and advocacy. Later writings tended to diminish (though not eliminate) the advocacy for and optimism about democracy; but a very heavy residue of democratic teleology remains.

The idea of semiauthoritarianism and the related but separate concepts of "hybrid" and "electoral authoritarian" regimes neatly illustrate this limited retreat. These terms have gained ground quickly partly because they no longer treat all political systems as democracies waiting to break out. But semiauthoritarianism is defined more by what it is not (full authoritarianism or democracy) than what it is; even when it is defined in positive terms, definitions feature what it borrows from fully democratic and fully authoritarian systems. This is even truer of "hybrid" regimes, which are defined largely in terms of how close they come to a fully liberal democracy.[11] Similarly, "electoral authoritarian" regimes still have elections as a defining characteristic (as if that is their most critical institution). With all these stripes of political systems, scholars are often deeply interested in what can transform them into democracies. Indeed, writings on electoral authoritarianism have two major themes—the first is to illustrate how the elections are cooked, and the second is to probe when and how the cooks can make fatal mistakes by losing elections they were supposed to win.[12]

These shortcomings should not lead us to abandon the concepts. Existing writings even address—albeit in passing—a puzzle that has drawn our attention already: the combination of the regularity of elections with complete stability in the results. Why constantly tinker with the rules of elections when the outcome is not in doubt? The answer seems fairly clear: the tinkering takes place precisely to ensure that the outcome remains beyond contestation. In some ways, this is the precise opposite of a democratic system as it relates to outcomes and rules. Valerie Bunce has noted that "we need to think of democracy as a two-part proposition, having uncertain results (or competition) but also having certain procedures."[13] Exploring how elections are designed and used in the Arab world can help us understand this process—and move beyond treating semiauthoritarianism as a residual category or a halfway house on a road with no particular direction.

## Negotiating the Terms of Opposition in the Arab World

In the semiauthoritarian systems of the Arab world, the important electoral struggles on which to focus—for both activists and analysts—are not the campaigns or the balloting but the organization and administration of elections. Regimes and oppositions argue, posture, and bargain continuously and without final agreement over who may run in elections, who will oversee the balloting, how votes will be translated into seats, who may observe the electoral process, how campaigns will be conducted, how candidates and parties can deliver their messages and what those messages may be, and what authorities of the elected body will be granted. As Andreas Schedler has written, "neither incumbents nor opponents will perceive manipulated elections as an 'equilibrium' solution that corresponds to their long-term interests. Rather, they will accept the rules of the electoral game as a temporary compromise, a provisional truce contingent on current correlations of force and open to revision in the uncertain future." He continues more formally, "The ambivalent and thus (usually) contested nature of flawed elections implies that elections do not unfold as simple games but as two-level games. . . . At the same time as incumbents and opponents measure their forces in the electoral arena, they battle over the basic rules that shape the electoral arena. Their struggle over institutional rules is not extraneous to but an integral part of their struggle within prevalent institutional rules, as the game of electoral competition is embedded within the meta-game of electoral reform."[14]

Schedler's emphasis on fluidity does not go far enough. Speaking of a "truce" suggests that the contest over rules is suspended during the campaign itself. In fact, even provisional rules on such issues are continuously tested, probed, and pushed on both sides. Even what are often referred to as "red lines" are hardly stable and accepted but are only the hazy and shifting front lines in a fluid contest.

The contest may be constant—offering even less respite than Schedler avers—but it is not equal. Regimes in a semiauthoritarian setting have the capability, virtually by definition, to impose rules. They are mildly limited to—or, better, steered toward—a particular set of rules by four factors. First, inertia plays a limited role. While regimes do tinker with rules, they generally use the last election as the starting point, because a legislative and bureaucratic residue generally remains.

Second, the desire for legitimacy—while widely exaggerated—does lead to feeble efforts to mimic some of the forms (if much more rarely the substance) of neutral (and increasingly internationalized) standards of electoral administration. International audiences in particular can be assured that there is some possibility of—and even concrete movement toward—reform by the presence of very bounded competition, especially if the tinkering can be cast in terms familiar to international audiences. Thus, Egypt set a high threshold for opposition parties to gain election in its 1985 parliamentary elections (initially 10% and then—under opposition pressure—8% of the national vote). The attempt to discourage the emergence of opposition parties was justified in terms of the German system (which actually sets a far lower benchmark). In 2005 it brought in an "electoral commission" that was designed to outflank demands for constitutionally mandated judicial supervision rather than allow truly independent oversight.

Third, semiauthoritarian regimes wish to have at least some opposition movements participate in the election. A total boycott is a negative (though not intolerable) outcome. Elections can serve to tame the opposition, in part by co-opting it but also by diverting its energies in fruitless electioneering. The first goal—co-optation—is rarely completely achieved, but regimes can often coax oppositions into complying with restrictive legal frameworks in return for the promise of limited toleration (and occasionally even a seat or two at a bloated cabinet table). The second goal—absorption of the opposition's energies—amounts to attracting dissident energies into legal political struggles rather than more radical ones. A mix of co-optation and absorption can have the added benefit of splintering an opposition; with no hope of a majority but some debatable hope of limited gains, oppositions tend to fragment.

Arab monarchies have become even more fond than republics of co-opting oppositions; often with a family monopoly on senior state positions and without their own party to mobilize support, monarchs tend to be more willing than presidents to reach out to tame oppositions and offer them seats in the cabinet. Morocco and Kuwait, for instance, have allowed formerly strident opposition critics into the government—in the former, socialists and nationalists who in the past have been very critical of the regime; and in the latter, Arab nationalists, liberals, and Islamist ministers who (sometimes in their youth, such as the late education minister Ahmad al-Rub'i) espoused extreme ideologies. Republics can play the same game, though they tend to be more selective; they are more likely to reward individual renegades (such as when Yasser Arafat appointed a former Hamas activist as a minister) than entire parties or movements.

Finally, and by far most important, regimes use rules to avoid the possibility of electoral defeat. Indeed, if they face defeat, they will hasten to break the rules that they had earlier set. In Algeria in 1992, the military prevented the completion of an election that the governing party was losing catastrophically. In Palestine in 2006—the exception that proves the rule—some members of the ruling party wished to cancel the election they thought they might lose. They failed to do so (in part because of a prevailing feeling among their colleagues that the party would still win), and their movement went down to an embarrassing defeat—and therefore promptly set to work to bring the new government down with a series of strikes, bureaucratic sabotage, preparation for armed action, and threat of unconstitutional action. In Egypt in 2005, the first round of three-tiered parliamentary elections went sufficiently badly for the regime party in the first stage that it deployed its security forces to prevent voters from reaching the polls in the next two rounds of voting.

Opposition movements are rarely naive about their opportunities in a semiauthoritarian system, especially as the game wears on. This leads often to intense internal debates about the desirability of participation and constant threats of boycotts and withdrawals. The threat of boycott is likely to be deployed for tactical reasons as well: in contrast to regimes that have many tools, opposition parties can generally affect the rules only by threatening to boycott. And thus this is precisely what they do—ad nauseum, histrionically, and up to (and even past) the last minute. In 2007 the Jordanian Islamic Action Front pulled out of municipal elections on the morning of election day—and then promptly resumed dithering over whether to boycott the parliamentary elections scheduled four months later (a dispute that even continued after the elections when party leaders squabbled over whether the party's secretary-general had accepted and implemented the leadership's decision). Just as a boycott is a negative but tolerable outcome for the regime, opposition movements regard boycotting an election they do not expect to win as an acceptable outcome. Indeed, knowing that victory is out of the question—at least for the short term—opposition movements in the Arab world look to elections to provide other benefits. With some important exceptions, opposition movements in the Arab world today generally prefer to avoid being driven underground or into illegal activity; most seek instead (for a variety of ideological and practical reasons) to use whatever openings exist in order to pursue their aims. If participation will not bring victory, at least it tends to bring increased tolerance, access to the public sphere, and a consequent ability to communicate with established constituencies and reach out to new ones. But virtually the only tool they have to press for marginal increases in openness is to threaten to pull out of the process altogether.[15] Even as they tire of the game, they generally continue to play it.

Thus, semiauthoritarian elections in the Arab world are generally accompanied by prolonged and indeterminate bargaining—explicit (in which leaders sit down, publicly or privately, to discuss rules) and implicit (through posturing, press releases, veiled warnings, hints, and threats). to Distinguishing one from the other is difficult—elections are often accompanied by rumors that the regime has cut deals with specific opposition movements (or even with specific leaders or factions within those movements). Egypt's 2005 parliamentary elections—like Jordan's 2007 parliamentary polling—were accompanied by widespread speculation that the leadership of the Muslim Brotherhood had negotiated the number of seats it would contest and win. Such rumors are likely far more common than explicit agreements they speculate about—in both the Egyptian and Jordanian cases, the results were hardly in accordance with the desires of at least one of the parties to the supposed deal—but conspiracy theorists are still closer to the mark than they may initially appear: the number of seats won by the opposition may not have been determined by an explicit deal, but the result is almost always deeply affected by the constant bargaining and maneuvering between government and opposition. The only illusion is that there is ever final agreement.

## Elections and Regime Type

We can now move from the murky world of Arab electoral politics to more general considerations of the role of elections in democratic, semiauthoritarian, and fully authoritarian systems and of our understanding of Przeworski's definition of democracy. If democracy is a system in which political parties can lose elections, then scholarly explorations of hybrid regimes, electoral authoritarianism, and semiauthoritarianism have stumbled on a second category of regimes whose defining characteristic is that opposition parties can organize, propagandize, canvass, convene, publish, and complain—but never win. And fully authoritarian regimes can be defined as those which do not allow the opposition to operate even in these ways.

To be sure, there are still significant gradations within each category (a democratic system, for instance, might tilt its elections against parties unfairly but still allow them a significant opportunity for winning). But there is still a clear distinction among the three kinds of regimes—two of them allow different parties to operate, and one of them allows different parties to win.

The borders between semiauthoritarianism on the one hand and democratic and fully authoritarian systems on the other are not purely qualitative—they depend in part in assessing (necessarily quite roughly) how much freedom parties have as well as how much the electoral rules are stacked toward specific outcomes. This combination of a quantitative and a qualitative dimension (however vaguely we have let the former be defined) is nicely captured by the "semiauthoritarian" label, which we will therefore retain.

This three-part scheme offers four important benefits beyond greater precision. First, if our interest is in elections, this division helps us understand the variations in their role, structure, and purpose. Second, for those interested in regime type, it helps us clarify and be more precise about an important development in many authoritarian systems that analysts and activists had noted in a wide variety of settings—the willingness of many regimes to move toward liberalization while blocking any attempts to move toward fully democratic competition. The shift was vaguely understood not because it was ineffable but because it had so many different names. Third, this definition of semiauthoritarinism explains the odd combination of electoral regularity with institutional and procedural instability. In an effort to fix the outcome and deploy their ability to use state resources for their own self-perpetuation, semiauthoritarian regimes often find themselves tinkering with the rules. Thus, many semiauthoritarian regimes always seem to be running to stay in place, confounding analysis by generating much motion but little movement. Finally, the schema points to the importance of political parties in determining the basic functioning of otherwise structurally similar political systems.

By directing our attention to the underexplored role of political parties in semiauthoritarian systems,[16] we may now appreciate the odd phenomenon—

common to Islamist parties in the Arab world today as well as Christian and socialist parties in semiauthoritarian European polities a century ago—in which the political parties that do best in such settings are precisely those that are not orientated primarily toward elections. Democratic lenses have so thoroughly conditioned us to see political parties as primarily electoral organizations that we often overlook the way that political parties and associated social movements in semiauthoritarian settings often view electoral competition as a secondary means for achieving their goals. Educational networks, voluntary associations, self-help groups, charitable activities, intellectual fora, the press, and professional associations often provide far more promising avenues for activities with much more immediate payoffs. Political parties in semiauthoritarian systems that focus only on elections are often paper organizations with a few supporters surrounding prominent personalities. And they generally garner few votes. But broad social movements with multiple organizational channels and well-organized constituencies—built up sometimes precisely because of the weak and incomplete nature of democratic procedures—often are far better poised to bring supporters to the polls as they can do in semiauthoritarian elections. The quintessential movement here is the Muslim Brotherhood, an organization that seems to thrive (as much as any opposition movement can) in the semiauthoritarian environment prevailing in many Arab countries.

Our understanding of semiauthoritarianism is thus enriched by our new understanding of Przeworski's definition. But what of our understanding of democracy?

## Elections and Democracy

Defining democracy as a system in which political parties lose elections seems at first glance to run very much counter to the cliché that democracy is more than elections. That cliché is often used in a deeply unsatisfying manner because it easily leads to associating democracy with a hodgepodge of political values and procedures that are deemed as valuable. And the cliché has the historically odd effect of combining popular sovereignty and majority rule with the very practices that it was so long charged with undermining—such as free speech, property rights, and tolerance. It seems to define any tension between democracy and an array of liberal values and virtues out of existence. A definition of democracy that moves beyond elections to a broad shopping list invests tremendous normative significance in democracy by robbing it of its analytical content.

Przeworski's definition would seem to do the opposite—at first glance, it strips democracy of many of its normative trappings and gives it analytical clarity by returning it to its original etymological meaning of rule by the people. But our consideration of elections and semiauthoritarianism can lead us to understand critical departures Przeworski makes from the classical definition—and how those departures give his conception normative power without diminishing its analytical utility.

Przeworski defines democracy in terms of partisan elections with uncertain outcomes. In some ways, this returns to the classical conception that democracy is simply rule by the people. But it does so incompletely because it insists on elections of leaders. Voting was part of democracy from the beginning, but parties and uncertain election of leaders were not. Partisanship was seen as a disease to be avoided. And democrats often worked to avoid electing leaders. They preferred instead to select leaders, when they had to do so, by lot partly because they recognized that elections hardly gave all individuals an equal opportunity to win.[17] And critics of democracy regarded democratic voting as either uncertain in the extreme (if a passionate and fickle mob set policy) or too certain to collapse in the face of persuasive but dictatorial demagogues. Przeworski's inclusion of political parties in his definition would have filled such democrats of the past (as well as their critics) with a degree of disgust, concerned as they were to guard against domination of the polity by self-interested groups that represented only a part of the community.

Thus, Przeworski's democracy—with its stress on partisanship, regular elections, and uncertain results—hardly resembles an ancient Greek or medieval Italian city-state. The older conceptions of democracy are still useful, though, because they serve to remind us of important but long-submerged suspicions of democratic systems. The image of democracy as being an unstable political system, governed by a mob ruling without regard to procedure, on the basis of short-term calculation, swayed by leaders who appeal to base interests, short-term impulses, and mercurial passions may have left only a few echoes and traces in current political and scholarly debates (living on, perhaps, in fairly gentle form in rarefied circles of political philosophy, in part inspired by Jürgen Habermas's work on the public sphere). But it does point to a perennial democratic problem that Przeworski's definition—with its subtle departures from the classical conception—helps sharpen. If the people are to rule, what are the mechanisms by which they can do so? In the classical world, the people did so collectively and directly in assembly. For Przeworski, that answer is outmoded: democracy today is a system in which people (now a plural rather than a collective) choose among parties in elections in which none is guaranteed victory.

The cliché that democracy is about more than elections therefore has some utility, but not unless we can be fairly specific and not overly loquacious or utopian on what else is needed to distinguish what is democratic from what is not. For Przeworski, elections are a necessary but not sufficient condition for democracy. But democracy is not simply everything we like. In addition to elections, we also need parties and uncertainty—but that is all. Elections without parties and uncertain outcomes are not enough to make democracy.

The classical critics of democracy who viewed democracy as likely to give birth to dictatorship did not have it quite right. The problem in the current world is not that mobs create dictators but that dictators create mobs. They do so by allowing voting in a manner that they hear their own voice echoed back to them—they hold elections that (in semiauthoritarian systems) they cannot lose and (in fully authoritarian systems) they do not even allow opponents to organize and speak to their potential supporters.

Of course, the various good things associated with democracy—such as the full panoply of civil and political liberties, property rights, and the rule of law—can certainly play a role in ensuring that parties can organize and that each of them can win (and, more critically, lose). But governments with democratic legitimacy can also limit, define, or ignore some or all of these good things as well—as critics of democracy have noted quite literally for thousands of years. Democracies may be stupid or evil when they limit the rule of law or property rights, but they are not necessarily undemocratic. Only when governments do so in such a way as to ensure that parties cannot organize or that an incumbent cannot lose are they no longer democracies.

## Conclusion: The Flashpoints of Semiauthoritarian Politics

We have now uncovered what might be seen as the fundamental constitutional flaw (from a democratic perspective) with Arab democracies. Formally democratic elements exist in all Arab political systems. But party competition and uncertain outcomes are missing. The problem is not so much one of ignoring official procedures (laws and regulations are violated but far more rarely than is often supposed) but of gaps in those procedures. In some sense, this may be another aspect of the problem discussed by Steven Fish elsewhere in this volume—the domination of the executive and the weakness of parliaments, the main forum in semiauthoritarian systems for partisan competition.

And it also explains why the central political struggles in recent years in the Arab world—especially in semiauthoritarian systems—focus so much on specific kinds of constitutional issues. Opposition activists—often at loggerheads with each other over a host of ideological, practical, and personal differences—have developed a strikingly common set of reform proposals: institute fairer and more equal competition (e.g., through more independent election commissions) and rein in executive authority. Recognizing that paper existence of plural party systems is insufficient so long as one dominant party is permanently wedded to senior state positions, Islamists, liberals, and nationalists of varying stripes have often postponed, downplayed, or abandoned grand ideological visions in favor of pursuing seemingly prosaic but actually potentially system-changing reform.

Finally, we now understand where politics is least likely to change—and get particularly nasty if it seems that change is possible. In semiauthoritarian systems in the Arab world, much motion but little real movement seems in the offing. New formal parties may be permitted, elections will continue, rules will be continually subject to tinkering, and noisy debates will continue.

But there will be two likely flashpoints where regimes will become particularly resistant and even ferocious. First, when existing parties become able to mobilize real constituencies, or when existing movements with constituencies link themselves to political parties, electoral systems become more difficult to manage. From this perspective, the problem with existing Islamist opposition movements comes not from a weakness in their commitment to democracy; it comes when they become overly committed to democratic change. That is precisely why the movements (which I earlier described as well suited for semiauthoritarian systems) also provoke particular attention and repression.

Second, certain kinds of constitutional reform—those which would make it possible for existing regimes to lose—will be rejected. Truly independent electoral commissions, constitutional courts that have true autonomy from the executive, and entrenched and fair electoral rules are the sorts of reforms that regimes are likely to see as existential threats. Opposition movements can ask for them only at the cost of being labeled as revolutionary or seditious by the semiauthoritarian rulers.

NOTES

1. In a sense, conceptual ambiguities even antedate the burgeoning interest in in-between regimes: when Thomas Carothers published an article declaring "The End of the Transition Paradigm" (*Journal of Democracy* 13, no. 1 [January 2002]: 5–21), the *Journal of Democracy* published an issue (13, no. 3 [July 2002]) on the responses he provoked—what is notable is that the authors disassociated themselves from the teleology of the "transition paradigm," implying or starkly claiming that it had never existed in the first place.

2. Freedom House, Radio Free Europe/Radio, *Liberty Undermining Democracy: 21st Century Authoritarians* (Washington, DC: Freedom House, 2009), p. 3.

3. See Daniel Brumberg, "The Trap of Liberalized Autocracy," *Journal of Democracy* 13, no. 4 (October 2002): 56–68; Steven Hydemann, *Upgrading Authoritarianism in the Arab World*, Saban Center analysis paper, Brookings Institution, October 2007; and Marina Ottaway, *Democracy Challenged: The Rise of Semiauthoritarianism* (Washington, DC: Carnegie Endowment for International Peace, 2003).

4. Adam Przeworski, *Democracy and the Market* (Cambridge: Cambridge University Press, 1991), p. 10.

5. On the nature of authoritarian politics in the Arab world, see Lisa Wedeen, *Ambiguities of Domination* (Chicago: University of Chicago Press, 1999). Recently some scholars have sought to go beyond the interest in the motivations of regimes and oppositions and explored the motivations of voters in authoritarian and semiauthoritarian elections. See, for instance, Lisa Blaydes, "Who Votes in Authoritarian Elections and Why? Determinants of Voter Turnout in Contemporary Egypt," paper presented at the 2006 annual meeting of the Middle East Studies Association, Philadelphia, 2006; and Tianjian Shi, "Voting and Nonvoting in China: Voting Behavior in Plebiscitary and Limited-Choice Elections," *Journal of Politics* 61 (1999): 1115–39. Significantly, these scholars—who work from the perspective of the voters themselves—do not show much interest in the legitimating features of the elections.

6. Barbara Geddes has posited political parties in authoritarian systems as vital counterweights to the military—and tellingly illustrated this view with two Arab examples (Egypt and Algeria). See "Why Parties and Elections in Authoritarian Regimes?" paper presented at the annual meeting of the American Political Science Association, Washington, DC, 2005.

7. Ellen Lust-Okar, "Elections under Authoritarianism: Preliminary Lessons from Jordan," *Democratization* 13, no. 3 (June 2006): 459; also Ellen Lust-Okar, *Structuring Conflict in the Arab World* (Cambridge: Cambridge University Press, 2005).

8. See Jill Crystal, *Oil and Politics in the Gulf* (Cambridge: Cambridge University Press, 1995), p. 89; also Mary Ann Tetreault, *Stories of Democracy: Politics and Society in Contemporary Kuwait* (New York: Columbia University Press, 2000).

9. Indeed, Geddes's influential paper on elections under authoritarianism did not focus on semiauthoritarian systems.

10. See, for instance, Steven Levitsky and Lucan A. Way, "The Rise of Competitive Authoritarianism," *Journal of Democracy* 13, no. 2 (April 2002): 51–65; Andreas Schedler, ed., *Electoral Authoritarianism: The Dynamics of Unfree Competition* (Boulder, CO: Lynne Rienner, 2006); and Ottaway, *Democracy Challenged.*

11. See, for instance, Levitsky and Way, "Competitive Authoritarianism."

12. See Schedler, *Electoral Authoritarianism.* See also his article "Elections without Democracy: The Menu of Manipulation," *Journal of Democracy* 13, no. 2 (April 2002): 36.

13. Valerie Bunce, "Comparative Democratization: Big and Bounded Generalizations," *Comparative Political Studies* 33, nos. 6-7 (August–September 2000): 714. In contrast to my analysis, however, Bunce sees hybrid regimes as combining uncertain results and uncertain rules. According to my argument, however, such regimes might better be seen as unstable democracies; there is a critical distinction between such regimes and those in which the results are certain.

14. Andreas Schedler, "The Nested Game of Democratization by Elections," *International Political Science Review* 23, no. 1 (January 2002): 109–10. While I find Schedler's general portrait of semiauthoritarian elections extremely helpful, I think his treatment of the subject is still focused too much on democratizing outcomes and also stresses legitimacy too greatly.

15. For an exploration of the boycott option, see Staffan I. Lindberg, "Tragic Protest: Why Do Opposition Parties Boycott Elections?" in Schedler, *Electoral Authoritarianism,* 149–64.

16. Jason Brownlee, *Authoritarianism in an Age of Democratization* (Cambridge: Cambridge University Press, 2007); Michel Penner Angrist, *Party Building in the Modern Middle East* (Seattle: University of Washington Press, 2006); and Ellen Lust-Okar and Amaney Ahmad Jamal, "Rulers and Rules: Reassessing the Influence of Regime Type on Electoral Law Formation," *Comparative Political Studies* 35, no. 3 (April 2002): 336–66.

17. See Bernard Manin, *The Principles of Representative Government* (Cambridge: Cambridge University Press, 1997).

# CHAPTER 3

# The Unexpected Resilience of Latin American Democracy

## Kathleen Bruhn

> "Is there any other point to which you would wish to draw my attention?"
> "To the curious incident of the dog in the night-time."
> "The dog did nothing in the night-time."
> "That was the curious incident," remarked Sherlock Holmes.
>
> *Arthur Conan Doyle, "Silver Blaze"*

Between 1979 and 1981, the Woodrow Wilson International Center brought together a number of prominent scholars in a series of conferences to analyze the transitions to democracy that had begun to occur in Latin America and Southern Europe. In 1986 this work culminated in a four-volume book, *Transitions from Authoritarian Rule,* which provided a seminal analysis of the process of democratization and would spark an explosion of studies on democratization around the world. During the next decade, as the "third wave" of democratization spread to new regions, the original insights of the *Transitions* team—based largely on Latin American and Iberian transitions—strongly influenced the themes and issues tackled by regional specialists on eastern Europe, Asia, and Africa.

These works emphasized the importance of strategic interactions between regime insiders and regime opponents and the contingent, uncertain nature of the transition period. Previous theories of democratization had focused on more slowly changing factors, such as the level of economic development, inequality, and political culture; the new generation of theorists downplayed such factors precisely in order to explain why, despite a negative context, democratic transition had occurred.

Yet because the structural context remained unfavorable, the future of democracy was questionable. In his introduction to the *Transitions* volume on Latin America, Guillermo O'Donnell noted that, "in most Latin American countries the dice are probably loaded in favor of repeated iterations of shaky and relatively short-lived democracy and ever-uglier authoritarian rule."[1] At that time, O'Donnell pinned his hopes on political learning: that having experienced the military regimes of the 1970s, more cruelly repressive than their predecessors, Latin Americans of all political persuasions would value democracy more and hesitate to call in the military to resolve future political crises.

Nevertheless, he and most other analysts of the new Latin American democracies saw a rocky road ahead to consolidation. Three threats assumed particular importance: the threat of reintervention by a politicized and still powerful military; the threat posed by the impact of economic crisis and neoliberal economic reforms; and the threat resulting from the Latin American combination of strong presidentialism with multiparty legislatures. Any of these threats could have posed a problem; together, they raised significant doubts about successful democratic consolidation.

Twenty years later, however, all of Latin America's vulnerable democracies have survived. None of the challenges once expected to be the downfall of at least a few of them produced more than a temporary interruption in constitutional government. While some presidents found themselves forced out of office before the end of their constitutional terms, these events did not result in long-term military governments taking power in their own right. What accounts for the surprising resilience of Latin American democracy despite the valid concerns raised by scholars of the first transitions?

As the oldest set of third wave democracies and the inspiration for many contemporary theories of democratization, Latin America's experience offers an opportunity to reevaluate the balance between structure and choice that led theorists of the early 1980s to expect transition but not consolidation. This chapter addresses how and why threats pointed out at the time of transition did not have the anticipated results. The argument highlights the continued importance of agency and, above all, changes in the international context in the consolidation phase. Second, the chapter looks briefly at some of the factors associated with Latin America's continuing pattern of unstable governments amid stable democratic regimes. The final section discusses the

implications of democratic survival in a structural context that remains unfavorable for democracy in many ways. In particular, it examines the role of
domestic institutions as potential threats to the quality (if not the continuity)
of democracy.

## Paper Tigers? The Armed Forces and Democracy in Latin America

Unsurprisingly, early evaluations of the prospects for democratic consolidation in Latin America worried most about renewed military intervention. In
contrast to later transitions in eastern Europe, virtually all of the Latin American transitions involved extrications from military rule. Most of these countries had already experienced more than one episode of military government.
The military was highly politicized and demonstrably willing to overthrow
democracy. Thus, O'Donnell and Schmitter described the process of convincing military governments to step down as "playing coup poker."[2] Successful
transition would most likely involve making a deal with the military to grant
immunity for past human rights violations in exchange for its withdrawal
from power.

O'Donnell and Schmitter favored broader prosecution despite the risks,
arguing that failure to confront the military's crimes would undermine the
ethical foundations of democracy. Other authors, such as Huntington, argued
that prosecuting military offenders was a pragmatic question dependent on
the power of the military. If the military were weak, prosecution might be
advisable (but only of the top leaders and immediately after gaining power);
otherwise, he discouraged "attempt[ing] to prosecute authoritarian officials
for human rights violations. The political costs of such an effort will outweigh
any moral gains."[3] Yet this debate mostly weighed the dangers of trying to
rein in powerful militaries against the dangers of leaving their power intact.
There was broad agreement that the armed forces posed a problem for democratic consolidation.

Assessing the military as a threat hardly required a leap of imagination. By
the 1980s, Argentina had experienced five successful coups in the twentieth
century (as had Ecuador, Haiti, and Honduras), Peru had seven, and Bolivia
(the champion) eleven. Even supposed bastions of democracy such as Chile
and Uruguay succumbed to military coups in the 1970s. In 1978 Wiarda noted

that "the incidence of Latin American coups has been so constant over such a long period of time" that coups had become a " 'normal' or 'regular' part of the political process."[4] The military had governed at least once in most of Latin America, sometimes for twenty or thirty years at a time. It had relinquished power to civilian elected governments only to retake power, often after a relatively short interval. Nordlinger's influential book *Soldiers in Politics* calculates that from 1951 to 1965, Latin America demonstrated a "recurring pattern of coups and military governments," with 70 percent of militaries who gave up power staging another coup within six years on average.[5] Military officers often saw themselves as more competent to lead than civilian politicians. They also had strong motives to resist civilian efforts to control or punish them after a democratic transition. Although the military governments of the 1970s were more repressive than previous regimes, analysts saw little reason to expect that the withdrawal of militaries from power in the early 1980s would be any more enduring than previous withdrawals had been.

And yet it was. As early as 1991, Robert Dix noted that the time between military interventions in Latin America had tripled compared to Nordlinger's 1950s data, with only one of the fourteen countries that had a democratic transition after 1979 experiencing a return to military rule.[6] As of 2008, no Latin American country was governed by the armed forces, and only one (Cuba) was classified as "not free" by Freedom House. Although in some countries the military sometimes supported popular mobilizations intended to force unpopular presidents out of power, it no longer sought to assume power directly, preferring instead to back civilian replacements.

We cannot attribute the strange passivity of the armed forces to a sudden surge in economic development, as earlier theories of democratic consolidation proposed. Although most countries did have higher GDP per capita by the 1980s than in earlier decades, the record of Latin American democracies in the three decades after World War II actually found that countries with higher development levels were more vulnerable to democratic breakdown.[7] Moreover, during the 1980s Latin America experienced its worst period of economic decline since the 1930s and had only fitful periods of growth in the 1990s. In previous decades, economic deterioration often provoked military intervention.[8] This time around, democratic regimes survived.

Four principal explanations have been offered to account for these patterns. The first was presented at the time of the transitions: Guillermo O'Donnell's "hope" that political learning might discourage both military and civilian elites from repeating the deadly experiences of the military governments of the 1970s. To some extent, changing values helped stabilize democracy. Certainly the Latin American Left gained a new appreciation for mere "bourgeois democracy" after having been subjected to repression and torture by bourgeois military governments. Dix also notes that the armed forces in many countries appeared scarred by the internal divisions inevitably associated with governing and seemed reluctant to take on such a role again.[9]

However, political learning alone cannot fully account for the suddenness and the breadth of changes in the military's role. Why did militaries and civilians unexpectedly learn in the 1980s not to repeat military rule but did *not* learn this lesson after similar interventions in the 1950s or 1960s? Why were countries that should have been less affected by "learning"—because their militaries were in power for less time, were more successful, and/or were less repressive—just as immune to repetition of military rule as countries whose experience was more searing?

Perhaps more importantly, there is evidence from mass surveys that Latin Americans remain less than fully committed to democracy. In 2001 majority support for democracy could be documented in only six of the seventeen countries polled by Latinobarometer.[10] While support for democracy has strengthened in recent years, developments since 2001 cannot account for the survival of democracy throughout the turbulent 1980s and 1990s. Moreover, satisfaction with democracy remains low: only a little more than a third of Latin Americans are happy with the way democracy works in their countries. Trust in political institutions (especially political parties) has declined everywhere, a theme to which we return later in the chapter. Though we lack truly comparable information about attitudes toward democracies in the 1960s, such cautious support for democracy today makes it unlikely that cultural change is the primary reason for military restraint.

A second explanation is that militaries learned to exercise power behind the scenes, sparing themselves the opposition that would result from taking over openly. Alfred Stepan warned about this possibility in his classic 1988 work, *Rethinking Military Politics*. Civilian control of the military, he noted, has two key dimensions: military contestation and military institutional prerogatives. The first dimension involves conflicts between military and civilian elites, ranging from mild grumbling up to a military coup. The second dimension "refers to those areas where, whether challenged or not, the military as an institution assumes they have an acquired right or privilege, formal or informal, to exercise effective control."[11] Situations where military prerogatives are high and contested he classifies as a "near untenable position for democratic leaders," likely to result in a coup. But the alternative is not automatically civilian control: one could also imagine situations where military prerogatives are high and generally not contested by civilians, a condition Stepan calls "unequal civilian accommodation."[12] Only where both military prerogatives and contestation were low would civilian control exist. Stepan was gloomy about the prospects, particularly in countries such as Brazil, where the military relinquished power in a strong position and with many of its institutional prerogatives intact.

Clearly, there are still countries in Latin America that could fairly be described as "unequal civilian accommodation." Yet the condition is rarer than early analysts expected. Even in Brazil—the country that inspired Stepan to issue his warning—later analyses suggested that civilians have made significant advances in reining in military influence.[13] In the first ten years after democratic transitions, the number of soldiers per thousand inhabitants declined in Argentina, Brazil, Chile, Peru, and Uruguay.[14] Military budgets also declined, in some cases significantly.[15] Argentina's military spending dropped from 6.4 percent of GDP in 1980 to 1.2 percent of GDP in 1996. In Chile, where the military left under very favorable conditions, the decline was similar, from 6.7 percent of GDP in 1980 to 1.6 percent of GDP by 1996. Since 2000, military spending has increased in some Latin American countries, most notably Venezuela, but Latin America on average spends less on its military than any other world region.[16] While far from powerless, militaries in Latin America generally have not acted as puppet masters behind the scenes. Rather, civilians have exercised increasing control over military budgets and missions.

A third explanation points to changes in the global political context, particularly the fall of communism and the end of the Cold War. The third wave may have begun in southern Europe and Latin America, but its spread to eastern Europe and Russia deprived the Latin American Left of a viable political model other than democracy. This, in turn, reduced the threat posed by domestic leftists to political order. During the twentieth century, Latin American militaries usually intervened in coalition with the Right. At least during the second half of the twentieth century, these coups often won the tacit or explicit support of a U.S. government afraid of Soviet expansion in the Western hemisphere, though as Brazinsky notes (in this volume), pre–Cold War

U.S. policy (especially under Wilson) may have been more prodemocratic. Where the United States once supported military governments that promised to defeat "communist" subversion, after 1989 it increasingly tolerated the election of leftist leaders and even threatened would-be coup leaders with the withdrawal of political and economic support if a coup was successful. Hyde's argument (in this volume) makes similar claims about the reasons for the international spread of elections.

This hypothesis cannot explain Latin American transitions but does a much better job than the previous two of explaining democratic survival, the simultaneous shift across Latin America away from military intervention, and the timing of this shift. Hunter even credits the willingness and ability of presidents to reduce military budgets and influence to the lack of international support for military government.[17] If the team that produced *Transitions from Authoritarian Rule* had foreseen the collapse of the Soviet Union, its predictions about the consolidation of democracy in Latin America would probably have been more optimistic. It should be noted, however, that this factor has little to do with traditional explanations of democratic survival, which rested on more stable characteristics such as the level of economic development or political culture. Rather, it suggests that democratic consolidation, like transition, was contingent on strategic factors, though not exclusively domestic factors. Instead, shifts in the global balance of power changed the calculations of key domestic actors such as the armed forces.

Yet the fall of communism was not the only event to rock Latin America in the 1980s. A fourth explanation for military reluctance to assume power credits, paradoxically, another global change that was initially seen as a threat to democratic survival: economic crisis and the widespread adoption of economic market reforms.

## Neoliberalism and Democracy in Latin America

In 1981, just as the wave of democratic transitions got underway, a sudden drop in the price of oil triggered a debt crisis in Mexico that spread rapidly throughout Latin America. During the 1970s, many Latin American countries borrowed heavily, becoming the most highly indebted developing region in the world by the beginning of the 1980s. Loss of confidence in Latin America's ability to repay these loans quickly dried up new sources of lending, which they had counted on to pay back old loans. Investment fell and economic growth stagnated. Most countries found themselves forced into debt rescue agreements with the International Monetary Fund (IMF), which required drastic cuts in public spending and further reduced domestic demand. Latin America entered a serious recession, later dubbed the "lost decade."

In response to the crisis, country after country began to adopt market reforms, often at IMF insistence, but also as a way to bring in new (mostly foreign) investment. The neoliberal package fundamentally reshaped the role of the state in economic development. Latin America had long championed state-led economic development, including strong trade protection, state subsidies of domestic industry, and price controls on basic items such as food and electricity to keep the cost of living low. The crisis of the Latin American economies in the 1980s called into question the viability of state-led development. More practically, continued state subsidies became untenable in a context of strict budget guidelines imposed by the IMF. In addition, given the collapse of domestic consumer spending, opening up trade barriers and seeking to increase exports became increasingly attractive as a means of restarting the economy. The discrediting of state economic planning in the Soviet Union further strengthened these trends.

However, neoliberal reforms came with a cost: short-term pain resulted as uncompetitive businesses and their workers lost out. Early analysts worried that the pressures resulting from market reform would overload Latin America's fragile new democracies because, according to Przeworski in his influential 1991 book, *Democracy and the Market*, "such reforms necessarily cause a temporary fall in aggregate consumption. They are socially costly and politically risky."[18] Przeworski's logic was straightforward. Economic reforms cause pain. Democratic governments are more vulnerable to negative public opinion than authoritarian governments because they face regular public elections. Public resistance to unpopular reforms could lead politicians to abandon market reforms or to try to avoid or manipulate elections. Przeworski noted that a clever politician might in the short term evade the trade-off by claiming not to have reformist intentions in order to get elected and then implementing reforms anyway. However, this style of politics would lead to voter distrust of politicians, weaken accountability, and ultimately undermine democracy.[19] Thus, he posed the question, Were market reforms and democratization compatible?

Neoliberal economic reforms did indeed result in suffering and widespread pain. Poverty and inequality rose in an already highly unequal region. Yet the political consequences for democracy and even market reformers were far less severe than anticipated. Politicians enthusiastically campaigned on antireform platforms, continued economic reforms in office—and got reelected. There were many protests against reforms, some of which forced out presidents before their term ended, but both reforms and democracy survived. It is empirically clear that neoliberal reforms did not doom Latin American democracies to return to military rule. But were market reforms supportive of democracy? It is possible that the survival of democracy is a mere coincidence: democracy survived because the military did not want to take over, not because neoliberalism and democracy are compatible. However, three scenarios posit a more direct connection between neoliberal reform and democratic stability.

The first scenario simply states that the pessimists got it wrong: democracies are not less capable than authoritarian regimes of carrying out successful neoliberal reforms.[20] In fact, they may even enjoy some advantages. Because the democratic policy-making process requires compromise and negotiation, economic reforms that do get adopted may be more legitimate. One version of this argument stresses that voters under some circumstances will actually support painful reforms despite the costs. Kurt Weyland, for example, draws on prospect theory to argue that support for radical and risky reforms is higher in a context of severe economic crisis.[21] Operating in a "domain of losses," people may choose a risky option that might improve their situation over the certainty of moderate loss (the status quo, economic crisis).

Similarly, Susan Stokes disputes Przeworski's claim that "neoliberalism by surprise" necessarily undermines democracy.[22] She argues that voters are quite willing to forgive politicians who campaign on one platform but implement another, as long as the policies help by the time the next election rolls around. Essentially voters are smarter, or perhaps more opportunistic, than pessimists gave them credit for. They will reward whatever works, including duplicity. Therefore, neoliberal reforms did not necessarily undermine support for democratic regimes. Market reformers did get reelected despite the economic pain caused by reforms, and even when politicians claimed during the campaign to oppose the reforms that they later carried out. In particular, policies that succeeded in controlling inflation enhanced the popularity and credibility of reformers.

The problems here are twofold. First, the level of public support for reforms cannot be readily predicted by either the severity of the economic crisis or the depth of reform. The same reforms that elicit a reaction in one country may not in another. Political institutions and the level of organization in civil society also play a significant role. Second, there are indications that, despite voters' apparent readiness to reelect neoliberal reformers, trust in political institutions and political parties in particular has declined in many countries, exactly as foreseen by Przeworski.

The second scenario argues that neoliberal reforms are only compatible with democracy because they marginalize the losers. Democracy survives by default. This argument accepts most of Przeworski's premises—that economic reforms cause hardship and anger at politicians—but adds that these same reforms make it much more difficult to organize opposition.[23] The pressures of survival deprive the very people most damaged by economic reforms of the resources and time to resist them, while rewarding the winners with political and economic spoils. The supporting coalition being more powerful, both reforms and reformers do well. In particular, market reforms and global economic competition weakened the organizations that might plausibly oppose neoliberalism, such as labor unions. The threat of losing jobs to foreign competition inhibited unions from more aggressively defending workers against the erosion of wages and working conditions that has accompanied market reform in Latin America.

The empirical result should be a general decline in social mobilization. Debate over the empirical record continues, however. Kurtz's 2004 *World Politics* article arguing that neoliberalism demobilizes was followed by Arce and Bellinger's 2008 piece in the same journal that argues the opposite, using the same empirical data and a slightly modified statistical model.[24] In large part, the controversy reflects the poor quality of data available for quantitative testing. There is no doubt, however, that there have been massive antiglobalization protests in many Latin American countries. Clearly, neoliberalism does not demobilize completely nor does it demobilize everyone. In fact, protests against neoliberal reforms are among the most important and consequential of the past decade, including cases that led to the removal from power of democratically elected presidents such as Jamil Mahuad of Ecuador and Gonzalo Sanchez de Lozada of Bolivia.

These examples also call into question the most optimistic proposal, which argues that neoliberalism not only poses no threat to democratic consolidation but has actually promoted it. This argument rests on two propositions: that free markets and free politics go together (a revised version of the modernization theories of the 1950s); and that the spread and apparent inevitability of market-oriented reforms have brought about an ideological convergence that greatly reduces the risk of polarization and breakdown. The first proposition relies in part on an analogy between preferences for choice in economics and choice in politics (people who have one will want the other) and in part on the pragmatic effects of liberating wealth creation from state protection. When market advantages rather than state policies determine who makes money, control of the state becomes less important. Losing elections is less consequential. Challenging the state carries less risk. In addition, the availability of money from diverse sources encourages competition among political alternatives and fuels the growth of parties.

There is anecdotal evidence linking capitalist entrepreneurs to support for opposition parties, particularly in Mexico and Brazil. However, despite many years of analyzing the role of capitalists in democracy, scholars have yet to find a consistent pattern over time in line with Moore's original dictum: no bourgeoisie, no democracy.[25] Still less evidence has been marshaled to support the idea that cultural shifts favoring democracy are caused by capitalist markets. If anything, in Latin America shifts toward democracy mostly preceded shifts toward capitalist markets (Chile and Mexico being important exceptions).

The second proposition points to the record of leftist presidents in many Latin American countries since the 1980s who governed under the same basic market model as their conservative predecessors. When leftists get elected these days, they are less likely to govern as Marxists would. They pose less threat to property rights or conservative economic interests. They can therefore be permitted to take power without facing a military coup.

It is true that ideological polarization has not declined in all cases. Against Peronist president Carlos Menem in Argentina or Ricardo Lagos in Chile, each of whom continued neoliberal reforms, we can set radical anti-neoliberal presidents such as Hugo Chavez of Venezuela or Evo Morales of Bolivia. Yet the exceptions are telling. The ability to export natural gas and petroleum is one of the most important factors distinguishing the two groups. Chavez has enough money as a result of Venezuela's oil to do what a series of Socialist presidents in Chile could not: defy international markets and the United

States. Weyland makes precisely this argument, that "the crucial factor is the boom and bust cycle of rentier states, especially the natural resource bonanza. . . . These rents discredit the neoliberal insistence on constraints . . . and stimulate radicalism and voluntarist attacks on the established socioeconomic and political order."[26] As a result, Bolivia, Ecuador, and Venezuela, as states with oil and natural gas, produced more radical leftist presidents than countries lacking these sources of wealth. For most states, however, as in the case of the military, the international context has shifted, changing the calculations of domestic actors in ways that were not foreseen by the earliest analysts of Latin American transitions.

## Presidents and Parliaments: Bucking the "Perils of Presidentialism"

The third threat was first proposed by Juan Linz, largely on the basis of his comparison of the Latin American and Spanish cases.[27] He called it the "perils of presidentialism." In a series of influential articles, he argued that Latin America's long record of repeated democratic breakdown could be traced in large part to the adoption of presidential regimes. Because of differences in the method of selecting the chief executive, presidential regimes faced more hazards than parliamentary regimes. In particular, he argued two main points.

*1. Presidential regimes are less able to respond to leadership crises created by incompetent leaders than parliamentary regimes are.* In parliamentary systems, the elected members of the legislature choose the prime minister. He does not serve a fixed term and can be removed if he loses the confidence of the majority of the legislature. In presidential systems, the chief executive is elected by popular vote for a fixed term. He does not serve at the pleasure of the legislature. Because of these differences, removing a corrupt, incompetent, or dictatorial prime minister is easy in parliamentary systems, requiring only a simple majority vote, but very difficult in presidential systems. Even though impeachment procedures usually exist, they often require multiple votes, supermajorities, approval of multiple legislative bodies, or a narrow definition of the conditions under which impeachment is possible (e.g., limiting it to actual criminal malfeasance rather than mere incompetence). Thus, opponents of an unpopular president—knowing that the congress can do little—could be tempted to turn to the military for help rather than wait out the president's term.

*2. Presidential regimes are prone to deadlock as a result of unresolvable confrontations between the executive and the legislative branch.* In parliamentary regimes a prospective prime minister must first form a majority coalition in the legislature, usually by offering smaller parties policy concessions as well as positions in the cabinet. Once she forms a coalition, the prime minister can draw on its support to approve her government's initiatives. If the coalition fails to back her, then the government falls, and a new parliamentary coalition forms. Members of a coalition are therefore highly motivated to cooperate with the prime minister or face a renegotiation of the coalition, or even new elections in which they might lose their seats.

In presidential systems, presidents and legislators are separately elected. There is no requirement that the president must enjoy the support of a majority of the legislature; in fact, this condition is rare outside of a two-party system such as that in the United States. Even there, the legislature is sometimes controlled by a majority of legislators from the party *opposing* the president, a situation called divided government. The more common combination in Latin America pairs presidents with minority legislatures (in which no party holds a majority of the seats). Both contexts, Linz argued, are prone to deadlock. In divided government, a legislative majority of the opposition can successfully block the president's proposals, and the president can veto legislative initiatives. In a fragmented legislature, presidents may fail to construct legislative majorities at all. There is little incentive for legislators to cooperate with the president because the government does not collapse if they fail to reach an agreement. It can become impossible to pass legislation, creating a crisis. Once again, the military may be seen as a means of breaking the deadlock. Even short of regime breakdown, presidents in this untenable position would be tempted to bypass the congress and approve policies by executive decree, thus weakening democratic government and raising the stakes attached to control of the presidency.

Linz's two points were immediately contested. In particular, critics pointed out, Linz based his theory largely on the Latin American cases. "If, however, his focus had been on instability in post-colonial Asia and Africa, the institutional villain would surely have been parliamentary systems."[28] Parliamentary systems could collapse too readily, give small and extremist parties too much influence, or empower legislative majorities with a winner-take-all ability to pass legislation without reference to the rights of minorities, something that could be especially damaging in ethnically divided societies.

However, empirical evidence based on cross-national samples tended to confirm Linz's suspicions, in that "parliamentary democracies had a rate of survival more than three times higher than that of presidential democracies."[29] The Latin American combination of presidentialism with multiparty legislatures seemed to create particularly serious problems.[30]

Some critics claimed that these results were biased by the inclusion of the stable European democracies (most of which are parliamentary); their analysis including only less developed countries found no significant relationship between presidentialism and democratic survival.[31] Still, recent studies have returned to Linz's early argument, that presidential regimes with strong executive powers are less likely to consolidate as democracies.[32]

Thus, the scholarly debate continues over the relative merits of presidentialism and parliamentarism, and the impact of combining them with various electoral and party systems. What is striking, however, is that over the past twenty years in Latin America—the region that inspired Linz's original theory—country after country has managed to survive corrupt, incompetent, destructive, and even crazy presidents without returning to authoritarian rule.

Both aspects of Linz's causal logic have been challenged. With respect to Linz's claim that presidentialism breaks down because it produces legislative deadlock, Cheibub argues that coalition formation is far from rare even in presidential democracies with minority legislatures, emerging 62 percent of the time in presidential democracies versus 77 percent of parliamentary democracies.[33] Thus, multiparty presidentialism is not doomed. In fact, a greater number of parties could also mean more flexibility in legislative alliances and could thus make governance easier. The real reason that presidentialism breaks down more often than parliamentarism, he argues, is that it typically emerges after military dictatorships, a problem he calls "the product of a historical accident . . . the Cold War and the role of the military in fighting it."[34] Left unexplained is why third wave presidential democracies that follow military rule are more stable than previous ones. However, Cheibub's emphasis on the military's role in democratic breakdown suggests that we should look to changes in the military for an answer rather than to the type of constitutional democracy adopted.

Perez-Liñan challenges the other half of Linz's causal story, that presidential systems are inflexible in the context of a crisis that pits the congress against the executive. From 1978 to 2003, 40 percent of Latin America's elected presidents were challenged by civilian actors, and 23 percent were removed from office before their term ended. In only two of these cases did the military play a critical role.[35] In some cases, popular protests and lack of congressional support made the president's position so untenable that he resigned and was replaced by a vice-president or a congressionally selected replacement. In others, the legislature went through a formal process of impeachment: between 1992 and 2004, six Latin American presidents were impeached, and four were removed from office. As a result, "democratically-elected governments [in Latin America] continue to fall, but in contrast to previous decades, democratic regimes do not break down."[36]

The reason for this new pattern of "stable presidentialism with unstable presidents" once more refers back to the new strategic context facing the armed forces, a factor that seems important in all three of our causal stories. On the positive side, Latin American presidential regimes have resolved deadlock and removed unpopular leaders without resorting to military intervention or—more particularly—military rule. On the negative side, these processes are extremely messy. Although Latin American legislatures are generally at or above the mean score on Fish and Kroenig's Parliamentary Powers Index (PPI), legislatures are often unable to use purely constitutional powers to resolve these crises. Nor are the most powerful countries according to the PPI necessarily more competent to block high-handed presidential action; Peru has one of the highest scores on the PPI (.66) but could not stop Fujimori from dissolving the congress and taking over in a "self-coup" in 1992.[37] Successful congressional action to remove a president required conditions beyond mere incompetence, including a scandal implicating the president directly and resulting in mass protests.[38] Latin American legislatures can punish bad presidential behavior but only after the fact and only at the cost of provoking a national crisis. What are the long-term effects on democracy of such repeated confrontations? Could these spectacles explain at least in part why Latin Americans have lost trust in both the legislature and the presidency? As Perez Liñan notes, it is still unclear whether such "crises without breakdown" are "signals of democratic erosion or democratic vitality."[39]

## Thieves of Trust: Threats to Democracy in the Modern Era

Thus far, this chapter has argued that the principal threats to democratic continuity foreseen by analysts at the time of the Latin American transitions have not had the devastating results that were anticipated. Yet, clearly, all is not entirely well: Latin American democrats cannot just declare victory and go home. In many countries, *government* remains unstable even if *democracy* as an outward form is preserved: fourteen of Latin America's elected presidents from 1978 to 2004, in nine separate countries, were removed from office before their term ended.[40] What have been the reasons for this continued poor performance? And could these threats eventually endanger the continuity of democracy itself? This section argues that the failure to construct adequate regulatory mechanisms for economic and political markets constitutes the principal threat to the stability of democratic government in Latin America.

In the economic marketplace, the most important "regulatory mechanism" for the purposes of understanding the fate of democracy involves the state's ability to tax sources of economic wealth fairly. Corporations have an interest in promoting reforms to improve the institutional capacity of states to enforce contracts and property rights, to administer justice, and perhaps even to enforce criminal laws that promote public safety—all areas in which Latin American democracies have much room to improve. Public concern about crime, in particular, is one of the most important sources of dissatisfaction with the performance of democracy today. But there is no necessary conflict between this goal and neoliberal reform. In contrast, corporations have no such interest in allowing themselves to be taxed, but democracy does. A taxation system that is even modestly progressive can reconcile people to high levels of economic inequality, financing social services and education that allow them to participate more effectively in markets and politics alike.

Latin American democracies are abysmally ineffective at taxing their own populations and are especially ineffective at taxing the rich. One of the key reasons for this inefficiency is another market failure: the existence of imperfect competition (oligopolies or monopolies) in many economic sectors. In economic terms, imperfect competition allows the advantaged monopolists to block mutually beneficial gains from trade in favor of gains to the monopolist. In political terms, imperfect competition often results from and perpetuates special relationships between state actors and the monopolist. In Mexico, for example, the telecommunications market is dominated by a single company, owned by a single businessman, Carlos Slim, who parlayed his connections with former Mexican president Carlos Salinas into monopoly control of this important domestic market.[41] As of 2010, Slim was the world's richest man according to *Forbes* magazine, due primarily to his control of the Mexican telecommunications market.[42] Three presidents who followed Salinas have been unable to chip away at this monopoly. Such wealthy entrepreneurs enjoy special access to the state, can escape state regulation and taxes, get special favors, and may determine which faction wins elections by financing their preferred candidates.

This kind of market failure has three consequences that endanger democracy. First, control of the state is no longer irrelevant to generating—and keeping—wealth. As a result, holding office becomes a potential source of enrichment, with corrupting effects on parties and politics in general, even if the billionaires in question are not engaged in illegal drug trafficking (as is one of the new 2009 billionaires listed by *Forbes*: Mexican cocaine mogul Joaquín "El Chapo" Guzmán).[43] Second, the inability of states to adequately tax these monopolistic capitalists leaves states either dependent on natural resource revenues or unable to provide goods demanded by the majority of the population. Third, to the extent that voters perceive this failure as a result of the state's complicity on behalf of the rich, the democratic state loses legitimacy.

Cynicism alone does not necessarily threaten democracy, but it can open the door to the kind of political adventurers who do. Democracy is about counting the number of votes. Whether or not the losers have the resources to mobilize against democracy, the existence of a large pool of unhappy potential voters may eventually tempt some ambitious politician to go after those votes. The resurgence of populist campaigning on the right as well as the left warns that at least some politicians think this pool may be growing.

To the extent that neoliberal reforms constrain populists from fulfilling their campaign promises, disillusionment with existing parties and politics is bound to grow. Although Przeworski's scenario of collapsing democracies may not have occurred, voters seem more inclined toward the solution once offered in the popular Argentinean reaction to the country's economic collapse in 2001: "¡Que se vayan todos!" (Kick them all out!). The growing number and popularity of antiparty, "outsider" candidates is evident in Coppedge's survey of electoral change in Latin America between 1982 and 1995. Virtually all of the biggest losers during this period were long-established parties, of both the Left and Right. But the biggest winners (one out of three) were personalistic parties, the often-temporary electoral vehicles of individual politicians. Half of the "emerging parties" founded after 1982 fit this description.[44]

In turn, as parties are further marginalized and weakened, politics becomes ever more praetorian and subject to democratic reversals. Parties are the regulatory mechanisms of the political marketplace. In Latin America, parties have always been weak compared to parties in the advanced industrial democracies. Party *systems* are less stable and institutionalized as well.[45] Mainwaring and Scully argue, with many others, that "the nature of parties and party systems shapes the prospects that stable democracy will emerge, whether it will be accorded legitimacy, and whether effective policy-making will result."[46] Parties are central to representation in modern mass democracy, affecting the quality of democracy itself, as well as the quality of governance.

However, the survival of democracy may also depend on the actions—or inactions—of political parties. In the post-1980s democracies in Latin America, parties have replaced militaries as *the* key actors determining the outcome of political crises. In some cases, parties are complicit in the extrajudicial removal of presidents; in others, they fail to stop the authoritarian power grab of a president. The case of Peru is particularly interesting because the temptation of great oil wealth cannot explain its turn toward more authoritarian politics. Instead, party system weakness contributed to the temporary collapse of democracy in Peru in 1992.[47] According to Levitsky and Cameron, the failure of the democratic opposition to coordinate effectively against Fujimori—a result of weak parties—stymied the theoretical ability of the Peruvian Congress to check presidential overreaching.[48] Despite Peru's high PPI score according to Fish and Kroenig, the Peruvian Congress could not even stop President Fujimori from dissolving it.

Similarly, Perez-Liñan argues that the ability of presidents to rely on what he calls a "legislative shield"—a loyal legislative coalition—can help him avoid impeachment or removal in the face of quite serious crises questioning his fitness to continue in office. The outsider president who lacks a party starts with a disadvantage. Not only are impeachments less likely to succeed when the president can count on a strong legislative party coalition, but political opponents may be less likely to attempt them. But stable legislative coalitions require stable parties to negotiate and coordinate them. Thus, governmental instability may be more characteristic of countries without strong party systems; in fact, half of the cases of preterm presidential removals after 1990 occurred in the countries listed by Mainwaring and Scully as the four weakest party systems in Latin America. None occurred in the three strongest party systems.[49]

It is impossible to miss the parallels to democratic reversal in post–Soviet Russia, where personalistic parties have accompanied the undermining of democratic regimes—in the case of Russia, to the point where Freedom House no longer characterizes the country as even partly free. Parties have longer-term interests that motivate them to check the ambitions of individual politicians. Similarly, Stokes finds that more established parties produce campaigns that are predictive of what they will actually do in office; newer parties in contrast are more often the home of message switchers, who campaign on one set of policy promises but govern with another set of policies.[50] Politicians simply are not as free to "wing it" when strong parties hold them accountable.

Social movements can play an important role in democratic representation, but they are unlikely to replace parties in this regulatory role. Civil society can hold politicians accountable, but because they typically lack mechanisms to control the future careers of politicians (as parties do, by virtue of their power over candidacies), they must use the more disruptive mechanisms at their disposal, such as the power to strike or to mobilize. Omar Encarnación refers to this phenomenon as a "civil society coup"; Perez-Liñan, more charitably, calls it "spasmodic accountability."[51]

Understanding how to build party systems that are capable of performing these regulatory and coordination functions remains an important task for scholars of third wave democracies. The European examples are unlikely to help us understand when and how parties "work" in developing countries because the historical conditions in which parties were first built differ from those facing new parties today. Among other things, the strong labor movements that anchored many European leftist parties are largely absent in the developing world and under pressure even in Europe itself. Levitsky and Cameron are pessimistic about the prospects for building parties at all in the postcollapse context in Peru, because of both the structural changes in Peruvian society and the success of past independent candidates. As they suggest, "contemporary party systems may prove to be somewhat like Humpty Dumpty: in the absence of crisis, they may persist, but if they happen to collapse . . . all the institutional engineering in the world may be insufficient to put them back together again."[52] Nevertheless, to the extent that party systems can move counter to entropy, it is worth studying their examples to learn under what conditions parties might become more functional as guardians of democracy.

## The Future of Democracy: Lessons from Latin America

This chapter has focused on threats to the stability of democracy. Analyses based on the lessons of Latin America helped shift scholarly analysis of democratic transitions away from traditional explanations based on socio-economic characteristics of societies and toward a more process-oriented analysis of democratic transition. However, because these scholars expected the structural characteristics of society to play a stronger role in consolidation, they predicted a grim and uncertain future for democracy in Latin America. That grim future did not, by and large, come to pass. As scholars have followed the development of Latin American democracies over the past twenty years, what have we learned about democracy and the factors that were expected to threaten it? In what follows, I offer four "lessons" from Latin America.

*1. Strategic choice matters for democratic survival as well as for transition.* It is, of course, a truism that the survival of democracy depends on what actors such as the military and civilian elites choose to do. The authors of *Transitions from Authoritarian Rule* argued that transition moments were unusually open to the effects of strategic choices made in a context of imperfect information and high uncertainty. In the story of democratic survival, however, such moments continued to occur. During a presidential crisis, when the legislature and president confront one another, what does the military do? Which side do wavering congressmen take? Does the president resign or fight on? The methods used to understand these decisions during a democratic transition could also be employed to understand decision making at other turning points; some crossroads are traversed more than once. The division of political choice into "normal" and "abnormal" politics may be overstated.

*2. Changes in the international environment systematically altered the strategic context for domestic political actors in ways that favor democracy.* Changes in the international context are the most significant factors explaining why the Latin American democratic transitions of the 1980s have lasted so much longer than previous democratic regimes. The importance of these factors has reached near-consensus status among scholars, although the positive impact of the end of the Cold War has much more support than the hypothetically positive impact of the spread of neoliberal reforms. Changes in the international context operated principally by changing the strategic payoffs for domestic political actors, not through direct pressure or sanctions. In particular, they decreased the risks of open democratic competition. When the military intervened in Latin America in the past, it usually did so as a result of a perceived security threat created by leftists organizing against the basic capitalist model; economic elites supported or instigated these coups because they feared challenges to property rights. The fall of the Soviet Union not only dried up a traditional source of funding for such radical organizations but also deprived them of their chief alternative to capitalism. The ideological spectrum narrowed. Most opponents of neoliberal reform (and there are many) accept at least some of the principles of a market economy. Market critics no longer pose as grave a policy threat to economic elites. Nor are they as viable a military threat without the moral and material support of the Soviet Union. The rapid shift of the Zapatista guerrilla army in Mexico from military action to political organization and dialogue reflected its weak resource base. What new banner did they wave to attract support? Not socialism, but democracy and indigenous rights. Security threats in Latin America today come primarily from organized crime and drug trafficking, not political dissidents.

The global spread of neoliberalism and democracy has also increased the costs to domestic military and civilian actors of seeking a return to military rule. In a context of neoliberal economic competition, the stability of a political regime can affect the rate of investment, both domestic and foreign, and the value of the country's currency. Although most of the transitions in Latin America predate neoliberal reforms, these changes made the subsequent interruption of constitutional order a more costly enterprise for economic elites, bolstering democratic survival. Similarly, the end of the Cold War, though it did not propel the transitions, may have increased the odds of democratic survival by reducing the willingness of the Latin American military's number one funder—the United States—to support military-authoritarian regimes. Once it no longer had to fear Soviet missiles in its back yard, the United States was free to support even fairly left-wing democracies. An example is the attempted coup in Guatemala in 1993. With the support of the military, Guatemalan president Jorge Serrano dissolved the congress and declared rule by decree. However, the United States refused to recognize his government, cut off aid, and threatened to impose trade sanctions. The military's support for Serrano evaporated. Less than a week later, it forced him to resign.

Although more likely to prop up tottering democracies than to create new ones, these changes in the strategic context help democrats more than authoritarians. Latin America's experience is thus a sign of hope for struggling democracies elsewhere that face similarly daunting economic and social challenges.

*3. Location, location, location: Neighborhood matters.* Nevertheless, Latin America's democracies are peculiarly favored by their regional circumstances. It is unreasonable to expect similar success rates elsewhere. Two features of the Latin American context seem especially important. First, the proximity of the United States and its role in regional security make Latin America quite different from Georgia or Kazakhstan, whose regional hegemon is undemocratic Russia. The kinds of regimes Russia wants to support are not necessarily (or even probably) democratic. Second, the proportion of democracies in Latin America is extremely high. Studies have shown that democratic neighbors substantially increase the likelihood of democratic transition and stability.[53] One analysis even found that the number of democratic neighbors predicts regime survival better than the level of economic development, the classic and most widely accepted correlate of stable democracy.[54]

This implies that money spent to support a newly democratic Cuba would have a higher probability of succeeding than money spent to support a democratic Georgia. It does not mean that one should not try to help democracies in less healthy parts of the world, but it does mean that it will cost more, take more time, and be more likely to fail. This also suggests that bringing in regional democratic actors is vital to new democracies. In the event of democratization in North Korea, for example, the United States should rely heavily on South Korea and other regional democracies to play a leading role. Again, international context does not guarantee a transition but does seem to stabilize democratic regimes.

*4. Stable democracy is not always very democratic.* Latin America's experience also highlights, however, that the mere avoidance of military rule does not mean that democracy is healthy. Studies of Latin American politics increasingly refer to these regimes as democracies with adjectives: illiberal, or hollow, or difficult, or partial, depending on the author. The implication of all of these adjectives is that democracy in Latin America is not fully democratic; that is, it does not provide citizens with the means to participate fully in selecting leaders and holding them accountable. One of the most useful concepts is "illiberal democracy," indicating countries that combine free and fair elections with restrictions on citizens' rights. Using Freedom House rankings, which score political and civil liberties separately, Zakaria notes that the number of countries that do better on political rights than civil liberties is rising.[55] Smith and Ziegler classified 40 percent of Latin American democracies from 1978 to 2004 as illiberal during at least one year.[56] And as of 2008, 17 percent of Latin American countries classified overall as "free" by Freedom House had a civil liberties ranking in the partly free range. An additional 44 percent had a ranking of partly free on both political rights and civil liberties.[57]

Why have Latin American democracies been so vulnerable to authoritarian practices even within the context of elections? Two of the leading candidates are military influence and overly strong presidents. Although these threats did not lead to the overthrow of democratic regimes as scholars in the 1980s feared, they may still undermine the quality of democracy. Scholarly research has increasingly turned its attention to these questions as opposed to the causes of democratic breakdown. Other research suggests that while economic development may not account for the survival of such a disparate group of democracies, it may help us understand which of them is likely to be healthier.[58]

Another important problem is institutional weakness or, more precisely, uneven institutional development across space and issue boundaries. For example, a great deal of attention has focused on the development of electoral institutions, those which run and monitor elections, to the point they are arguably stronger and more institutionally developed than comparable institutions in developed democracies, where trust rather than elaborate security measures undergirds the legitimacy of elections. However, the infrastructure for the ordinary administration of justice is far less institutionally developed. One of the primary reasons for the low scores of many Latin American democracies on civil rights is precisely this deficiency in the police and court systems. Police forces run rampant over the rights of individuals, court systems release the guilty (rich) and imprison the innocent (poor), if they get around to prosecuting cases at all, and politicians are under considerable pressure from both economic elites and ordinary citizens to adopt harsh measures to reduce crime at any cost as public insecurity grows.

A related question receiving attention is the issue of transitions within electoral democracy, from illiberal to liberal democracies or vice versa. Do the conditions and processes that helped explain transitions from authoritarian rule also help us explain when a regime is likely to suffer setbacks or advances in democratic quality? How rare are these shifts? If illiberal democracy is not just a transitional stage toward liberal democracy but a stable regime type in itself, as Zakaria suggests, then the costs of achieving formal democracy may be quite high.

The consequences could be even greater if elections legitimize exclusion, inequality, and poverty. In 1987 Terry Karl warned that deals between authoritarians and democratizers to achieve transition could result in "frozen" democracies, unable to address key concerns of their citizens or to allow meaningful popular participation. More recently, she has called inequality "the greatest threat facing democracy in the Americas."[59] While economic welfare is not part of the definition of democracy, critics have long claimed that democracy, like religion, may serve as an opiate of the masses, distracting them from meaningful change. More recent critics of the effects of neoliberalism use different language, but their concerns are similar: how can democracy be real to people when international constraints limit economic policy choices, states have become increasingly irrelevant to economic decision making, and multinational companies have larger "GDPs" than most nations? The risk here is not authoritarian rule, but a democracy emptied of significance. People can make choices but only on irrelevant issues, not on the issues that matter to them most. This contradiction may help account for the Latin American paradox, that "the military has stayed in its barracks and civilian elites seem to want to keep them there, yet [public] support for democracy and its institutions is diminishing."[60] If these trends continue, we may witness not the sudden death of Latin American democracy by coup but its slow erosion from within.

Smith and Ziegler are more optimistic. They argue that "free and fair elections are the Achilles' heel of illiberal democracies."[61] Transformation of illiberal democracies into more liberal ones typically occurred in the context of presidential elections and performance failures (such as hyperinflation). In response, angry voters chose reformers who promised more accountability. It should be noted, however, that angry voters also supported Fujimori's *auto-golpe* (self-coup) in the hope that strong leadership could fix the problems that weak democracy had failed to solve.

Much research remains to be done. New measures of democracy, more sensitive to shifts within the democratic spectrum, must be developed. Nevertheless, if we assume the worst—democracy survives, but only as illiberal or hollow democracy—it may still be worth having, or at least better than the alternatives available to countries whose structural and political context militate against full democracy. Even illiberal democracies do not typically perform as poorly on human rights measures as nondemocracies. And to the extent that even bad democracies may contain within their own procedures a possible cure, the institutionalization of elections matters.

NOTES

1. Guillermo O'Donnell, "Introduction to the Latin American Cases," in Guillermo O'Donnell, Philippe C. Schmitter, and Laurence Whitehead, eds., *Transitions from Authoritarian Rule: Latin America* (Baltimore: Johns Hopkins University Press 1986), pp. 14–15.

2. Guillermo O'Donnell, Philippe C. Schmitter, and Laurence Whitehead, *Transitions from Authoritarian Rule: Tentative Conclusions about Uncertain Democracies* (Baltimore: Johns Hopkins University Press, 1986), p. 24.

3. Samuel Huntington, *The Third Wave: Democratization in the Late Twentieth Century* (Norman: University of Oklahoma Press, 1991), p. 231.

4. Howard Wiarda, *Critical Elections and Critical Coups: State, Society, and the Military in the Processes of Latin American Development* (Athens: Ohio University Center for International Studies, 1978), p. 43.

5. Eric Nordlinger, *Soldiers in Politics: Military Coups and Governments* (Englewood Cliffs, NJ: Prentice-Hall, 1977), p. 207.

6. Robert Dix, "Military Coups and Military Rule in Latin America," *Armed Forces and Society* 20, no. 3 (Spring 1994): 441.

7. The original proponent of this theory was, of course, Guillermo O'Donnell in his book, *Modernization and Bureaucratic-Authoritarianism: Studies in South American Politics* (Berkeley: Institute of International Studies, University of California, 1973). However, recent work tends to confirm this finding. See Luis Gonzalez, "Political Crises and Democracy in Latin America since the End of the Cold War," Kellogg Institute Working Paper no. 353, December 2008, http://kellogg.nd.edu/publications/workingpapers/WPS/353.pdf.

8. See Egil Fossum, "Factors Influencing the Occurrence of Military Coups in Latin America," *Journal of Peace Research* 4, no. 3 (1967): 228–51; Martin Needler, *Political Development in Latin America: Instability, Violence, and Evolutionary Change* (New York: Random House, 1968).

9. Dix, "Military Coups and Military Rule in Latin America."

10. Data from www.worldpublicopinion.org/pipa/articles/brlatinamericara/328 .php?nid=&id=&pnt=328&lb=brla, accessed September 24, 2008.

11. Alfred Stepan, *Rethinking Military Politics: Brazil and the Southern Cone* (Princeton: Princeton University Press, 1988), p. 93.

12. Ibid., p. 100.

13. See Wendy Hunter, *Eroding Military Influence in Brazil: Politicians against Soldiers* (Chapel Hill: University of North Carolina Press, 1997).

14. These countries both experienced a third wave transition *and* did not make this transition in a context of civil war, which inflates military spending and people under arms in the pretransition period.

15. James Wilkie, ed., with Eduardo Aleman and José Guadalupe Ortega, *Statistical Abstract of Latin America,* vol. 38 (Los Angeles: University of California, 2002), pp. 384–89, 397.

16. http://yearbook2005.sipri.org/ch8/ch8.

17. Hunter, *Eroding Military Influence in Brazil.*

18. Adam Przeworski, *Democracy and the Market: Political and Economic Reforms in Eastern Europe and Latin America* (New York: Cambridge University Press, 1991), p. 136.

19. Ibid., p. 186.

20. For example, José María Maravall, "The Myth of the Authoritarian Advantage," in Larry Diamond and Marc F. Plattner, eds., *Economic Reform and Democracy* (Baltimore: Johns Hopkins University Press, 1995): 13–27; Barbara Geddes, "Challenging the Conventional Wisdom," in ibid.: 59–73.

21. Kurt Weyland, "Risk-Taking in Latin American Economic Restructuring: Lessons from Prospect Theory," *International Studies Quarterly* 40, no. 2 (June 1996): 185–207; Kurt Weyland, "Swallowing the Bitter Pill," *Comparative Political Studies* 31, no. 5 (October 1998): 539–69.

22. Susan Stokes, *Mandates and Democracy: Neoliberalism by Surprise in Latin America* (New York: Cambridge University Press, 2001).

23. Kenneth M. Roberts and Erik Wibbels, "Party Systems and Electoral Volatility in Latin America: A Test of Economic, Institutional, and Structural Explanations," *American Political Science Review* 93, no. 3 (September 1999): 575–90; Marcus J. Kurtz, "The Dilemmas of Democracy in the Open Economy: Lessons from Latin America," *World Politics* 56 no. 2 (January 2004): 262–302.

24. Moises Arce and Paul Bellinger Jr., "Low Intensity Democracy Revisited: The Effects of Economic Liberalization on Political Activity in Latin America," *World Politics* 60 (October 2007): 97–121.

25. Barrington Moore, *Social Origins of Dictatorship and Democracy: Lord and Peasant in the Making of the Modern World* (Boston: Beacon Press, 1966).

26. Kurt Weyland, "The Rise of Latin America's Two Lefts: Insights from Rentier State Theory," *Comparative Politics* 41, no. 2 (January 2009): 146.

27. Juan J. Linz, "The Perils of Presidentialism," in Larry Diamond and Marc F. Plattner, eds., *The Global Resurgence of Democracy*, 2nd ed. (Baltimore: Johns Hopkins University Press, 1996).

28. Donald Horowitz, "Comparing Democratic Systems," in Diamond and Plattner, *The Global Resurgence of Democracy*, p. 144.

29. Alfred Stepan and Susan Skach, "Constitutional Frameworks and Democratic Consolidation? Parliamentarism versus Presidentialism," *World Politics* 46 (October 1993): 10. See also Adam Przeworski, Michael Alvarez, José Antonio Cheibub, and Fernando Limongi, "What Makes Democracies Endure?" *Journal of Democracy* 7, no. 1 (January 1996): 47.

30. Scott Mainwaring, "Presidentialism, Multipartism, and Democracy: The Difficult Combination," *Comparative Political Studies* 26, no. 2 (July 1993): 198–229.

31. Timothy J. Power and Mark Gasiorowski, "Institutional Design and Democratic Consolidation in the Third World," *Comparative Political Studies* 30, no. 2 (April 1997): 123–56; Timothy J. Power and Mark Gasiorowski, "The Structural Determinants of Democratic Consolidation," *Comparative Political Studies* 31, no. 6 (December 1998): 740–72.

32. Mikhail Baliaev, "Presidential Powers and Consolidation of New Postcommunist Democracies," *Comparative Political Studies* 39, no. 3 (2006): 375–98.

33. José Antonio Cheibub, *Presidentialism, Parliamentarism, and Democracy* (New York: Cambridge University Press, 2007), pp. 6, 79.

34. Ibid., p. 23.

35. Aníbal Pérez-Liñán, *Presidential Impeachment and the New Political Instability in Latin America* (New York: Cambridge University Press, 2007), p. 187.

36. Ibid., p. 1.

37. M. Steven Fish and Matthew Kroenig, *The Handbook of National Legislatures: A Global Survey* (New York: Cambridge University Press, 2009), www.polisci.berkeley.edu/faculty/bio/permanent/Fish,M/PPIScores.pdf, accessed March 15, 2009. See also Fish, chapter 5 in this volume.

38. Pérez-Liñán, *Presidential Impeachment and the New Political Instability in Latin America*, p. 13.

39. Ibid., p. 201.

40. Ibid., p. 61.

41. In 2007, *Fortune* magazine estimated that Slim's companies control more than 90% of the telephone landlines in Mexico and 70% of the cell phone market. http://money.cnn.com/2007/08/03/news/international/carlosslim.fortune/index.htm?postversion=2007080614, accessed August 3, 2010.

42. www.forbes.com/2010/03/09/worlds-richest-people-slim-gates-buffett-billionaires-2010-intro_slide_2.html?partner=yahoo.

43. www.forbes.com/2009/03/11/worlds-richest-people-billionaires-2009-billionaires-intro.html.

44. Michael Coppedge, "Political Darwinism in Latin America's Lost Decade," in Larry Diamond and Richard Gunther, eds., *Political Parties and Democracy* (Baltimore: Johns Hopkins University Press, 2001), p. 185.

45. For Mainwaring and Scully, strong parties are crucial to the institutionalization of a stable party *system*, but the two concepts are distinct. Stable party systems involve "stability in interparty competition" and "acceptance of parties and elections as the

legitimate institutions that determine who governs"—both system characteristics—as well as "parties that have somewhat stable roots in society" and "party organizations with reasonably stable rules and structures." Scott Mainwaring and Timothy R. Scully, eds., *Building Democratic Institutions: Party Systems in Latin America* (Stanford, CA: Stanford University Press, 1995), p. 1.

46. Ibid., p. 2.

47. Henry A. Dietz and David Myers, "From Thaw to Deluge: Party System Collapse in Venezuela and Peru," *Latin American Politics and Society* 49, no. 2 (Summer 2007): 59–86.

48. For Levitsky and Cameron, one of the key functions of political parties is coordination, facilitating the "ability of democratic oppositions to maintain a united front" and to mobilize collective action to sustain democracy. The failure of the coordination factor in Peru allowed Fujimori to dismiss the Congress. See Steven Levitsky and Maxwell Cameron, "Democracy without Parties? Political Parties and Regime Change in Fujimori's Peru," *Latin American Politics and Society* 45, no. 3 (Fall 2003): 5.

49. The fourth strongest party system on the Mainwaring and Scully list (*Building Democratic Institutions*) is Venezuela, which experienced an interruption in 1993. However, the complete collapse of the Venezuelan party system within five years suggests that party system weakness may have played a role here as well.

50. Stokes, *Mandates and Democracy*.

51. Omar Encarnación, "Venezuela's 'Civil Society Coup,'" *World Policy Journal* 19, no. 2 (Summer 2002): 38–56; Pérez-Liñán, *Presidential Impeachment and the New Political Instability in Latin America*, p. 13.

52. Levitsky and Cameron, "Democracy without Parties?" p. 25.

53. Daniel Brinks and Michael Coppedge, "Diffusion Is No Illusion: Neighbor Emulation in the Third Wave of Democracy," *Comparative Political Studies* 39, no. 4 (May 2006): 463–89.

54. Przeworski et al., "What Makes Democracies Endure?" p. 43.

55. Fareed Zakaria, "The Rise of Illiberal Democracy," *Foreign Affairs* 76, no. 6 (November–December 1997): 24.

56. That is, 40% of all country-years, a measure that includes one year for each country. Thus, if one had 10 countries and 10 years, the total number of country-years would be 100. Peter Smith and Melissa Ziegler, "Liberal and Illiberal Democracy in Latin America," *Latin American Politics and Society* 50, no. 1 (Spring 2008): 31–57.

57. www.freedomhouse.org. Based on my calculations of the eighteen continental Latin American democracies.

58. Scott Mainwaring and Aníbal Pérez-Liñán, "Regime Legacies and Democratization: Explaining Variance in the Level of Democracy in Latin America, 1978–2004," Kellogg Institute, Working Paper no. 354, University of Notre Dame, December 2008; Cynthia McClintock and James H. Lebovic, "Correlates of Levels of Democracy in Latin America during the 1990s," *Latin American Politics and Society* 48, no. 2 (Summer 2006): 29–59. Both articles find that GDP per capita is a significant predictor of the quality of democracy as measured by Freedom House scores.

59. Terry Lynn Karl, "Economic Inequality and Democratic Instability," *Journal of Democracy* 11, no. 1 (January 2000): 156; Terry Lynn Karl, "Petroleum and Political Pacts: The Transition to Democracy in Venezuela," *Latin American Research Review* 22, no. 1 (1987): 63–94.

60. Frances Hagopian, "Conclusions: Political Performance, Political Representation, and Public Perceptions of Contemporary Democracy in Latin America," in Frances Hagopian and Scott Mainwaring, eds., *The Third Wave of Democratization in Latin America: Advances and Setbacks* (New York: Cambridge, 2005), p. 320.

61. Peter Smith and Melissa Ziegler, "Liberal and Illiberal Democracy in Latin America," *Latin American Politics and Society* 50, no. 1 (Spring 2008): 46.

# CHAPTER 4

# Sustaining Party Rule in China

## Coercion, Co-optation, and Their Consequences

*Bruce J. Dickson*

Throughout the past three decades and more, China has experienced a period of rapid economic growth and dramatic social change. The "reform and opening" policies championed by Deng Xiaoping in the late 1970s triggered domestic economic activities and integration into the global economy, raising living standards and enhancing China's international status. These reforms entailed the retreat of the state from the market and the daily lives of most Chinese. The centrally planned economy, a hallmark of communist regimes, was gradually and incrementally replaced by a market economy and private ownership. Whereas the Maoist state controlled where people lived and worked and monitored what they thought and did, the post-Mao state relinquished control over many of these personal choices, creating a private realm and a dynamism in society that matched the economic activities that were pushing China rapidly toward modernization.[1]

With these economic and social developments came expectations of political change. Throughout the post-Mao period, China watchers anticipated that the pace of political reform would sooner or later catch up with reforms in the economic and social realms. Just as economic reform had liberalized the state's control over the economy, most observers expected that the political liberalization would inevitably emerge. Scholars and journalists examined China for signs of liberal inclinations among the political leaders and indicators of civil society and democratic sentiments within society. Chinese intellectuals also called for democratization to accompany economic modernization. At the very beginning of the reform era, China's best-known dissident, Wei Jingsheng, offered an eloquent call for democratization, which he saw as the prerequisite for economic and social progress. "Without [democracy], not only is further development impossible, but even preserving the level of development already attained would be very difficult."[2] The conventional wisdom shared by observers inside and outside China was that political reforms leading to democracy were inevitable.

However, the Chinese Communist Party (CCP) has not been a passive actor in the process of economic and social change. It has defied predictions of its demise and called into question the logic that economic and political reforms must go together. The search for signs of imminent democratization led many observers to overlook, or at least underappreciate, the ability of the CCP to adapt to the changes in the economy and society, changes that were the goal of its own "reform and opening" policies.[3] While using coercive measures to prevent organized demands for political change emanating from outside the party, the CCP has also been able to generate popular support from economic growth, the co-optation of new elites, and the adoption of populist policies to balance the competing goals of growth and equity. China's recent experience shows how countries can become increasingly prosperous economically while remaining steadfastly authoritarian politically.

Rather than focus on the prospects for democratization in China, it is more useful to understand the strategies being utilized to reproduce and sustain the current authoritarian regime. This chapter explores the CCP's strategy for survival and the viability of that strategy in the future. Two key themes run through this chapter. First, like all authoritarian regimes, China's is sustained in part by the use of coercion against critics and opponents. In contrast to the past, however, the regime's use of coercion is now more selective and targeted. For most people in contemporary China, the hand of the state is less prominent than in the past. Second, coercion alone does not sustain authoritarian rule in China. The CCP also generates support by improving living standards through rapid economic growth, integrating new elites into the political system, and providing a range of public goods to the population at large. Whereas most authoritarian regimes provide private goods to their key supporters, the CCP adds a distinctive twist: it is also increasing the supply of public goods, such as education, access to information, and basic infrastructure, that benefit society as a whole. By comparing the CCP's current strategy with that of the Maoist era, and with those of other countries in the recent past, we can gain a better appreciation of the sustainability of authoritarian rule in China; the factors that either promote or undermine that strategy; and, by extension, the prospects for regime change in China.

## What Sustains Authoritarian Regimes?

Scholars studying the persistence of authoritarian regimes have noted several key characteristics. Abundant natural resources, especially oil, have allowed some regimes to survive without needing to court popular support. Oil reserves generate ample revenues to fund government operations, and oil exports also generate international support that dampens criticism of regime practices. These revenues also allow these governments to expand and strengthen military and security forces to suppress internal threats and defend against external enemies.[4] Patrimonial practices reward family members and political supporters with key jobs and the rents those jobs control.[5] Regime leaders may use wedge tactics against their political opponents, coercing and manipulating the opposition rather than co-opting them or entirely repressing them.[6]

These comparative insights have limited utility for understanding the reproduction of authoritarian rule in China. China is a net importer of energy and most other raw materials, so the government lacks the resources to finance state activities and solicit international support. Although it has dramatically increased its spending on military and security forces, it has done so through taxes and trade. While personal connections are still an essential part of informal politics in China, official appointments are increasingly based on merit (a necessary if not always sufficient condition). Rather than dividing the political opposition, the CCP has attempted to eliminate it, aggressively defending its monopoly on political organization. While much of the scholarly attention has shifted to the study of hybrid regimes, China remains a prominent example of what Larry Diamond refers to as a "closed political regime": it lacks meaningful elections, and all positions of political influence are controlled by the ruling party.[7]

But putting the right label on China's political system obscures the changes over time in its survival strategy and in its relationship with society. Focusing on coercive tools alone misses a crucial fact about politics in China: the CCP continues to rule because it not only has been able to eliminate or at least suppress all viable alternatives but also enjoys a remarkable degree of popular support. Like other autocratic regimes, it relies on coercion to repress threats to its rule and criticism of its policies. But unlike many other autocratic regimes, China maintains its hold on power not simply by coercion. It also has been able to generate a large degree of popular support for the goals of its economic reform policies, even though there has been severe dissatisfaction with the inequality and corruption that have accompanied rapid economic growth. It has co-opted new elites into the political system in order to elicit their support, or at least prevent the formation of an organized opposition.

## The CCP's Coercive Powers

Coercion has been a key part of the reproduction of the communist regime in China, as it is in all authoritarian regimes. The intensity and scope of coercion in China have varied considerably over time. During the Maoist era (1949–76), particularly during the antirightist movement in the late 1950s and the Cultural Revolution, the CCP actively sought out and harshly punished alleged class enemies and opponents of Chairman Mao in particular. These were not simply state-led political campaigns; one of the hallmarks of the Maoist style of politics, best exemplified by the Cultural Revolution, was the mobilization of the masses into the political arena to implement repressive policies. All members of society were called on to identify political enemies. Although the key targets of these campaigns were party and government officials, anyone could be implicated and punished for "counterrevolutionary" thoughts or actions. To accentuate the obedience to Mao, people were expected to implicate friends, colleagues, and even family members as enemies of the people. This bred suspicion and uncertainty throughout the state and society, preventing a collective challenge to Mao and his supporters. While this practice was successful in repressing real and imagined political threats, it also created doubt about the intentions and wisdom of Mao and other CCP leaders. As the country veered between periods of radical political goals and pragmatic economic development, actions and statements that were encouraged during one campaign turned into grounds for repression in the next one. By the time of Mao's death in 1976, most members of China's state and society had grown weary of the constant turmoil and uncertainty. As new leaders succeeded Mao, the strategy and tactics used to keep the CCP in power also shifted.

To clearly demarcate the post-Mao era from the politics of the past, the CCP announced the end of class struggle in 1978. In its place, the party adopted the goal of economic modernization as its key task. This announcement was significant for several related reasons. First, it brought an end to the repression and punishment of alleged counterrevolutionaries and "capitalist roaders." With the shift toward economic development, the CCP no longer treated capitalists as class enemies but instead as key sources of political support. Second, practical results replaced ideological propriety as the standard for judging the correctness of policies. Rather than seek inspiration from Marx or Mao, post-Mao leaders experimented with a variety of economic reforms, abandoning those that failed and adopting for nationwide implementation those that produced economic growth. "Seek truth from facts" became the mantra of the initial post-Mao era to signal the emphasis on results rather than ideological orthodoxy. Nevertheless, the CCP has continued to justify its reforms with ideological language. Third, the end of class struggle created political normalcy within both state and society. The repeated cycles of purging and rehabilitating party and government officials were largely abandoned. Individual leaders occasionally were removed from office for political "mistakes" (Hu Yaobang, Zhao Ziyang) or for personal opposition to top leaders (Chen Xitong, Chen Liangyu), even though the people purged for personal opposition were normally charged with corruption as justification for their ousters. The end of class struggle also resulted in the depoliticization of everyday life for most Chinese. An individual's taste in music, clothing, or hairstyle was no longer viewed as a political statement or a reflection of class sentiments. This led to a predictability in political and social life that was missing from most of the Maoist era.

With the shift in policy, the CCP under Deng Xiaoping's leadership pursued economic "reform and opening" policies: gradually, it reduced the role of central planning in the economy in favor of market forces and opened the country to the international economy. Despite these dramatic changes, the hallmark of China's political system did not change: it remains a one-party dictatorship. The CCP actively monitors its environment for signs of political opposition and aggressively represses it. Public calls for democratization have consistently led to arrest, imprisonment, and occasionally exile. To preserve its monopoly on political organization, the CCP harshly cracks down on efforts to create organizations outside the party's control, for example, the Chinese Democracy Party, independent labor unions, and religious groups and churches. Coercion is not used as often as in the past, nor does it affect as many people as before, but it remains part of the CCP's repertoire for remaining in power. Just as economic transformation was part of Deng's legacy, so too was his insistence that reform and opening be done under the unchallenged authority of the CCP.

In order to repress and even preempt political challenges without relying entirely on coercive powers, the CCP more commonly increases the difficulty of collective action by restricting access to what Bueno de Mesquita and Downs call "coordination goods," which are "public goods that critically affect the ability of political opponents to coordinate but that have relatively little impact on economic growth."[8] These include political rights, such as freedom of speech and freedom of assembly; human rights, such as habeas corpus and freedom to travel; a free press, which provides access to information not controlled by the state; and advanced education, which increases the ability to organize and communicate more effectively. The challenge for authoritarian leaders comes in strategically restricting access to these kinds of goods without undermining the economy. In this respect, China has been an exemplar of this strategy. It carefully monitors communication on the Internet for political content. It pressures companies such as Google and Yahoo to limit information and even images found in searches from within China and to share information with the state about their users. The rule of law is weakly enforced, especially for politically sensitive cases: people are imprisoned without formal charges; when they are charged, their legal right to communicate with their lawyers and family is often denied; and their trials may be held in closed court. All broadcast media are still state owned, allowing it to limit the stories that can be reported and to punish the journalists who ignore these restrictions. While higher education has become more popular, colleges and universities remain state controlled, which deters political activities among college students, who risk unemployment after graduation if they run afoul of the state.

In absolute terms, China highly restricts coordination goods. However, the state's control over each of these goods has diminished in the post-Mao era. The state no longer controls speech as it did during the Maoist era, when casual remarks could subject people to vicious political accusations and punishment, and where people were mobilized during repeated political campaigns to mouth the currently favored slogans, only to be expected to denounce those slogans—and even be punished for voicing them—in subsequent campaigns. In contemporary China, there are still limits on what people can publish, but people readily criticize local officials and policy implementation. The freedom of movement, heavily restricted in the Maoist era, is now a routine part of life for most Chinese. A large migrant population has been a key characteristic of the post-Mao era, as more than 100 million people have flocked to cities from the countryside in search of better-paying jobs in the industrial and service sectors. The ability to travel abroad for work, study, or leisure has also grown higher. The Chinese population has become much more mobile, for short- and long-term stays, within the country and abroad. Opportunities to attend colleges and universities have also expanded exponentially in the post-Mao era. During the Cultural Revolution decade, China's universities were essentially closed, creating a "lost generation," which was denied the chance for higher education. In the post-Mao period, in contrast, the number of college graduates has increased steadily. In 1990 only 3.4 percent of college-age students (between eighteen and twenty-two years of age) enrolled in college, but by 2006 that percentage had increased to 22 percent.[9] The CCP not only encourages young people to attend college but also uses college campuses as its main site for recruiting new party members. For both economic and political reasons, the CCP is investing in human capital.

In short, the CCP continues to restrict coordination goods, but they are in greater abundance now than in the recent past. Although the *level* of coordination goods in China is far below that enjoyed in democratic countries, the *trend* over time has been a dramatic increase in these goods. Both the restricted level and the rising trend must be appreciated in order to assess the CCP's strategy. For most people in China, the reach of the state is less pervasive, less intrusive, and less arbitrary, but for those who challenge the CCP's political monopoly, the state remains repressive and severe.

Two key coordination goods—access to information and the ability to organize—merit closer attention. First of all, the Chinese state devotes a tremendous amount of its political resources to restricting access to information. Most broadcast and print media remain under state ownership and are subject to censorship if party leaders decide information is politically sensitive or embarrassing to the regime. At the same time, the number of newspapers and magazines has exploded by tenfold during the reform era, making it more difficult to monitor what gets broadcast and printed. Moreover, the commercialization of the media has encouraged some enterprising journalists and editors to investigate stories of corruption and malfeasance that attract widespread attention and thereby boost revenue from circulation and advertising. The state also tries to limit the flow of information on the Internet. It restricts access to the Internet to prevent people's ability to retrieve and share information that does not meet the party line. It does so through a variety of means: blocking access to certain Web sites; requiring users of Internet cafés to register their names so the state can monitor their online activities; and monitoring Internet bulletin boards and blogs for political content, often taking down postings as soon as they appear and arresting the people who posted them. It also tries to monitor the use of text messages for political purposes: rather than scanning messages before they are delivered, it reportedly stores and later analyzes them for political content.

This is an ongoing cat-and-mouse game between the state and political activists. As the state restricts access to Web sites, technologically savvy users find new ways around the "Great Firewall" through proxy servers and other technological means.[10] To fool software programs that detect political contact, users sprinkle their postings with symbols (such as % and #) in between characters and rely on homonyms and euphemisms to avoid detection. For example, to organize protests against plans to build a maglev train in Shanghai, people sent text messages that they were "going shopping" at a specific time and place. Moreover, the number of Chinese who access the Internet has grown exponentially in recent years, from an estimated 22.5 million in 2000 to 298 million in 2008.[11]

The CCP does not fully restrict access to the Internet because of a basic dilemma: it wants to constrain the use of the Internet for political purposes while still making it available for leisure and especially for economic purposes. The costs of coercion—of completely blocking access to the Internet for any and all purposes—outweigh the benefits: prohibiting access to all users would affect most Chinese, who use the Internet for communication and gaming, not just those involved in political activities, and would create strong resentment. Moreover, the state recognizes the economic potential of the Internet and does not want to deny access for business use. As a result, it attempts to cope with the challenges presented by the Internet without completely repressing those who utilize it.

In addition to limiting access to information, the CCP limits the ability to form new organizations. Most observers note the weakness of China's civil society. There is no organized political opposition. An attempt to form a China Democracy Party in the late 1990s led to jail terms of more than ten years apiece for its organizers. There are few active dissidents within China, and most of the best-known dissidents either are in jail or were forced into exile during the 1990s. Those that remain active are often harassed with repeated searches of their homes and confiscation of their computers and papers, tailed

by police when they leave their homes, kept under house arrest, and sometimes imprisoned for short or long periods of time. Not only do China's dissidents pay a high price for their political activities, but they also enjoy little
public support. Whereas dissidents in other authoritarian regimes—such as
Vaclav Havel, Nelson Mandela, and Aung San Suu Kyi—were held in high
regard as symbols of popular resistance, critics of the Chinese government
are more often seen by their fellow citizens as unpatriotic. China's dissidents
therefore face not only repression by the state but also resentment from other
members of society.

Key social groups in China also face challenges in obtaining an organized
voice independent of the state. There are no independent labor unions; in
fact, the call for autonomous labor unions during the 1989 demonstrations
was a nonnegotiable issue from the perspective of party hard-liners, and labor
activists received harsher punishments—including even execution—than
student organizers. Efforts to create labor unions not tied to the official All-
China Federation of Trade Unions have been consistently and forcefully repressed, even as the plight of labor worsened as a consequence of wide-scale
privatization. There is no organization for farmers, either state sponsored or
autonomous. Although the largest share of China's population still lives in
the countryside, they have no organization that represents their interests or
speaks on their behalf.

The CCP attempts to raise the cost of collective action without preventing
organized activities altogether. If civil society is viewed as an autonomous
realm capable of pressuring the state to instigate political reform, or even of
leading to the overthrow of the regime, then China's civil society is indeed
weak. But China also has a flourishing and increasingly diverse civil society
that is often overlooked and underestimated because it is not organized for
overtly political purposes. China has a wide variety of professional groups,
business associations, sports and hobby clubs, homeowners associations, and
the like. Many of these are closely monitored by the state, and their activities
and even existence are dependent on the state's approval. Consequently, they
lack the degree of autonomy that nongovernmental organizations in other
countries normally possess.[12] Because they are not organized to oppose the
regime, they are often excluded from discussions of civil society in China.
These kinds of groups are often seen as essential for stable democracies but
do not seem influential in bringing about political change. That is why it is

useful to unpack the concept of civil society by differentiating the political realm that is in opposition to the state from the economic realm that fosters more cooperative relations between state and society. The economic realm is what Putnam had in mind, and what Foley and Edwards referred to as "civil society I": this type of civil society can help stabilize current regimes instead of challenging them.[13] Although their arguments were based primarily on democratic countries, the same logic may well apply to authoritarian regimes. In other words, as the number and variety of professional, civic, and cultural associations continue to grow in China, they may actually contribute to the reproduction of the incumbent authoritarian regime rather than pose a challenge to it.

Even the "civil society I" in China is partly constrained by the state. Organizations must register with the state, and the state often rejects these applications. Moreover, there is a corporatist logic to the state's treatment of these groups. In most cases, it insists that only one organization representing a certain interest or cause can exist in a given community; when more than one exist, they are pressured to merge or disband. Civil society organizations are also monitored by state agencies or even directly controlled by them. For example, most business associations fall under the jurisdiction of the CCP's United Front Department, which is in charge of relations with nonparty individuals and groups, and their offices are often within government buildings.

What Foley and Edwards called "civil society II" is the political realm that uses dissent and protest to oppose the state. This realm is in short supply in China. The absence of an organized opposition enhances the CCP's control but presents a potential problem for a future transition. When political change occurred in other countries, it was often the consequence of negotiations between state and opposition groups. The absence of organized political groups and an identifiable political opposition in China, or of an opposition leader who is widely seen as representing society, as was the case in other authoritarian regimes, could create the potential for political instability during a messy transition. That was part of the CCP's dilemma in responding to the 1989 demonstrations: when it tried (albeit half-heartedly) to enter a dialogue, it was not clear who could legitimately speak on behalf of the protesters. Without an "honest broker" who could enforce a compromise if one were reached, negotiations had little chance of success. A similar dynamic would likely prevail if another political opening were to occur, because the basic features of the political system—the monopoly of political organization by the CCP—remains unchanged.

Whereas other authoritarian parties adopt a "divide and conquer" approach to their opposition,[14] the CCP uses repression and exclusion to cope with political threats. The CCP has not attempted to sow divisions between moderate and radical opposition leaders in order to seek cooperation from the former against the latter. Because its institutional characteristics do not fit the concept of electoral authoritarianism (it does not allow opposition parties, and national leaders and the legislature are not chosen through general elections), it cannot rely on those familiar tactics.[15] Instead, it uses harassment, imprisonment, and in some cases exile to repress and exclude dissidents and critics. It is more willing to accept criticism of its quality of governance and ability to implement its policies and co-opts critics who suggest ways of ruling better, but it does not tolerate critics who suggest it should rule differently, in particular by abandoning the current political institutions in favor of democratic ones.

In sum, coercion remains a key feature of authoritarian rule in China, as it is for all authoritarian regimes. However, coercion is costly; it risks antagonizing people who are otherwise apolitical or potential supporters of the regime. This was a contributing factor in the democratization of countries such as Brazil: when the targets of repression were armed rebels, the population was supportive, but once the children of the urban middle class also were targeted, popular support shifted away from the regime in favor of democratization. A similar trend happened during the Cultural Revolution, in which the victims included people who were innocent of all accusations against them and others whose punishment far outweighed their alleged crimes, leading to widespread cynicism and disillusionment. In China's case, however, the post-Mao leaders were determined to reconcile the state's relationship with society but without democratizing the regime. Consequently, over time, coercive power has been used more selectively to sustain the CCP. In contrast to the Maoist era, coercion is used against a narrower range of people. Political elites are no longer subject to ideologically oriented purges, and the population as a whole is no longer terrorized by recurring political campaigns. When post-Mao leaders announced the end of class struggle and the beginning of economic reform, they also signaled their intention to reconcile state with society and to allow a wider range of economic and social activities than were tolerated under Mao. One limit remained, however: the CCP's monopoly on political power was inviolable. The CCP has consistently and often harshly punished those who posed a direct challenge to its authority. But coercion alone is not the only factor that sustains the CCP. We must also consider the factors that generate popular support among select groups and the population at large.

## Generating Popular Support in China

One of the great paradoxes of contemporary China—and there are many—is the remarkably high level of popular support for a regime that often seems so incapable of effective governance. Stories abound of widespread corruption, of environmental degradation and social dislocation resulting from rapid growth, of growing income disparities, of health crises brought on by lack of regulation and restrictions on the flow of information, and of popular protests against these practices. And yet, study after study has found tremendous popular support for the government. Most recently, a global survey by the Pew Research Center found that 86 percent of those surveyed in China believed the country was moving in the right direction; in contrast, just over 20 percent in the United States believed the same things.[16] This finding is not an anomaly; it is consistent with several academic studies.[17]

What accounts for this high level of popular support for a government that lacks transparent institutions, is not accountable to the people it governs, and in a variety of ways seems to have delivered such poor governance? On the one hand, the CCP has focused on economic development not only as its key task but also, by extension, as its main source of legitimacy. The beneficiaries of economic reform—private entrepreneurs and the broader middle class— have strong incentives to support the status quo.[18] In addition, the modernization of the country and its growing integration into the international system— symbolized most vividly by the 2008 Summer Olympics—strengthened nationalist sentiment and popular support for the CCP and its reform policies. On the other hand, recent efforts to adopt more populist policies to address the growing economic inequalities and other externalities of rapid growth are designed to distribute the benefits of economic reform more widely, reduce the political instability that grew from the late 1990s, and above all increase popular support among the population at large.

# The Politics of Inclusion: Co-opting New Elites into China's Political System

Co-opting new elites into a political party or other type of organization is a common way of both adapting and preventing external challenges. As Ken Jowitt observed, Leninist parties adopt more inclusive practices as they move from revolutionary goals to developmental goals.[19] The key question for the adaptability and survivability of the ruling party is what kinds of elites are being co-opted? When Leninist parties co-opt intellectual and political elites, the result may be the eventual transformation of the party, as the co-opted elites push for political change from within the party.[20] In contrast, China has targeted economic and technical elites for co-optation. These elites are less likely to pose an imminent political challenge to the party and, moreover, are necessary allies in the goal of economic development. In other words, co-opted elites from "civil society I" are less likely to pose challenges to the status quo than those from "civil society II."

As the CCP shifted from waging class struggle to developing the economy, it needed new sets of elites with appropriate skills for its new policy goals. Whereas educated elites were often persecuted during the Maoist era, they became the focus of the CCP's recruitment efforts. Whereas other authoritarian regimes were sustained in part by allocating jobs in the government and security forces to political allies, family members, and other cronies, these patrimonial policies declined in the post-Mao period relative to meritocratic practices.[21] The renewed emphasis on expertise and minimum professional standards meant that educational qualifications and professional experience were also part of appointing and promoting party, government, and military officials. Favoritism still comes into play, but meritocratic qualifications are a necessary if not sufficient condition for official appointments. With this emphasis on expertise, universities became a primary recruitment area for the CCP; as a result, it brought many of China's best and brightest into the regime and solidified their support for the status quo.

The gradual privatization of the economy also changed the relationship between state and society and brought new sets of elites into the political system. During the 1980s, the CCP popularized the slogans "to get rich is glorious" and "take the lead in getting rich" to signal its support for both economic prosperity and the individual and regional equalities that resulted. The CCP operationalized these slogans in two ways: first, it encouraged CCP members to go into the private sector and lead by example, demonstrating that engaging in business would not result in retaliation and punishment as it had under Mao; second, it began co-opting successful entrepreneurs into the CCP. The rise of an independent business class is often seen as a potential threat to an authoritarian regime. Huntington earlier noted the danger posed by the "diversification of the elite resulting from the rise of new groups controlling autonomous sources of economic power, that is, from the development of an independently wealthy business and industrial middle class."[22] In post-Mao China, the CCP did not wait passively for the private sector to generate the anticipated opposition; it actively integrated political and economic elites in order to sustain its hold on power. Entrepreneurs were no longer "capitalist-roaders," ripe for repression as in the Maoist era, but partners in building a modern economy.

As economic liberalization progressed and the private sector grew, many observers began to predict that the CCP would inevitably initiate political liberalization. As Barrington Moore observed for early developers, the emergence of an urban bourgeoisie led to democratic outcomes as these new economic elites demanded representation and accountability to defend their property rights and limit the state's interference in the economy. But in China, as for many late developers, the relationship between business and the state is not as conflictual as Moore portrayed: both have an incentive to encourage economic development. As a result, China's capitalists have not acted as agents of political change as they did in early developers but instead have helped defend the status quo.

The personal ties, common interests, and shared policy preferences of China's economic and political elites make it difficult to speak of antagonistic relations between business and the state. Many private entrepreneurs have previous ties with the state, as either party and government officials, state-owned enterprise managers, or rank-and-file party members. Whereas the sons and daughters of high-ranking party, government, and military officials followed their parents into similar careers in the past, the children of incumbent leaders have all gone into business and, in the case of the daughters of President Hu Jintao and Prime Minister Wen Jiabao, also married prominent business leaders. This cozy relationship between the CCP and the private sector has contributed to the weak social mobilization for political change.[23]

This close relationship between the state and business does not make China's experience unique—far from it. Capitalists in most late developers have not been eager advocates of democratization, and when they have supported political change, they have not been first movers. China's experience matches previous research on the role of capitalists in political change: they are often so closely tied to the regime and so dependent on it for their success that they have little incentive to seek increased democratization.[24] They already have close ties to the state and enjoy official support, making the advantages of a more democratic system uncertain at best. So long as the CCP pursues economic development as its key task and relies upon the private sector as the source of that growth, China's capitalists are likely to remain allies of the state and a key source of political support.

## Populist Commitments to Balance Growth with Equity

During the 1990s, China pursued a rapid growth policy that favored coastal cities and paid less attention to rural and inland areas. In addition, the CCP actively embraced the private sector by encouraging its members to go into business, co-opting successful capitalists, and privatizing many state-owned enterprises. To indicate its support for the private sector more concretely, it adopted the "Three Represents" slogan, which was popularized by Jiang Zemin, who was CCP general secretary and president during this time. According to the "Three Represents," the CCP first of all represented the "advanced productive forces," a euphemism for the urban economic and high-tech elites, in addition to "advanced culture" and the interests of the "vast majority of the Chinese people." The consequence of this elitist strategy was rapid growth but also growing inequality and rising instability. Whereas China had one of the world's lowest levels of inequality in the late 1970s at the start of the reform era, by 2005 its Gini coefficient as a measure of inequality had climbed to 46.9, making China more unequal than the United States and most other developing countries.[25] That sudden and dramatic rise in inequality helped fuel social tensions, which in turn created political protest. Between 1999 and 2005, the number of protests throughout the country grew from 39,000 to 87,000. China's leaders discovered for themselves what Karl Polanyi had noted about the earlier economic development of Europe: too much emphasis on freeing market forces brings damage to the society at large. Since 2002, when the "fourth generation" of leaders, represented by Hu Jintao and Wen Jiabao, came into office, the CCP has changed its elitist approach to rapid growth and attempted to balance the policy goals of growth and equity. It is still determined to sustain high rates of growth but is trying to achieve more equitable and balanced growth.

The CCP's renewed commitment to equitable growth has been shown in a variety of ways. It provided direct income subsidies to rural residents and lowered taxes to boost the incomes of those who continue to live in the countryside. It began to invest more aggressively in the areas of central and western China that had not yet enjoyed the benefits of its reform and opening policies. It adopted a new labor law, designed to protect workers against unfair labor contracts and harsh working conditions. It began devising a "Green GDP" index to try to calculate the environmental cost of rapid growth.

These new populist policies were designed to reduce growing inequalities and, indirectly, political instability. Whereas during the high-growth 1990s the CCP under Jiang Zemin promoted the slogan of achieving a "relatively prosperous society" (*xiaokang shehui*), under the leadership of Hu and Wen it instead pursued a "harmonious society" (*hexie shehui*), showing the new priority on balance and order. Although not all CCP leaders supported this new approach,[26] the consensus among top leaders seemed to be that rather than swinging between opposing policy goals, they needed to be seen as complementary.[27] One indication that this new policy orientation was successful in building public support comes from the Pew survey mentioned earlier: in 2002, when the transition from Jiang to Hu and Wen began, only 38 percent of the country believed the country was moving in the right direction, but by 2007, 86 percent thought so. Studies have also found that high levels of satisfaction with material and social life are closely correlated with regime support in China as elsewhere.[28]

Although the "harmonious society" sought by the CCP under Hu and Wen symbolized the commitment to equity and balanced growth, it also has a coercive element. When protests arise, local leaders try to negotiate a settlement and bring the protests to a close. Tens of thousands of laid-off workers in the rust belt city of Liaoyang protested over unpaid severance and pensions, and local leaders responded with promises to provide job retraining and a portion of the unpaid commitments. Similarly, in response to rural protests over land grabs, local officials have often agreed to give additional money to the people who have lost their farmland and sometimes their homes, although these amounts are normally well below the true value of the land (and well below what developers pay to local governments for the rights to the land). But when material incentives have not been enough to restore order, the CCP has used coercive means to end the protests and punish the protesters.[29] In Liaoyang, three alleged leaders of the protests were arrested and received lengthy jail sentences in order to deter similar protests from arising. Local leaders have received orders from the central leadership of the party to limit the number of protesters who register complaints with higher-level leaders; local police are often sent to provincial capitals and even Beijing to arrest protesters and force them to return home. "Harmonious society" may sound benign, but it also has a dark side for those who threaten harmony with continued protests.

## Building Legitimacy

In order to enhance its popular support, the CCP has also tried to enhance its legitimacy. Legitimacy seems to be more important to leaders than it does to scholars, perhaps because it is such a difficult concept to measure effectively and because, as Przeworski has pointed out, its absence has had minimal negative effect on the survival of many regimes.[30] But for regimes that do not want to rely primarily on coercive threats to remain in power, seeking popular support entails building bases of legitimacy.

After being in power for almost sixty years, the CCP draws less and less legitimacy from its revolutionary victory in 1949.[31] Similarly, the cult of personality centered on the late Chairman Mao no longer legitimizes the regime, even though his picture remains on the currency and hangs over Tiananmen Square (as well as the rear view mirrors of many taxi drivers!). Instead, the CCP relies primarily on what is often referred to as "performance legitimacy," the result of its economic policies over the past several decades. The implicit social contract of the post-Mao years has been that the party-state would reduce political controls over everyday life and allow people to pursue economic prosperity in exchange for political quiescence. In other words, the CCP would abandon the Marxist goals of the Maoist era as long as it could retain the Leninist monopoly on political power. With the notable exceptions of student protests in 1986 and the 1989 protests that drew support from a wider spectrum of society and even important parts of the state, that social contract has largely remained intact. Indeed, many of the supporters of the 1989 protests later revised their earlier support for political change, because they believed that the economic growth of the 1990s would not have been possible under a new regime. Regardless of whether this counterfactual is valid, it reinforces a point made earlier: there is little societal support for promoters of political change because most of society is focused on material pursuits. The views of many in China mesh with the principle tenet of modernization theory: they believe that China is not yet ready for democracy because its economy is still too underdeveloped and its population is still too rural and culturally backward. These comments are commonly heard in official speeches as well as casual conversations. This belief also supports the current regime: if people believe democratic change would be premature, they are unlikely to pursue it or support those who do.

The CCP's economic reforms over the past three decades have resulted in sustained growth rates, rising standards of living (especially in coastal cities), and greater integration into the international system. This performance legitimacy in turn has produced greater nationalistic sentiment, a feeling that China has finally "stood up" after more than a century of being victimized by foreign influences. This is exemplified by both the patriotic pride of hosting the Olympics and the more virulent reactions to real and perceived insults from abroad, such as the media coverage of the Tibetan uprising in spring 2008. This nationalism also contributes to popular political support because the CCP's reform and opening policies are credited with both domestic prosperity and international prestige.

At the same time, these nationalist sentiments can threaten the state's diplomatic relations and indirectly undermine popular support if the state looks weak in defending China against real or perceived slights. Anti-Japanese feelings have repeatedly triggered public protests, which complicate the state's effort to forge closer economic ties with Japan. When U.S. planes bombed the Chinese embassy in Belgrade in 1999, the Chinese public reacted with outrage, pillorying the U.S. embassy in Beijing with rocks and bottles in a somewhat orchestrated attack.[32] When French president Sarkozy criticized China's harsh response to protests in Tibet and suggested a boycott of the Olympic Games, Chinese citizens protested against French commercial operations in China, in particular Carrefour, almost beating to death one passer-by in the mistaken belief he was French. In each case, the official media signaled it would no longer permit protests and encouraged all involved to focus on preserving stability and promoting the economy. Nationalism has therefore been a source of popular support for the regime, but China's leaders recognize that nationalist sentiments can be fickle, quickly turning against the state they previously supported if society believes the state is too weak to defend the nation's interests against foreign threats.

A second dimension of the CCP's legitimacy comes from traditional sources. Institutions and practices that were repressed and persecuted in the Maoist era reemerged in the reform era. Temples have been restored and rebuilt as centers of local religious and social interaction. The study of Confucian philosophy and traditions was revived in the reform era; in recent years, China has also been establishing Confucian institutes around the world in its pursuit of soft power. Even CCP slogans have roots in China's Confucian past: Deng's call to "seek truth from facts" was not new; it was written by Mencius (and also appeared above the door to Mao's home in Yanan during the revolution). Jiang Zemin's "relatively prosperous society" and Hu and Wen's "harmonious society" are also common phrases and themes in Confucian writings.[33] In 2008, traditional holidays, such as the dragon boat festival in early summer, became official holidays. Above all, the CCP has utilized the traditional fear of chaos to propagate the idea that only its leadership can hold the country together.

Although the regime in China does not meet the Weberian standards of legal-rational legitimacy, the CCP has become increasingly institutionalized over time.[34] Whereas top-level party meetings occurred sporadically under Mao, party congresses now meet every five years, plenary sessions of the central committee meet at least one a year, and the Politburo meets at least once a month (and the agenda for these meetings is now covered by the official media). The policy influence of party "elders"—that is, retired officials who still enjoy informal authority—have diminished in favor of incumbent leaders. Party and government officials are now subject to mandatory retirement ages and term limits. As noted earlier, official appointments are increasingly based on merit and less on patrimonial favors. In addition to these aspects of the CCP's institutionalization, which deal primarily with internal political and organizational matters, the CCP has also introduced a variety of institutions for regulating interactions between state and society, including local elections and channels for reporting grievances to the party and government. While these institutions do not meet the standards expected of a democratic polity, and often frustrate the Chinese citizens who utilize them but are unable to get their complaints resolved,[35] they nevertheless indicate the CCP's intent to be more responsive to society while still being unwilling to be accountable to it.

## Prospects for Political Change

The CCP has been able to adapt its institutions and ideology to China's rapidly changing environment. Will it be able to continue to adapt and survive, or has it simply delayed its ultimate fate? As noted at the beginning of this chapter, previous predictions of either regime collapse or inevitable democratization in China proved unfounded, so following in those footsteps is undoubtedly foolhardy. But what would cause the CCP's current strategy for survival to become unworkable in the future? First of all, the appearance of a sudden economic or political crisis may threaten its hold on power. Economic crises have often preceded regime change, and the CCP is aware of such a threat. CCP leaders are most worried about a sudden and dramatic economic crisis, such as began in 2008. So long as party leaders can credibly blame the economic problems on the market—especially the downturn in the export market—and not on their policies, public dissatisfaction will likely not become politicized and turn against the state.[36] Indeed, CCP leaders, including Prime Minister Wen Jiabao, pointedly blamed the mismanagement of the U.S. economy as the cause of China's problems and questioned whether China would continue to see the U.S. economy as a safe investment. Moreover, the economic downturns mostly affect the "floating population" of workers who migrated from the countryside to the cities in search of work. Most of them were employed in export industries or on construction sites. As factories closed when foreign demand declined and construction slowed after the building boom leading up to the 2008 Olympics, many migrants returned to the rural areas but hoped to venture out again when the economy picked up. Because rural migrants are poorly organized and incapable of generating public support among other urban workers, their discontent may not crystallize into a threat to the regime.[37]

A related potential threat would be the emergence of horizontal links between localized protests. In recent years, large-scale protests have been increasingly common, but they have focused on mostly local and material grievances, such as unpaid severance pay and pensions, the collection of excessive taxes and fees by local officials, expropriation of land for redevelopment without adequate compensation to existing residents, and more generally the failure of local officials to abide by and implement central laws and regulations.[38] These protests have been isolated events, even though they have similar causes. To the extent that protesters linked their causes in more widespread collective action, these individual brush fires could combine into a more dangerous conflagration. For this reason, the CCP has limited media reporting on local protests and has punished the political entrepreneurs who disseminate successful strategies and tactics to new areas. When local protests are combined with more widespread economic problems, the potential for collective action may increase, despite the challenges of successful communication, coordination, and organization against the state.

A more serious threat would be a split within the political elite. In democratic polities, elections provide the option to replace a country's leaders without changing the political system. In authoritarian regimes such as China's where leaders are not accountable to voters, changing the regime itself may be the only way to change the leaders. Alternatively, a split within the leadership may emerge at a time of crisis, which may further weaken regime integrity and make it vulnerable to a popular upsurge. While often slow to respond to past crises, such as the SARS crisis in 2003 and the devastating earthquake in Sichuan in 2008, the CCP has proved able to swing into action once the top leaders achieve a consensus and signal to lower-level officials what is necessary. Whereas factional divides were a hallmark of the Maoist era and helped precipitate the 1989 demonstrations, in more recent years the top leaders have successfully presented a united front to the public. Differences over policy and personnel matters continue to fester below the surface, but party leaders have not sought public support against their rivals. Were such an effort to occur, all bets on regime survival would be off.[39]

From a more long-term perspective, an additional challenge to continued CCP rule comes from changing social values. Economic development is leading to the rapid industrialization and urbanization of the country, bringing with it changes in where people live and work, the information they have access to, and the expectations they develop. For the current older generations in China, memories of the not-too-distant past have shaped views of the present: for most Chinese, the political environment has become more relaxed, the economic situation more promising, and the future promises more of the same. As these cohorts are replaced by younger ones that did not experience the turmoil of the Maoist years, the life they have led becomes the benchmark for their assessment of the present and expectations for the future. Will they remain satisfied with a political system that deprives them of the freedoms and liberties enjoyed by other countries, especially the East Asian democracies? Will the very success of the CCP's economic reform policies serve to undermine support for its Leninist political system in the long run? If the insights of modernization theory are correct, the answer to these questions may very well be yes.[40] So far, the CCP has been able to adapt itself to these types of challenges; whether it remains able to do so will be the ultimate test of its longevity.

## Conclusion

Authoritarian regimes rely on a variety of tools to remain in power. In China, this first of all has included coercive means. The CCP has repeatedly asserted its right to rule without a legitimate opposition and has zealously defended its monopoly on political opposition. But the CCP has not relied on coercion alone, and the importance of coercion relative to other factors has diminished over time. As a consequence of the change in the party's mission after Mao died and the rise of reform-oriented leaders, the CCP has sought to enhance its political power by generating popular support among key sectors of society as well as the population at large. While China still lacks the extent of political freedoms and civil liberties enjoyed in democratic regimes, compared to its own past the country is freer and more open than at any time in memory. While the *level* of freedom and liberty remains low, the *trend* is toward more. This is what makes so many in China believe the country is moving in the right direction and allows the CCP to rely less on coercion and more on popular support to remain in power.

NOTES

1. The literature on China's economic reforms is vast. A good introduction is Barry Naughton, *The Chinese Economy: Transitions and Growth* (Cambridge, MA: MIT Press, 2007).

2. Wei Jingsheng, "The Fifth Modernization: Democracy," in *The Courage to Stand Alone: Letters from Prison and Other Writings* (New York: Penguin, 1997), p. 210. Wei was arrested soon after the publication of this essay and spent most of the next two decades in jail before being forced into exile in 1997.

3. Andrew J. Nathan, "Authoritarian Resilience," *Journal of Democracy* 14, no. 1 (January 2003): 6–17; David Shambaugh, *China's Communist Party: Atrophy and Adapta-*

*tion* (Berkeley and Washington, DC: University of California Press and Woodrow Wilson Center Press, 2008); Bruce J. Dickson, *Wealth into Power: The Communist Party's Embrace of China's Private Sector* (New York: Cambridge University Press, 2008).

4. Michael L. Ross, "Does Oil Hinder Democracy?" *World Politics* 53, no. 3 (April 2001): 325–61.

5. Eva Bellin, "The Robustness of Authoritarianism in the Middle East," *Comparative Politics* 36, no. 2 (January 2004): 139–57.

6. Ellen Lust-Okar, "Divided They Rule: The Management and Manipulation of Political Oppression," *Comparative Politics* 36, no. 2 (January 2004): 159–79.

7. Larry Diamond, "Thinking about Hybrid Regimes," *Journal of Democracy* 13, no. 2 (April 2002): 21–35.

8. Bruce Bueno de Mesquita and George W. Downs, "Development and Democracy," *Foreign Affairs* 84, no. 5 (September–October 2005): 77–86.

9. Ministry of Education of the People's Republic of China, "Gross Enrollment of Rate of Schools by Level," www.moe.edu.cn/edoas/website18/87/info33487.htm, accessed April 21, 2009.

10. Guobin Yang, "Contention in Cyberspace," in Kevin O'Brien, ed., *Popular Protest in China* (Cambridge, MA: Harvard University Press, 2008), pp. 126–43.

11. China Internet Network Information Center, *Statistical Survey Report on the Internet Development in China*, 2009, http://www.cnnic.net.cn/uploadfiles/pdf/2009/3/23/131303.pdf, accessed April 21, 2009.

12. Tony Saich, "Negotiating the State: The Development of Social Organizations in China," *China Quarterly*, no. 161 (March 2000): 124–41; Qiusha Ma, *Non-governmental Organizations in Contemporary China: Paving the Way to Civil Society?* (New York: Routledge, 2005).

13. Robert Putnam, *Making Democracy Work* (Princeton: Princeton University Press, 1993); Michael W. Foley and Bob Edwards, "The Paradox of Civil Society," *Journal of Democracy* 7, no. 3 (July 1996): 38–52.

14. Lust-Okar, "Divided They Rule."

15. Andreas Schedler, ed., *Electoral Authoritarianism: The Dynamics of Unfree Competition* (Boulder: Lynne Rienner, 2006).

16. *The 2008 Pew Global Attitudes Survey in China* (Washington, DC: Pew Research Center, 2008).

17. Jie Chen, *Popular Political Support in Urban China* (Stanford: Stanford University Press, 2004); Wenfang Tang, *Public Opinion and Political Change in China* (Stanford: Stanford University Press, 2005); Jie Chen and Bruce J. Dickson, *Allies of the State: China's Private Entrepreneurs and Democratic Change* (Cambridge, MA: Harvard University Press, 2010).

18. Teresa Wright, *Accepting Authoritarianism: State-Society Relations in China's Reform Era* (Palo Alto: Stanford University Press, 2010).

19. Ken Jowitt, "Inclusion," in *New World Disorder: The Leninist Extinction* (Berkeley: University of California Press, 1992), pp. 88–120.

20. This was the experience in Hungary and Taiwan; see Patrick H. O'Neil, "Revolution from Within: Institutional Analysis, Transitions from Authoritarianism, and the Case of Hungary," *World Politics* 48, no. 4 (July 1996): 579–603; and Bruce J. Dickson, *Democratization in China and Taiwan: The Adaptability of Leninist Parties* (Oxford: Oxford University Press, 1997).

21. Bellin, "The Robustness of Authoritarianism in the Middle East." For the change in recruitment and promotion practices in China, see Nathan, "Authoritarian Resilience," pp. 9–11.

22. Samuel P. Huntington, *Political Order in Changing Societies* (New Haven: Yale University Press, 1970), p. 20.

23. Kellee Tsai, *Capitalism without Democracy: The Private Sector in Contemporary China* (Ithaca: Cornell University Press, 2007); Bruce J. Dickson, *Wealth into Power: The Communist Party's Embrace of China's Private Sector* (New York: Cambridge University Press, 2008).

24. Dietrich Rueschemeyer, Evelyne Huber Stephens, and John D. Stephens, *Capitalist Development and Democracy* (Chicago: University of Chicago Press, 1992); Peter Evans, *Embedded Autonomy: States and Industrial Transformation* (Princeton: Princeton University Press, 1995); Meredith Woo-Cumings, ed., *The Developmental State* (Ithaca: Cornell University Press, 1999); Eva Bellin, "Contingent Democrats: Industrialists, Labor, and Democratization in Late-Developing Countries," *World Politics* 52, no. 2 (January 2000): 175–205.

25. United Nations Development Program, *Human Development Report, 2007/2008* (New York: Palgrave Macmillan, 2007), p. 282. The Gini coefficient is a measure of economic inequality, with 0 representing perfect equality and 100 representing perfect inequality.

26. A notable exception to this consensus was Chen Liangyu, a Politburo member and party leader of Shanghai, which had benefited the most from the coastal strategy of the 1990s. He openly ridiculed the notion of balanced growth and advocated that the old strategy be maintained. He was subsequently arrested for corruption (the diversion of money from Shanghai's pension fund into risky real estate developments), but his real crime was challenging the policy priorities of Hu and Wen.

27. Bruce J. Dickson, "Beijing's Ambivalent Reformers," *Current History* 103, no. 674 (September 2004): 249–255; Cheng Li, "The New Bipartisanship within the Chinese Communist Party," *Orbis* 49, no. 3 (Summer 2005): 387–400.

28. Ronald Inglehart, *Modernization and Postmodernization: Cultural, Economic, and Political Change in 43 Societies* (Princeton: Princeton University Press, 1997); Chen and Dickson, *Allies of the State*.

29. Philip Pan, *Out of Mao's Shadow: The Struggle for the Soul of a New China* (New York: Simon and Schuster, 2008); Yongshun Cai, "Power Structure and Regime Resilience: Contentious Politics in China," *British Journal of Political Science* 38, no. 3 (July 2008): 411–32.

30. Adam Przeworski, "Some Problems in the Transition to Democracy," in Guillermo O'Donnell, Philippe C. Schmitter, and Laurence Whitehead, eds., *Transitions from Authoritarian Rule*, vol. 3: *Comparative Perspectives* (Baltimore: Johns Hopkins University Press, 1986).

31. Bruce Gilley, "Legitimacy and Institutional Change: The Case of China," *Comparative Political Studies* 41, no. 3 (March 2008): 259–84; Wang Zhengxu, "Political Trust in China: Forms and Causes," in Lynn T. White, ed., *Legitimacy* (Singapore: World Scientific, 2005): 113–39.

32. The government provided buses to bring college students from the university district in northwest Beijing to protest in front of the U.S. embassy, allotting each group a certain amount of time to shout and throw objects. Observers disagreed over whether

this showed official complicity in the protests or the government's efforts to channel the protests and prevent them from spiraling out of control.

33. Elizabeth J. Perry, "Chinese Conceptions of 'Rights': From Mencius to Mao—and Now," *Perspectives on Politics* 6, no. 1 (March 2008): 37–50.

34. Nathan, "Authoritarian Resilience"; Shambaugh, *China's Communist Party*.

35. Lianjiang Li, "Political Trust and Petitioning in the Chinese Countryside," *Comparative Politics* 40, no. 2 (January 2008): 209–26.

36. Marc Blecher, "Hegemony and Workers' Politics in China," *China Quarterly*, no. 170 (June 2002): 283–303.

37. Ching Kwan Lee, "Is Labor a Political Force in China?" in Elizabeth J. Perry and Merle Goldman, eds., *Grassroots Political Reform in Contemporary China* (Cambridge, MA: Harvard University Press, 2007), pp. 228–52.

38. Elizabeth J. Perry and Mark Selden, eds., *Chinese Society: Change, Conflict, and Resistance*, 2nd ed. (London: Routledge, 2003); Thomas Bernstein and Xiaobo Liu, *Taxation without Representation in Contemporary Rural China* (New York: Cambridge University Press, 2003); O'Brien, *Popular Protest in China*.

39. Bruce J. Dickson, Bruce Gilley, Merle Goldman, and Dali L. Yang, "The Future of China's Party-State," *Current History* 106 (September 2007): 243–51.

40. Henry S. Rowen, "When Will the Chinese People Be Free?" *Journal of Democracy* 18, no. 3 (July 2007): 38–62; see also the comments by Minxin Pei and Dali L. Yang in the same issue. See also Gilley, "Legitimacy and Institutional Change."

# CHAPTER 5

# Fighting Reversion

## Strong Legislatures as the Key to Bolstering Democracy

### M. Steven Fish

The failure of once-promising neodemocracies is one of the most salient trends in contemporary world politics. The euphoria of the early 1990s, when nearly the whole world seemed to be democratic, democratizing, or on the cusp of democratization, has given way to the realization that maintaining open politics is a mighty task.

While fixed or relatively stable conditions such as socioeconomic development and culture undoubtedly affect democratization's prospects, the role of institutions has also received considerable attention. After all, people can do little to transform a country's level of development or culture, at least in the short run, but they can craft and build institutions. Electoral rules, the division of power between central and subnational authorities, and the independence of the judiciary have been scrutinized for their effects on democratization's fate. While these institutions may be important, I hold that a single institutional factor has special significance: the strength of the national legislature. Whether the constitutional system is formally classified as "presidential," "parliamentary," or "semipresidential" is of less consequence than the actual amount of power vested in the legislature. Using recently published data on the powers of parliaments around the world, I argue that a robust legislature is the institutional key to avoiding reversion to authoritarianism. I examine the cross-national evidence on the link between the power of legislatures and the fate of democracy, focusing particularly on Africa and the postcommunist region. After weighing the evidence, I consider why strong legislatures are so important for robust democratization. The benefits of a muscular legislature for democracy are many, but the most important is the laudable effect that a strong assembly has on constraining overweening presidents, who have emerged as open government's most formidable antagonists in recent decades.

## Thinking about and Measuring the Powers of Parliaments

Acute observers have long viewed strong legislatures as the institutional guarantors of open politics. Benjamin Constant, in many respects the founder of modern liberalism, remarked nearly two centuries ago: "Undoubtedly no liberty can exist in a large country without strong, numerous, and independent assemblies. . . . It is representative assemblies alone that can infuse life into the political body."[1] A century later, as the kaiser faltered and Germany faced the end of its political order in the wake of World War I, Max Weber, a father of modern social science, urged his countrymen to adopt a British-style parliamentary system. Weber regarded parliamentary supremacy as crucial to democratization, and democracy as essential to the recovery of national greatness.[2]

In writings on democratization in recent decades, the role of parliament has not figured prominently. Civil society, the judiciary, and subnational units of government have overshadowed the legislature. Some writings have maintained a focus on legislatures, but much of the debate has taken the form of a debate over whether presidential, semipresidential, or parliamentary (or, in the expanded typology, presidential, president-parliamentary, premier-presidential, or parliamentary) systems are best for advancing democratization. Scholars spar over whether a unified executive (found in most parliamentary systems) is better than a division of powers (found in many presidential systems), and whether an executive who lacks a fixed term in office (as in most parliamentary systems) is better than one who has a fixed term (as in most presidential systems). Often these debates include discussion of what types of party systems function best in conjunction with given types of constitutional systems, as well as whether this or that type of party system is most conducive to democratization.

Lost in much of this debate, however, is the simpler—and potentially more vital—question of who's got the power. Does the president hold all (or most) of the cards, or does the legislature? Or is power fairly evenly divided between the two? After all, where power resides might shape the outcome of democratization more than whether or not the executive has a fixed term. Generally speaking, the advocates of parliamentarism favor lodging more power in the parliament, and the advocates of presidentialism like strong presidents. But scholars' arguments usually focus less on the straightforward question of where power is vested than on secondary matters, such as the interplay between the branches of government and the nexus between constitutional orders and party systems.

Several problems account for the faintness of debate over the big question. The first is a shortage of data. Until recently we have lacked quantitative data on the strength of legislatures and presidents that cover all or most of the world. Without such data, it has been difficult for comparative political scientists to test whether a stronger legislature is better or worse for sustaining progress in fledgling neodemocracies. We had criteria for classifying constitutional systems as presidential, semipresidential, or parliamentary but lacked data on which agency or branch had how much power. The second shortcoming stems from some scholars' misconceptions of how power is constituted in parliamentary systems. At least among specialists on established democracies, some scholars tended to draw such a thick line between the government and members of parliament who do not serve in government in parliamentary systems that they came to equate the power of backbenchers in parliament with the power of the parliament in the polity. Doing so distorted our understanding of what constitutes power and where it resides. Some scholars have even claimed, for example, that the U.S. Congress is far more powerful than the British Parliament, because in Britain the dominant members of the leading party enjoy initiative in legislative matters, leaving lower-ranking members of the ruling party and members of the opposition largely in the role of critics. In the United States, according to such thinking, many members of Congress are less constrained by executive (meaning presidential) power. Yet such logic overlooks that in Britain the interparty contest over executive power is determined by the outcome of *parliamentary* elections, that the government is made up of members of *Parliament* who must be elected in their own constituencies, that the chief executive (the prime minister) serves at the pleasure of a majority of members of *Parliament* and can be deposed at any moment by a shift in the will of parliamentarians, that the government ultimately answers to *Parliament* alone, and that the leaders of *Parliament* are the central figures in the central government. Indeed, with the exception of the ceremonial functions reserved to the queen, Parliament ultimately holds most of the power lodged in the central government in the United Kingdom. None of this can be said of the United States, which does have a reasonably strong legislature, but one that nevertheless shares power with a puissant, independently elected president who can run the executive branch with relatively little regard for the will of Congress.

Many observers did not make this conceptual error, and parliamentary systems usually—and rightly—have been regarded as generally providing for stronger legislatures than do presidential systems. Still, conceptual confusion, as well as data shortage, has hindered progress in understanding where power resides. A dearth of information on where power resides, in turn, has limited our grasp of whether the people's ability to maintain control over governmental power is affected by where political power is vested in governmental institutions.

Such obstacles need not detain us any longer. A recently published study provides data on the power of national legislatures in nearly all of the world's countries with a half-million or more inhabitants.[3] We can use the data to assess the powers of parliaments in cross-national perspective. The data are based on a thirty-two-item survey that assesses legislatures' sway over the executive, institutional autonomy, authority in specific areas, and institutional capacity. The survey aims to measure the power of the national legislature in the polity as a whole. It does not fall prey to the conceptual problems discussed earlier, which underestimate the power of parliaments in parliamentary systems by equating the influence of backbenchers in the parliament with the power of parliament in the political system. The data take the form of a Parliamentary Powers Index (PPI) and range from 0 (powerless legislature) to 1 (all-powerful legislature).

The data are rough and imperfect. Measuring the power of a governmental body or state agency—or, for that matter, assessing the strength of "the state" in general—is an inexact enterprise. Still, the data furnish us with fodder for investigating the fundamental question of how the strength of the legislature affects democracy and democratization.

## The Strength of the Legislature and the Openness of the Polity: An Initial Look

Before examining the quantitative data, we may make several preliminary observations. The first is that most of the world's old, established democracies have constitutional systems that are based on the supremacy of the national legislature. In much of continental Europe, elections for legislatures are conducted (at least partially) on the basis of proportional representation, meaning that voters vote for parties rather than people. In the United Kingdom, Canada, and Australia, voters vote for people rather than parties; legislators are elected as individuals from districts. Regardless of their method of election, however, legislatures are the center of political life, and executive authority depends on the outcome of parliamentary elections. The United States is the exception among the old democracies; it is the only major country with a presidential system.

Among younger democracies, parliamentary government also appears to predominate. In Asia, the career of democracy is measured in decades and not centuries. Still, Asia does include two major countries that have enjoyed more or less continuous democracy since the late 1940s. Those two countries, Japan and India, have parliamentary systems. In the contemporary Middle East and North Africa, the only countries with anything resembling a robust tradition of open politics are Turkey and Israel, both of which have parliamentary systems as well. Even in the absence of quantitative data, it is not difficult to see why some observers regarded parliamentary systems as more conducive than presidential systems to open politics.

The PPI confirms that most systems we have traditionally categorized as parliamentary indeed have stronger parliaments than those that we have regarded as presidential, though there is great variation within the categories, and some presidential systems do have legislatures that are more powerful than some polities whose constitutions are formally parliamentary. Use of the PPI to measure the strength of the legislature also confirms that stronger legislatures are closely associated with greater political openness. Figure 5.1 shows a simple correlation of the PPI and a three-year average for 2005–7 in Freedom House (FH) freedom scores for all countries in the world that had populations of at least 500,000 people as of the year 2000. Freedom House presents its scores as running from 1 (most free polity) to 7 (least free polity). Here I flip the scores for more intuitive presentation, so higher scores represent greater political openness. The correlation is very high. The strength of the legislature and political openness are closely, and positively, related.

Still, even if there may be a causal relationship between the legislature's strength and political openness, we cannot automatically infer that stronger parliaments necessarily produce higher FH scores. The causal arrow may point the other way. Demonstrating the direction of causality is difficult. In

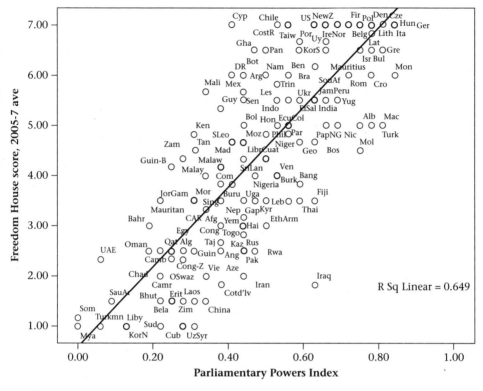

*Figure 5.1.* Political Openness and Parliamentary Powers, World

reality, it probably runs both ways. The extent of political openness at the time of the adoption of the rules that defined the powers of the legislature—what I will call the "constitutional moment"—may affect the powers vested in the legislature. One might expect dictatorships, for example, to provide for weak legislatures and to vest most power in the chief executive, the military, leadership of a dominant party, or another hegemonic actor. The relationship between the legislature's strength and the extent of democracy poses a potential endogeneity problem, meaning that what we are treating as the causal variable may be at least partially caused by the dependent variable, or what we are trying to explain.

There are several ways to probe the direction of causality. Detailed studies that trace the history of cases can be of use. Statistical techniques that can help tease out causal direction include instrumental variables regression. But we do not have the space here to do in-depth case analysis, and locating good instruments for analyzing the problem at hand is exceedingly difficult. So here we will keep it simple. We will acknowledge that the extent of political openness probably has some effect on the strength of the legislature. We will merely probe for evidence on whether the causal arrow also may point the other way, from the strength of the legislatures to the openness of the political regime.

We cannot rule out the possibility that the relationship is spurious. Definitively demonstrating causality would require rigorously controlling for a host of independent variables. It is conceivable that socioeconomic conditions, the transformation of the political party system, or some other factor could simultaneously and independently strengthen (or weaken) legislatures and open (or close) political regimes across cases. Given the small number of cases and the short period of time under examination, as well as limitations in the quality of our data, rigorously controlling for other possible determinants of political openness is difficult, and we do not attempt to do so. The causal argument presented here is therefore meant to be treated as a proposition backed by some evidence rather than a fact established by sophisticated empirical test.

Investigation is facilitated by focusing on countries that defined their parliaments' powers at some identifiable point that was neither in the distant past nor in the immediate past. The authors of the PPI, from which we draw our data on the powers of parliament, traced changes in the constitutional powers of parliaments back to about 1990. Before that time, we cannot say with any certainty what the powers of legislatures were. Yet we also want data on the strength of legislatures that lag behind the data we use to measure the extent of political openness, which are the most recent FH scores. That way we can specify what the extent of democracy was at the constitutional moment—that is, when the powers of parliaments were defined—and compare those relationships with the relationships between the power of parliament and the extent of democracy in the most recent years. If we select only cases where the PPI did not change at all between the constitutional moment and the past few years, we can hold the power of the legislature constant. If the correlation between the power of the legislature and the level of democracy is substantially higher now than it was at the time that the powers of the parliament were defined, we will have a bit of evidence that the power of parliament has some independent effect on the level of political openness. If, on the other hand, the correlation between the PPI and the most recent FH scores is no higher now than it was when the constitutions that defined legislatures' powers were adopted, we will lack evidence that stronger legislatures make for stronger democracies. We will be left with little or no evidence that the strength of parliament has an independent effect on cross-national variation in trajectories of democratization.

## The Strength of the Legislature and the Openness of the Polity: Evidence from Two Regions

In order to investigate the question, we examine data from two world regions: Africa and the postcommunist area (meaning eastern Europe and the former Soviet Union). These regions provide particularly fertile ground. They, and only they, experienced a wave of constitution making during the past quarter century during which countries redefined the powers of their governmental institutions. What is more, the regional waves occurred at the same time; in both, they happened in the 1990s. In Africa, roughly half of all polities adopted new constitutions in the 1990s; in the postcommunist region, nearly all did. While Latin America also experienced a regional wave of democratization in which most countries underwent regime change virtually simultaneously (in the 1980s), far fewer countries there adopted whole new constitutional orders. Most tinkered with the fundamental laws they already had in place, often restoring provisions from older documents that had been scrapped or ignored by authoritarian rulers. Much the same may be said of East and Southeast Asia, which underwent a surge of democratization between the early 1980s and the late 1990s.

In both Africa and the postcommunist region, some countries that adopted new constitutions in the 1990s subsequently made constitutional changes that altered one or more of the powers of the legislature measured in the PPI. In order to hold parliamentary powers constant, we include only countries whose legislatures neither gained nor lost powers, according to the criteria for assessment used in the PPI, after the year 1999. We therefore include only countries that adopted fresh constitutions in the 1990s *and* that did not alter the provisions that define the powers of the legislature after 1999. Thus, we have a lag of at least six years between the time of the establishment of the legislatures' powers and our measure of political openness, which is a three-year average of annual FH scores for the years 2005–7. We also exclude countries for which we lack FH scores for the year of the constitution's adoption. This problem obtains for several countries of the former Yugoslavia, which adopted constitutions at or just before the time they gained national independence. After whittling down the universe according to these criteria, we are left with twenty-three African countries and sixteen postcommunist countries.

Tables 5.1 and 5.2 contain the relevant data for African and postcommunist polities, respectively. The tables show the PPI, the FH score at the time of the constitutional moment, the year the constitution was adopted, and the change in FH scores between the year of the constitutional moment and the average of the FH scores for 2005–7. Because the FH scores are inverted such that higher scores represent more political openness, higher scores in the second column represent more-open polities. Positive scores in the fourth col-

*Table 5.1.*   Data on Parliamentary Powers and Political Openness: African Countries

| Country | Parliamentary Powers Index | Freedom House Score (inverted) at Time of Constitution's Adoption (base year) | Date of Adoption of Constitution | Difference in Freedom House Score, 2005–7 Average Minus Base Year |
|---|---|---|---|---|
| Benin | .56 | 3.00 | 1990 | 3.00 |
| Burkina Faso | .53 | 2.50 | 1991 | 1.50 |
| Central African Republic | .34 | 4.50 | 1994 | −1.17 |
| Chad | .22 | 2.50 | 1996 | −0.50 |
| Ethiopia | .50 | 2.50 | 1994 | 0.50 |
| Gabon | .44 | 4.50 | 1991 | −1.50 |
| The Gambia | .31 | 1.50 | 1996 | 2.00 |
| Ghana | .47 | 3.00 | 1992 | 3.50 |
| Guinea | .31 | 2.50 | 1990 | 0.00 |
| Lesotho | .53 | 4.50 | 1993 | 1.00 |
| Madagascar | .41 | 4.00 | 1992 | 0.67 |
| Malawi | .38 | 5.50 | 1994 | −1.33 |
| Mali | .34 | 5.50 | 1992 | 0.17 |
| Mauritania | .31 | 1.50 | 1991 | 2.00 |
| Mozambique | .44 | 2.00 | 1990 | 2.67 |
| Namibia | .50 | 5.50 | 1990 | 0.50 |
| Niger | .50 | 3.00 | 1999 | 1.83 |
| South Africa | .63 | 6.50 | 1996 | −0.17 |
| Sierra Leone | .41 | 2.50 | 1991 | 2.17 |
| Sudan | .22 | 1.00 | 1998 | 0.00 |
| Togo | .38 | 2.50 | 1992 | 0.17 |
| Uganda | .44 | 3.50 | 1995 | 0.00 |
| Zambia | .28 | 3.50 | 1996 | 0.83 |

Table 5.2. Data on Parliamentary Powers and Political Openness: Postcommunist Countries

| Country | Parliamentary Powers Index | Freedom House Score (inverted) at Time of Constitution's Adoption (base year) | Date of Adoption of Constitution | Difference in Freedom House Score, 2005–7 Average Minus Base Year |
|---|---|---|---|---|
| Albania | .75 | 3.50 | 1998 | 1.50 |
| Azerbaijan | .44 | 3.00 | 1992 | −0.50 |
| Belarus | .25 | 2.00 | 1996 | −0.50 |
| Bosnia | .63 | 2.00 | 1995 | 2.67 |
| Bulgaria | .78 | 5.50 | 1991 | 1.00 |
| Czech Republic | .81 | 6.50 | 1993 | 0.50 |
| Estonia | .75 | 5.00 | 1992 | 2.00 |
| Hungary | .75 | 4.50 | 1989 | 2.50 |
| Kazakhstan | .38 | 2.50 | 1995 | 0.00 |
| Lithuania | .78 | 5.50 | 1992 | 1.50 |
| Poland | .75 | 6.50 | 1997 | 0.50 |
| Russia | .44 | 4.50 | 1993 | −2.00 |
| Slovenia | .75 | 5.50 | 1991 | 1.50 |
| Tajikistan | .31 | 1.00 | 1994 | 1.50 |
| Turkmenistan | .06 | 1.50 | 1992 | −0.50 |
| Uzbekistan | .28 | 2.00 | 1992 | −1.00 |

umn represent movement toward greater openness between the constitutional moment and 2005–7. Negative scores indicate movement in the direction of political closure.

We may start by having a look at the relationship between the legislature's powers and political openness at the constitutional moment. Here we treat the legislature's powers, measured by the PPI, as the dependent variable, under the assumption that more open polities adopted constitutions that provided for stronger legislatures. We first examine Africa. Figure 5.2 provides a scatterplot that shows the relationship.

As the figure shows, there is a positive correlation between the powers vested in parliament and the openness of polities at the time of constitutions' adoption. Countries that had more favorable FH scores at the time they adopted their fundamental documents vested more power in their legislatures.

Yet the correlation is hardly overwhelming. Burkina Faso, Benin, Niger, and Ghana had FH scores that marked them as authoritarian polities at the time

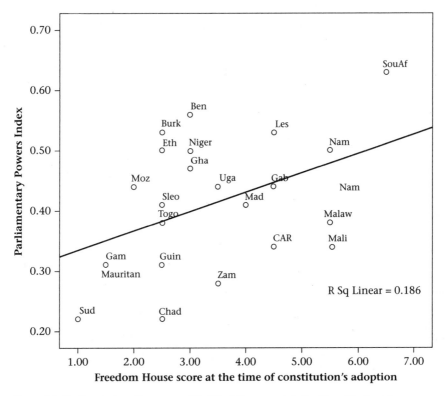

*Figure 5.2.* Parliamentary Powers and Political Openness at the Constitutional Moment, African Cases

they adopted their constitutions, but each country vested substantial power in its legislature. The Central African Republic, Malawi, and Mali were much more democratic at the moment they adopted their constitutions, but none vested great power in parliament. If the extent of democratization determined the powers that countries vested in their legislatures, we would expect the correlation between FH scores and the PPI to be higher than what we see in figure 5.2.

Let us see what the relationship between the two variables was at a later date. Now we treat the PPI as the independent variable. Here we are turning the causal arrow around, working with the hypothesis that the power that countries vested in their legislatures affected FH scores at a later date. The dependent variable is the three-year average for FH scores for 2005–7. The average gap between the time of the constitution's adoption and the midpoint of the FH scores' average (2006) is about twelve years. For some countries, such as

Benin, Guinea, and Namibia, the gap is as much as sixteen years. These countries adopted their constitutions in 1990. The smallest gap is for Niger, which adopted its constitution seven years before 2006. If the powers of parliament have an independent effect on trajectories of regime change, we would expect the correlation between recent FH scores and the PPI, which reflects constitutional measures adopted in the 1990s, to be higher than the correlation between the PPI and FH scores at the time that parliament's powers were defined.

Figure 5.3 shows the relationship. The correlation is quite high. There are some outliers. Mali is more democratic than one would expect it to be, given its weak parliament, and Ethiopia is considerably less democratic than one would anticipate given its stronger parliament. But figure 5.3 shows a much more intimate relationship between political openness and parliamentary powers than figure 5.2 does. It provides a bit of evidence that the power of

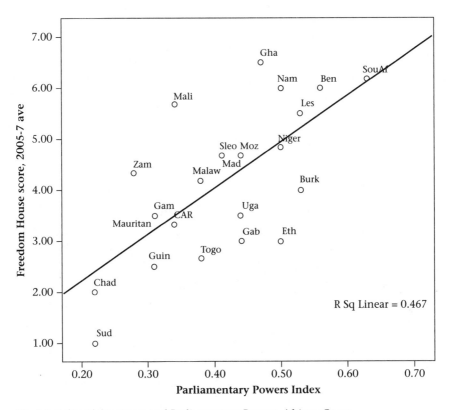

*Fig. 5.3.* Political Openness and Parliamentary Powers, African Cases

parliaments, as defined in constitutions adopted in the 1990s, predicts political openness in the mid- to late 2000s more accurately than political openness at the time of the adoption of constitutions predicts the powers vested in parliaments.

What about the postcommunist region? Do we find a similar pattern there? Here we repeat the operations we just conducted for the African cases. Figure 5.4 is analogous to figure 5.2, and figure 5.5 is analogous to figure 5.3.

As figure 5.4 shows, the correlation between the powers granted to parliament and the openness of polities at the constitutional moment is very high, much higher than it was in the African cases. In the postcommunist region, the countries that had undergone more democratization by the time they adopted their constitutions clearly furnished their legislatures with more power than did countries in which democratization had been less extensive.

Yet the correlation shown in figure 5.5 is even higher than that in figure 5.4. In figure 5.5, there are no outliers. There is virtually a one-to-one relationship between the powers of parliament as established between 1989 and 1998, on the one hand, and FH scores in 2005–7. The even-closer tie shown in figure 5.5 suggests that stronger parliaments may have contributed to more extensive democratization after the constitutions were adopted and the powers of parliament established.

## Changes in Political Openness and the Strength of the Legislature

We may explore further by calculating the change in FH scores between the constitutional moment and 2005–7, and see if there is a correlation between this change and the PPI. The far-right columns of tables 5.1 and 5.2 show the changes in FH scores between the constitutional moment (treated as the "base year") and 2005–7. Figure 5.6 plots the relationship between the changes in FH scores shown in these tables and the PPI for all the African and postcommunist countries under examination. As the figure shows, there is a relationship. The correlation is not overwhelming, but it is notable. It is, moreover, positive. Countries that adopted institutional arrangements that provided for stronger legislatures in the 1990s generally ended up progressing further (or regressing less) on democratization than those that adopted arrangements that created weaker legislatures.

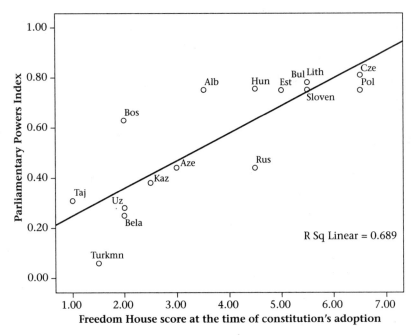

*Fig. 5.4.* Parliamentary Powers and Political Openness at the Constitutional Moment, Postcommunist Cases

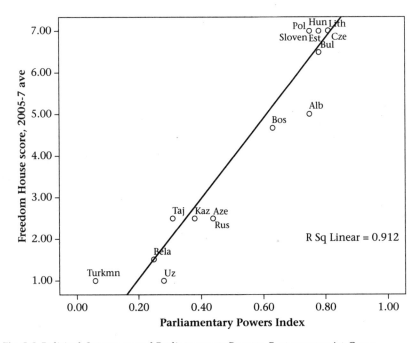

*Fig. 5.5.* Political Openness and Parliamentary Powers, Postcommunist Cases

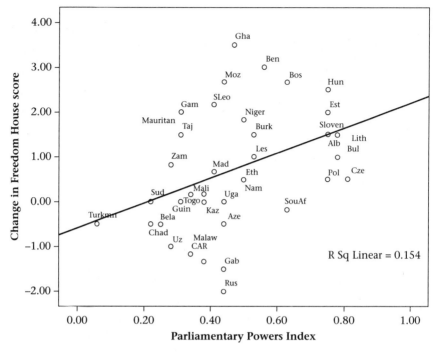

*Fig. 5.6.* Change in Political Openness and Parliamentary Powers

The strength of the legislature is undoubtedly only one of several (or many) factors that influenced cross-national variation in trajectories of political regime change. It might not have been the most important factor. What is more, all we have shown here are correlations. Definitively demonstrating causality, if it is possible, would require better data and more sophisticated methods than we have used here. But the evidence does suggest the possibility of a causal link and gives grounds for productive speculation about how stronger representative assemblies might advance open government and weaker ones undermine it.

## How Do Weak Legislatures Inhibit Democratization?

Strong legislatures may aid democratization in many ways.[4] Perhaps the most important is by balancing and blocking overweening executives. Legislatures that are vested with less power are often incapable of standing up to executive arrogation, even when members of the legislature desire to do so.

In order to appreciate the importance of checking executive power for avoiding backsliding toward authoritarianism, let us take a look at the identity of the agents of democratization's reversal. There are five possible culprits: the masses, who may undermine open politics by staging uprisings or revolutions; insurgents, who may undo democratization by waging civil war; foreign powers, which many block democratization by invasion or by sponsoring antidemocratic movements or regimes; the armed forces, which may toss elected civilians out of power or, more subtly, marginalize them; and, finally, chief executives, who may undermine open politics by engaging in despotic action, usually in the form of attempts to aggrandize themselves and quash opponents.

One of the most remarkable things about political change in the decades since the "third wave" of democratization began in the mid-1970s is how commonly the fifth agent, the chief executive, is at fault for democratization's demise or nonoccurrence. Scholars who studied the first half of the twentieth century were accustomed to viewing restive masses as a big hazard to neodemocracies. The triumph of communists or fascists with broad popular backing in interwar Russia, Germany, and Italy, among other countries, appeared to show that the people are a major threat. Throughout the postwar period, insurgencies, including separatist movements in countries with contested borders, seem to have ruined opportunities for political opening in many polities, most notably in Africa and Southeast Asia. During the height of the Cold War, foreign powers often seemed to be a serious impediment to democratization. The U.S.- and British-backed coup in Iran in 1953, the U.S.-sponsored coup in Guatemala in 1954, and the Soviet–Warsaw Pact invasion of Czechoslovakia in 1968 were examples of great powers intervening to block democratization that they regarded as inimical to their own strategic or economic interests. During the first four decades of the postwar period, the military also often acted as democracy's antagonist. Indeed, during the 1960s and 1970s, most of South and Central America came under the rule of men in epaulets, as generals and colonels threw elected officials out of office. The military was a strikingly prominent obstacle to open rule in many polities in Africa, Asia, and the Middle East as well.

In recent decades, however, men attired in cravats rather than workshirts, guerilla garb, foreign military uniforms, or the military uniform of the home country have been democracy's staunchest antagonists. Prime ministers have sometimes played the part of the bad executive, but perhaps because they are often more constrained by their own parties or by the legislature, they have been far less prominent as gravediggers of democracy than have presidents and monarchs.

A brief review of the African and postcommunist countries that experienced deterioration or no improvement in FH scores displays the dynamic. Of the twenty-three African cases included in our study, seven had FH scores in 2005–7 that were the same as or lower than they had been at the time of their constitution's adoption in the 1990s. In four of the seven cases, despotic presidents, more than any other agent, were responsible for democratization's failure. In Gabon, President Omar Bongo has been the main culprit. After a partial opening at the beginning of the 1990s, Bongo used all manner of chicanery, including rigging elections and intimidating or buying off opposition, to reverse liberalization. In Guinea, which had a decidedly authoritarian regime throughout the 1990s and the current decade, the central actor in blocking democratization has also been the president. Lansana Conté, by strangling and manipulating opposition and turning the state apparatus into his personal fief, has played the role that Bongo has in Gabon. Malawi underwent substantial liberalization in the mid-1990s, achieving FH scores that placed the country in Freedom House's category of "free polities" between 1993 and 1998. Thereafter, however, Bakili Muluzi, who held the presidency from 1994 until 2004, and Bingu wa Mutharika, who succeeded Muluzi in 2004, gradually pulled the country back toward more closed rule. Neither president acted as despotically as Gabon's Bongo or Guinea's Conté. But each Malawian executive, and Mutharika in particular, pursued actions that gradually stifled Malawi's nascent democracy. For example, in 2007 Mutharika shut down parliament without consulting the speaker, postponed local elections, targeted critical media outlets, and pressured high-ranking judges whose rulings he did not like. In Uganda, as in Guinea, the problem has been more the persistence of authoritarianism than backsliding from democracy, but again democratization's main antagonist has been the president. Yoweri Museveni, using the full arsenal of patronage, intimidation of opponents, dubious referenda that allow him to remain in office decade after decade, and pressure on the media, has ensured nondemocratization in Uganda.

In some cases, one can identify culprits besides sitting presidents. In Gabon, for example, the French army's commitment to maintaining the status quo has undoubtedly aided Bongo. Still, in each of these four cases, presidents have been the central agent of democratization's failure. In none of these countries may mobilized masses, insurgencies, foreign powers, or military interventions be considered the main cause.

This generalization does not hold for all seven African countries that experienced backsliding or no progress. In the Central African Republic, insurgencies and the armed forces have been democratization's biggest foes. Early in the current decade, government forces of President Ange-Félix Patassé fought insurgents commanded by General François Bozizé, who overthrew Patassé. Bozizé's government forces, as of this writing, are battling insurgents, many of them marauding thugs from neighboring Sudan. While neither Patassé nor Bozizé are champions of democracy, they are not necessarily the primary culprits for the regression from the partially open regime that the Central African Republic had in the 1990s to the authoritarian one that is in place today. Chad never enjoyed anything resembling an open regime, but blame for its failure to democratize may be laid at the feet of the same actors as derailed the Central African Republic's experiment with democracy. While Chad's longtime president, Idriss Déby, has done everything in his power to thwart democratization and plunder his country, insurgencies have been as big a block to open government as the high-handed president has. In South Africa, the very slight movement away from democracy that occurred in the past several years may be due to the less-than-always-democratic ways of the country's perplexing former president, Thabo Mbeki, though Mbeki may not be at fault. South Africa, at any rate, maintained a high level of political openness during the 2000s. The backsliding it experienced was very mild and does not count as a case of failed democratization.

Thus, in four of the seven African cases for which we find evidence of diminution or no improvement in political openness, overweening presidents were the main culprits. In two cases insurgencies were at least largely to blame, and in one case it is difficult to pin the blame on any single actor.

In the postcommunist region, the culpability of chief executives is even more unequivocal. Six of the sixteen postcommunist countries experienced reversion or no improvement in their FH score between their constitutional moments and 2005–7. In every case, chief executives were the paramount problem. In Azerbaijan, Heydar Aliyev thwarted his country's tentative opening in the early 1990s and presided over the consolidation of a personalistic regime. The regime continues in force under Aliyev's son, Ilham, to whom

Heydar handed off the presidency shortly before his death in 2003. In Belarus, which underwent a more extensive political opening than Azerbaijan in the early 1990s, the author of democratization's demise was Aleksandr Lukashenko. After winning the presidency in 1994, Lukashenko initiated what would become a relentless drive to stamp out independent media, snuff out opposition, and convert elections into charades. Kazakhstan's, Turkmenistan's, and Uzbekistan's presidents, Nursultan Nazarbayev, Saparmurat Niyazov, and Islam Karimov, respectively, personally nipped in the bud what little liberalization occurred in the early post-Soviet period and dragged their countries from Soviet-style authoritarianism to sultanism. In Russia, democratization went much further than in Central Asia but was similarly undermined by the president. After experiencing substantial political opening in the early 1990s, Russia reverted to authoritarianism. During the 1990s, President Boris Yeltsin presided over a gradual erosion of press freedoms and integrity of electoral practices. His successor, Vladimir Putin, finished off democratization with a bang. He cracked down on opponents, converted most mass media into a mouthpiece for his administration, and turned elections into shams.

In none of the cases of reversion in the postcommunist region did any actor other than the president bear primary responsibility for reversion, though in several cases one can identify a supplemental actor. In Azerbaijan, intervention by the military in 1993 helped usher Heydar Aliev, a former first secretary of the republic's Communist Party during Soviet times, back to power. Still, the military really acted on Aliev's behalf rather than the reverse, and Aliev's control over the military became amply evident as the 1990s wore on. In Belarus, the dictatorship has received aid from Russia, showing that foreign powers have not been irrelevant to Belarus's democratic reversal. But the Russian government's support for Belarus's authoritarian regime has taken the form of aid to Lukashenko, and even in times when the relationship between Lukashenko and Moscow was strained, Belarusian authoritarianism remained sturdy. President Lukashenko, rather than intervention by Russia or any other external actor, has been the main agent of democratization's derailment in Belarus. The insurgency in Chechnya in southern Russia and the appearance of the threat of an incipient Islamist insurgency in Uzbekistan may have contributed to democratization's failure in those two countries. But in neither country were insurgencies the prime agent of reversion. In fact, in both countries, presidents' use of the insurgencies as pretexts to bolster already expansive presidential powers, more than the insurgencies themselves, caused political closure. In general, mobilized masses, insurgents, interventionist militaries, and foreign powers played, at most, supporting roles in reversing or aborting democratization in the postcommunist region. Chief executives—in all cases, presidents—were the culprits.

The role of legislatures' weakness was evident in many cases of failed democratization in both regions. In some countries, such as Guinea and Kazakhstan, high-handed presidents used their expansive powers and the relative debility of the legislature to ensure subservient majorities in the legislatures. In such cases, the legislature's constitutional weakness facilitated, and in turn was compounded by, docile majorities that supported presidents unconditionally. In other cases, such as Malawi and Russia, parties that opposed the president at times formed majorities or substantial minorities in the legislature but usually proved unable to counterbalance executive dominance because of the lopsided interbranch balance of power.

The numbers help capture the institutional situations in the backsliders. Across the thirty-nine African and postcommunist countries under review in this chapter, the average PPI score is .47. Among the seven African and six postcommunist countries that experienced no movement or negative movement in terms of regime change between their constitutional moment and 2005–7, all but one have PPI scores that are below the mean score of .47. South Africa is the only exception. Only it, among the backsliders, has a PPI that is higher than .47. And South Africa does not really represent a case of democratic failure, as mentioned earlier.

Benin, Namibia, Lithuania, and Poland provide examples of contrasting cases. Each has withstood the presence of arrogant presidents without backsliding toward authoritarianism. In these countries, legislatures enjoy substantial power. Each country has a PPI of .50 or higher. Legislatures were able to push back against presidential arbitrariness and help preserve liberties and electoral fairness in the process.

Each of these four countries has a president whose mandate derives from direct popular election, not from election by parliament. Benin and Namibia have presidential systems; Lithuania and Poland have semipresidential systems. The president in each country, just as the president of the United States does, has real, not just ceremonial, powers. Each of these systems includes a separation of powers. Yet in each country, as in the United States, the legislature has enough muscle to countervail presidential pretensions. These examples suggest that robust democratization does not require the fusion of executive and legislative power that is characteristic of pure parliamentarism. In parliamentary systems, the danger of executive arrogance may be particularly low because prime ministers (and presidents who owe their job to the legislature) are typically more accountable to the legislature than are executives who enjoy an independent mandate. Still, even in systems in which the president is elected directly and enjoys broad control over the executive branch apparatus, a legislature that is strong enough to challenge and check the president can be sufficient to safeguard open politics. The point is that a strong legislature, not a weak executive or the fusion of executive and legislative power such as is found in pure parliamentarism, is the institutional key to bolstering democracy.

Beneficent presidents who firmly grasp their own fallibility and perceive where their own ambitions and popular interests diverge are wonderful. But they are also virtually unknown. They are much less reliable guarantors of open politics than are muscular legislatures that are capable of resisting presidential imperiousness.

Legislatures' roles in balancing presidents may be even more important in fledgling democracies than they are in established ones. In the latter, the courts sometimes provide an additional check on an overbearing executive. But powerful, independent judiciaries are a rarity in developing countries. Seldom do the courts enjoy the power to rein in executives that they sometimes do in, for example, the United States. Furthermore, the spirited, sturdy independent societal organizations that are found in abundance in many advanced industrialized countries are often absent or inchoate in regions such as Africa and the postcommunist world. With neither powerful judiciaries nor vigorous civil societies in place, neodemocracies often have no major force apart from the national legislature to check presidential pretentions.

## What Is to Be Done?

From the standpoint of improving the prospects of democracy, the implication of the analysis is clear. Strong legislatures are the institutional key. Avoiding reversion means vesting substantial power in the national legislature. Would-be democratizers in developing countries face many tasks, including building civil society, crafting electoral rules, and controlling the armed forces. But if they do not found a national legislature vested with substantial powers, the people are unlikely to retain their voice in how their countries are ruled; toothless legislatures are authoritarianism's staunchest ally.


NOTES

1. Benjamin Constant, *Political Writings*, ed. Biancamaria Fontana (Cambridge: Cambridge University Press, 1988), pp. 194, 197.

2. Max Weber, "Parliament and Government in a Reconstructed Germany," in Max Weber, *Economy and Society*, ed. Guenther Roth and Claus Wittich (Berkeley: University of California Press, 1978), pp. 1381–1469.

3. M. Steven Fish and Matthew Kroenig, *The Handbook of National Legislatures: A Global Survey* (New York: Cambridge University Press, 2009).

4. M. Steven Fish, *Democracy Derailed in Russia: The Failure of Open Politics* (New York: Cambridge University Press, 2005), pp. 224–43.

# Part II. Democracy and Development

## INTRODUCTION

Is there a relationship between economic development and the structure of the political system? Are democracies more or less likely to prosper? Do they need prosperity to thrive? The connection between political system and the economy has been a preoccupation of social science since its inception. And the connection seems to be driven home hard in the contemporary world, where most advanced industrial societies are democracies; the record of democratic governance in the developing world is more uneven and seems to be especially sketchy and unstable in the world's poorest countries. There seems to be a relationship. What is it?

While scholarly interest in democracy in other domains waxed and waned over time, research on the relationship between democracy and development has been fairly steady over the past forty years. However, there have been cycles in thought, or at least in the general consensus within the academic community, regarding the relationship between development and democracy. Those cycles have produced more sophisticated questions and provoked the use of more sophisticated methods. But it is not clear that they have led to any broad conclusions.

There are four reasons for the indeterminacy and vagueness in this field.

First, the critical concepts themselves are not merely general but also shift from researcher to researcher. On the political side of the ledger, are we most interested in rule of law, popular sovereignty, transparency, elections, inclusionary politics, or perhaps some combination of all of these? On the economic side, are we concerned with overall level of prosperity, growth, class structure, or policies promoting growth and development?

Second, the complexity of the subject has not prevented (indeed, it sometimes seems to encourage) facile assumptions. It is quite common in public and even policy discussions to elide the distinctions between all the concepts mentioned in the previous paragraph so that free markets, economic growth, elections, and liberal political institutions all come to be regarded—generally unconsciously but sometimes consciously—as various aspects of a single phenomenon. To be sure, presidential inaugural addresses and eight-hundred-word newspaper columns are hardly places for fine distinctions and nuanced conceptual parsing, and scholars are less likely to be as cavalier with their terminology and unspoken assumptions. But the tendency of such prevailing ideas to color research questions remains, as two chapters elsewhere in this volume show. A sometimes unhelpful connection between modernization theory and American policy is examined by Gregg Brazinsky; and Bruce Dickson shows how assumptions about political change in China stemming from economic change have been far more often made than vindicated.

Third, the general record of democratic and economic performance has also colored the scholarly mood. The general optimism of modernization theory gave way to pessimism in the 1970s and early 1980s as economic development appeared to bolster a number of authoritarian regimes, particularly in Latin America and Asia. In addition, the success of developmental states in Asia lent credibility to the argument that authoritarianism may be advantageous for rapid economic development, and thus that development might need to precede democracy. However, the transition to democracy experienced by many of these countries during the third wave revived a sense of optimism in the 1980s and 1990s and led some academics to wonder whether modernization theory was essentially right after all. At the same time, the spread of democracy in many poor countries undermined the argument (endorsed by some strains of modernization theory) that development had to precede democratization. The ability to find cases that seemed to support any side in the debate helped ensure that research on the relationship between development and democracy remained a growth industry throughout the 1990s.

Finally, the connection between democracy and development is difficult because there are so many possible causal relationships. Is a certain level of development a necessary or merely facilitating condition for democracy? Is it more likely to create or sustain a democracy? Does the relationship vary with the level or nature of economic development? Is democracy likely to lead to immediate gains in development while creating long-term problems—or is the reality just the opposite?

Such conceptual and empirical complexity is likely to make it impossible to support any extremely broad and categorical claim of the kind favored by pundits. But the essays in this second part are designed to show that we can still speak intelligently about the relationship and come to greater understandings of the way that the two are linked. We are aided in this regard by two developments. First, social scientists have grown increasingly rigorous in their thinking and sophisticated in their methods. Second, the dramatic increase in the number of democracies as a result of the third wave also provided new opportunities to test the basic propositions.

Since the late 1990s, numerous studies have questioned some of the broad claims that have been made in the past—for instance, that there is no evidence either that economic development causes democracy or that authoritarianism is necessary for economic development. Instead, even while seeking to make general statements, they have refined our thinking. For instance, the most famous of the studies (led by Adam Przeworski) concludes that while development does not generate democracy, it does contribute to the potential stability of existing regimes, particularly already democratic states.[1]

The contributors to this section try to follow in the footsteps of such work by casting their arguments broadly and examining a large number of cases using a variety of techniques—but to specify, refine, and test empirical claims with considerable care. The broadest essay, perhaps, is the one by José Cheibub (part of Przeworski's initial team) and James Vreeland, whose examination of the evidence shows at best an uncertain relationship between economic growth and the emergence of democracy but also a far stronger body of evidence suggesting that development helps sustain democracy.

Second, Staffan Lindberg and Sara Meerow examine the emerging claim of a "resource curse"—instead of focusing broadly on the level of economic development or on economic growth (as earlier generations of scholars sometimes tended to do), they join the effort to focus on a more specific relationship—in this case, the effects of dependence on natural resources for economic performance. And they distinguish as well between achieving and sustaining democracy. While much of the work on the resource curse has focused on oil-rich states, especially (but not exclusively) those in the

Middle East, Lindberg and Meerow look to sub-Saharan Africa, a region with a rich experience with democratization over the past two decades. And they find not only that "African countries that are economically dependent on natural resources are most likely to remain authoritarian" but also that "if and when they do take steps to liberalize, they are at much greater risk of reverting back to a more authoritarian state than non-resource-rich countries."

Finally, John Gerring examines not what produces democracy but the policy outcomes that democracies produce. He works to introduce nuance into the claim that democracies perform better. He notes that the benefits of democratic governance are not likely to be felt immediately but only to emerge over time—yet too often policy makers and scholars have focused on short-term and immediate effects. He finds that a longer-range view produces a notable finding—the benefits of democracy for policy performance turn out to be real and significant. Or, in short, while a country's level of democracy in a single year may not immediately explain the level of growth the next year, there is still strong support for a more patient optimism "that democratic regimes, over the long haul, will provide better governance than authoritarian regimes."

NOTE

1. Adam Przeworski, Michael E. Alvarez, José Antonio Cheibub, and Fernando Limongi, *Democracy and Development: Political Institutions and Well-Being in the World, 1950–1990* (Cambridge: Cambridge University Press, 2000).

# CHAPTER 6

# Economic Development and Democratization

## José Antonio Cheibub and James Raymond Vreeland

The correlation between economic development and democracy is probably among the strongest we find in the social sciences. No matter what measures of political regime and economic development are employed, a positive correlation between them is always present in the data. Higher levels of economic development are associated with democracy, lower levels with autocracy. Why is there such a strong relationship between economic development and democracy? Many people assume the answer has to do with "democratization"—the *emergence* of democracy. It is commonly accepted in public political discourse that economic development causes democracy to emerge. Yet the relationship between development and political regime is not so straightforward. Five distinct arguments have been proposed by scholars:

1.  The relationship between economic development and democratization is real, causal, and positive: *economic development causes democracy to emerge.*
2.  The relationship between economic development and democratization is real, causal, and negative: *economic development causes democracy to collapse.*
3.  The relationship between economic development and democratization is real but not causal: *economic development does not cause democracy to emerge but rather contributes to its survival.*
4.  The relationship between economic development and democratization is spurious: *there is no causal relationship, and the correlation is driven by outside factors.*
5.  The relationship between economic development and democratization is real but reversed: *democracy causes economic development.*

Proposition 1 is at the core of "modernization theory," which emerged in the late 1950s. If true, then economic development should eventually cause democracy to emerge throughout the world. This theory was used in part to justify the U.S. Cold War foreign policy of supporting open economic relations with friendly dictatorships, even providing them with foreign aid.[1] In the 1990s, it was used by the Clinton administration to justify inviting China into the World Trade Organization. Proposition 1, however, was challenged from the very beginning by proponents of proposition 2. They questioned whether economic development caused truly sustainable democracies to emerge and whether newly emerging democracies would simply collapse under the requirements for continued rapid economic development and all of the social upheaval that came along with it.

This debate continued for decades until the mid-1990s when proposition 3 turned the debate on its head. Its proponents suggested that economic development did not cause democracy to emerge. Instead, the relationship between economic development and democracy was driven by a connection between economic development and the *survival* of democracy. Put bluntly, democracies emerge under all sorts of conditions, but they never collapse in countries that have reached a certain level of economic development.

This new interpretation did not go unchallenged. While agreeing that economic development causes democracy to survive (proposition 3), some scholars proposed new evidence supporting the original modernization formulation that economic development causes democracy to emerge (proposition 1). Most recently, some scholars have rejected the connection entirely, suggesting proposition 4—that the correlation between economic development and political regime is entirely spurious—or, in other words, the relationship is really driven by other factors.

All along there were those who examined proposition 5: democracy causes economic development. Splashes in this literature, however, seem to be connected with current events. From the 1960s to the early 1980s, as dictatorships in Asia rapidly developed and democratically elected governments in Latin America were overthrown in the name of progress, many scholars supposed that democracy was a hindrance to economic development because of its lack of a centralized authority. Then developing democracies began to surpass their autocratic peers, and scholars proposed that democracy was actually good for economic development because it provided secure property rights. These changing views were even reflected in the findings of empirical studies: the majority of studies published before 1988 concluded that dictatorships are better for development, while no study published between 1987 and 1992 found support for this conclusion.[2]

We agree with Gerring, who argues in chapter 8 of this volume that it is rather implausible that political regime can influence a country's developmental trajectory over the short or even medium run. He contends that the effects of political institutions unfold over a long period of time. On average, annual economic growth is about the same under both regime types—although Przeworski et al.[3] have shown that democracies and dictatorships do appear to grow in different ways. These authors show that dictatorships display more variance in income growth—more miracles and more failures—while democracies tend to avoid extremes. Dictatorships tend to grow through greater exploitation of labor by suppressing wages, while democracies make more efficient use of technology. But in the end, rates of economic growth under both regimes are not that different, especially after one takes into account the fact that democracies tend to exist under better economic conditions. And this leads us back to the question of how economic development affects democratization. Thus, we leave readers interested in proposition 5 to explore other work,[4] while we focus on propositions 1 through 4 in this chapter.

The objective of this chapter is thus to examine the theoretical and empirical foundations of each of these propositions. Readers should note that a real debate is taking place among scholars, which has major implications for policy makers. If proposition 1 is correct, then democracy promotion should continue as it did during the Cold War—support the economic development of autocracies. If proposition 3 is correct, however, then democracy promotion should focus instead on promoting its survival in existing democracies—support the economies of developing world democracies. If proposition 2 or 4 is correct, then perhaps democracy promotion should not focus on promoting economic development at all. With the collection of new data and the development of new statistical techniques, the scholarly literature has become quite sophisticated. The payoff for mapping out the field, indicating the areas of consensus and disagreement, and suggesting questions for future research may be high. And the implications of this research can have a real impact on foreign policy discussions.

Before we proceed, we need to define what we mean by democracy and to clarify an important concept: the dynamics of political regimes. Thinking about the dynamics or changes of political regime draws attention to the distinction between the establishment of democracy and its sustainability.

We say that a country is a democracy if the choice of rulers proceeds through competitive or, alternatively, contested elections. The emphasis on competitiveness and contestation is meant to draw attention to the idea that not all countries holding elections qualify as democratic. The legislature and the executive must be filled by elections;[5] there must be alternatives presented in these elections; and when incumbents lose, they must abide by the results and allow alternation in power. Contested elections are ex ante uncertain, ex post irreversible, and repeatable.[6]

The question about the *emergence* of democracy is, What accounts for the relevant actors' decision to allow such a process to begin? Thus, we consider the impact that economic development may have on "democratization"; or the establishment of democracy; or, equivalently, the emergence of democracy; or, still equivalently, the breakdown of a dictatorial or authoritarian regime with a transition to democracy. Yet another way to think about the emergence of democracy is that it is the opposite of the survival of an authoritarian regime. In this sense, we broadly investigate the same question that Dickson addresses in this volume with his detailed case study of how the Communist Party in China is sustaining its single-party rule through coercion and co-optation. (Note that China is doing this despite unprecedented levels of economic development, making the case even more germane for our chapter.)[7]

Democracy is *sustained* when the actors who were involved in allowing a competitive election to take place choose to abide by the results and, after the agreed upon term of rule expires, choose to allow another competitive election to take place, and, after the election, choose to abide by the results, and so on.[8] Thus, we consider the impact that economic development may have on the sustainability of democracy or, equivalently, the survival of democracy. The converse is also addressed: the survival of democracy implies that there is no breakdown of democracy; or, equivalently, emergence of a dictatorial or authoritarian regime; or, still equivalently, transition to authoritarianism.

Economic development need not have the same effect on both the emergence and the survival of democratic regimes. This important observation was implicit in the early empirical work on democracy starting in the late 1950s, but it was not clarified until the mid-1990s, when it was made explicit for both theoretical and statistical studies. Today, this observation has become standard in all cutting-edge work on democracy.

Note that the observation that emergence and survival of democracy may be caused by different factors has an important implication for the way that we define political regime. The distinction between the establishment and the sustainability of democracy implies a discrete moment that marks the regime transition.[9] If we want to analyze the factors that lead to the emergence of democracy as distinct from the factors that lead to its maintenance, it does not make sense to think of democracy as an inherently continuous attribute of just any regime. To be sure, there are different types of democracies and different types of dictatorships.[10] But we do not consider different types of dictatorships to be more or less democratic than others. Either a regime fills the executive and legislature through contested elections or it does not. If it does not, it is simply not a democracy. Similarly, we do not examine the quality of democracy among regimes that do fill the executive and legislature through contested elections, though there are certainly differences among them. Why some democracies have more political and economic freedom than others is certainly an interesting and important question, but our focus is on questions of regime transition—the miraculous moments when ballots, paper or electronic, truly determine the fate of political leaders—and the tragic moments when they stop doing so.

This view of political regime is not uncontroversial. Other contributors to this volume suggest alternative conceptions.[11] In other work (with Jennifer Gandhi of Emory University), we discuss our conception of political regime at length and contrast it to other measures.[12] For the purposes of this chapter, it suffices to emphasize that when studying transitions to and from democracy, a categorical conception of political regime is required so that the moment of transition can be clearly identified.

With this in mind, we begin by considering propositions 1 and 2— development causes democracy or it does not. We then turn to the argument that development causes democracy to survive, as well as the recent challenges bringing back revised versions of modernization theory. Finally, we consider the evidence that the relationship is entirely spurious, driven instead by country fixed effects.

## Economic Development Causes Democracy: Modernization Theory

Proposition 1—economic development causes democracy to emerge—is famously known as "modernization theory," which is rooted in a broad social theory.[13] The narrower question of how economic development affects democracy was first examined by Lipset.[14] The original argument took several forms, but the basic idea was that as countries develop economically, social structures become too complex for authoritarian regimes to manage—individuals' outlooks change, technological change endows owners of capital with some autonomy and private information, complex labor processes require active cooperation rather than coercion, and civil society emerges. At some specific point in this process, dictatorship collapses, and democracy emerges as the alternative.

One important challenge for modernization theory is to identify precisely this point at which one can expect dictatorships to collapse and democracies to emerge. Przeworski et al. noted that "if modernization theory is to have any predictive power, there must be some level of income at which one can be relatively sure that the country will throw off its dictatorship."[15]

This issue was recognized by Neubauer early in the empirical study of democratization.[16] For him, "certain levels of 'basic' socio-economic development appear to be necessary to elevate countries to a level at which they can begin to support complex, nation-wide patterns of political interaction, one of which may be democracy. Once above this threshold, however, the degree to which a country will 'maximize' certain forms of democratic performance is no longer a function of continued socio-economic development."[17] Jackman, in turn, finds that there is a point of inflection in the democracy curve after which the effect of economic development at least levels off.[18] Finally, Lipset, Seong, and Torres find an N-shaped pattern, allowing for a negative effect of economic development on democratization at moderate levels, after which the impact becomes, again, positive.[19] None of these authors, however, attempted to identify the point in the process of economic development where the inflection in the democracy curve takes place; and, as we will see, those who looked were not able to find anything.

For either data or theoretical limitations, the first generation of empirical studies seeking to test the modernization hypothesis did not consider regime dynamics but rather used cross-sectional data. In other words, they took a snapshot of the world at a given moment in history and compared the level of per capita income across democracies and dictatorships. From the observation that the democracies were significantly richer than the dictatorships, inferences about the effect of the *process* of economic development were made.

In all fairness, it should be said that, from a theoretical point of view, this was not entirely incorrect. According to modernization theorists, the process of transformation that makes a traditional society into a modern one is universal and unilinear. Cross-sectional development variation arises only because countries are located at different points in this universal and unilinear process; an underdeveloped country today is nothing but the developed country yesterday. In this sense, the use of cross-sectional data to test the modernization hypothesis would be legitimate because it would capture countries at different *stages* of development.

Only if the view of a unilinear modernization process is abandoned do the limitations of cross-sectional data for testing the modernization hypothesis become apparent. Arat, for example, has shown that the positive relationship between economic development and democracy found in a cross section of countries is compatible with within-country relationships that can take any form.[20] In her study of 124 countries for the period 1948–77, she found that, in spite of a strong positive aggregate correlation between development and democracy, only 30 experienced a growth in the level of democracy over time as economic development increased. In 52 countries the two variables displayed no relationship, and in 42 countries the level of democracy actually decreased with the level of economic development.

Beyond the work correlating economic development to democracy, there is little research that seeks to explicitly test the (direct or indirect) mechanisms whereby economic development is supposed to affect democratization. Lipset's original article was replete with stories that connect the two. Economic development leads to democratization via education, which affects people's outlook by making them more rational, moderate, and tolerant, all alleged requisites for a democracy to emerge and exist. Economic development also leads to democratization via its effects on the class structure: it not only expands the middle classes—something that seems to be axiomatically beneficial for democracy—but also reduces the lower classes' discount rate (thus making them less radical) and increases the upper classes' tolerance for redistributive demands. Finally, economic development leads to a more complex civil society and the consequent creation of a network of voluntary organizations that serve as democracy's training ground and protection against the state.[21] We do not mean to say that no one has explored these topics of research. There is a vast literature, too large to be cited here, focusing on the impact of development on education, on social stratification, and on civil society. Perhaps not as large, but still significant, is the literature that connects these aspects to democracy. Yet, to our knowledge, there is little that explicitly seeks to test whether the relationship between economic development and democratization happens via the effect of the former on education, the class structure, or civil society, which then affects the latter.

There are two notable exceptions. One is the work of Inglehart, who, in a number of publications, has argued that economic development affects people's belief systems, placing them closer to the more "democratic" poles of a two-dimensional attitudinal space.[22] For him, even though there are some "cultural zones" that exert an independent impact on the democratic attitudes of citizens across the globe, economic development is probably the single most important factor accounting for democratic attitudes and, by implication, the emergence of democracy.[23] The second exception is provided by Rueschemeyer, Stephens, and Stephens, who argue that the reason economic development leads to the emergence and maintenance of democracy is that it expands and politically strengthens the working class, which happens to be the only class with an unambiguous preference for democracy.[24] These exceptions notwithstanding, the most famous studies supporting modernization theory have focused exclusively on the correlation between level of economic development and democracy.

These days, there is a healthy recognition that one needs to show more than simply the existence of a correlation between economic development and democracy to claim support for modernization theory. The basic claim of modernization theory has always been one about regime dynamics, and it is now understood that an empirical test of its main claim requires that this be taken into consideration. After all, the modernization claim is a strong one. Its main proposition is not simply that economic development will be positively correlated with democratization. Rather, the proposition is that economic development will *lead* to democratization and that the effect will be a strong one, if not the strongest among all the other factors that may also *cause* the emergence of democracy. We return to this issue later in this chapter, but here it is sufficient to note that, in the context of modernization theory, democracy is the culmination of a global process of transformation that we call development. Even if we are able to correctly capture economic development empirically—a topic that we bracket by asserting that per capita income level, the variable that is most often used in empirical analyses, is a sufficiently acceptable indicator of economic development—the expectation that emerges out of modernization theory is that the impact of economic development on democratization will overshadow all other effects.

## Development Does Not Always Lead to Democracy

To refute modernization theory, some scholars sought to establish not that economic development would inevitably lead to authoritarianism but simply that there were some conditions under which development would actually lead to dictatorship and not democracy. Lipset himself mentioned that rapid economic development can be destabilizing. This brings us to proposition 2: economic development causes democracy to collapse. Barrington Moore Jr., Samuel Huntington, and Guillermo O'Donnell have developed the three best-known arguments along these lines.[25]

Moore argued that there was more than one path to modernity and that these paths did not always end in democracy. The circumstances that in England led to the marketization of labor relations and the dilution of the landed aristocracy's power in response to the stimulus of capitalist development were unique and were the only ones that would "naturally" lead to the emergence of democracy. Absent an exogenous shock—such as the 1789 revolution in France that destroyed the repressive system of labor relations—capitalist development would lead either to what was called "modernization from above," a process of development characterized by the repression of labor by the state in alliance with the landed aristocracy, or to a "communist revolution," where labor would take over the state to repress the landed aristocracy. Neither of these two last alternatives was democratic, even though they resulted from the onset of the very process of modernization. A simplistic summary of Moore's argument is his famous statement, "no bourgeoisie, no democracy," though this does not do justice to the nuances of his argument. The existence of a strong independent bourgeoisie is a necessary, but not sufficient, condition for economic development to lead to democratization; and for many societies, with or without a bourgeois class, economic development may lead to authoritarianism under fascism or communism.

Huntington called attention to the importance of institutions in the process of modernization. For him, the process of modernization is inherently unsettling of existing social relations. In the absence of strong political institutions able to absorb, control, and guide those it displaces, modernization leads to praetorian politics. Improving economic circumstances lead to mass economic and political demands that an underdeveloped state cannot meet. Inequality makes socialism attractive, leading to the establishment of a one-party socialist state. Huntington's advice to the West during the Cold War was thus to support non-Communist one-party states, encouraging the development of robust political institutions able to withstand the destabilizing force of rapid economic development. He did not promise that economic development would lead to democracy; for Huntington, whereas modernity may be associated with democracy, modernization may not.

Finally, O'Donnell, not unlike de Schewnitz,[26] has argued that dependent development, such as experienced by Latin American countries in the 1950s and 1960s, eventually faces constraints that can be overcome only by the force of an authoritarian regime. After an "easy" phase of economic development driven by the local production of previously imported consumer goods (called import-substitution-industrialization, or ISI), countries face a bottleneck that cannot be addressed in the context of a democratic system that is based on a nationalist ideology and the political mobilization of urban workers. A "coup coalition" thus emerges that is ready to implement the bitter policies necessary for further economic development. Democracy becomes a casualty of modernization. Thus, dictatorships emerged in the 1960s and 1970s in countries such as Argentina, Brazil, Chile, and Uruguay not because of their lack of development but, rather, precisely because they were successful in generating a domestic industrial sector. These dictatorships emerged as the vehicles for the implementation of the next development phase.

There are several difficulties with these arguments. With respect to Moore, it is hard not to read it (particularly as interpreted by Skocpol)[27] as a story in which nondemocratic outcomes are a function of relatively weak modernizing impulses. In this light, England, France, Germany, and China simply represent different levels of economic development on a scale going from high to low. Thus, in a manner not unlike what modernization theory would suggest, differences in political regimes are due to modernizing impulses that are varied in their strength—in other words, to differences in levels of economic development.

As for Huntington, the level of political development required to sustain economic development and thereby steer a country to democracy is not at all apparent. He has little to say about the process of institution building itself, about the moment when a country's institutions can be considered to be ready to face the test of mass politics, and when nondemocratic institutions can safely be replaced by new, democratic frameworks. He often defines "institutionalization" tautologically in terms of the expected outcome, "order." Still, Huntington's claim about the dangers of early democratization resonates with recent work that points to the perils of introducing contested elections in some countries when conditions are not ready.[28] Yet, like Huntington, those who make this kind of argument fail to realize the apparent paradox involved in a situation in which institutions that will enable democracy must be created under nondemocratic systems; they also fail to provide a clear way for identifying ex ante when a society would be ready to "be allowed" to democratize.[29]

Finally, O'Donnell's account of the emergence of South American authoritarian regimes in the 1960s and 1970s has been challenged in terms of its historical accuracy and implicit inevitability.[30] Although O'Donnell's argument is compelling given its premises, the premises themselves are questionable. For example, the notion that the "deepening" of import substitution industrialization could not be achieved under democratic conditions because it required sharp reduction of wages and consumption expenditures has been shown to be untrue, both then and now (see the vast literature on economic reforms under democracy).[31]

One difficulty that pertains to all of these arguments is that the aggregate evidence linking economic development to democracy—the evidence that a correlation between the two exists—is simply overwhelming and is not really altered by the existence of cases that deviate from the general pattern. At most, what these critics of modernization theory establish is that (1) economic development may happen in a way that will not bring about all the associated transformations that modernization theory postulated would happen together; and (2) there are factors other than economic development that need to be present for development to lead to democracy. For Moore, the key additional factor is the class structure. For Huntington, the key additional factor is institutionalization. And for O'Donnell, the key additional factor is the international relationship of the country to global capitalism. Yet the core proposition of modernization theory—that given a certain type of development, democracy will emerge—is not fundamentally challenged.

## Development and the Survival of Democracy

Adam Przeworski has argued that democracy is a contingent outcome of conflict.[32] It emerges as the result of the interaction between regime and nonregime actors who come to accept that their best strategy is to delegate the decision about who will rule to a device that requires periodic competition for popular votes. The conditions that will make these actors choose this strategy cannot be reduced to any one factor. Actors will make the choice to institute periodic competitive elections for choosing rulers under conditions of high and low economic development, ethnic diversity, resource wealth, income inequality, asset specificity, revolutionary threat, geopolitical intimidation, or any other factor one may want to name.

This represents a radical departure from modernization theory. The claim is that the emergence of democracy is idiosyncratic or random with respect to economic development. How can such a claim be made in the face of an overwhelming correlation between democracy and development? The answer lies in regime dynamics. The correlation is driven by a connection between economic development and the survival of democracy. Democracy may emerge under all sorts of circumstances, but when it exists in poor countries, it is fragile and may well collapse. When democracy exists above a certain level of economic development, however, it never collapses. By thinking explicitly in a dynamic way, it is easy to see that the sustainability of democracy is what may drive the democracy and development connection, as distinct from the emergence story offered by modernization theorists. This is our proposition 3: economic development does not cause democracy to emerge but rather contributes to its survivability.

In empirical work with Fernando Limongi, José Antonio Cheibub, and Mike Alvarez, Przeworski has argued that the following is true regarding the relationship between economic development and political regimes:[33]

- There is a strong relationship between level of economic development (as measured by per capita income) and the incidence of democracy: level of development alone correctly predicts 77.5 percent of current regimes in a sample of 138 countries between 1950 and 1990. When the impact of economic development on the incidence of democracy is compared with that of other factors (whether the country was founded after 1950, whether the country had been a British colony, whether the country had experienced a democratic breakdown in the past, the proportion of Catholics, Protestants, and Muslims in the population, the degree of ethnolinguistic fractionalization, the degree of religious fractionalization, and the proportion of democracies in the world), it turns out that development is what best predicts the incidence of democracy.

- The bivariate relationship between economic development and the probability of a transition to democracy is curvilinear: transitions to democracy are less likely at very low and very high levels of economic development. This means that economic development destabilizes dictatorships at intermediate levels.
- Many dictatorships survived at relatively high levels of economic development. To put it differently, whatever the supposed threshold for dictatorships to become democracy, many dictatorships passed it in good health.
- Many dictatorships fell, that is, many democracies were established, at low levels of economic development.
- Of the countries that experienced development under dictatorships, some never democratized, whereas others eventually became democratic, but much later and at very different income levels. Only a few, actually five out of twenty, did experience what modernization theory would have expected.
- Per capita income has a strong impact on the survival of democracy: the probability that a democracy will die falls monotonically as per capita income increases, reaching (approximately) zero when income is higher than $7,000 (1985 PPP$).[34]
- The effect of per capita income on the survival of democracy is strong, even in the presence of other economic, political, social, cultural, and historical factors considered simultaneously. The effect of per capita income on transitions to democracy is positive and statistically significant, although it is orders of magnitude smaller than the effect of income on democratic survival.
- Thus, for the 1950–90 period, there is, at most, a curvilinear relationship between economic development and the emergence of democracy; at the same time, there is a monotonically declining relationship between economic development and the endurance of democracies.

- This pattern is also observed for the pre-1950 period. Given the limited availability of data, one finds for the period before 1950 that democracy was established at very different levels of development, that is, that there was no clear development threshold after which democracy became inevitable; that democratic reversals (transitions to dictatorship) did occur and that they were more likely in countries where democracy was established when they were very poor; and that democracy tended to survive past 1950 (and survive until today) in countries where they were established at higher levels of income. Thus, the pre-1950 pattern seems to be the same as the post-1950 one: no development threshold for the establishment of democracy, unstable democracies in poor countries, and endurance in rich countries.

Understandably, these findings have been theoretically and empirically challenged by subsequent scholarship.[35] The gist of these critiques is that Przeworski et al. misinterpret the evidence, fail to consider the limitations of their data, and/or are blinded by their zeal to refute the modernization hypothesis. Two of the most direct and detailed critiques are represented in work by Boix and Stokes and Epstein et al., to which we now turn.[36]

## Modern Work on Modernization Theory

The best-known critiques of the empirical work of Przeworski and colleagues are the studies by Carles Boix and Susan Stokes, as well as the study by David Epstein, Robert Bates, Jack Goldstone, Ida Kristensen, and Sharyn O'Halloran.

Boix lays the theoretical groundwork for the empirical research of Boix and Stokes.[37] Boix provides a game theoretic mechanism for modernization theory. He argues that level of economic development, income distribution, and—importantly—asset specificity together impact the probability of the emergence of democracy.

Asset specificity refers to the extent to which investments in the production of a good are locked in to the production of that specific good, or whether the investment may contribute to the production of various different goods. For example, investments in oil pipelines are highly specific, whereas investments in education are not.

Where asset specificity is high and the income distribution is highly skewed, such as in many countries rich in oil or other natural resources, the wealthy members of a society face severe distributional consequences for allowing popular sovereignty, and they have no credible threat to flee the country. Thus, it is in the self-interest of the rich to pay high costs of repressing democracy, maintaining dictatorial rule.[38] To put it bluntly, if the rich of a country derive their incomes from what is in the ground, they must defend it against the redistributive demands of democracy because they cannot flee the country with this source of income.

Suppose, however, that asset specificity is low, and the rich derive their income from high levels of skill (as do many in South Africa, for example). Then the rich have a credible exit threat. If the rich flee the country, taking their productive capacity along with them, they can severely harm the national economy. This credible threat restrains the distributional demands of the poor and may make democracy possible even in countries with relatively low levels of economic development, such as India. Asset specificity aside, if distributional demands diminish at higher levels of economic development, Boix argues that economic development should make democracy more likely both to emerge and to survive.

Yet, how can Boix and Stokes claim that development causes democracies to emerge in the face of the evidence presented by Przeworski, Alvarez, Cheibub, and Limongi (henceforth PACL)? They argue that PACL's empirical inferences are questionable because they are based on a small number of wealthy dictatorships and that, if data from a longer period of time are considered, the effect of development becomes more apparent. They furthermore argue that the effect of development is contingent on accounting for other factors, some of which are identified by the theory proposed by Boix. Once these important variables are included in the analysis, they argue, economic development clearly causes democracy.

Epstein and colleagues take a different approach. Rather than propose a new variant of modernization theory, they take issue with the conception of democracy employed by PACL. They argue that one should acknowledge the existence of a middle category of political regimes and that, if one does so, the data show a connection between economic development and the emergence of democracy. Thus, theirs is purely an empirical issue and rests on a defensible middle category of political regime.

As the work by Przeworski and colleagues delivered a severe blow to modernization theory, these new studies represent an exciting new challenge and a vigorous defense of the old school of thought. The new studies themselves, thus, deserve scrutiny as we enter into the next round of the debate. We thus consider their contributions one by one.

## Dwindling Numbers, Sample Bias, and Omitted Variables

This subsection's title lists the three empirical objections raised by Boix and Stokes to the analysis of Przeworski and Limongi and PACL:[39]

1.  The inferences are shaky because they are based on a small number of wealthy dictatorships.
2.  While the findings may be true for the post-1950 period, they do not hold for a larger time span (e.g., since the middle of the nineteenth century).
3.  Finally, PACL fail to consider important variables that, when included in their analysis, clearly demonstrate that economic development causes democracy.

We examine each of these claims in turn.

*Dwindling Numbers.* Boix and Stokes object to two statements PACL make on the basis of their data. They react, first, to the assertion that dictatorships at the highest levels of per capita income have lower probabilities of democratizing than those at moderate levels of per capita income, a statement that obviously contradicts modernization theory. Second, they react to the observation that few dictatorships experienced development for a relatively long period of time and then democratized.

Regarding the first statement, Boix and Stokes correctly argue that inferences made on the basis of small numbers—as with transitions to democracy at high levels of economic development—should be treated with caution. Such inferences can change drastically with the addition or subtraction of only a few instances of the event of interest. Given the small number of wealthy dictatorships in PACL's dataset, one or two additional cases of authoritarian collapse could change the overall picture substantially, making the relationship between economic development and transitions to democracy resemble the one described by modernization theory.

Although a possibility, this is, however, all that it is. Short of wishing for an alternative world, there is little one can do about the fact that only a few dictatorships exist at high levels of economic development. One of the things one can do is to explain why the world is as it is.

Boix and Stokes object to the second statement—that few dictatorships experienced development for a relatively long period of time and then democratized—on the grounds that this, in fact, constitutes evidence in support of modernization theory. Here is their argument:

> Assume . . . that both endogenous and exogenous mechanisms are at work [in the process of democratization]. Then there may be few dictatorships left at a high level of income precisely because development at lower levels of income already helped turn them into democracies and then helped keep them democratic. . . . Przeworski and Limongi count as countries "that developed under authoritarianism and became 'modern'" only ones that achieved a per capita income of $4,115. But it is not obvious to us why countries that move from a per capita income of $1,000 to $2,000, or from $2,000 to $3,000, and so on are failing to undergo development. If they are developing, and if dictatorships collapse and are replaced by democracies as they achieve development at these lower levels, then their absence from the pool of dictatorships at higher levels of income does not refute endogenous modernization but instead supports it. Indeed, from this perspective the anomaly is not that the number of dictatorships that became rich and then democratized is small, but that some dictatorships survived at all, despite earlier development.[40]

The reason the dataset contains few wealthy dictatorships, Boix and Stokes argue, is that most dictatorships that experienced some amount of development, even if paltry, had already democratized and remained democratic. Boix and Stokes thus change the main theoretical claim of modernization theory from being one about the effects of *levels* of development on democratization to one about the effects of *changes* (or perhaps long-term trends) in the level of development. From this perspective, what matters is that per capita income increases, even if from a very low level. Development, in this sense, is a process and not a condition; thresholds become irrelevant because the "democratizing" effects of development—that is, of a change of per capita income—will be felt even by very poor countries.

If this is the case, then the relevant variable for explaining democratization should be changes in per capita income and not levels of per capita income. Yet, the evidence supporting a positive relationship between changes in per capita income and democratization is at best weak. PACL find that changes in per capita income affect both democracies and dictatorships: economic growth is always good as it makes both regimes less likely to change (although the effect is stronger for the latter than for the former). Acemoglu et al., in turn, find that changes in per capita income have no effect on democracy, whether the time span one adopts is 10, 50, or 100 years.[41] Alternatively, Quinn and Gassebner, Lamla, and Vreeland find that short-run changes in per capita income, that is, economic growth, makes democratization less likely because it helps dictatorships survive in office.[42] This turns modernization theory on its head.

Our skepticism notwithstanding, the challenges of Boix and Stokes are worthy of empirical investigation. We consider a variant of the Boix and Stokes statistical model and find that for a poor dictatorship—with per capita income of just $100—the chances it will democratize are small: about 1 out of 100. With per capita income of $5,000, the chances of democratization increase to 1 out of 75. With per capita income of $12,000, the chances of democratization increase to about 1 out of 40. So, the best estimate is that by increasing income the chances of democratization nearly triple. But in order for this to happen, per capita income must increase by 120 times, going from $100 to $12,000.

In the history of the modern world, a change in per capita income of this magnitude has never happened. The closest is Japan, which entered the sample with a per capita income of $1,768 in 1952 and reached a per capita income of $14,317 in 1990, an eightfold increase in per capita income. Five other countries—Canada, Finland, West Germany, Luxembourg, and Norway—experienced an increase in per capita income slightly higher than $10,000 between 1950 and 1990. Of course, these cases do not represent good examples for modernization theory because they were all democracies to begin with. At the same time, twenty-four countries ended the period with per capita incomes below those with which they had started, and forty-four saw their incomes increase by less than $1,000 between the times that they were first and last observed. The average country between 1950 and 1990 had its per capita income increase by 2.1 times, far below the 120-fold increase that our estimates suggest are necessary to raise the probability of a transition to democracy from about one out of 100 to about one in 40.

Given these estimates and realistic expectations about economic growth, should we embrace the claim that development sets in motion a number of processes that will, soon enough, lead to the emergence of democracy? When we also consider that the relationship is highly uncertain from a statistical point of view, our answer is no.

*Sample Bias.* The second empirical objection that Boix and Stokes raise to PACL's analysis is that it was limited to the 1950–90 period. Extending the analysis back to the mid-nineteenth century, they argue, reveals that the impact of economic development on democratization is positive and very strong. Yet, further data analysis of the 1850 to 1949 period (not presented here but available on request) shows that the result is driven by a small number of western European cases in the late nineteenth century.

First consider the period 1901–49.[43] It turns out that this period is much like the 1950–90 period analyzed by PACL. Economic development has no effect on transitions to democracy, democracy emerged at high and low levels of economic development, and economic development did have an effect on the survival of democracy, substantially reducing the probability of a democratic breakdown.

Given that per capita income does not cause democratization in the 1900–49 sample, the effect that Boix and Stokes found for the 1850–1949 period must be due to what happens between 1850 and 1900. Here, the effect of economic development on the emergence of democracy is indeed positive.[44] Substantively, the effect is strong: the probability of a democratic transition increases from virtually zero to 0.42 when per capita income goes from $100 to $3,000. The statistical significance of this finding, however, is marginal, which means that we cannot have much confidence in the result.[45]

Why is our confidence low? To begin with, there are not many observations. For the eighteen countries in the sample, data on per capita income are available for only 259 yearly observations of nondemocracies out of a possible 2,345 observations—so nearly 90 percent of the data are missing. Eleven of the countries have data for 1850, but no country has data for the period between 1851 and 1870—so we are really analyzing the period 1871–1900. Most of these data (222 of the observations) come from eight western European countries: the United Kingdom, Belgium, the Netherlands, Germany, Austria, Italy, Sweden, and Denmark. Moreover, there is not much variation. There are only three transitions to democracy in this period for which per capita income information is available: the United Kingdom (1885), Belgium (1894), and the

Netherlands (1897). As these transitions occurred at relatively high levels of per capita income, we see a positive relationship; but it is not a relationship with high statistical significance. Note that Boix and Stokes do not control for other variables because data are not available. It may well be that if we could control for other factors, the correlation would be even weaker.

Thus, to review, the effect of per capita income on transitions to democracy is not statistically significant for the period 1950–90, is not statistically significant for the period 1901–49, and is only marginally statistically significant for the period 1850–1900.

*Omitted Variables.* Boix and Stokes's last empirical objection to PACL is that it suffers from omitted-variable bias. Specifically, they argue that there are two variables that PACL did not include in their analysis and which hindered democracy from emerging as a result of economic development: whether the country was rich in oil, and whether the country was in eastern Europe under the influence of the Soviet Union.[46]

As we saw earlier, Boix proposes that the effect of per capita income on democratization may be contingent on the degree of asset specificity in a country.[47] If the economic elites (or "the rich") within a country derive their income from highly specific assets, such as oil (as they do in many Middle Eastern countries), then they will stop at nothing to repress democracy. They fear that democracy will lead to massive expropriation by governments supported by the poor. But if the rich derive their income from their skills and education, as is true for countries such as India and South Africa, redistributive demands are tempered even under democracy. Alienation of the rich may lead to emigration, damaging prospects for economic growth. Recognizing this, even democratic governments supported by the poor will resist the temptation of massive expropriation. So, anticipating moderate redistributive demands, the rich may acquiesce to demands for democracy.

Boix and Stokes also propose that international relations may matter. Specifically, they suggest that countries under the influence of the Soviet Union may have been less likely to democratize despite their levels of economic development because the Soviet Union exerted "powerful pressures" against democratization in eastern Europe "and did so consistently through almost the entire period covered by the Przeworski data set."[48] They suggest, therefore, the importance of accounting for whether a country was under Soviet influence.

Had PACL accounted for oil-rich and Soviet dictatorships, Boix and Stokes argue, they would have found a positive and substantial effect of per capita income on democratization in the period between 1950 and 1990. Boix and Stokes conclude that "once we control for the exogenous factors of international politics and factor endowments, economic development makes democratization more likely."[49] To account for these factors, they drop observations of Soviet and oil-producing countries from the analysis.

It is true that if one drops *most* of the observations of Soviet dictatorships and all of the oil-rich dictatorships, the effect of per capita income on the emergence of democracy is statistically significant. Yet, Boix and Stokes fail to drop *all* of the observations of countries that were Soviet dictatorships—they keep the precise observations for the years in which these countries transitioned to democracy: Bulgaria in 1990, Czechoslovakia in 1990, and Hungary in 1990. This is an understandable and unintended technical mistake: because their model is dynamic, they should drop observations of countries that *were* Soviet dictatorships the previous year, but they actually dropped observations that *are* Soviet countries in a given year, so the Bulgaria, Czechoslovakia, and Hungary transitions are included even though they transitioned from Soviet dictatorships.[50] What is surprising is that if we drop just these three observations, as Boix and Stokes should in accordance with their theory, then the effect of per capita income on the emergence of democracy is *not* statistically significant.

More generally, we caution against excluding cases according to important variables (rather than controlling directly for the potential effects of these variables in the statistical analysis). If we exclude sufficient cases, we can get any results we want. This could become absurd, with the researcher choosing to analyze only the authoritarian regimes in which small merchants accumulated sufficient capital to increase productivity and provide a general increase in material well-being; in which the capital accumulated was mobile rather than fixed; in which the population was ethnically homogeneous and shared a religion that emphasized individual values and the pursuit of happiness through hard work; in which institutions that allowed an elite to compete for power and get habituated with competition were in place before the emergence of mass politics; in which the middle class expanded and started to forcefully demand that the shackles of dictatorship be removed; in which . . . the process of economic development took place in just the right way as to lead to democratization as posited by modernization theory. At the limit, one is left with the cases of which Lipset spoke, located in "northwest Europe and their English-speaking offspring in America and Australasia," where "the conditions related to stable democracy . . . are most readily found."[51]

Still, Boix and Stokes make an important contribution in drawing attention to the effect of asset specificity—particularly oil—on democratization. More generally, there is a growing literature on the effect of the "resource curse" on political regime and economic development. The question is addressed by Lindberg and Meerow in this volume. It has long been known that the presence of natural resources can lead an economy to divert investment away from potentially productive sectors, ultimately undermining economic development. Ross, as well as Jensen and Wantchekon, have shown that the presence of oil hinders the emergence of democracy.[52] Gassebner et al. show that oil is one of a very few variables that robustly predict democratization, with a negative effect.[53] The resource curse may also hurt democracies. Collier and Collier and Hoeffler argue that the resource curse can hurt democracy more than autocracy because it is more likely to breed violent conflict and instability under democracy.[54] We find some of the evidence that oil has a direct impact on the dynamics of political regimes convincing. The evidence that the effect of economic development is contingent on the presence of oil is plausible in theory, but robust empirical evidence supporting this claim is lacking.

The broad evidence in support of a strong effect of economic development on democratization is weak at best, even after the extension of the sample to the nineteenth century and the inclusion of variables that had been left out of the analysis before. This effect is often not statistically significant. When it is significant, it is either substantively small—particularly in view of the expectations derived from modernization theory—or based on a dataset that is problematic.

## Partial Democracies

Epstein et al.'s major innovation is to employ a measure of political regime that classifies cases into three categories: democracy, partial democracy, or autocracy. For this, they need an alternative measure to PACL's binary one. They use POLITY, a commonly used measure of regime, particularly in the quantitative literature in international relations.

Though POLITY runs from −10 to +10, often researchers choose to "dichoto-mize" the measure between cases that are greater than +6 or +7 and cases that are less than +6 or +7. While such an approach produces a measure that is broadly correlated with the PACL measure, it is problematic when it comes to studying regime transitions because there is no obvious threshold for a switch in regime types. The extremes are easy to agree on—there are obvious democ-racies, such as the United Kingdom, and obvious dictatorships, such as North Korea. But the precise timing of the transition from dictatorship to democ-racy and back again is not obvious without crisp, explicit, and replicable rules for coding transitions, such as provided by the PACL measure.[55]

What constitutes a "transition" in the POLITY scale is further complicated by the fact that it actually combines five different component variables that measure different facets of a polity. The measure combines variables that code, for example, the relationship between the executive and the legislature, how the executive is recruited, whether there are elections, and whether there is political violence. The combination of all of these different facets of a polity results in several objectionable claims. For example, if a country moves from totalitarianism into civil war, it is coded as more "democratic" because politi-cal violence is considered to be a form of political participation that is absent under totalitarianism.[56] As another example, countries that fill the chief ex-ecutive through coups are considered more "democratic" than countries that have monarchies because the selection process is theoretically more open. In our view, we would not consider any of these situations more or less demo-cratic. Rather, we would simply suggest that they are different situations within the same category of nondemocracy.[57]

These critiques notwithstanding, Epstein et al.'s uniqueness in the transi-tions literature is to propose a "trichotomization" of the POLITY scale over the intervals [-10, 0], [+1, +7], and [+8, +10]. They estimate the probability of a transition from dictatorship to democracy and the probability of a transition from partial democracy to democracy. They also consider breakdowns of de-mocracy, estimating the probability of a transition from democracy to either partial democracy or dictatorship.

Epstein et al. emphasize two main aspects of their findings: (1) that they have "demonstrated that higher incomes per capita significantly increases the likelihood of democratic regimes, both by enhancing the consolidation of existing democracies and by promoting transitions from authoritarian to democratic systems"; and (2) that the category of "partial democracies" emerges from their analysis "as critical to understanding democratic transitions."[58] According to them, "These are 'fragile' democracies, or perhaps 'unconsolidated democracies.' Whatever one wishes to call them, they emerge from our analysis as critical to the understanding of democratic transitions. More volatile than either straight autocracies or democracies, their movements seem at the moment to be largely unpredictable. One of our major conclusions, then, is that it is this category—the partial democracies—upon which future research should focus."[59]

What are partial democracies? For Epstein et al., as we have seen, partial democracies are political regimes that score between +1 and +7 in the POLITY measure. They justify the decision to partition the POLITY measure in this way by arguing the following: there are no cases of a country with a total score of 7 or below and a maximum value in any of the five component measures; the classification "correspond[s] well with those employed by others"; and the analysis "is robust to changes in the cut points."[60] This last point is precisely the problem. Their findings with respect to "partial democracies" are robust to all different cut points of the POLITY measure, making their findings *too* robust to provide any real analytical traction over their question.

To explain, following the Epstein et al. suggestion to focus research on "the partial democracies," we expand the cut points in step-by-step increments from the [+1, +7] interval all the way out to the [−9,+9] interval. Thus, partial democracies are variously defined to encompass as few as 811 observations (when the POLITY interval is [+1, +7]) and as many as 4,503 (when the POLITY interval is [-9, +9]). It turns out that no matter what interval we use, the qualitative findings reported by Epstein et al. do not change. Most importantly, the estimate of the impact of economic development on the probability of a transition toward democracy always remains positive and significant (and actually larger) as the definition of partial democracies expands. The effect of economic development on the survival of democracy is also positive and significant as long as the upper bound of partial democracy is +8 or lower.

When full democracies are coded as the cases scoring +10, and autocracies as the cases scoring −10, the effect of economic development on the survival of democracy is positive but not significant, whereas the effect of economic development on the emergence of democracy is both positive and significant. Recall that the latter really indicates the effect of per capita GDP on transitions from autocracy or partial democracy to full democracy. An examination of the data demonstrates that many of the cases included as partial democracies in the more expansive definitions violate whatever conceptual understanding one may have of these political regimes. There is certainly no consensus in the literature. Hegre et al. consider the full scale of POLITY in their analysis of middle regimes, estimating their significance parametrically, while Fearon and Laitin define the middle interval as running [–5, +5].[61] Yet, in the Epstein et al. analysis, the key result holds no matter what cut points are used. Ironically, we thus lose analytical traction over the question of midlevel regimes. There are, it seems, situations in which coefficients can be just too robust for them to be of any use.

We suggest that careful, conceptually driven, dissection of the POLITY index is required to understand what is going on in the data. Of the many aspects of democratization conflated in the measure—political violence, constraints on the chief executive, the selection of rulers—we need to understand which ones are correlated with economic development and whether the correlation is driven by the emergence and/or the survival of democracy. Until such a better understanding of the findings of Epstein et al. appears, we remain unconvinced.

We conclude that economic development does not exert a strong effect on democratization, though we find convincing its strong impact on democratic survival. This proposition has been recently further corroborated by an analysis of the emergence and survival of democracy in which the impact of fifty-eight other factors were analyzed for robustness. After evaluating 1.7 million regressions of the emergence of democracy and 1.4 million for the survival of democracy, Gassebner et al. concluded that per capita income *is not* among the most robust determinants of the transition to democracy, but that it *is* one of three robust factors accounting for the survival of democracy.[62]

In our view, the best statistical techniques and the best data collection efforts have not been sufficient to generate convincing evidence that the effect of economic development on democratization is substantively significant. True, there is an effect, in the sense that estimated coefficients are positive and, at times, statistically significant. Under some specifications, the effect is curvilinear—development destabilizes middle-income dictatorships but not very poor or very rich ones. But in no case is the effect of economic development—as measured by per capita income—consistent with what would be expected if modernization theory, in any of its incarnations, were true.

When it comes to the emergence of democracy, there are some cases that conform to proposition 1 (economic development goes along with democratization), some that conform to proposition 2 (economic development goes along with the entrenchment of autocracy), and many other cases where we observe little change at all. The lack of a clear relationship may be due to a lack of a causal connection between economic development and democratization, but it also may be because the causal connection is more complex than scholars have thus far analyzed. Economic development may unleash both prodemocracy forces and also undemocratic forces. Democratizing forces may include increasing levels of education and labor processes that become too complex to be controlled by an autocracy; it may also include a diverse civil society that is simply too strong to be dominated through autocratic forms of control. Undemocratic forces may include a growing insecurity among the winners from economic development who fear the expropriation of their gains, increasing inequality resulting in a growing sentiment of relative deprivation among labor and the poor, and an increase in factionalism across society too deep for peaceful elections. If economic development can simultaneously lead to both prodemocratic and undemocratic forces, we may not observe a consistent, prevailing movement in favor of democracy. Nevertheless, this does not mean that development is necessarily neutral with respect to democratization—we may need to further break down its effects, sorting out the democratic and undemocratic forces. Theoretical models such as those of Rosendorff, Boix, and Acemoglu and Robinson are helpful in identifying how these forces may interact.[63] Yet, as for testing these theories, unfortunately history has not given us sufficient data to work with, as the work by Boix and Stokes demonstrates. Still, we look forward to future research along these lines.

In the meantime, PACL's statement, in our view, still stands: "The conclusion reached thus far is that whereas economic development under dictatorship has at most a non-linear relationship to the emergence of democracies, once they are established, democracies are much more likely to endure in more highly developed countries."[64]

## Country-Specific Effects and Spurious Correlation

Given all that has been written about the relationship between development and democracy, proposition 4, put forward by Acemoglu, Johnson, Robinson, and Yared is a radical one: the relationship between democracy and development is spurious.[65] In other words, there is no causal connection between democracy and development at all. Development causes neither the emergence nor the survival of democracy. The apparent connection between democracy and development is really driven by other factors, which independently cause both.

Focusing on former European colonies, Acemoglu and his colleagues argue that the institutional structure built at the moment of colonization (which they see as a "critical juncture" in the history of these countries) created divergent development paths, which persisted through time: one path was characterized by economic failure and repressive forms of governments, whereas the other was characterized by economic success and democratic forms of government (in particular, forms of government that impose constraints on the executive power). Once these divergent paths are taken into consideration, they claim, the relationship between development and democracy disappears: development is related neither to the probability of transition to democracy nor to the sustainability of democracy.

This is an exciting proposition—it challenges everything that has been said about the relationship between economic development and democracy by social scientists in the past fifty years. It is also a proposition that is based on an empirical claim that is not necessarily valid.[66]

Acemoglu and his colleagues argue that the reason previous studies have found a significant effect of economic development on transitions to and away from democracy is that they failed to take into consideration the impact of country-specific factors on both income and democracy. These factors, they argue, are historical in the sense that they are the result of events (critical junctures) that took place in a country's distant past and whose implications are still felt today because "institutions have a tendency to persist."[67] They address this issue by estimating models of regime transition including country fixed effects and find that, once this is done, the impact of per capita income disappears entirely: it matters neither for the emergence of democracy nor for the survival of democracy.

A country "fixed effect" may be due to any of a large number of a country's attributes that are fixed over time.[68] While political regime and economic development are examples of attributes that may change over time for most countries, other attributes of the country are more fixed (with some notable exceptions), such as its date of independence, the characteristics of the founding population, the language, the borders, its geographic features, its latitude and longitude, and the list goes on. Because these features do not vary over time, it is hard to disentangle which one or ones may have causal power in a given setting. Typically, scholars use a "fixed effects model" as a diagnostic to test the robustness of their findings and remain agnostic as to which specific attribute of a country the fixed effects may really be capturing. Acemoglu et al. take their analysis a step further, however, speculating as to the precise causal mechanism that the fixed effects capture.

Acemoglu et al. support their claim that these fixed effects capture the historical events that took place around critical junctures by showing that they, the country fixed effects, are themselves correlated with variables that are correlated with the institutional structures created at the moment of European colonization and the development paths that countries subsequently embarked on. Specifically, the country fixed effects are correlated with settler mortality rates at the time of colonization, indigenous population density in 1500, the average constraint on the executive in the country's first ten years after independence,[69] and the date of independence. The intuition behind their argument is that two major contributors to democratization are the strength of civil society and the structure of political institutions (meaning the constraint on the executive branch of government), and—because of exogenous factors—these developed the furthest in western Europe. Where western Europeans settled in large proportions and survived, so did their civil society and institutions. These factors contributed to both economic prosperity and democratization.

The estimates of country fixed effects thus play a crucial role in the analysis of Acemoglu and colleagues; these estimates are used not only to eliminate the findings that per capita income causes democracy to emerge and survive but also to support their alternative claim that what really matters is the developmental path that countries embarked on at the moment of European colonization.

Yet a problem with the country fixed effects approach is that we really cannot distinguish the civil society and institutions that settlers bring with them from any other factor associated with the country, such as its resource endowment, latitude and longitude, size, and strategic importance.

Even more problematic for the country fixed effects approach is that many countries in the period under study (1950–90) did not experience any political regime change. They spent the entire period either as democracies or as dictatorships. Because they do not vary over the periods in which they are observed, these cases effectively do not count when a country fixed effects approach is employed. One can think of the problem this way: what is the probability of observing a transition to democracy given that a country is always observed as a dictatorship? The answer is zero. What is the probability of observing a transition to dictatorship given that a country is always democracy? Again, the answer is obviously zero. We appear to "learn" nothing from these cases, so they drop out of the analysis. But do we really learn nothing from these cases?

Note, importantly, that the countries for which there is no variation in regime are not randomly distributed around the world: the countries that were first observed as democracies and remained democratic during the 1950–90 period tended to be relatively wealthy, whereas the countries that were first observed as dictatorships and remained dictatorships during the same period tended to be relatively poor. So, when we introduce country fixed effects, we drop key cases with respect to the question of economic development and democracy: a large number of poor dictatorships and rich democracies is dismissed, and the estimation of the impact of per capita income on transition to and from democracy is disproportionately based on observations of countries with middle levels of per capita income. Thus, given this country fixed effects setup, the lack of a statistically significant impact of per capita income should come as no surprise.

These issues are far from having been settled, and our goal here is simply to recognize the importance of the proposition put forward by Acemoglu and his colleagues and, at the same time, call attention to some of the issues that arise from their analysis. Their work represents an important contribution to the literature on democratization to which students and scholars should be attentive.

## Conclusion

From our original five propositions, we reject all but the third one: that economic development causes democracy to survive. We accept proposition 3 in a broad sense because the evidence is clear and convincing. As for the other propositions, we acknowledge that there are several cases that fit each story and even some nonrobust systematic evidence in favor of them. Yet, the preponderance of the evidence is against them.

If development (per capita income) affects democratization, its status is not privileged with respect to other factors that may also affect democratization—past democratic breakdowns, participation in international organizations, short-term economic performance, natural resources, the ethnic composition of the population, historical legacies, diffusion, and so on.[70] Yet development does appear to sustain democracy: countries that democratize at higher levels of development are virtually certain to continue living under democracy, whereas countries that democratize at lower levels of development still face significant odds that democracy will be overthrown.

At a general level, democracy emerges either because one actor who happens to prefer democracy is politically successful or because there is a balance of forces among relevant actors so that no one can impose its preferences over the others. There are multiple reasons why the existence of such an actor or of such a balance of forces exists. Sometimes it is because economic development favored a democratic actor (the working class for Rueschemeyer, Stephens, and Stephens or the middle class for Lipset),[71] which led to the emergence of conflicts over democracy. But other times these reasons have nothing to do with economic development: the military government decides that the political system is too centralized and sets in motion a process that, against its own preferences, ultimately leads to an alternation in power via competitive elections (as occurred in Brazil);[72] or geopolitical considerations, among others, importantly shape the decisions of the dominant party to implement political reforms (as in Taiwan);[73] or the military, which is unable to govern the country or win an international war of its own making, gives up power (as in Argentina);[74] or a civil war ends militarily in a way that induces warring factions to accept power-sharing agreements,[75] or neighbors and regional partners are becoming increasingly democratic.[76] Whatever the reason, there is nothing predetermined about the outcomes of interactions revolving around the establishment of democracy. As many analyses of democratic transitions have demonstrated, transition games are characterized by a multiplicity of equilibria, including the establishment of a democratic regime and the perpetuation of an authoritarian one.

Thus, democratization is the product of many causes, and it is inherently uncertain. Should we then give up on theorizing about it? The answer, of course, depends on what we mean by theorizing. If the goal is to generate a theory that is able to unambiguously answer why democracies emerge and, on the basis of this answer, generate predictions about when it will emerge, we find that theorizing is doomed, and we should just as well go do something else. If, however, the goal is to identify different mechanisms for the emergence of democracy and characterize the conditions under which these mechanisms are more or less likely to operate, then we have a long and, we hope, fruitful agenda in front of us.[77]

In the meantime, for those interested in what policy makers should be doing at this moment, we acknowledge that there is a great deal of interest in promoting democracy among many governments, international organizations, and nongovernmental organizations. Given all that we now know about the relationship between economic development and democratization, we cannot sanction the policy advice of modernization theory, which is that if we promote economic development in poor dictatorships, eventually democracy will emerge. We can suggest, however, that efforts might be better spent in promoting the survival of democracy rather than its emergence.

NOTES

For helpful comments and suggestions we thank Sheri Berman, Nathan Brown, Svitlana Chernykh, John Gerring, Craig Kauffman, Fernando Limongi, Cynthia McClintock, Milan Svolik, and all the participants in the "Future of Democracy" workshops at George Washington University. We also thank Carles Boix, as well as Robert Bates, David Epstein, and Jack Goldstone for making their respective datasets available to us. Finally, we express our gratitude to the anonymous reviewer, who provided nothing but excellent suggestions, all of which we incorporated. The chapter is a stronger contribution as a result.

1. Robert Packenham, *Liberal America and the Third World: Political-Development Ideas in Foreign Aid and Social Science* (Princeton: Princeton University Press, 1973); Nils Gilman, *Mandarins of the Future: Modernization Theory in Cold War America* (Baltimore: Johns Hopkins University Press, 2004).

2. Adam Przeworski and Fernando Limongi, "Political Regimes and Economic Growth," *Journal of Economic Perspectives* 7, no. 3 (Summer 1993): 60.

3. Adam Przeworski, Michael Alvarez, José Antonio Cheibub, and Fernando Limongi, *Democracy and Development: Political Institutions and Well-Being in the World, 1950–1990* (Cambridge: Cambridge University Press, 2000), chap. 3.

4. For example, Przeworski et al., *Democracy and Development*, chaps. 3–5; Robert J. Barro, *Determinants of Economic Growth: A Cross-Country Empirical Study* (Cambridge, MA: MIT Press, 1997). For more recent work, see John Gerring, Philip Bond, William T. Barndt, and Carola Moreno, "Democracy and Growth: A Historical Perspective," *World Politics* 57, no. 3 (2005): 323–64; Torsten Persson and Guido Tabellini, "Democracy and Development: The Devil in the Details," *American Economic Review* 96, no. 2 (2006): 319–24; and Gerring, chapter 8 in this volume.

5. Indirect elections for the executive in the case of parliamentary systems.

6. Przeworski et al., *Democracy and Development*, p. 16.

7. For readers interested in the survival and adaptation of authoritarian rule in China, we also recommend Pierre Landry, *Decentralized Authoritarianism in China: The Communist Party's Control of Local Elites in the Post-Mao Era* (New York: Cambridge University Press, 2008). For a comparison of the survival of authoritarianism in Cuba to China (and Vietnam), see Eusebio Mujal-León, "Can Cuba Change? Tensions in the Regime," *Journal of Democracy* 20, no. 1 (2009): 20–35.

8. Note that the decision about whether to abide by the results has to be made by *all* actors, losers and winners. Winning is relative to one's expectation, and there may be situations in which the winner of an electoral contest (say, the party that got the most votes) is not satisfied with the results. Recall Park Chung Hee in South Korea, who "lost" elections in 1971 in the sense that he did not obtain a majority as large as the one he thought necessary; consequently, he closed congress and wrote a new constitution.

9. For an alternative view, see Kenneth A. Bollen and Robert W. Jackman, "Democracy, Stability, and Dichotomies," *American Sociological Review* 54 (1989): 438–57.

10. For work on different types of dictatorships and their survival, see Jennifer Gandhi, *Political Institutions under Dictatorship* (New York: Cambridge University Press, 2008). For work on different types of democracy and their survival, see José Antonio Cheibub, *Presidentialism, Parliamentarism, and Democracy* (New York: Cambridge University Press), and Fish, chapter 5 in this volume.

11. See, for example, chapter 5 by M. Steven Fish and chapter 7 by Staffan I. Lindberg and Sara Meerow, both in this volume.

12. José Antonio Cheibub, Jennifer Gandhi, and James R. Vreeland, "Democracy and Dictatorship Revisited," *Public Choice* 143, nos. 1-2 (April 2010): 67–101.

13. Talcott Parsons, *The Social System* (Glencoe, IL: Free Press, 1951).

14. Seymour Martin Lipset, "Some Social Requisites of Democracy: Economic Development and Political Legitimacy," *American Political Science Review* 53, no. 1 (1959): 69–105.

15. Przeworski et al., *Democracy and Development*, p. 97.

16. Deane E. Neubauer, "Some Conditions of Democracy," *American Political Science Review* 61, no. 4 (1967): 1002–9.

17. Ibid., p. 1007.

18. Robert W. Jackman, "On the Relation of Economic Development to Democratic Performance," *American Journal of Political Science* 17, no. 3 (1973): 611–21.

19. Seymour Martin Lipset, Kyoung-Ryung Seong, and John Charles Torres, "A Comparative Analysis of the Social Requisites of Democracy," *International Social Science Journal* 45, no. 2 (1993) 155–75.

20. Zehra F. Arat, "Democracy and Economic Development: Modernization Theory Revisited," *Comparative Politics* 21, no. 1 (1988): 21–36.

21. This summary follows Diamond's interpretation of Lipset; Larry Diamond, "Economic Development and Democracy Reconsidered," in G. Marks and L. Diamond, eds., *Reexamining Democracy: Essays in Honor of Seymour Martin Lipset* (Newbury Park, CA: Sage, 1992).

22. Ronald Inglehart and Christian Welzel, *Modernization, Cultural Change and Democracy: The Human Development Sequence* (New York: Cambridge University Press, 2005).

23. Ronald Inglehart and Wayne E. Baker, "Modernization, Cultural Change, and the Persistence of Traditional Values," *American Sociological Review* 65, no. 1 (February 2000): 19–51.

24. Dietrich Rueschemeyer, Evelyne Huber Stephens, and John D. Stephens, *Capitalist Development and Democracy* (Chicago: University of Chicago Press, 1992).

25. Barrington Moore Jr., *Social Origins of Dictatorship and Democracy: Lord and Peasant in the Making of the Modern World* (Boston: Beacon Press, 1966); Samuel P. Huntington, *Political Order in Changing Societies* (New Haven: Yale University Press, 1968); and Guillermo O'Donnell, *Modernization and Bureaucratic-Authoritarianism: Studies in South American Politics* (Berkeley: Institute of International Studies, University of California, 1973).

26. Karl de Schweinitz Jr., *Industrialization and Democracy: Economic Necessities and Political Possibilities* (Glencoe, IL: Free Press, 1964).

27. Theda Skocpol, "A Critical Review of Barrington Moore's *Social Origins of Dictatorship and Democracy*," in Theda Skocpol, *Social Revolutions in the Modern World* (New York: Cambridge University Press, 1994), pp. 25–54.

28. See, for example, Jack Snyder, *From Voting to Violence: Democratization and Nationalist Conflict* (New York: W. W. Norton, 2000).

29. For more on this debate, see Sheri Berman, "How Democracies Emerge: Lessons from Europe," *Journal of Democracy* 18, no. 1 (2007): 28–41, and "The Vain Hope for 'Correct' Timing," *Journal of Democracy* 18, no. 3 (2007): 14–17; Thomas Carothers, "Misunderstanding Gradualism," *Journal of Democracy* 18, no. 3 (2007): 18–22; Francis Fukuyama, "Liberalism versus State-Building," *Journal of Democracy* 18, no. 3 (2007): 10–13; and Edward D. Mansfield and Jack L. Snyder, "The Sequencing 'Fallacy,' " *Journal of Democracy* 18, no. 3 (2007): 5–10.

30. In reference to historical accuracy, see Karen L. Remmer and Gilbert W. Merkx, "Bureaucratic-Authoritarianism Revisited," *Latin American Research Review* 17, no. 2 (1982): 3–40; Robert Kaufman, "Industrial Change and Authoritarian Rule in Latin America: A Concrete Review of the Bureaucratic-Authoritarian Model," in David Collier, ed., *The New Authoritarianism in Latin America* (Princeton: Princeton University Press, 1979), pp. 165–254. In reference to implicit inevitability, see Argelina Figueiredo, *Democracia ou Reformas? Alternativas Democráticas a Crise Política, 1961–1964* (Rio de Janeiro: Paz e Terra, 1993); Youssef Cohen, *Radicals, Reformers, and Reactionaries: The Prisoner's Dilemma and the Collapse of Democracy in Latin America* (Chicago: University of Chicago Press, 1994).

31. See also Kaufman, "Industrial Change and Authoritarian Rule in Latin America," and James R. Kurth, "Industrial Change and Political Change: A European Perspective," in Collier, *The New Authoritarianism in Latin America*, pp. 319–62.

32. Adam Przeworski, "Democracy as a Contingent Outcome of Conflict," in Jon Elster and Rune Slagstad, eds., *Constitutionalism and Democracy* (Cambridge: Cambridge University Press, 1988).

33. Przeworski et al., *Democracy and Development*.

34. PPP stands for "purchasing power parity." This measure of per capita income accounts for the fact that nontraded goods and services (e.g., haircuts) may have similar values in different countries, even though the price, according to nominal exchange rates, may be quite different. Countries with large vibrant domestic economies and low

labor costs, such as China and Brazil, have higher levels of economic development than the nominal exchange rate would indicate.

35. The theoretical critique is that Przeworski et al. do not offer an explanation of why economic development sustains democracy, that is, why political actors choose not to revert the result of contested elections at high levels of income. We do not address this issue here as our goal is to evaluate the empirical claims about the relationship between economic development and democratization. One such explanation is provided in Adam Przeworski, "Democracy as an Equilibrium," *Public Choice* 123 (2005): 253–73.

36. Carles Boix and Susan C. Stokes, "Endogenous Democratization," *World Politics* 55 (July 2003): 517–49; David L. Epstein, Robert Bates, Jack Goldstone, Ida Kristensen, and Sharyn O'Halloran, "Democratic Transitions," *American Journal of Political Science* 50, no. 3 (July 2006): 551–69.

37. Carles Boix, *Democracy and Redistribution* (New York: Cambridge University Press, 2003).

38. Rosendorff makes a related theoretical argument supported by the case of South Africa; B. Peter Rosendorff, "Choosing Democracy," *Economics & Politics* 13 (2001): 1–29. On the question of income distribution, Desai et al. show that policy making in highly unequal democracies is dramatically different from that in more egalitarian democracies; Raj M. Desai, Anders Olofsgård, and Tarik Yousef, "Democracy, Inequality, and Inflation," *American Political Science Review* 97, no. 3 (2003): 391–406.

39. Adam Przeworski and Fernando Limongi, "Modernization: Theories and Facts," *World Politics* 49 (1997): 155–183; Przeworski et al., *Democracy and Development*.

40. Boix and Stokes, "Endogenous Democratization," p. 524.

41. Daron Acemoglu, Simon Johnson, James Robinson, and Pierre Yared, "Income and Democracy," *American Economic Review* 98 (2008): 808–42. They do find, however, that if one adopts a 500-year time span, the relationship between change in per capita income and democratization is positive, although they make an argument that this relationship is very likely to be spurious. We take this finding with some skepticism as we find it hard to meaningfully talk about democracy 500 years ago.

42. Dennis P. Quinn, "Democracy and International Financial Reform: The Paradoxical Consequences of International Economic Reforms in Non-democracies," mimeo, Georgetown University McDonough School of Business, 2009; Martin Gassebner, Michael J. Lamla, and James Raymond Vreeland, "Extreme Bounds of Democracy," KOF Working Paper No. 224, 2009.

43. Przeworski et al., *Democracy and Development*, pp. 103–6, also analyzed the period 1901–49, relying on descriptive statistics. Unlike Boix and Stokes, they do not estimate inferential statistics given the complications with the data.

44. We do not analyze the effect of per capita income on democratic breakdown for the 1850–1900 period because all democracies—for which data are available—survive. As a matter of fact, there is one democratic breakdown in the period—France in 1852—but per capita income is not available.

45. The finding holds only at the 0.10 level of statistical confidence and is rejected at the conventional 0.05 level.

46. This first variable is derived from Boix's version of modernization theory outlined previously; Boix, *Democracy and Redistribution*. Note that PACL already exclude

from their dataset (the same used by Boix and Stokes to produce their table 6), six countries in which the ratio of fuels exports to total exports exceeded 50% in 1984–86. They do so "because the patterns of economic development for countries that rely for most of their income on oil are *sui generis*"; Przeworski et al., *Democracy and Development*, p. 77. These countries are Bahrain, Kuwait, Oman, Qatar, Saudi Arabia and the United Arab Emirates.

47. Boix, *Democracy and Redistribution*.

48. Boix and Stokes, "Endogenous Democratization," p. 535.

49. Ibid., p. 535.

50. For technical readers: Boix and Stokes drop observations if their Soviet indicator is equal to one, but they should drop observations if their *lagged* Soviet indicator is equal to one. Otherwise, transitions from Soviet dictatorships to democracy—Bulgaria, Czechoslovakia, and Hungary—all count as transitions at relatively high incomes. But all of the years that the Soviet dictatorships survived and for which we have data on income—Bulgaria 1981–89, Czechoslovakia 1961–89, and Hungary 1971–89, again at relatively high incomes—get dropped. To bring this into more detail, Boix and Stokes argue that they exclude Soviet-dominated countries (rather than using an indicator variable to identify these countries) because such a variable would be perfectly collinear with the regime variable: all Soviet-dominated countries are also authoritarian; ibid., n. 31. This, however, is true only if "Soviet-domination" is taken to be a time-invariant factor, which it is not. Now, given that it varies over time, the proper way for this variable to be entered into the Markov model—the model that both PACL and Boix and Stokes estimate—is lagged by at least one year: what matters for regime dynamics is not that the country was dominated by the Soviet Union this year but that it was dominated by it last year. Once this is done, the results reported by Boix and Stokes disappear.

Other countries under the influence of the Soviet Union also democratized in the period (e.g., Poland in 1989 and Romania in 1990). These countries, however, do not appear in the Boix and Stokes dataset because income data for these years are not available.

51. Seymour Martin Lipset, *Political Man: The Social Basis of Politics* (Garden City, NY: Doubleday, 1960), p. 57.

52. Michael L. Ross, "Does Oil Hinder Democracy?" *World Politics* 53 (2001): 325–61, and "But Seriously: Does Oil Really Hinder Democracy?" mimeo, UCLA Department of Political Science, 2008; Nathan Jensen and Leonard Wantchekon, "Resource Wealth and Political Regimes in Africa," *Comparative Political Studies* 37 (2004): 816–41. For a more nuanced view, see Thad Dunning, "Resource Dependence, Economic Performance, and Political Stability," *Journal of Conflict Resolution* 49, no. 4 (2005): 451–82.

53. Gassebner, Lamla, and Vreeland, "Extreme Bounds of Democracy." The argument about oil has also been applied to other natural resources. See, for example, Ricky Lam and Leonard Wantchekon, "Dictatorships as a Political Dutch Disease," mimeo, Department of Politics, New York University, 1999; Michael L. Ross, "How Does Natural Resource Wealth Influence Civil War? Evidence from Thirteen Cases," *International Organization* 58, no. 1 (2004): 35–67; Macartan Humphreys, "Natural Resources, Conflict, and Conflict Resolution: Uncovering the Mechanisms," *Journal of Conflict Resolution* 49, no. 4 (2005): 508–37; Piivi Lujala, Nils Petter Gleditsch, and Elisabeth Gilmore, "A Diamond Curse? Civil War and a Lootable Resource," *Journal of Conflict Resolution* 49,

no. 4 (2005): 538–62. On the question of oil and democracy in the Middle East, see Gassebner, Lamla, and Vreeland, "Extreme Bounds of Democracy," who argue that the paucity of democracy in the region is due to factor endowments, not culture. For more on the political institutions in the region, see Ellen Lust-Okar, *Structuring Conflict in the Arab World: Incumbents, Opponents, and Institutions* (New York: Cambridge University Press, 2005); and Nathan J. Brown, *Constitutions in a Nonconstitutional World: Arab Basic Laws and the Prospects for Accountable Government* (Albany: State University of New York Press, 2001).

54. Paul Collier, *The Bottom Billion: Why the Poorest Countries Are Failing and What Can Be Done about It* (New York: Oxford University Press, 2007), chap. 3; Paul Collier and Anke Hoeffler, "Testing the Neocon Agenda: Democracy in Resource-Rich Societies," *European Economic Review* 53, no. 3 (2009): 293–308; and Paul Collier and Anke Hoeffler, "Democracy and Resource Rents," mimeo, Department of Economics, University of Oxford, 2005.

55. See Cheibub, Gandhi, and Vreeland, "Democracy and Dictatorship Revisited," for a comparison of the PACL and Polity measures.

56. See Monty G. Marshall and Keith Jaggers, *Polity IV Project: Political Regime Characteristics and Transitions, 1800–2000* (www.cidcm.umd.edu/inscr/ polity/), cited in James Raymond Vreeland, "The Effect of Political Regime on Civil War: Unpacking Anocracy," *Journal of Conflict Resolution* 52, no. 3 (2008): 401–25.

57. To be clear, we view the Polity data collection project as an admirable effort, and take issue with the ways in which the data have been combined and employed in the transitions literature and political science more generally. The conceptualization, transparency, and quality of the Polity data are superior to that of another oft-used measure, Freedom House. The Freedom House measure of political regime has so many problems, there is not space here to address them all. Chief among the problems are: (1) numerous component variables are conflated into the measure in an ad hoc manner; (2) the data for the separate component variables are not publicly available; and (3) the coding rules change from year to year, and prior years are not updated according to the new rules, rendering the variable useless for cross-temporal work (e.g., regime dynamics). See Gerardo L. Munck and Jay Verkuilen, "Conceptualizing and Measuring Democracy: Evaluating Alternative Indices," *Comparative Political Studies* 35, no. 1 (2002): 5–34; Vreeland, "The Effect of Political Regime on Civil War: Unpacking Anocracy"; and Cheibub, Gandhi, and Vreeland, "Democracy and Dictatorship Revisited." In defense of the organization that produces the Freedom House measure, its primary purpose is not scholarship but rather the advocacy of "freedom." Serious scholars of political regime should avoid Freedom House.

58. Epstein et al., "Democratic Transitions," p. 566.

59. Ibid.

60. Ibid., p. 555.

61. Håvard Hegre, Tanja Ellingsen, Scott Gates, and Nils Petter Gleditsch, "Toward a Democratic Civil Peace? Democracy, Political Change, and Civil War, 1816–1992," *American Political Science Review* 95, no. 1 (2001): 33–48; James Fearon and David Laitin, "Ethnicity, Insurgency, and Civil War," *American Political Science Review* 97, no. 1 (2003): 75–90.

62. Gassebner, Lamla, and Vreeland, "Extreme Bounds of Democracy." Interestingly, Gassebner et al. do find evidence that a positive *change* in per capita income is associated

with the survival of dictatorships. So, economic growth actually prevents the emergence of democracy, which goes directly against proposition 1 and may be somewhat consistent with proposition 2. For a thorough empirical and theoretical investigation of this phenomenon, see Quinn, "Democracy and International Financial Reform."

63. Rosendorff, "Choosing Democracy"; Boix, *Democracy and Redistribution*; and Daron Acemoglu and James Robinson, *Economic Origins of Dictatorship and Democracy* (New York: Cambridge University Press, 2005).

64. Przeworski et al., *Democracy and Development*, p. 103.

65. Daron Acemoglu, Simon Johnson, James Robinson, and Pierre Yared, "Reevaluating the Modernization Hypothesis," unpublished manuscript, Cambridge, 2007; Acemoglu et al., "Income and Democracy."

66. Furthermore, the proposition is based on data that have been questioned. The data Acemoglu and his associates use to support their claim about the importance of critical junctures, specifically the critical juncture represented by the onset of European colonization of the rest of the world, are not entirely free of problems. There is an ongoing debate regarding Acemoglu's coding decisions, which we want to avoid here. Albouy, probably the most systematic of the critics of their data efforts, calls attention to the fact that there may be a bias in the coding decisions of the settler mortality rates toward assigning high values to countries that have "bad" institutions today; David Albouy, "The Colonial Origins of Comparative Development: An Investigation of the Settler Mortality Data," Center for International and Development Economics, Berkeley, 2006, Paper C04'138. For the beginning of the debate, see Daron Acemoglu, Simon Johnson, and James Robinson. "The Colonial Origins of Comparative Development: An Empirical Investigation," *American Economic Review* 91, no. 5 (2001): 1369–1401. See Daron Acemoglu, Simon Johnson, and James Robinson, "Reply to the Revised (May 2006) Version of David Albouy's 'The Colonial Origins of Comparative Development: An Investigation of the Settler Mortality Data,'" unpublished manuscript, Cambridge, 2006, for their reply to Albouy's charges. For a different critique, see John R. Freeman and Dennis P. Quinn, "The Economic Origins of Democracy Reconsidered," paper presented at the annual meeting of the American Political Science Association, Boston, 2008.

67. Acemoglu et al., "Reevaluating the Modernization Hypothesis," p. 5.

68. To ground this discussion in more of a statistical jargon, a "fixed effects" model is equivalent to including a separate variable that uniquely indentifies each country. So, if there are 135 countries in the sample, 134 additional variables are de facto included to "control" for the "Algeria" effect, the "Angola" effect, and all the way down to the "Zambia" effect, and the "Zimbabwe" effect.

69. The data on this factor actually come from one of the components of the POLITY measure of political regime.

70. On diffusion and democracy, see Zachary Elkins and Beth A. Simmons, "On Waves, Clusters, and Diffusion: A Conceptual Framework," *Annals of the American Academy of Political and Social Science* 598, no. 1, (2005): 33–51; also see Covadonga Meseguer, *Learning, Policy Making, and Market Reforms* (New York: Cambridge, 2009). On globalization and democracy, see Quan Li and Raphael Reuveny, "Economic Globalization and Democracy: An Empirical Analysis," *British Journal of Political Science* 33, no. 1, (2003): 29–54.

71. Rueschemeyer, Stephens, and Stephens, *Capitalist Development and Democracy*; Lipset, *Political Man*.

72. Bolivar Lamounier, "Opening through Elections: Will the Brazilian Case Become a Paradigm?" *Government and Opposition* 19, no. 2 (1984): 167–77.

73. Bruce J. Dickson, *Democratization in China and Taiwan: The Adaptability of Leninist Parties* (Oxford: Oxford University Press, 1998).

74. Gerardo Luis Munck, *Authoritarianism and Democratization: Soldiers and Workers in Argentina, 1976–1983* (University Park: Pennsylvania State University Press, 1998); Terry Karl, "Dilemmas of Democratization in Latin America," *Comparative Politics* 23, no. 1 (1990): 1–21.

75. Bumba Mukherjee, "Why Political Power-Sharing Agreements Lead to Enduring Peaceful Resolution of Some Civil Wars, but Not Others?" *International Studies Quarterly* 50, no. 2 (2006): 479–504.

76. Daniel Brinks and Michael Coppedge, "Diffusion Is No Illusion: Neighbor Emulation in the Third Wave of Democracy," *Comparative Political Studies* 39, no. 4 (2006): 463–89.

77. In this chapter, we have exclusively focused on development as a determinant of political regime. Students and policy makers who are curious about other factors might consider starting with studies that have a regional angle, such as Berman, "How Democracies Emerge"; Gregg Brazinsky, *Nation Building in South Korea: Koreans, Americans, and the Making of a Democracy* (Chapel Hill: University of North Carolina Press, 2007); Valerie Bunce, "Rethinking Recent Democratization: Lessons from the Postcommunist Experience," *World Politics* 55 (2003): 167–92; M. Steven Fish and Omar Choudhry, "Democratization and Economic Liberalization in the Postcommunist World," *Comparative Political Studies* 40, no. 3 (2007): 254–82; Henry E. Hale, "Regime Cycles: Democracy, Autocracy, and Revolution in Post-Soviet Eurasia," *World Politics* 58, no. 1 (2005): 133–65; Henry E. Hale, "Democracy or Autocracy on the March? The Colored Revolutions as Normal Dynamics of Patronal Presidentialism," *Communist and Post-Communist Studies* 39 (2006): 305–29; Francis Hagopian and Scott Mainwaring, eds., *The Third Wave of Democratization in Latin America: Advances and Setbacks* (New York: Cambridge University Press, 2005); Staffan I. Lindberg, *Democracy and Elections in Africa* (Baltimore: Johns Hopkins University Press, 2006); and John C. Pevehouse, *Democracy from Above: Regional Organizations and Democratization* (New York: Cambridge University Press, 2005), among many others.

# CHAPTER 7

# Persistent Authoritarianism and the Future of Democracy in Africa

## *Staffan I. Lindberg and Sara Meerow*

Africa is in many ways one of the most exciting and interesting places in the world today when it comes to studying dictatorship and democracy. When the "third wave" hit the African continent there was an outburst of optimistic scholarship voicing hopes for a "second liberation"[1] that soon turned into sour commentaries on the lack of "real" change.[2] The picture is in reality mixed with some countries moving ahead and becoming more free (e.g., Ghana) while others drag their feet (e.g., Nigeria) or regress (e.g., Zimbabwe). About a quarter of all the world's states are found on the continent and it accordingly has produced a wide variety in terms of political institutions and outcomes. Out of sub-Saharan Africa's forty-eight countries, about twenty can today be considered relatively democratic by a minimum standard definition, while another twenty or so are electoral authoritarian in various guises from Nigeria to Zimbabwe, and five countries are decisively autocratic (Angola, Ivory Coast, Eritrea, Somalia, Swaziland). Table 7.1 provides a snapshot of the state of elections and democracy in Africa as of 2008.

Democratization in Africa after the end of the Cold War was first analyzed comprehensively by Bratton and van de Walle in their seminal contribution emphasizing mobilization of civil society and popular protest before "founding elections" as the key explanatory factor to successful transitions.[3] Later research has, however, demonstrated that that finding was not robust.[4] Most democratization processes in Africa have been prolonged, and rather than marking the end of transitions, "founding" elections have more often been their starting point. Repetition of electoral processes, even if flawed to begin with, and without interventions by a coup or similar event, have been driving democratization forward.[5] Similar dynamics that go against the orthodoxy of our understanding of the key factors of democratization have been found

*Table 7.1.* African Regimes, Number of Successive Elections Held, and Freedom House Political Rights (PR)/Civil Liberties (CL) Score, 2008

| | No Elections | PR | CL | One Election | PR | CL | Two Elections | PR | CL | Three Elections | PR | CL | Four or More | PR | CL |
|---|---|---|---|---|---|---|---|---|---|---|---|---|---|---|---|
| (Electoral) autocracies | Angola | 6 | 5 | Burundi | 4 | 5 | Nigeria | 4 | 5 | Burkina Faso | 5 | 3 | Gabon | 6 | 4 |
| | Ivory Coast | 6 | 5 | Central African Rep. | 5 | 5 | Sudan | 7 | 7 | Cameroon | 6 | 6 | Togo | 5 | 5 |
| | Eritrea | 7 | 6 | Democratic Rep. Congo | 6 | 6 | | | | Chad | 7 | 6 | Zimbabwe | 7 | 6 |
| | Somalia | 7 | 7 | Guinea Bissau | 4 | 4 | | | | Djibouti | 5 | 5 | | | |
| | Swaziland | 7 | 5 | Mauritania | 6 | 5 | | | | Eq. Guinea | 7 | 7 | | | |
| | | | | Rwanda | 6 | 5 | | | | Ethiopia | 5 | 5 | | | |
| | | | | Rep. of Congo | 6 | 5 | | | | Gambia | 5 | 4 | | | |
| | | | | | | | | | | Guinea | 7 | 5 | | | |
| Electoral democracies | | | | Liberia | 3 | 4 | Comoros | 3 | 4 | Kenya | 4 | 3 | Benin | 2 | 2 |
| | | | | Sierra Leone | 3 | 3 | Lesotho | 2 | 3 | Malawi | 4 | 4 | Botswana | 2 | 2 |
| | | | | | | | Niger | 3 | 4 | Mozambique | 3 | 3 | Cape Verde | 1 | 1 |
| | | | | | | | | | | São Tomé | 2 | 2 | Ghana | 1 | 2 |
| | | | | | | | | | | South Africa | 2 | 2 | Madagascar | 4 | 3 |
| | | | | | | | | | | Tanzania | 4 | 3 | Mali | 2 | 3 |
| | | | | | | | | | | Uganda | 5 | 4 | Mauritius | 1 | 2 |
| | | | | | | | | | | | | | Namibia | 2 | 2 |
| | | | | | | | | | | | | | Senegal | 3 | 3 |
| | | | | | | | | | | | | | Seychelles | 3 | 3 |
| | | | | | | | | | | | | | Zambia | 3 | 3 |
| Mean rating | | 6.6 | 5.6 | | 4.8 | 4.7 | | 3.8 | 4.6 | | 4.7 | 4.1 | | 3.0 | 2.9 |

among the postcommunist countries, and more generally across the globe, in the post–Cold War era.[6] Yet, there are other factors that we need to take into account, and natural resource abundance perhaps is one of the most important.

Oil and minerals provide the majority of energy supplies and raw materials for manufacturing. Their prices have immediate effects on financial markets and foreign direct investment, and they are only growing in geostrategic importance between the world's major and emerging powers. With increasing demand, a nation with vast natural resource reserves could potentially harness momentous resources for developmental purposes. Because democracy tends to survive in more affluent countries,[7] this should also be good news for democracy. However, many studies reveal that rather than encouraging economic development, abundant natural resources, in particular oil wealth, actually hinder development and prevent democratization.[8]

This chapter first discusses some of the established literature on the effects of natural resource abundance on democratization and then shows how an empirical analysis of the relationship supports the theoretical expectations. We also reveal an underresearched aspect of the "resource curse." On the basis of data from the forty-eight African countries over the past twenty-four years (1985–2008), we find that if such "cursed" states, against the odds, manage to make substantial gains in terms of democracy, they are dramatically more likely than other states to backslide and revert to authoritarianism. Natural resource richness not only tends to prevent democratization but also is a major factor in democratic backsliding and erosion of democratic gains.

Finally, we move to a multivariate analysis of democratization in Africa that is based on what the literature has found to be some of the main explanatory factors. In the end, we find that three factors stand out as the main factors systematically related to democratization: repetitive elections and significant levels of aid together push democratization and sustain democracy, while the resource curse prevents liberalization and undermines democratization.

## Resource Abundance and Democracy

Quite a body of research has developed on oil-rich states in the Middle East,[9] Latin America,[10] and globally.[11] While theories dealing with the resource curse have come to a relative agreement that resource dependency perpetuates authoritarianism and causes increased risk of internal violent conflict, there is no clear consensus among scholars as to why this is the case. The (then) seemingly counterintuitive finding that states at the receiving end of the largest sum of wealth ever transferred without war continue to be some of the most economically and politically unstable in the world was first labeled the "paradox of plenty."[12] What turns the blessing of abundant natural resources into a curse? While many resource curse theories have it that natural resource–dependent states tend to have a higher propensity for political instability and conflict[13] (even if the causal stories differ to some extent),[14] there is increasing evidence that it actually increases the durability of authoritarian regimes. In contrast to Karl's earlier study, Smith and Omgba for example, find that oil wealth increases the durability of regimes.[15] The causal argument is that stability is achieved if the government either maintains control of the extraction or monopolizes the revenue from resources to prevent the breeding of economically independent opposition groups.[16] Rather than simply attributing the so called Dutch Disease to shortsighted economic mismanagement and selfishness, it is a conscious effort on the part of ruling elites to maintain power and prevent conflict.[17]

The contemporary literature thus suggests that resource-abundant states are in a high-risk zone of persistent authoritarian rule preventing democratization. This "preventive" effect consists in part of strengthening existing authoritarian regimes' coercive and patronage power and in part of creating incentives for another extractive dictatorship in the case of regime breakdown.[18] Large "unearned" revenues go directly to the state, and elites can use them relatively freely to build the coercive power of the state to deter potential opposition groups. They are also in a position to freely expand patronage to co-opt social forces, thus further concentrating power at the state level.[19] Rapid expansion and centralization of the national government are almost inevitable,[20] and these new means are typically used to perpetuate authoritarian rule. Natural resource revenue also tends to fund and encourage corruption, which further undermines political development when potential opposition forces are "bought off."[21]

Ross for example, finds that significant oil exports negatively affect the likelihood of democracy even when controlling for income, Islam, membership in the OECD, past regime type, and geographic region, noting that the effect appears stronger on poor states than on rich ones.[22] The results support the "rentier state" argument that governments of resource-rich countries can dampen public pressure for democratization by reducing the need for taxation, increasing government spending and patronage, and discouraging the formation of nongovernmental groups.[23] But there is also support for the thesis that governments use natural resource profits to build up their security forces and generally squelch opposition and protests.[24] Given that these findings are stronger for poor countries, one would imagine that the "preventive" effects of the resource curse on democratic development would be exacerbated in the poverty-stricken countries in Africa. This is closely related to Wantchekon's concept of the incumbency advantage: the incumbents receiving large oil profits to distribute at their discretion to pay off the opposition, encourage support with patronage, or create security forces to crush any protests or coup attempts.[25] His argument is corroborated by a study of 141 countries showing a negative correlation between natural resource exports and the likelihood of democracy.[26] In another study, Jensen and Wantchekon find that disparities in the democratic development of resource-rich and resource-poor countries are even more evident after Africa's wave of political reforms in the 1990s, thus further supporting the idea that resource dependence impedes the development of democracies.[27]

Smith similarly suggests two major causal trajectories among resource-rich countries that both support authoritarianism, even if his explanations differ somewhat from the previously mentioned authors.[28] He claims that "durable authoritarian" regimes were characterized by a relatively stable coalition of power brokers undergirding the regime before discovery and exploitation of natural resources, and thus these regimes had no need to rely primarily on repression or patronage once oil was discovered. Because such regimes are able to ride out the roller coaster of economic booms and busts,[29] democratization is prevented. "Vulnerable authoritarianism," on the other hand, emerges when the oil industry precedes or coincides with the foundation of the regime, creating incentives for elites with short time horizons to extract as much wealth as possible as fast as possible. Hence, they tend to maintain power by repressive means and use as little patronage as possible, thus providing at best unreliable loyalty. When the economy is in crisis, the institutions are not in place to maintain such governments, and thus they are more often overthrown. Yet, when vulnerable authoritarian governments fall, they are typically succeeded by a new extractive authoritarian regime.[30] Thus, in both cases we would expect natural resource abundance to have a preventive effect on democratization. In the twenty-one oil-exporting countries Smith studies, only five actually experience regime transitions. Smith's findings are especially relevant to this chapter, as three out of the five regime transitions his study includes take place in African countries: one in the Republic of Congo and two in Nigeria.[31] The Republic of Congo has since experienced two further periods of instability and currently receives among the worst Freedom House ratings on the continent. Nigeria experienced two military coups in the 1990s and has since 1999 barely managed to uphold a competitive electoral authoritarian regime.

The existing theories thus all share the notion that large unearned revenues from concentrated natural resources should have a preventive effect on democratization. We therefore set out to test this hypothesis with regard to Africa's forty-eight states over the past twenty-four years. If the resource curse theory's prediction about a preventive effect on democratization applies to Africa, states that are dependent on natural resources should be more authoritarian than those without resources.

But this does not exhaust the theoretical possibilities. If the resource curse has only a preventive effect, this effect should vanish once liberalization has taken off and a country has started to democratize. Backsliding after initial democratization is thus a different theoretical issue. If (against the odds) resource-abundant countries start to liberalize and move toward democracy, their characteristics should make it more likely that gains will erode and liberalizing regimes will fall back into authoritarianism.

Only Jensen and Wantchekon have directly alluded to the idea that resource wealth also decreases the chances of liberalization efforts succeeding,[32] but there has not been empirical research done on whether resource wealth makes it more likely that a liberalizing country will fall back into authoritarianism. There are several reasons why one would expect backsliding to occur. Liberalization involves increasing the amount of information open to the public, as well as more unconstrained reporting of such information in media. This factor on its own should reduce the rent opportunities available to elite actors and the possibilities for them to channel such resources in undisclosed patronage networks. These are only tendencies, of course, and no one expects anything but relative changes. Nevertheless, the possibilities should be obvious to rulers and thus pose a potential threat. At the same time, political liberalization opens up the possibility of more free civic and political organization that, in effect, should increase the need for rulers to spend more on patronage and public goods provisions. It would be in their strategic interest to prevent this by reversing liberalization. In resource-rich countries of the rentier state kind, the capabilities associated with coercive force and strong patronage networks should make such efforts particularly "successful." In short, political liberalization in states dependent on natural resources should be more frequently stalled and should lead to backsliding more often than in other states.

There are several reasons for the focus on Africa. Although much research has been done on the political effects of the resource curse theory, the issue of regional causal heterogeneity versus universal claims remains an empirical question that should be investigated, not assumed. At the same time, the wave of democratization starting in the 1990s has enlarged the number of people living in relative freedom manifold, and for the first time in decades, most African economies have been experiencing significant economic growth over the past ten to fifteen years. The potential resource curse effects thus threaten strategic interests, as well as human political and economic freedom. In addition to supplementing the existing literature, the implications of any findings could extend to leaders questioning how best to encourage the liberalization and development of a violent and troubled continent.

Finally, the rapid expansion of the ore, oil, and mineral industries in a large number of African nations is increasingly affecting the political and strategic significance of the continent. Africa has about 12 percent of the world's oil supply and accounts for 19 percent of U.S. oil imports, with projections that this figure will rise to 25 percent in the near future. Energy production, not surprisingly, has almost doubled since 1970 and is expected to increase by another 68 percent by 2020.[33] Recently, oil prices, conflicts in the Middle East, changes in Latin American oil-producing countries such as Venezuela, and the increasingly assertive stance by the world's leading producer of oil and natural gas—Russia—have pushed Western countries to invest more in Africa. The continent is also rich in many precious metals that are in increasing demand such as gold, cobalt, and copper. An estimated 30 percent of Africans live in a resource-rich country, while that number is an average of 11 percent for the other developing nations.[34] Increased oil, mineral, and ore profits for the poor and underdeveloped countries on the continent thus should cause severe resource curse effects. Anecdotal illustrations seem to corroborate this expectation. In Angola, crude oil exports brought $7.1 billion into the country in 2000, representing 89.4 percent of the fiscal revenue. Over the period of 1985 to 2007, oil, ores, and minerals represented on average 99.7 percent of merchandise exports in Angola, while the country's average combined Freedom House political rights and civil liberties score was only 2 on a scale from 0 to 12 for the same twenty-three-year period, designating it as staunchly authoritarian.[35] In Botswana, on the other hand, oil and minerals account for an average of 7 percent of merchandise exports during the period 1985–2007, and the country has the only regime that has been consistently democratic (in fact, since independence in 1966), with a mean Freedom House political rights and civil liberties score of 10.3 over that time. Similarly, Ghana has liberalized from a score of 1 to 11 in those years, and it too is not overly dependent on concentrated natural resource exports, seeing as fuel and minerals, despite significant gold extraction, account for just over 16 percent of merchandise exports. These are only illustrations, of course; hence, we turn to a systematic evaluation of the two hypotheses.

## Measuring Resource Dependence

Typically, a state under a general resource curse is defined as one that is economically dependent on a single or a few capital-intensive, depletable resources with a large rent capacity, the spoils of which go directly to the state as part of a foreign-controlled, high-wage economy.[36] Karl uses the World Bank's definition of an oil-exporting country as one in which petroleum accounts for at least 10 percent of the GDP and 40 percent of total merchandise exports. We do not limit our investigation to only oil-abundant states because none of the hypothesized effects discussed previously are specific to oil dependency, and therefore the independent variable is a measure of the extent to which the states' economies are dependent on the export of a range of natural resources, using data from the World Bank Development Indicators (WBDI). To determine resource dependency, the average value of fuel, ores, and minerals (as a percentage of merchandise exports) is calculated for the period from 1985 to 2007, based on the years with data available for each country.[37] To differentiate whether a state is heavily dependent on natural resources, we use the World Bank definition, drawing the line at 40 percent of merchandise exports.[38] The result is that sixteen, or one-third, of the forty-eight African states fall under the label of "resource-curse countries" (see table 7.2).

Table 7.2.  Resource Dependency in Africa

| Country | Resource-Curse Country? | Mean Oil, Ores, and Minerals (as % of merchandise exports 1985–2007) |
|---|---|---|
| Angola | Yes | 99.70 |
| Benin | No | 12.87 |
| Botswana | No | 7.08 |
| Burkina | No | 1.75 |
| Burundi | No | 2.28 |
| Cameroon | Yes | 43.91 |
| Cape Verde | No | 36.87 |
| Central African Rep. | No | 21.80 |
| Chad | Yes | n.a. |
| Comoros | No | 0.38 |
| Democratic Rep. Congo | Yes | n.a. |
| Congo | Yes | 89.89 |
| Cote d'Ivoire | No | 13.00 |
| Djibouti | No | n.a. |
| Equatorial Guinea | Yes | n.a. |
| Eritrea | No | n.a. |
| Ethiopia | No | 2.19 |
| Gabon | Yes | 80.23 |
| Gambia | No | 1.46 |
| Ghana | No | 16.66 |
| Guinea | Yes | 69.28 |
| Guinea Bissau | No | 4.61 |
| Kenya | No | 14.89 |
| Lesotho | No | n.a. |
| Liberia | Yes | n.a. |
| Madagascar | No | 8.51 |
| Malawi | No | 0.26 |
| Mali | No | 3.79 |
| Mauritania | Yes | 44.7 |
| Mauritius | No | 0.61 |
| Mozambique | No | 28.50 |
| Namibia | No | 10.79 |
| Niger | Yes | 44.28 |
| Nigeria | Yes | 96.76 |
| Rwanda | No | 20.84 |
| São Tomé | No | n.a. |
| Senegal | No | 25.95 |
| Seychelles | Yes | 45.08 |
| Sierra Leone | Yes | n.a. |

(continued)

*Table 7.2.  (continued)*

| Country | Resource-Curse Country? | Mean Oil, Ores, and Minerals (as % of merchandise exports 1985–2007) |
|---|---|---|
| Somalia | No | n.a. |
| South Africa | No | 21.33 |
| Sudan | Yes | 40.11 |
| Swaziland | No | 0.78 |
| Tanzania | No | 6.48 |
| Togo | No | 33.16 |
| Uganda | No | 4.13 |
| Zambia | Yes | 74.53 |
| Zimbabwe | No | 15.57 |

Our starting point is 1985 because before this time data are limited and the years following mainly represent the post–Cold War era. The average value over the period is used rather than any single year's data in order to get a more theoretically valid measure. The figures on merchandise exports fluctuate greatly from year to year in many states, especially in developing nations in general, and in states exporting various forms of raw materials and natural resources in particular. For the Seychelles, for example, mineral and fuel exports in 1985 represent 82 percent of exports, but in 2003 just 20 percent. If the 1985 figure was used, Seychelles would be extremely resource dependent, but according to the data from 2003 it would not. Similarly, in 2003 minerals and fuels accounted for 53 percent of Cameroon's merchandise exports, making it resource rich; yet they represented just 18 percent in 1986. Resource curse studies using data from only a single year, because of the variable annual statistics, are susceptible to skewed estimations of real effects.[39] We therefore follow Jensen and Wantchekon in employing an independent variable calculated using the average fuel, mineral, and metal exports as a percentage of merchandise exports over an extended period.[40] They also use data from the WBDI but for the period from 1970 to 1995.[41]

This variation is a serious concern. None of the theories suggest that the resource curse effects should materialize or disappear following fluctuations over one year or a few years. To the contrary, all causal claims are based on longer-term processes, and using a measure that captures resource dependence over an extended period of time is the most valid option. Time-series analyses can in such instances produce results that are hard to interpret in terms of the theory, when a significant number of units have large variations on the independent variables from year to year affecting the estimations, while most of the theoretical claims are about nonlinear effects of sustained resource wealth. The nonlinearity is something we also wish to take seriously. No theory is suggesting that a small amount of natural resources should make any difference. It is not as if we expect that an increase in "dependence" on natural resources from, say, 5 percent to 8 or even18 percent would lead to a symmetric increase in the negative effects observed from a very large dependence on these resources. The suggested cutoff point by most authors is 40 percent, which is when we expect the negative effects to start materializing. We therefore created a threshold measure (level of resource curse) equivalent to the theoretical expectations, where a combined average value of exports of fuel and minerals less than 40 percent of merchandise exports is given the value of zero in the statistical analysis. Any figure above that threshold retains its factual value. We also created a dummy variable (resource-curse country?) for resource-curse countries where the same threshold is used and resource dependent countries are coded one.

## Liberalization and Democratization

In order to measure democracy, we take as our point of departure the classic definition of a democracy as that of the "polyarchy," which requires free contestation and general public participation.[42] In operational terms, we need a graded scale, rather than a dichotomous measure, in order to be able to measure both levels of democracy and changes indicating liberalization even in the face of a less-than-democratic state of affairs in a country. A reasonable and widely used measure of "polyarchy" is the Freedom House political rights and civil liberties scores.[43] The Freedom House scores have been shown to correlate strongly with other alternative measures of democracy, such as the Polity IV used by Wantchekon.[44] We construct three alternative measures. Because the independent variable is being averaged over a twenty-three-year period, it would seem logical to measure the similarly long-term effects on democracy. Allowing for some time lag, the first dependent variable is the average country-year Freedom House combined ratings for the twenty-year period 1989–2008.[45] But it could be argued that the time lag should be longer and that what is more interesting is the effect on democracy in the latter part of the period. We therefore also constructed a variable measuring the average combined scores from the past decade (1998–2008). Finally, we also took this argument to its extreme and used the single-year combined country-score for 2008.[46] If the results regarding the "prevention hypothesis" are similar for these three different measures, the findings should be relatively robust.

To test the "fall-back hypothesis," a different measure is needed. When average scores for the entire period are examined, resource-poor Burkina Faso is deemed more authoritarian than resource-rich Zambia; however, looking at the scores over time, Burkina Faso shows a clear liberalizing trend while Zambia makes some gains from 1989 to 1992 but then falls back by 1997. To test the fallback hypothesis, we thus examine the data from 1989 to 2008 for the combined civil liberties and political rights scores and classify all states' trajectories into one of three categories. States with scores constantly lower (worse) than 6 with little improvement are deemed *authoritarian*. A score of 6 on the scale from 0 to 12 is used as the cutoff point because, according to Freedom House, states with a an average Freedom House (original) score of 4 are considered "transitional government or hybrid regimes," which would equate to a 6 in our reversed, combined civil liberties and political rights measure. Countries that show a clear liberalizing trend, indicating steady improvement over time, and that either remain at or finish out the period with a score of 6 or better are categorized as *liberalizing*.[47] The final category, labeled *fallback*, includes all those states which are fluctuating greatly by beginning to liberalize (improving 4 or more points) and then falling back (2 or more points).

If natural resource dependency prevents democratization by not only making initial transitioning difficult but moreover, and in particular, diminishing the likelihood of reform success, the analysis of Freedom House scores over a twenty-year period should reflect this. Those states which have significant amounts of oil and minerals should be overrepresented in the authoritarian category. But we are particularly interested in the fallback and liberalized categories. If the hypothesis about a fallback effect is true, countries with high natural resource dependency should be overrepresented in the fallback category.

## Double Pains: Preventing Liberalization and Reversing Democratization

A bivariate analysis of the direct relationship between resource dependence and the average level of democracy, as well as the level of democracy in

*Table 7.3.* Relationship between Resource Curse and Level of Democracy

| | Freedom House[a] | | |
|---|---|---|---|
| | 1989–2008 | 1998–2008 | 2008 |
| Level of resource curse[b] | | | |
| Pearson's | –.359 | –.334 | –.330 |
| $p$ | .012 | .021 | .022 |
| $N$ | 48 | 48 | 48 |

[a] The years for Freedom House refers to the year of measure; the reports were published in the following year (hence, "2008" refers to the ranking of 2009). Values represent political rights plus civil liberties ratings combined, reverted into a 0–12 scale.

[b] If average share of merchandise exports made up of oil, ore, and minerals in 1985–2006 is less than 40 percent, the country is coded "0," if above 40 percent the actual value is used (missing values for four countries imputed with mean of the latter group).

2008, shows a strong and negative impact of the resource curse (table 7.3). African states that are more dependent on natural resources have a record of being clearly more authoritarian than their less-endowed counterparts over a long period.[48] In short, this initial analysis provides a strong support for the hypothesis of a preventive effect of natural resource curse on democratization.

As an alternative means of analysis, an ANOVA comparison of means was conducted using our dummy variable for resource-curse countries (table 7.4). Again we find that the resource-rich countries have lower Freedom House scores, regardless of measure, and the differences are statistically significant.

Before subjecting these findings to multivariate tests, we consider the fallback hypothesis. As shown in table 7.5, trends in Freedom House scores over time indicate a very strong relationship in the expected direction. Resource-curse countries not only are overrepresented in the category of authoritarian states, as the "preventive effect" hypothesis predicts, but are also highly (and statistically significantly) overrepresented in the category of countries that liberalized early but have since fallen back and become authoritarian again. While 44 percent of resource-curse countries have remained consistently authoritarian over the period, only 25 percent of other states are found in this category. Another 50 percent of the states dependent on natural resources are found in the category of countries that have liberalized but fallen back, while only 19 percent of the other states end up in this predicament. In short, there seems to be a strong fallback effect at work, in addition to the preventive effect already discussed in the literature.

Table 7.4.  Comparison of Means

| | "Resource-Curse" Country? | | |
| | No | Yes | ANOVA-F and p |
| --- | --- | --- | --- |
| Freedom House[a] | | | |
| 1989–2008 | | | |
| Mean | 5.69 | 3.37 | 8.739 |
| SD | 2.81 | 1.95 | .005 |
| 1998–2008 | | | |
| Mean | 6.22 | 3.88 | 7.083 |
| SD | 3.13 | 2.28 | .011 |
| 2008 | | | |
| Mean | 6.41 | 3.94 | 6.607 |
| SD | 3.26 | 2.86 | .013 |
| N | 32 | 16 | |

[a] The years for Freedom House refer to the year of measure; the reports were published in the following year (hence, "2008" refers to the ranking of 2009). Values represent political rights plus civil liberties ratings combined, reverted into a 0–12 scale.

Table 7.5.  Resource Dependence and Liberalization, N (%)

| | Authoritarian | Fallback | Liberalized | Total |
| --- | --- | --- | --- | --- |
| "Resource-curse" country? | | | | |
| No | 8 (25) | 6 (19) | 18 (56) | 32 (100) |
| Yes | 7 (44) | 8 (50) | 1 (6) | 16 (100) |
| Total N | 15 | 14 | 19 | 48 |

Note: Chi square value = 11.508; $p = .003$.

Expressed differently, 47 percent ($N = 7$) of the fifteen authoritarian states are resource-dependent countries, while they make up only 33 percent of the total number of states. Out of the fallback states, 57 percent, or eight out of the fourteen, are rich in natural resources, and a mere 5 percent, or one out of the nineteen liberalized countries, is a resource-rich state. The differences are statistically significant ($p < .01$) and thus support the hypothesis that resources hinder democratic development and liberalization in two ways: they make it likely that a country remains authoritarian and, if liberalization is successfully initiated, make it highly likely that it will eventually fail.

If we take another perspective on these figures, the differences are put in even starker relief. There were almost no differences between the two groups in terms of the share of countries that liberalized at first (64 % of resource-rich countries and 75 % of resource-poor states), but there was *a vast disparity* in how successful these reforms were. In the subsample to which the fallback effect should apply (countries that liberalized), 89 percent of the resource-curse countries fell back into authoritarianism compared to only 25 percent of resource-poor states. In terms of success rates, only 11 percent of resource-dependent countries succeeded with liberalization compared to 75 percent of the other countries. In short, resource-dependent countries in Africa are much less likely to attempt any form of substantial political liberalization, and when they do so, they almost always fail and fall back into authoritarianism.

Finally, we checked these findings for a potential source of spuriousness. If some resource-dependent countries manage to diversify their economies and then became more democratic, then our analyses would classify them as not resource dependent and democratic to support our hypotheses, whereas, in fact, such cases would speak against them. In the available data from 1985 to 2007, we find only two cases of substantial diversification in Africa. Togo managed to reduce its dependence on minerals and ores from around 50 percent to less than 10 percent during the period. Its overall average is lower than 40 percent of merchandise exports, so it is not classified as a resource-curse country. Hence, it is not a source of spuriousness. The other case is the Seychelles, which reduced its dependence on oil exports from more than 80 percent in 1985 to less than 20 percent in 2003, whereafter its dependence went up to more than 35 percent again over the course of the following five years. It is classified as a resource-curse country in the analysis and is the only case in table 7.5 of such countries that successfully liberalized. Again, it is therefore not a source of spurious relationships. Finally, we also exchanged the Freedom House scores for Polity IV to check if our findings were sensitive to choice of democracy indicator, but none of our findings were substantially altered.

## Explaining Democratization in Africa?

We need to subject the findings about the negative impact of natural resource wealth in Africa to more sophisticated testing. In the following we therefore use as the dependent variable the level of political development along the autocracy-democracy scale as of 2008, as indicated by the combined Freedom House scores for that year on our reversed scale. To capture the threshold nature of the expected relationship with natural resource wealth, we use both of the measures previously discussed in detail. The first alternative explanation of democratization we need to control for is what has been called the "democratization-by-elections" thesis.[49] The operationalization is easy, and we use Lindberg's measure of the number of successive elections (without interruption of a coup or similar event) from 1989 (or the start of a multiparty electoral regime immediately before that) to January 2007.[50] Another obvious suspect for an intervening variable or factor behind possible spurious findings is international influences. In Africa, it is reliance on foreign aid that, through political conditionalities, could be suspected to be instrumental in pressuring authoritarian regimes into both holding elections and improving the level of democracy.[51] This hypothesis has been the object of studies claiming a zero relationship[52] but also others demonstrating a positive relationship.[53] We use the commonly accepted measure of total overseas aid in current U.S. dollars based on data provided by the World Bank, but we seek to achieve a better standardization for cross-national comparison. In terms of providing means for public goods, order, and patronage that can reasonably mitigate domestic pressures for reform, the value should be calculated per capita. We thus use total annual aid per capita as the baseline. However, such values also vary substantially on a year-to-year basis and regimes want to stay in power for the long run. In order to compensate for short-term fluctuations and to capture the possibility of the influence of donors that may take years to materialize, but also to allow for some amount of time lag between the independent variable and the outcome, we calculate the average annual per capita aid from 1989 to 2006.

The modernization hypothesis, originally phrased by Lipset, that the more well-to-do a nation is, the more likely it will sustain democracy, must certainly also be included.[54] Rowen, for example, observed that in 1990—around the time this study takes as its empirical departure—among the twenty-eight countries with a per capita income more than $8,000 per year, only Singapore was rated less than free by Freedom House.[55] Many studies have corroborated the thesis through measures of modernization based on economic indicators,[56] while the earlier studies used a range of social as well as economic indicators.[57] We measure level of development by the typical measure of GDP per capita adjusted for purchasing power parities, using data from the WBDI from 1989 in order to allow for substantial time-lagged effects to materialize.

One of the most influential recent studies, however, claims modernization theory has little if any explanatory power to offer.[58] Instead, it suggests that democracies are much more likely to survive under prosperity. Similarly, it has been claimed that economic development facilitates progress of democratization.[59] In order to assess this possible confounding effect, we include GDP per capita adjusted for purchasing power parities with data from 1998. If higher levels of economic development help democracies survive, a reasonable point of measuring this seems to be about halfway through the time period. Because of collinearity problems, this factor is assessed in a separate model. In addition, average annual growth rates from the ten-year period from 1996 to 2005, with data also from the World Bank, are used to test for regime performance on the basis of the established idea that good performance should act as a stabilizer and prevent democratic breakdowns.

Another robust finding has been the consistently negative impact of Islam, found both in Lipset's early article[60] and in later additions.[61] To assess the importance of this variable, the more or less constant share of the population that adheres to Islam is employed in the model with data from Bratton and van de Walle's dataset.[62] Another and related issue recently high on the agenda is ethnolinguistic fractionalization, where the debate on the soundness of various measures has been hotly contested.[63] Regardless of that debate, however, a high level of fractionalization has been thought to impede democratization by infusing the polity with high stakes that are in fierce competition in more traditionally based societies. The ethnic heterogeneity index from Ellingsen is used,[64] which also has a distinct advantage in providing coverage of all cases.

Finally, Lipset et al., in the aftermath of the revolutionary changes in eastern Europe and Africa after 1989, tested the influence of popular mobilizations on democratization.[65] In Africa, this became the perhaps most renowned finding from Bratton and van de Walle's study: that popular protests were one of the key driving forces in the introduction of democracy on the continent.[66] This finding has been questioned, however, by using the original dataset,[67] but it is still influential in the literature and therefore merits closer scrutiny, and it is included using Bratton and van de Walle's own measure of the number of politically motivated protests from 1985 to 1994.[68] Using this set of variables, we ran a total of five models.[69]

Reading table 7.6 in which the statistically significant results have been put in bold, a pretty unambiguous picture of democratization in Africa after

*Table 7.6.* Explaining the Level of Democracy in Africa: The Resource Curse and Other Factors

| Variable | Indicators | Dependent Variable: Freedom House Combined Political Rights and Civil Liberties, 2008[a] | | | | |
|---|---|---|---|---|---|---|
| | | Model 1 | Model 2 | Model 3 | Model 4 | Model 5 |
| Resource curse | Level of resource curse[b] | −.036 (.015) *.021* | −.032 (.015) *.044* | −.022 (.012) *.081* | | |
| | Resource-curse country[c] (dummy) | | | | −2.914 (1.028) *.008* | −1.853 (.842) *.033* |
| Elections | Number of successive repetitive elections as of January 2007 | .677 (.343) *.058* | .743 (.348) *.041* | .727 (.215) *.002* | .683 (.328) *.046* | .712 (.211) *.002* |
| International influence | Average total value of aid per capita (current U.S.), 1989–2006 | .021 (.011) *.052* | .023 (.010) *.039* | .016 (.007) *.025* | .026 (.010) *.017* | .016 (.007) *.018* |
| Economic development | GDP per capita/PPP, 1989 | .000 (.000) *.825* | | | | |
| | GDP per capita/PPP, 1998 | | .000 (.000) *.421* | | .000 (.000) *.615* | |
| Regime performance | Average GDP growth, 1996– 2005 | .206 (.163) *.217* | .208 (.161) *.207* | | .195 (.153) *.212* | |
| Religion | Moslems share of population, ca. 1985 | −.009 (.015) *.554* | −.012 (.015) *.425* | | −.004 (.015) *.805* | |
| Ethnicity | Ethnic fractionaliza- tion index, ca. 1990 | .016 (.022) *.481* | .011 (.022) *.637* | | .014 (.021) *.503* | |
| Popular mobilization | Number of popular protests, 1985–1994 | .041 (.063) *.522* | .043 (.062) *.494* | | .055 (.060) *.363* | |

(*continued*)

*Table 7.6.*   (*continued*)

| Variable | Indicators | Dependent Variable: Freedom House Combined Political Rights and Civil Liberties, 2008[a] | | | | |
|---|---|---|---|---|---|---|
| | | Model 1 | Model 2 | Model 3 | Model 4 | Model 5 |
| | Constant | 2.121 | 2.355 | 3.127 | 2.017 | 3.274 |
| | | (1.843) | (1.839) | (.885) | (1.758) | (.866) |
| | | *.259* | *.211* | *.001* | *.261* | *.000* |
| | Adjusted $R^2$ | .337 | .350 | .346 | .413 | .368 |
| | Significance | *.008* | *.006* | *.000* | *.002* | *.000* |
| | N | 38 | 38 | 47 | 38 | 47 |

*Sources:* Lindberg, *Democratization by Elections*; Lindberg, *Democracy and Elections in Africa*; Bratton and van de Walle, *Democratic Experiments in Africa*; CIA World Fact Book (various years); and World Bank Development Indicators.

*Note:* The top number in each cell is an unstandardized B coefficient, the middle figure in parenthesis is the standard error, and the lower in italics is a *p*–value. Figures in bold are significant at .10-level.

[a] The political rights and civil liberties rankings were released by Freedom House in early 2009. The variable was constructed by adding the two ratings and then reversing the scale from a 14 (worst) to 2 (best) scale to a 0 (worst) to 12 (best) in order to make the reading of coefficients more intuitive.

[b] If the average share of merchandise exports made up of oil, ore, and minerals in 1985–2006 is less than 40%, the country is coded "0"; if it is more than 40%, the actual value is used (missing values for four countries imputed with mean of the latter group).

[c] Coded as "0" if the average share of oil, ore, and minerals of merchandise exports is less than 40% and "1" if average share is more than 40%.

the end of the Cold War emerges. One conclusion of this exercise is unavoidable: regardless of their quality, the longer the series of elections are, the higher the level of democracy is. Repetitive electoral processes uninterrupted by military interventions or similar events seem, indeed, to unleash a series of processes that furthers democratization, and if they are combined with high dependence on international aid (supposedly accompanied by governance conditions), so much the better. In terms of the independent average effect, three additional successive elections result in an overall improvement in Freedom House scores of about two full points on the scale from 0 to 12. An increase of about $50 per capita in international aid improves the leverage for donors and international agencies to push for another full point improvement. The big counteracting factor is resource dependence. Being a resource-curse country on average results in an average score that is two to three points lower. Expressed differently, increasing the percentage of dependence on oil, minerals, or metals as measured here, from 40 to 70 percent on average, results in a decrease in political rights and civil liberties by a at least one full point.

These are merely statistical calculations, of course, with little direct resemblance to how the process actually unfolds on the ground in these countries, but it nevertheless gives an indication of the key positive and negative factors that *systematically* affect the prospects of democratization across countries in Africa. Besides the always-present possibility of omitted-variable bias, the rest of the story is in the error term. The best-fit model in table 7.6 has an explained variance of about 40 percent. That is relatively high for an exercise of this kind but also tells us that (unless we have missed some major systematic factors) a large proportion of the key to successful democratization in Africa must be sought in idiographic factors. We thus like to acknowledge the importance also of identifying and theorizing those factors in research based on small-$N$ case studies.

The negative findings regarding some of the better-established and more thoroughly researched factors impacting democratization also merit some discussion. It is unavoidable to note that modernization, as observed by Przeworski et al. on a global level, does not contribute to an increase in the level of democracy, nor does regime performance, ethnic fractionalization, or even large shares of the population adhering to Islam.[70] Leaders of the free world should consider paying attention to Africa because part of the answer of how to combine a religious orientation toward Islam with support for democracy might be found here.

## Conclusions and Reflections

Over the past few decades there have been major political changes throughout the world, and the proliferation of multiparty elections in former authoritarian states is the most tangible evidence of this global transformation. According to Freedom House,[71] 119 nations are now electoral democracies, meaning they live up to a minimum definition of polyarchic democracy.[72] The electoral revolution is nowhere more evident than in Africa. Out of 48 countries, 23 could in 2008 be considered electoral democracies by a minimal procedural definition, as compared to 4 in 1990, while 20 were electoral hybrids in various guises from Nigeria to Zimbabwe. Almost 300 national-level elections have been held on the continent since the end of the Cold War,[73] illustrating that the spread of de jure multiparty elections in Africa, as elsewhere in the world, is an indisputable trend.

In response to the proliferation of multiparty elections, a wide range of academics have increasingly focused their attentions on, for example, the relationship between elections and democratization, women's roles, civil rights, economic growth, war, corruption, parties and party systems, ethnicity, and the citizenry.[74] Recently, several regional as well as global studies have come to the conclusion that elections play an important causal role in furthering democratization and consolidation.[75] There is thus an increasingly articulate literature reiterating the importance of electoral institutions and processes in democratization and consolidation of democracy. Overall, the results reported here suggest that the resource curse phenomenon concerning the relationship between natural resource dependency and authoritarianism applies to Africa, providing strong support for the hypothesis that resource-rich states are less democratic than resource-poor ones in Africa.[76] Theorizing about a fallback effect, our empirical analysis also finds that among those states that begin to take steps and liberalize, resource-rich states are extremely likely to fall back, leading to democratic breakdown.

In light of the final analysis that shows the positive impact of holding elections and repeating the process, and the leverage that international aid seems to give international actors, this study concludes that African countries that are economically dependent on natural resources are most likely to remain authoritarian, but if and when they do take steps to liberalize, they are at much greater risk of reverting back to a more authoritarian state than non-resource-rich countries.

This critical finding has serious implications for democracy in Africa. Many countries in Africa are becoming increasingly reliant on natural resources, especially oil, to fuel their economies, while simultaneously being pressured to liberalize and democratize further. In the context of this study, it would seem that these two goals are mutually exclusive. If the past twenty-four years are any indication, states should not expect to reap the economic rewards of high fuel prices and also to achieve a peaceful transition to a liberal democracy. If a state allows resources to dominate its economy, it can instead expect either continued authoritarianism or democratic breakdown. Thus, it would seem that even the promise of natural resources is politically damaging and that the discovery of natural resources threatens even seemingly established democracies in Africa. The future implications on democracy for states such as São Tomé and Ghana, who are now discovering natural resources, should be considered by all those who have a vested interest in the triumph of democracy in Africa.

NOTES

1. George Ayittey, *Africa Betrayed* (New York: St. Martin's Press, 1992); Goran Hyden and Michael Bratton, eds., *Governance and Politics in Africa* (Boulder, CO: Lynne Rienner, 1992).

2. Thomas Carothers, "Democracy without Illusions," *Foreign Affairs* 76 (1997): 85–99; Richard Joseph, "Democratization in Africa after 1989: Comparative and Theoretical Perspectives," *Comparative Politics* 29, no. 2 (1997): 363–82.

3. Michael Bratton and Nicolas van de Walle, *Democratic Experiments in Africa: Regime Transitions in a Comparative Perspective* (Cambridge: Cambridge University Press, 1997).

4. Staffan I. Lindberg, "Problems of Measuring Democracy: Illustrations from Africa," in Göran Hydén and Ole Elgström, eds., *Development and Democracy: What Have We Learnt and How?* (London: Routledge, 2002), chap. 7.

5. Staffan I. Lindberg, *Democracy and Elections in Africa* (Baltimore: Johns Hopkins University Press, 2006).

6. Valerie J. Bunce and Sharon L. Wolchik, "Favorable Conditions and Electoral Revolutions," *Journal of Democracy* 17, no. 4 (2006): 5–18; Valerie J. Bunce and Sharon L. Wolchik, "Opposition versus Dictators: Explaining Divergent Election Outcomes in Post-Communist Europe and Eurasia," in Staffan I. Lindberg, ed., *Democratization by Elections: A New Mode of Transition* (Baltimore: Johns Hopkins University Press, 2009), pp. 246–68; Marc M. Howard and P. G. Roessler, "Liberalizing Electoral Outcomes in Competitive Authoritarian Regimes," *American Journal of Political Science* 50, no. 2 (2006): 365–81; Andreas Schedler, "The Nested Game of Democratization by Elections," *International Political Science Review* 23, no. 1 (2002): 103–22; Andreas Schedler, "Sources of Competition under Electoral Authoritarianism," in Lindberg, *Democratization by Elections*, pp. 179–201; Jan Teorell and Axel Hadenius, "Elections as Levers of Democracy? A Global Inquiry," in Lindberg, *Democratization by Elections*, pp. 77–100.

7. Adam Przeworski, Michael Alvarez, José Antonio Cheibub, and Fernando Limongi, "What Makes Democracies Endure?" *Journal of Democracy* 7, no. 1 (1996): 39–55.

8. See, for example, Richard M. Auty, ed., *Resource Abundance and Economic Development* (New York: Oxford University Press, 2004); Paul Collier and Anke Hoeffler, "Resource Rents, Governance, and Conflict," *Journal of Conflict Resolution* 49, no. 4 (2005): 625–33; Michael L. Ross, "Does Oil Hinder Democracy?" *World Politics* 53, no. 3 (2001): 325–61; Leonard Wantchekon, "Why Do Resource Abundant Countries Have Authoritarian Governments?" Yale University, Leitner Center Working Paper (2002), pp. 99–12.

9. Lisa Anderson, "Democracy in the Arab World: A Critique of the Political Culture Approach," in Rex Brynen, Bahgat Korany, and Paul Noble, eds., *Political Liberalization and Democratization in the Arab World: Theoretical Perspectives*, vol. 1 (Boulder, CO: Lynne Rienner, 1995), pp. 77–92; Jill Crystal, *Oil and Politics in the Gulf: Rulers and Merchants in Kuwait and Qatar* (New York: Cambridge University Press, 1990).

10. Terri L. Karl, *The Paradox of Plenty: Oil Booms and Petro-States* (Berkeley: University of California Press, 1997).

11. Wantchekon, "Why Do Resource Abundant Countries Have Authoritarian Governments?"; Michael L. Ross, "Does Oil Hinder Democracy?" *World Politics* 53 (2001): 325–61.

12. Karl, *The Paradox of Plenty*, p. xv.

13. See, for example, Collier and Hoeffler, "Resource Rents, Governance, and Conflict"; Nathan Jensen and Leonard Wantchekon, "Resource Wealth and Political Regimes in Africa," *Comparative Political Studies* 37, no. 7 (2004): 816–41; Karl, *The Paradox of Plenty*; Ross, "Does Oil Hinder Democracy?"

14. This literature argues that resource dependence is associated with conflict in several ways. First, natural resource rents can be used to finance the conflict; see Collier and Hoeffler, "Resource Rents, Governance, and Conflict," p. 632. Second, they can be a motivating factor in secessionist movements, as resource-rich regions attempt to concentrate and control the profits among themselves, and conversely, resource-poor regions fight to keep them within their borders; see James D. Fearon, "Primary Commodity Exports and Civil War," *Journal of Conflict Resolution* 49, no. 4 (2005): 483–507. While such conflicts often are patterned along ethnic, religious, or class divisions, differences are more likely to escalate into violence when groups are competing for valuable shares of resource revenue; Nicholas Shaxson, "Oil, Corruption, and the Resource Curse," *International Affairs* 83, no. 6 (2007): 1123–40. Instability in the oil market and sudden price shocks provide another risk factor in inducing conflict, as discontent and economic crisis lead to violence; Collier and Hoeffler, "Resource Rents, Governance, and Conflict," p. 632; Karl, *The Paradox of Plenty*. Additionally, if the extraction of resources is not tightly controlled by the government, rebels can use it to finance their insurgency, thus leading to heightened conflict; Richard Snyder, "Does Lootable Wealth Breed Disorder? A Political Economy of Extraction Framework," *Comparative Political Studies* 39, no. 8 (2006): 943–68.

15. Benjamin Smith, "The Wrong Kind of Crisis: Why Oil Booms and Busts Rarely Lead to Authoritarian Breakdown," *Studies in Comparative International Development* 40, no. 4 (2006): 55–76; Luc Desire Omgba, "On the Duration of Political Power in Africa: The Role of Oil Rents," *Comparative Political Studies* 42, no. 3 (2009): 416–36.

16. Thad Dunning, "Resource Dependence, Economic Performance, and Political Stability," *Journal of Conflict Resolution* 49, no. 4 (2005): 451–82.

17. The Dutch Disease typically refers to the phenomenon where an initial economic boom allows increased government spending on macroeconomic projects, while other sectors of the economy are neglected; Karl, *The Paradox of Plenty*, p. 228. The influx of money allows citizens to rely on imported foreign goods and leads to greater abandonment of traditional subsistence farming, as workers move into the many civil service positions financed by oil. Large exports of oil, or other minerals or ores, simultaneously drive up the exchange rate, making exports of other goods unprofitable while imports become cheaper. In general, agriculture and other traditional industries are neglected in favor of the more immediately lucrative resource extraction. As a result, no enduring economic infrastructure is developed (Ross, "Does Oil Hinder Democracy?" p. 336), local production is discouraged, and pacifying the population leads to foreign debt, often as a result of extensive borrowing against future resource revenue to cover budget deficits.

18. See, for example, Jensen and Wantchekon, "Resource Wealth and Political Regimes in Africa"; Smith, "The Wrong Kind of Crisis."

19. See, for example, Ellen Lust-Okar, "Elections under Authoritarianism: Preliminary Lessons from Jordan," *Democratization* 13, no. 3 (2006): 455–70; and Ellen Lust-Okar, "Legislative Elections in Hegemonic Authoritarian Regimes: Competitive Clientelism and Resistance to Democratization," in Lindberg, *Democratization by Elections*, pp. 226–45.

20. Karl, *The Paradox of Plenty*, p. 59.

21. Shaxson, "Oil, Corruption, and the Resource Curse."

22. Ross, "Does Oil Hinder Democracy?" p. 349.

23. Ibid., pp. 332, 348.

24. Ibid., p. 351.

25. Wantchekon, "Why Do Resource Abundant Countries Have Authoritarian Governments?" p. 10.

26. Ibid., p. 20.

27. Jensen and Wantchekon, "Resource Wealth and Political Regimes in Africa."

28. Smith, "The Wrong Kind of Crisis."

29. Ibid., p. 56.

30. Ibid., p. 55.

31. Ibid., pp. 55, 71.

32. Jensen and Wantchekon, "Resource Wealth and Political Regimes in Africa."

33. "Energy in Africa," U.S. Department of Energy, www.eia.doe.gov/emeu/cabs/Archives/africa/africa.html.

34. Robert H. Bates, *When Things Fell Apart: State Failure in Late-Century Africa* (New York: Cambridge University Press, 2008), p. 135.

35. The Freedom House scores represent a graded measure for both political rights and civil liberties, combining fifteen criteria to rank each state on a 1 to 7 scale, with 7 being the worst and 1 the best for each, and the totals ranging from 2 to 14. Here we have calculated the average of combined scores over the period in question, but throughout we used a reversed scale from 0 to 12 to make it more intuitive, where 0 represents the worst score and 12 the best. For further information on Freedom House's rankings and methodology, see www.freedomhouse.org.

36. Karl, *The Paradox of Plenty*, p. 47.

37. We also used alternative specifications of this variable to check for robustness of our findings. Thus, we used both measures that took into account only years with data on both minerals and fuel exports, as well as a combined measure that does not exclude years with missing figures and separate means for fuel and ore and mineral exports respectively. The substantive findings reported in this chapter remain essentially unchanged regardless of measure.

38. For the ten countries for which the WBDI does not provide data (Chad, Democratic Republic of Congo, Djibouti, Equatorial Guinea, Eritrea, Lesotho, Liberia, São Tomé, Sierra Leone, and Somalia), resource dependence is determined using economic information from the CIA Factbook, various years.

39. Benjamin Smith, "Oil Wealth and Regime Survival in the Developing World," *American Journal of Political Science* 48, no. 2 (2004): 232–46; Ross, "Does Oil Hinder Democracy?"

40. Jensen and Wantchekon, "Resource Wealth and Political Regimes in Africa."

41. There are serious limitations in data availability before 1985, however, which in our view create a large potential selection bias with unknown effects. Hence, we limit our period to 1985 to 2007.

42. Robert Dahl, *Polyarchy: Participation and Opposition* (New Haven: Yale University Press, 1971).

43. Larry Diamond, "Elections without Democracy: Thinking about Hybrid Regimes," *Journal of Democracy* 13, no. 2 (2002): 21–35; Howard and Roessler, "Liberalizing Electoral Outcomes in Competitive Authoritarian Regimes"; Lindberg, *Democracy and Elections in Africa*; Bratton and van de Walle, *Democratic Experiments in Africa*.

44. Wantchekon, "Why Do Resource Abundant Countries Have Authoritarian Governments?" We also ran our models using the Polity IV scores as basis for classification of regimes and as the dependent variable. All our findings remain substantially unchanged with this alternative.

45. We added the ratings for each of the two scales going from 7 (worst) to 1 (best) making a scale from 14 to 2, then reversed it to make for more intuitive readings of the result. The resulting scale runs from 0 (worst) to 12 (best).

46. It should perhaps be noted that the ratings of 2008, for example, were released by Freedom House in early 2009 and listed as such. This anomaly sometimes causes some confusion over which values have actually been used.

47. In this part of the analysis, the liberalizing category includes the countries that have become democracies for reasons of parsimony.

48. We also ran the same analysis using the alternative specifications for mineral and ore, and oil dependency only, and the results show that while the relationship between fuel exports and democracy and ore and mineral exports and democracy are both not statistically significant on their own, the correlation is stronger for fuel. This supports Collier and Hoeffler's belief that oil, because of the unstable price market and profit potential, has a heightened resource curse effect; Collier and Hoeffler, "Resource Rents, Governance, and Conflict."

49. Lindberg, *Democracy and Elections in Africa*; Staffan I. Lindberg, "The Power of Elections in Africa Revisited," in Lindberg, *Democratization by Elections*, pp. 25–46; Schedler, "The Nested Game of Democratization by Elections."

50. Lindberg, "The Power of Elections in Africa Revisited."

51. We test for this rather than the dependency-type argument that a higher rate of economic reliance on the more developed states in terms of trade and capital investments affects democratization negatively; see Axel Hadenius, *Democracy and Development* (Cambridge: Cambridge University Press, 1992). Although corroborated recently by Li and Reuveny on a global scale, the most significant influence of the international arena for most African rulers is arguably aid; Quan Li and Rafael Reuveny, "Economic Globalization and Democracy: An Empirical Analysis," *British Journal of Political Science* 33 (2003): 29–54.

52. See, for example, Bratton and van de Walle, *Democratic Experiments in Africa*.

53. See, for example, Staffan I. Lindberg, "Problems of Measuring Democracy: Illustrations from Africa," in Hydén and Elgström, *Development and Democracy*, pp. 122–38.

54. Seymour Martin Lipset, "Some Social Requisites of Democracy: Economic Development and Political Legitimacy," *American Political Science Review* 53, no. 1 (1959): 69–105.

55. Henry S. Rowen, "The Tide Underneath the 'Third Wave,'" in Larry Diamond and Marc Plattner, eds., *The Global Resurgence of Democracy* (Baltimore: Johns Hopkins University Press, 1996), p. 309.

56. Ross Buckhart and Michael Lewis-Beck, "Comparative Democracy: The Economic Development Thesis," *American Political Science Review* 88, no. 4 (1994): 903–10; John B. Londregan and Keith T. Poole, "Does High Income Promote Democracy?" *World Politics* 49, no. 1 (1996): 56–91; Mark J. Gasiororwski and Timothy J. Power, "The Structural Determinants of Democratic Consolidation," *Comparative Political Studies* 31, no. 10 (1998): 740–72.

57. Lipset, "Some Social Requisites of Democracy"; Philip Cutwright, "National Political Development: Measurement and Analysis," *American Sociological Review* 28, no. 1 (1963): 42–59.

58. Adam Przeworski, Michael Alvarez, José Antonio Cheibub, and Fernando Limongi, *Democracy and Development: Political Institutions and Well-Being in the World, 1950–1990* (Cambridge: Cambridge University Press, 2000), p. 137.

59. Mark Gasiorowski, "Economic Crisis and Political Regime Change: An Event History Analysis," *American Political Science Review* 89, no. 4 (1995): 882–97.

60. Lipset, "Some Social Requisites of Democracy."

61. See, for example, Ross, "Does Oil Hinder Democracy?"

62. Michael Bratton and Nicolas van de Walle, *Political Regimes and Regime Transitions in Africa, 1910–1994*, Computer file, ICPSR version, No. 6996 (Michigan: Inter-University Consortium for Political and Social Research, 1996).

63. See, for example, Kanchan Chandra, *Why Ethnic Parties Succeed: Patronage and Ethnic Headcounts in India* (Cambridge: Cambridge University Press, 2004); Shaheen Mozaffar, James R. Scarritt, and Glen Galaich, "Electoral Institutions, Ethno-political Cleavages, and Party Systems in Africa's Emerging Democracies," *American Political Science Review* 97, no. 3 (2003): 379–90; Daniel Posner, "Measuring Ethnic Fractionalization in Africa," *American Journal of Political Science* 48, no. 4 (2004): 849–64; James Scarritt and Shaheen Mozaffar, "The Specification of Ethnic Cleavages and Ethnopolitical Groups for the Analysis of Democratic Competition in Contemporary Africa," *Nationalism and Ethnic Politics* 5, no. 1 (1999): 82–117.

64. Tanja Ellingsen, "Colorful Community of Ethnic Witches' Brew? Multiethnicity and Domestic Conflict during and after the Cold War," *Journal of Conflict Resolution* 44, no. 2 (2000): 228–49.

65. Seymour M. Lipset, "The Social Requisites of Democracy Revisited," *American Sociological Review* 59 (February 1993): 1–22.

66. Bratton and van de Walle, *Democratic Experiments in Africa*.

67. Lindberg, "Problems of Measuring Democracy: Illustrations from Africa."

68. Bratton and van de Walle, *Democratic Experiments in Africa*.

69. Those are the models reported in table 7.6. We also ran the same models using Polity IV data, as well as models using alternative specifications of resource dependency, regime performance, and ethnicity. The substantial findings were not significantly changed by any of these alterations.

70. Przeworski et al., *Democracy and Development*.

71. Freedom House Ratings of Political Rights and Civil Liberties, "Methodology," 2009, www.freedomhouse.org.

72. Dahl, *Polyarchy: Participation and Opposition*.

73. Lindberg, "The Power of Elections in Africa Revisited."

74. Without any pretense of doing justice to all contributions or being representative, a list of this new kind of research on democracy published only in the past few years includes the following. On executive, judicial, and electoral systems and consociationalism, see René Lemarchand, "Consociationalism and Power Sharing in Africa: Rwanda, Burundi, and the Democratic Republic of the Congo," *African Affairs* 106 (2007): 422; Staffan I. Lindberg, "Consequences of Electoral Systems in Africa: A Preliminary Inquiry," *Electoral Studies* 24, no. 1 (2005): 41–64; Gazibo Mamoudou, "The Forging of Institutional Autonomy: Electoral Management Commissions in Africa," *Canadian Journal of Political Science* 39, no. 3 (2006): 611–31; Scott D. Taylor, "Divergent Politico-Legal Responses to Past Presidential Corruption in Zambia and Kenya: Catching the 'Big Fish,' or Letting Him off the Hook?" *Third World Quarterly* 27, no. 2 (2006): 281–301; Peter von Doepp, "Politics and Judicial Assertiveness in Emerging Democracies: High Court Behavior in Malawi and Zambia," *Political Research Quarterly* 59, no. 3 (2006): 389–99.

On women and politics, see Gretchen Bauer and Hannah E. Britton, eds., *Women in African Parliaments* (Boulder, CO: Lynne Rienner, 2006); Andrea Cornwall and Anne Marie Goetz, "Democratizing Democracy: Feminist Perspectives," *Democratization* 12, no. 5 (2005): 783–800; Shireen Hassim, *Women's Organizations and Democracy in South Africa: Contesting Authority* (Madison: University of Wisconsin Press, 2006); Staffan I. Lindberg, "Democratization and Women's Empowerment: The Effects of Electoral Systems, Participation, and Repetition in Africa," *Studies in Comparative International Development* 38, no. 1 (2004): 28–53; Mi Yung Yoon and Sheila Bunwaree, "Women's Legislative Representation in Mauritius: 'A Grave Democratic Deficit,'" *Journal of Contemporary African Studies* 24, no. 2 (2006): 229–47.

On capitalism, development, and democracy, see Alison J. Ayers, "Demystifying Democratization: The Global Constitution of (Neo)Liberal Polities in Africa," *Third World Quarterly* 27, no. 2 (2006): 321–38; Stephen F. Burgess, "The Impact of Structural Adjustment and Economic Reform on the Transition Process in East Africa," in Paul J. Kaiser and F. Wafula Okumu, eds., *Democratic Transitions in East Africa: A Comparative and Regional Perspective* (London: Ashgate, 2004), pp. 120–41; Mamoudou Gazibo, "Foreign Aid and Democratization: Benin and Niger Compared," *African Studies Review* 48, no. 3 (2005): 47–67; Thomas A. Koelble and Edward LiPuma, "The Effects of Circulatory Capitalism on Democratization: Observations from South Africa and Brazil," *Democratization* 13, no. 4 (2006): 605–31.

On war, corruption, clientelism, and democracy, see Charles H. Blake and Christopher G. Martin, "The Dynamics of Political Corruption: Re-examining the Influence of Democracy," *Democratization* 13, no. 6 (2006): 1–14; Stephen Ellis, "The Roots of African Corruption," *Current History* 105, no. 691 (2006): 203–8; Mushtaq H. Khan, "Markets, States, and Democracy: Patron-Client Networks and the Case for Democracy in Developing Countries," *Democratization* 12, no. 5 (2005): 707–24; Terrence Lyons, *Demilitarizing Politics: Elections on the Uncertain Road to Peace* (Boulder, CO: Lynne Rienner, 2005); Philip G. Roeder and Donald Rothchild, eds., *Sustainable Peace: Power and Democracy after Civil Wars* (Ithaca: Cornell University Press, 2005); Camilla Sandbakken, "The Limits to Democracy Posed by Oil Rentier States: The Cases of Algeria, Nigeria, and Libya," *Democratization* 13, no. 6 (2006): 135–52.

On various features and effects of party systems, see Matthijs Bogaards, "Counting Parties and Identifying Dominant Party Systems in Africa," *European Journal of Political Research* 43 (2004): 173–97; Gero Erdmann, "Party Research: Western European Bias and the 'African Labyrinth,'" *Democratization* 11, no. 3 (2004): 63–87; Goran Hyden, "Barriers to Party Systems in Africa: The Movement Legacy," paper presented at the 48th annual conference of the African Studies Association, Washington, DC, November 17–20, 2005; John Ishiyama and John James Quinn, "African Phoenix? Explaining the Electoral Performance of the Formerly Dominant Parties in Africa," *Party Politics* 12, no. 3 (May 2006): 317–40; Michelle Kuenzi and Gina Lambright, "Party Systems and Democratic Consolidation in Africa's Electoral Regimes," *Party Politics* 11, no. 4 (2005): 423–46; Adrienne LeBas, "Polarization as Craft: Party Formation and State Violence in Zimbabwe," *Comparative Politics* 38, no. 4 (2006): 419–38; Staffan I. Lindberg, "Institutionalization of Party Systems? Stability and Fluidity among Legislative Parties in Africa's Democracies," *Government and Opposition* 42, no. 2 (2007): 215–41; Carrie Manning, "Assessing African Party System Consolidation: Ideology Versus Institutions," *Party Politics* 11, no. 6 (2005): 707–27; Minion K. C. Morrison, "Ghana's Political Parties: How Ethno/Regional Variations Sustain the National Two-Party System," *Journal of Modern African Studies* 44, no. 4 (2006): 623–47.

Voter and citizen attitudes are the topic of a host of Afrobarometer working papers and journal articles. See Peter Mwangi Kagwanja, "Power to Uhuru: Youth Identity and Generational Politics in Kenya's 2002 Elections," *African Affairs* 105, no. 418 (2006): 51–75; Staffan I. Lindberg and Minion K. C. Morrison, "Are African Voters Really Ethnic or Clientelistic? Survey Evidence from Ghana," *Political Science Quarterly* 123, no. 1 (2008): 95–122; Devra C. Moehler, "Public Participation and Support for the Constitution in Uganda," *Journal of Modern African Studies* 44, no. 2 (2006): 275–308.

On ethnicity, culture, and religion and democracy, see Elliott Green, "Ethnicity and the Politics of Land Tenure Reform in Central Uganda," *Commonwealth and Comparative Politics* 44, no. 3 (2006): 370–88; Tobias Hagmann, "Ethiopian Political Culture Strikes Back: A Rejoinder to J. Abbink," *African Affairs* 105, no. 421 (October 2006): 605–12; John N. Paden, *Muslim Civic Cultures and Conflict Resolution: The Challenge of Democratic Federalism in Nigeria* (Washington, DC: Brookings Institute, 2005); Anne Pitcher, "Forgetting from Above and Memory from Below: Strategies of Legitimation and Struggle in Postsocialist Mozambique," *Africa* 76, no. 1 (2006): 88–112; Daniel Posner, *Institutions and Ethnic Politics in Africa* (Cambridge: Cambridge University Press, 2005); Benjamin F. Soares, "Islam in Mali in the Neoliberal Era," *African Affairs* 105, no. 418 (2006): 77–95.

For general studies of elections and democratization, see Gretchen Bauer and Scott D. Taylor, *Politics in Southern Africa: State and Society in Transition* (Boulder, CO: Lynne Rienner, 2005); Clark C. Gibson, "Of Waves and Ripples: Democracy and Political Change in Africa in the 1990s," *Annual Review of Political Science* 5 (2002): 201–21; Lindberg, *Democracy and Elections in Africa*; Richard Sandbrook, "Origins of the Democratic Developmental State," *Canadian Journal of African Studies* 39, no. 3 (2005): 549–81; Nicolas van de Walle, "Elections without Democracy: Africa's Range of Regimes," *Journal of Democracy* 13, no. 2 (2002): 66–80. Some efforts to understand issues like party systems have suffered from methodological problems undermining findings but that is to be expected when new ground is being broken; Shaheen Mozaffar and James

R. Scarritt, "The Puzzle of African Party Systems," *Party Politics* 11, no. 4 (2005): 399–421.

75. See, for example, Bunce and Wolchik, "Favorable Conditions and Electoral Revolutions"; Axel Hadenius and Jan Teorell, "Authoritarian Regimes: Stability, Change and Pathways to Democracy, 1972–2003," *Journal of Democracy* 18, no. 1 (2007): 143–57; Howard and Roessler, "Liberalizing Electoral Outcomes in Competitive Authoritarian Regimes"; Leslie Anderson and Lawrence Dodd, *Learning Democracy* (Chicago: University of Chicago Press, 2005); Lindberg, *Democracy and Elections in Africa*; Schedler, "The Nested Game of Democratization by Elections."

76. Ross "Does Oil Hinder Democracy?"; Wantchekon, "Why Do Resource Abundant Countries Have Authoritarian Governments?"

# CHAPTER 8

# Democracy and Development
## Legacy Effects

*John Gerring*

While the book thus far has focused primarily on the causes of democracy, this chapter focuses on its possible consequences. What is the effect of regime type on economic growth, infrastructure, human capital, social equality, and overall quality of life?[1] Broadly speaking, does democracy promote development, or is it development neutral or perhaps even a negative factor in development?

The question is of obvious importance in an era when democracy is an avowed priority for the United States and other foreign aid donors. The general presumption is that the causal effects of democracy on development are, on balance, positive. Yet the scholarly evidence for this proposition is thin. Political scientists, economists, and sociologists generally view the effect of regime type on development as inconsistent. Whether democracies produce better governance than autocracies is not clear. Indeed, some argue, with an eye toward the East Asian newly industrializing countries (NICs), that economic growth is most likely to be achieved through a period of strict authoritarian rule, deemed necessary to instill discipline in the labor force, to prioritize long-term savings and investment over current consumption, and to resist the rent-seeking pressures of organized groups.[2] Democracy is often associated with policy sclerosis[3] and with skewed political representation, a situation in which relatively educated and well-organized voters (e.g., public-sector unions and urban elites) are able to monopolize state resources and prevent measures to redistribute resources to the rural poor.[4] Democracy may also encourage a clientelist, rent-seeking style of politicking in which side payments to special interests trump the provision of collective goods.[5] Democracy may even open the floodgates to ethnic conflict, social disorder, and war.[6] In short, there are many reasons—and a considerable amount of anecdotal evidence—to suggest that democracy does not stimulate positive development outcomes.[7]

Evidence for these skeptical judgments is drawn from case studies[8] and from cross-national statistical studies. The latter have focused, in particular, on democracy's effect on per capita GDP, where the standard finding is that regime type has no net impact on growth.[9] Even with respect to human development, where one might expect a stronger relationship, there is skepticism. It is true that democracies spend more on social policies, but it is not clear that there is a robust association between spending levels and policy achievements in the developing world (e.g., longer life expectancy, lower infant mortality, and higher literacy). The social policy bucket may be very leaky.[10] Thus, while democracies appear to be less prone to domestic policy disasters such as widespread famine,[11] their accomplishments in less visible policy areas is less impressive. Democracy, from the perspective of many academic studies, is not a solution for developmental ills in the poorer regions of the world.[12]

Democracy might still be defended for other reasons, for example, because it enhances citizen participation, civil liberty, civil society, and perhaps even happiness.[13] Yet, while these are important achievements, they may not be sufficient to inspire enthusiasm among those currently forced to live on less than one or two dollars a day—roughly half of the world's present population. In summarizing the results of a recent poll in eighteen Latin American countries, the authors note that "the preference of citizens for democracy is relatively low; many Latin Americans value development above democracy and would even stop supporting a democratic government if it proved incapable to resolving their economic problems."[14] Indeed, the demand for "food first" sounds more sensible than the call for "democracy first." Democracy is emphatically not equivalent to justice; it is, at best, a component of justice.[15] Thus, it would be wrong for First World actors to presume that a democratic organization of politics is preferable for countries in the developing world if another regime type promises greater material reward.[16]

Is democracy a luxury to be enjoyed only by countries rich enough to afford it? My argument against this proposition hinges on a matter of conceptualization and measurement, as well as a larger theory of regime dynamics. I begin by sketching the overall argument; proceed to a discussion of possible causal mechanisms; and then review empirical findings, based largely on cross-national statistical tests.[17]

## The Argument

The academic literature, just reviewed, offers scant reason to believe that democracy fosters development. What is notable about these empirical probes is that they focus largely on the immediate or short-term causal effects of regime type. Whether a country is democratic or authoritarian today is expected to influence its developmental trajectory in the next year or decade (as defined by a study's research design).[18]

Upon reflection, this expectation is rather implausible. A change in regime is unlikely to produce significant modifications in policies and policy outcomes in the years immediately following a regime change. Indeed, democratic transitions are often periods of extreme instability and unpredictability. It would be perplexing, therefore, if the performance of countries moving from authoritarian to democratic rule were substantially improved during a period of transition.

To the contrary, the effects of political institutions are likely to unfold over time—sometimes a great deal of time—and these temporal effects may be cumulative in nature. Regimes do not begin again, de novo, with each calendar year. Where one is today depends critically upon where one has been before. Countries build their political institutions over long periods of time.

Historical work suggests that democracy and authoritarianism construct deep legacies, extending back several decades, perhaps even centuries.[19] It follows that we should concern ourselves with the accumulated effect of these historical legacies, not merely with a country's contemporary regime status.

In this fashion, a second dimension—time—must be introduced to our judgment of the relationship between regime type and governance outcomes. For purposes of discussion, I posit four ideal types: (A) old authoritarian regimes, (B) young authoritarian regimes, (C) young democratic regimes (newly democratized countries), and (D) old democratic regimes. There is also a corresponding set of transition options among these four regimes, as illustrated in figure 8.1. My supposition is that the quality of governance increases from A to B, from B to C, and from C to D. The worst-governed polity is an old autocracy, the best-governed polity an old democracy—all other things being equal.

Of course, both dimensions are matters of degree. The concepts "old democracy," "young democracy," etc. are simply heuristic tools. An infinite number of regimes may fall in between these ideal types—and, equally important,

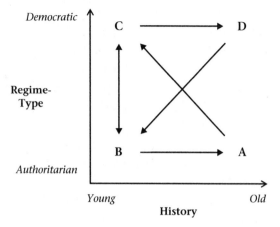

*Figure 8.1.* Regime Types in Time. *Note:* A = old autocracy; B = young autocracy; C = young democracy; D = old democracy. Arrows represent possible regime transitions.

there are no theoretical end points. Figure 8.1 is therefore constructed as a line graph rather than a 2×2 matrix.

To summarize the argument thus far: democracy is a good thing, and its goodness is cumulative. The more a country has of it, the better off it will be, all other things being equal. The less a country has of it, the worse off it will be, ceteris paribus. It follows that one ought to consider democracy as a *stock* rather than as a *level*. Stock measures the accumulation of democratic experience over time, so it comprises both dimensions displayed in figure 8.1: regime type (a country's degree of democracy-authoritarianism at a given point in time) and regime history (how long it has possessed those characteristics). The expectation is, the greater a country's stock of democracy is, the greater its "flow" of good governance will be.

What, then, is the *theory*? In what ways might a country's democratic stock contribute to its developmental potential? Identifying causal mechanisms is a daunting task. The theoretical variable of interest—"democracy"—evidently encompasses a wide range of features, and the policies and policy outcomes associated with "development" are even broader in scope. As a result, the causal story is quite complex. Democracy, insofar as it matters for development, probably affects these myriad outcomes through *multiple* channels.

The following discussion is limited to mechanisms that are likely to have important implications across a variety of policy areas. These pathways include civil society, accountability, learning, empowerment, consensus, and institutionalization. Naturally, some mechanisms are more important for some policy areas, and others will have greater ramifications for other policy areas. Even so, they are correctly regarded as general in purview.

These are not new ideas, and they are not especially controversial. Few are likely to quarrel with the claim that democracies enjoy stronger civil societies, greater accountability, greater opportunities for learning, more social empowerment, greater societal and elite-level consensus, and higher levels of political institutionalization, on average, relative to similarly situated autocracies. The contribution of the following discussion is to highlight a fairly simple point. These factors are the product not of democracy per se but rather of democratic experience, that is, prolonged experience living under a democratic constitution. The development of these virtues takes time, sometimes a great deal of time. Viewed from a historical perspective, the causal relationship between democracy and development becomes eminently plausible. This is what I hope to accomplish in the following discussion, which remains provisional (because few of these causal mechanisms can be tested empirically).

## Civil Society

The creation of a strong civil society—a sphere independent from politics and from the market—is very difficult under circumstances of authoritarian rule. Indeed, neither the strong authoritarian state nor the weak authoritarian state can effectively guarantee the flourishing of voluntary associations. In the first instance, the institutions of the state or ruling party tend to pervade all public deliberations, as in China, Eritrea, and the former Soviet Union. In the second instance (of weak authoritarian rule), there is no space safe for public deliberations because there is no public order. This would describe Congo under Mobutu or present-day Myanmar. Thus, it may be argued that civil society is premised on the existence of a democratic regime.

Evidently, voluntary associations representing diverse purposes, interests, and ideals do not spring up immediately following the declaration of multiparty elections. In some cases, there is scarcely a semblance of civil society before the instauration of multiparty competition. In other cases, where such organizations are already in place, it takes considerable time for them to gain traction, that is, to reach out to new constituencies and to mobilize resources. It takes time for nongovernmental organizations (NGOs) that are focused on the quality of governance to carve out their respective roles, to establish their independence, to gain knowledge of complex issues, to create knowledge networks, and to develop a reputation for perspicacity and probity. Here one might consider the example of the United States, a country blessed with a dense and varied community of civic-minded NGOs, including organizations such as the New York Times, the AARP, the Children's Defense Fund, the League of Women Voters, and the ACLU. Each has come to play an influential role in the development of public policy; however, their present status and prestige is a function of many decades of hard work and many reversals. The achievement of a robust civil society is neither immediate nor automatic. Even in comparatively well-educated and wealthy societies, such as the former Soviet bloc states, the development of civil society seems to lag well behind the installation of multiparty competition.[20]

Over time, however, the density, diversity, and competence of voluntary associations are likely to grow—under conditions of democratic rule. Indeed, despite the decline of party organization in some long-standing democracies, the general pattern of civil society in older democratic polities is one of persistence and vitality. In developing societies, the positive trend over time is even more marked (though the evidence collected to date is not systematic).[21] Thus, it seems fair to regard civic associations as a development fostered, over time, wherever political institutions are democratic.

## Accountability

Where conditions of democracy hold, I also expect that mechanisms of accountability will become more established.[22] The longer such conditions hold, the stronger these mechanisms are likely to be. This issue is often conceptualized as a principal-agency relationship, where the electorate is understood as the principal and elected officials (acting through appointed members of the bureaucracy) as the agent.

It is important to appreciate that in order for mechanisms of accountability to be fully operative several conditions must hold: the agent must be identifiable and relatively coherent (otherwise, there is no person or persons to reward or punish); the principal must have monitoring capacity; the electorate must constitute a large portion of the population in a polity; and, most importantly, mechanisms by which the principal can regularly reward or punish the agent must be available.

It follows almost apodictically that mechanisms of accountability are likely to be weak and/or limited in an authoritarian regime. To be sure, there may be an identifiable agent. However, this agent will be difficult to monitor because authoritarian regimes generally do not operate in a transparent fashion. Equally important, the class of principals is very small, extending perhaps to the military, an aristocracy, a landowning class, or an ethnic group. In any case, the "selectorate" is much smaller than the potential electorate. Of course, citizens can exact revenge upon an irresponsible leader by overthrowing the regime. But this is a crude, irregular, and generally ineffective mechanism of accountability and operates (to the extent that it operates at all) only in the most extreme cases of malfeasance. This means that the class of issues to which mechanisms of accountability can be said to apply in a dictatorship is limited to those of concern to the selectorate and/or those which might provoke the broader citizenry to the point of open revolt.

Thus, as with civil society, it seems reasonable to regard democracy as a *necessary condition* of accountability. However, I do not view these two concepts as interchangeable. Indeed, numerous democratic polities show evidence of extremely weak mechanisms of accountability. For my purposes, what is significant is that this sort of pathology seems to be much more common among newly established democracies than among older democracies. This is explainable once one considers the delicate institutional mechanisms needed to secure effective accountability and the time that is required for these institutions to develop.

Political parties are often viewed as mechanisms of accountability, for they connect elected officials with voters and also organize the work of elected officials. And yet a recently democratized regime is likely to have no fully institutionalized political parties, or at best only a single well-organized party (which is likely to dominate political affairs). Mechanisms of accountability are virtually impossible to establish until at least two parties have recognized labels, coherent (more or less) cadres of supporters, and a semblance of a policy agenda. Rival teams, vying for power, are the essence of accountability within a democratic framework.

One might also consider the question of accountability from the perspective of elective leaders. From the outset, leaders in a democratic polity are likely to pay verbal homage to what they imagine the electorate wants. However, these rhetorical flourishes may be merely rhetorical unless and until leaders realize that they might be punished or rewarded for what they do once in office. The establishment of accountability thus requires multiple iterations of an electoral cycle. It requires time for the assignment of responsibilities—for example, between executive, legislature, and judiciary, between elective and unelective bodies, between national and subnational authorities—to become clear. Until then, there is no agent that can plausibly be praised or blamed for its performance. It takes time for mechanisms of "horizontal" accountability to develop.[23] Most important, it takes time for electoral institutions to develop such that the electorate can exact revenge (or heap rewards) upon officeholders.

The accountability relationship between elites and masses is particularly evident in the arena of economic policy for the simple reason that the fate of the economy is a high-salience issue. Here, if anywhere, mechanisms of electoral accountability should be operative.[24] Perhaps the most important lesson that democratically elected elites learn is that growth performance matters for their political future. They are more likely to retain their jobs if the country prospers, and very likely to lose their jobs if it does not.[25] Note that in new democracies, politicians frequently adopt short-term policies intended to pay off political supporters and stimulate the economy during election seasons.[26] Short-term goals dominate because there is no assurance that elites would be able to make good on longer-term promises. However, once elites and voters have experienced several electoral and economic cycles, longer time-horizons may come to prevail. Voters who have directly experienced the effects of populist economic policies are likely to be skeptical of claims that soaking the rich, inflating the economy, abrogating debt agreements, or resorting to massive expropriation of property will enhance their livelihoods.[27] Indeed, various studies have shown it takes time for voters in a newly democratized country to begin to link their votes to the country's economic performance. Economic voting appears only as the electorate develops trust in new institutions and begins to treat elected politicians as guardians of the economy.[28] Consequently, leaders in established democracies may be willing to impose sacrifices over the short term to facilitate stronger growth performance over the course of their administration.[29] Thus, as democratic experience accumulates, I expect a slow transition away from a populist style of politics and policy making. As a result, I expect countries with longer democratic histories to institute better policies than transitional democracies or authoritarian regimes.

## Learning

Politics is not simply a product of power and interests. It is also, to some considerable extent, a product of cognition, that is, of learning.[30] Learning refers here to any cognitive development that is rational (a product of reason), true (as near as one can tell), and helpful in realizing basic values or objectives (assumed to remain fixed). For example, citizens may learn that a party or politician is corrupt, or that a party's promises are credible (or noncredible). Politicians may learn that a particular issue is of great salience to the electorate, or that it should be framed in a particular way in order to be palatable to the electorate. And politicians and citizens may learn that one policy works better than another to achieve a given policy objective. These are all examples of learning as it pertains to the political sphere.[31] Over time, politicians learn to be better politicians, and citizens learn to be better citizens (given whatever policy priorities they may hold).

My expectation is that there are more opportunities for learning in a democratic context than in an authoritarian context. As already observed, policymaking processes in authoritarian regimes are usually closed (nontransparent), and generally monopolized by a small number of elite actors—typically, a single leader and his or her coterie (though they may be assisted by a large bureaucracy).[32] There is generally little turnover among the leadership cadre, and when turnover does occur, for example, by natural death or by coup, it is not the sort propitious for policy learning. In a democracy, by contrast, opportunities for learning are much greater because the policy process is more open, the number of actors is greater (each of whom may bring a different perspective to a policy problem),[33] leadership turnover happens more frequently (inducing stochastic variation in public policies), and it happens in a context where new elites can build upon prior experience, while distancing themselves from perceived failures. Whenever an election turns out the old leadership team and installs a new leadership team, there is an opportunity to attempt new policies or to retry old policies (under a new guise). Democratic legitimacy is repeatedly renewed by virtue of the electoral mechanism.[34]

Under these circumstances, opportunities for learning—by masses and elites—are great. However, because learning takes time, its benefits should accrue over time, as democratic stock accumulates. Consider that political learning is largely experiential. Because general theories of politics and policy making offer only the most general guidance (and few politicians pay heed to political science anyway), citizens and policy makers must learn by doing. And undoing. A new policy is tried, its effects are evaluated, and a new course of action is considered. Occasional bold experiments are followed by long periods of muddling through. Learning occurs in the political realm as new issues are trotted out before the electorate, the framing of these issues is adjusted, leaders enter and exit the political stage, and the public's response—via elections and opinion polls—is registered. The process is time-consuming and error-prone. "Lessons" are learned only after many miscues. Not only must governing politicians learn what constitutes good policy; voters must also learn to recognize good policy. There may even be a third stage, during which politicians learn that voters have learned to distinguish good policies from bad.[35] This is why old democracies should be more "learned" than young democracies.

## *Empowerment*

The formal basis of power in a democracy is votes, a fact that separates this regime type from an autocracy, where power is generally based on factors such as coercion, money, loyalty, and connections—all of which privilege certain segments of the populace over others. Even though power in a democracy does not rest solely on votes, votes matter quite a lot. Every citizen has equal power while standing in the polling booth, and this central fact may prompt political elites to pay more attention to those without money, status, connections, or other resources than they would in other circumstances.

Second, because every citizen's vote matters, we can expect that political conflicts in a democracy exhibit an expansionary quality. Just as the loser of a fight appeals for support from the crowd, a losing faction is likely to appeal to those who were not initially involved (or perhaps even aware) of the conflict. Thus, while most political conflicts begin in small spheres, and may be restricted to elite players, outsiders are continually being appealed to. Their participation is demanded. And this expansionary quality of conflict in a democracy promises to reach out to previously excluded groups. E. E. Schattschneider called attention to the "contagiousness" of conflict, viewing democracy as "the greatest single instrument for the socialization of conflict."[36]

For this reason, the vote-seeking dynamic of multiparty democracy should lead politicians from both parties—but especially from the losing (or minority) party—to craft policy platforms appealing to voters who are currently excluded, or poorly served, by established parties. There is a natural affinity between an out-party and an out-group. Both are excluded; both need each other to realize their goals. So long as the out-party is allowed to campaign freely (as even the most minimal definitions of democracy presume), leaders of that party should find their natural constituency among the discontented. While autocracies characteristically seek to limit access to the public sphere, democracies generally seek to expand access—registering voters, getting them to the polls, educating them on the issues, and seeking their allegiance. In this fashion, competitive multiparty democracies integrate new citizens into the polity and give alienated citizens a reason to participate.

Finally, it is important to note that the institutions of democracy are, in form and *in spirit*, egalitarian, for democracy presumes the political equality of all citizens.[37] Once it is accepted that all citizens are equal members of a polity, gross discrimination against certain members will be difficult to sustain—by virtue of the fact that it runs counter to the norms and values of the polity. In this way, the status of citizenship may lead to greater respect across social groups and greater inclusion of out-groups. Similarly, citizenship may serve as a template and a political fulcrum for out-groups to assert their rights within a community.[38]

Thus, for both normative and practical reasons, democracies should do a better job of representing out-groups, and this ought to contribute to the social and economic empowerment of these groups, whether defined by social class, ethnicity, race, religion, language, caste, or sex. Case study analyses suggest that campaigns for social justice undertaken by working classes, peasants, and ethnic and racial minorities are much more common—and much more successful—in democracies than in autocracies.[39] Authoritarian rule has generally not led to a popular acceptance of the principle of minority rights; nor has it led to an enhancement in the status of minority groups in most countries. These groups have remained, for the most part, cultural outsiders. Rarely, have they been included in the process of governance. Often, they have been actively repressed.[40]

Of course, none of these processes is quick or easy. Indeed, they may take a good deal of time to materialize. Consider that the American civil rights movement appeared a century and a half after the establishment of democratic rule and almost a century after the principle of equal suffrage was enunciated. Thus, like other mechanisms leading to better governance, the empowerment of out-groups is likely to be more characteristic of old democracies than of new democracies, where xenophobic and parochial tendencies often hold sway.[41]

## Consensus

Over time, the operation of a democratic system is likely to lead to greater consensus in a society, on matters of both policy and basic constitutional principle.[42] This does not mean that contending ideologies will disappear.[43] It means, rather, that there will be areas of agreement that stretch across the major parties and social groupings and that such areas of disagreement as persist are less likely to engender violent conflict. With growing consensus on fundamental issues, the regime should enjoy a higher level of legitimacy (though this is an exceedingly difficult concept to measure).

The argument for consensus is not self-evident. A large literature on democratic overload posits that democracy engenders costly and destabilizing power struggles among subgroups.[44] And the literature on democratization is replete with examples of the difficulties encountered by newly democratizing countries—particularly when those countries are poor or ethnically divided or where the issue of nationality is open to question.[45] The problem of democratization in the modern era is enhanced by a surfeit of expectations, accumulated over many years. Citizens have been told to expect great achievements from self-government, and they generally expect these goods to materialize in a hurry. It is the fashion of political leaders during the long and dangerous struggle for democracy to overpromise, and transitions offer little preparation for the humdrum nature of everyday politics. Thus, when the transition finally occurs, it may be greeted with extravagant expectations. Almost inevitably, democracy experienced is never quite the same as democracy envisioned.[46] The democratic process of give-and-take among competing priorities may seem to barter away what had initially been gained, a corruption of the democratic ideal into brokerage politics. Needless to say, such disillusionment does not augur well for political stability. In addition, democratization frequently stimulates a surge of demands on the part of previously quiescent and perhaps even actively repressed groups. These might be lower classes, excluded ethnic or racial groups, or some other category of out-group.[47] Such mobilizations from below may be destabilizing and may have negative externalities for the climate of social and economic opportunities.[48]

I am not making any claims about the conditions under which new democracies will survive or fail. My point is simply that, if they do survive their tumultuous youth, democratic societies are likely to experience a tempering of political conflict. Consider that the inclusionary tendencies of democratic polities (noted in the previous section) create opportunities for elite members of all sizable social groups. These are the cadres who assume leadership positions in social movements, political parties, and perhaps even revolutionary insurrections. Once granted a taste of political power as leaders of legitimate (and legal) entities, these elites may find it in their interest to work within, and to uphold, the democratic polity. It is not just a matter of personal gain (the power and pelf they may receive from their leadership position) but also a matter of political logic; they are now in a position to bargain, to achieve real gains for their social group and/or their policy agenda.

Additionally, the relatively open nature of deliberation in an established democracy may diminish the appeal of conspiracy theories, which tend to flourish in the deep fog of authoritarian rule.[49] It is possible to know, with a reasonable degree of certainty, who is in charge and who is responsible for a given decision. Over the long run, the openness of a democracy may serve as the strongest weapon against intrigue and, indeed, against any surprising political developments. Where all parties can express their views and organize freely and where a vigilant press reports on all salient political developments, the uncertainties of politics are greatly reduced.

In any case, whatever centripetal tendencies are inherent in democracy are more likely to be in evidence when those democratic arrangements have been in operation for some time. For these reasons, the thesis of democratic overload is much more compelling when applied to new democracies than when applied to old. New democracies tend to be boisterous, obstreperous affairs. Established democracies, by contrast, tend to be more restrained. In particular, the norm of incremental change is more likely to be accepted. Thus, given sufficient time and given a sufficient degree of political institutionalization, democracies are likely to develop greater consensus than authoritarian regimes.

## Institutionalization

"The major role of institutions in a society is to reduce uncertainty by establishing a stable . . . structure to human interaction," according to Douglass North.[50] Well-functioning political institutions should serve to resolve society's coordination problems.[51] In order to do so, institutions must be sufficiently institutionalized, that is, functionally differentiated, regularized (and hence predictable), professionalized (including meritocratic methods of recruitment and promotion), rationalized (explicable, rule based, and nonarbitrary), and infused with value.[52] The process of institutionalization is thus closely linked to the achievement of *rule of law*, where

> 1) laws [are] general; 2) laws [are] promulgated (publicity of the law); 3) retroactivity is . . . avoided, except when necessary for the correction of the legal system; 4) laws [are] clear and understandable; 5) the legal system [is] free of contradictions; 6) laws [do] not demand the impossible; 7) the law [is] constant through time; and 8) congruence [is] maintained between official action and declared rules.[53]

All of these ideas—nebulous though they may be—contain a similar underlying logic, articulated by Weber's concept of legal-bureaucratic rationality.

Despite their ambiguity, there seems little reason to doubt the assertion that the quality of governance hinges crucially on the degree to which institutions of government embody the intertwined ideals of legal-bureaucratic rationality and rule of law. These are key ingredients in the establishment of secure property rights, which underpin growth in a capitalist economy. While a limited rule of law has been successfully established in some authoritarian states, it is usually difficult to maintain and can never—by definition—bind the ultimate decision makers. In no autocracy is it possible for present-day rulers to effectively constrain decisions taken by their successors. This means that long-term credible commitment is virtually impossible. By contrast, the institutionalization of power in a democratic regime is closely linked to the establishment of rule of law. The same forces that rationalize channels of power also tacitly endorse the rule of law—so much so that a fully institutionalized polity is impossible to imagine in the absence of rule of law (which is why both concepts are included under the same rubric).

The historical dimension seems especially important when considering these issues. In an authoritarian setting, a Hobbesian sort of order may be established by fiat, backed up by force. Rule by coercion, insofar as it is successful, can be imposed without loss of time and without negotiation; the threat of force is immediate. Consequently, there is less need for highly institutionalized procedures for reconciling differences and establishing the force of law. The sovereign may rule directly. Indeed, relatively few authoritarian regimes in the modern era are highly institutionalized—even those that have enjoyed sovereignty for many years. Ethiopia, one of the world's oldest nations, has yet to develop a well-articulated set of governing institutions.

As in most authoritarian states, power remains highly personalized and informal.[54]

In contrast, virtually all long-standing democracies have highly developed, highly differentiated systems of rule, involving both formal bureaucracies and extraconstitutional organizations such as interest groups, political parties, and other nongovernmental organizations. Arguably, the length of time a democracy has been in existence serves as a rough indicator of its degree of institutionalization.[55] It takes a long time to institutionalize a system of rule in which the populace is sovereign. Somehow, everyone must agree upon (or at least agree to respect) the imposition of society-wide resolutions that involve uneven costs and benefits. Establishing procedures for negotiation among rival constituencies and organizations takes a good deal of time and no little struggle. An electoral law, for example, is not fully institutionalized until patterns of mass and elite behavior have adapted to the statutory or constitutional rules, and those rules are infused with value (legitimacy). However, once a stable equilibrium becomes established, it should be more efficient in resolving differences and finding optimal solutions than would be fiats imposed from above.

The institutionalization of power, including the rule of law, is critical to the evolution of democracies, while it is only incidental to the evolution of autocracies. Autocrats have neither the means nor the motivation to constrain the arbitrary nature of their rule.

## Overview

I have argued that democracy, if maintained over time, is likely to foster civil society, accountability, learning, equality, consensus, and the institutionalization of power. If this argument is plausible, secondary benefits should also materialize, as alluded to in the foregoing narrative. These secondary benefits include greater political stability, longer time-horizons, a more credible commitment to policies (once adopted), and greater legitimacy accorded to political leaders and to government policies. And this, in turn, should eventuate in better governance policies and policy outcomes across a wide range of policy areas. These putative interrelationships are summarized in figure 8.2.

The argument for a democratic "development effect" is quite plausible if one considers regime type through a historical lens–schematically, democracy + time = development. Of course, this is a highly simplified view of what

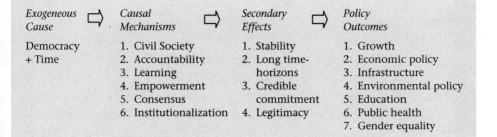

| Exogeneous ⇨ Cause | Causal ⇨ Mechanisms | Secondary ⇨ Effects | Policy Outcomes |
|---|---|---|---|
| Democracy + Time | 1. Civil Society<br>2. Accountability<br>3. Learning<br>4. Empowerment<br>5. Consensus<br>6. Institutionalization | 1. Stability<br>2. Long time-<br>   horizons<br>3. Credible<br>   commitment<br>4. Legitimacy | 1. Growth<br>2. Economic policy<br>3. Infrastructure<br>4. Environmental policy<br>5. Education<br>6. Public health<br>7. Gender equality |

*Figure 8.2.* Overview of the Argument

is bound to be an extraordinarily complex set of causal relationships. Several of these complexities deserve notice.

First, the key theoretical variable of interest—"democracy"—is exceedingly difficult to define. In my view, minimalist democracy (multiparty competition) is good for development, but the deepening of democracy (including, e.g., civil liberties, rule of law, and multiple avenues of participation) is even better. Thus, a continuous conception of this key concept is adopted; countries are more or less democratic across a variety of dimensions. For ease of exposition, I sometimes refer to democracies and autocracies as if they were crisp categories, that is, regime types. However, my theoretical conception of democracy is *non*-dichotomous. The breadth of this concept introduces some degree of ambiguity into the causal theory, for it is not clear what the "treatment" might consist of. The saving grace is that most of the recognized components of democracy co-vary, so that even a loose conceptualization of the concept does not introduce a large degree of error into the empirical analysis.

Second, the six causal mechanisms identified by the theory are also highly abstract. As a consequence, they are rather difficult to measure and hence to test. They also have a tendency to overlap with one another. It is difficult to say, for example, where "learning" begins and "institutionalization" ends. Even so, they represent conceptually distinct causal mechanisms that are hypothesized to have strong effects on a wide range of policy and governance outcomes. Although one might prefer a more concise theoretical framework, this should not tempt us to abandon accuracy and comprehensiveness. Insofar as democracy affects development, it seems quite likely that all six of the causal pathways may be at work.

Finally, there are undoubtedly multiple feedback loops in the diagram sketched in figure 8.2. For example, the policy and developmental outcomes listed in the diagram are by no means independent of each other. Economic policies affect growth, and growth presumably affects everything else, to name only one example. A second type of feedback loop concerns the effect that developmental outcomes might have on a country's regime type. A country's economic success, for example, may affect its ability to achieve, or maintain, a democracy (a matter that is disputed among scholars). These feedback loops lie outside the purview of the theory (though, naturally, they pose problems for causal attribution).

## Empirics

The foregoing theory has been tested repeatedly in the past several years by a group of scholars at work on a coordinated project. Following is a brief summary of the methodology employed in these analyses, and the results obtained to date.[56]

The first task is to identify measurable indicators of good governance— "prodevelopment" policies and policy outcomes—in the areas of interest. Thus, economic growth is measured by the GDP per capita growth rate. Economic policy is captured by trade openness, foreign direct investment, and investment risk. Infrastructure is measured by electricity grids. Environmental policy is measured by $CO_2$ and sulfur emissions. Education is measured by primary, secondary, postsecondary, and higher educational attainment. Public health is measured by the infant mortality rate. Gender equality is measured by female population (as share of total population), life expectancy ratio (female/male), fertility (total births per woman over the course of her lifetime), female labor force participation rate, and schooling gap (female/ male).

The theoretical variable of interest, democratic stock, is created by adding up each country's Polity2 score (a twenty-one-point index drawn from the Polity IV dataset) from 1900 to the present year, with a 1 percent annual depreciation rate.[57]

Analyses begin in the earliest year for which data are available—generally in the 1950s or 1960s—and extend to 2004. Samples include all sovereign and semisovereign countries for which sufficient data are available.[58] Annual data are employed wherever the evidence permits.

In the benchmark statistical model, a measure of good governance (as listed previously) is regressed against democratic stock, democratic level (the conventional, contemporaneous measure of regime type), urban population (as a percentage of total population), GDP per capita (natural logarithm), and agricultural production (as a percentage of total GDP), along with country and year fixed effects. This benchmark model is adjusted to include additional control variables, where warranted. And these results are subject to extensive robustness tests.

Table 8.1 summarizes the results of these cross-national regression tests. The first column lists the general outcome of interest, along with the indicator(s)

*Table 8.1.*  Summary of Empirical Tests

| Outcome and Indicators | Causal Effect | Robustness |
|---|---|---|
| Economic growth | | |
| GDP per capita growth rate | + | High |
| Economic policy | | |
| Trade openness | + | Medium |
| Foreign direct investment | + | Low |
| Investment risk | + | High |
| Infrastructure | | |
| Electricity | + | High |
| Environmental policy | | |
| $CO_2$ | + | High |
| Sulfur emissions | + | Medium |
| Education | | |
| Total schooling | 0 | Low |
| Higher education | + | Low |
| Pupil/teacher ratio | + | Low |
| Primary school attained | 0 | |
| Secondary school attained | 0 | |
| Public health | | |
| Infant mortality | + | High |
| Gender equality | | |
| Female population (% of total) | + | Low |
| Life expectancy ratio (F/M) | + | Medium |
| Fertility rate | + | Medium |
| Female labor force participation | + | Low |
| Schooling gap (F/M) | 0 | |

employed to measure that outcome. The second column shows the presumed impact of democracy stock on that outcome, as revealed in the benchmark statistical model. Relationships are judged positive/negative if they surpass 90% significance in a two-tailed test. The direction of this impact is understood according to the impact on *development*—not its correlation with the dependent variable. Thus, although democracy stock is negatively correlated with infant mortality, the corresponding column is marked "+" because this is a positive developmental outcome.

The third column indicates the general robustness of this finding across a variety of specification tests. These include testing democratic stock and democratic level separately (rather than together in the same model), introducing a ten-year lag for the democratic stock variable, the inclusion of a trend variable (rather than year fixed effects), a lagged dependent variable, a cross-sectional model (removing country fixed effects and including a variety of additional variables to control for cross-country heterogeneity), three-year time increments (rather than the usual annual data structure), an Arellano-Bond dynamic panel estimator, special codings of the key theoretical variable, the exclusion of newly independent countries (those without a long regime history, by virtue of their recent appearance), the exclusion of countries with the highest and lowest levels of democratic stock, the exclusion of countries from different parts of the world (Asia, Latin America, Africa, OECD, Middle East and North Africa, respectively), a democratic stock variable constructed upon a binary measure of democracy (rather than the continuous measure used in the benchmark model), a democratic stock variable constructed with a 5 percent annual depreciation rate (rather than the usual 1%), a reduced form model, and a "kitchen sink" model (including all plausible regressors, in addition to the benchmark model). Note that the high, medium, and low coding of results also reflects an intuitive judgment about the plausibility of the findings in light of the empirical model: how plausible is the identification strategy, in light of potential threats to inference?

Results provide considerable validation for the historical thesis. Although many of these outcomes show a weak or null relationship to a country's current (or previous) level of democracy, most of the chosen policies and policy outcomes show a positive and fairly robust relationship to a stock measure of democracy.

Of course, some results are stronger than others. Economic performance, measured by a country's per capita growth rate, is robustly associated with democratic stock. By contrast, economic policy outcomes are less strongly correlated with the predictor of theoretical interest. This, in turn, suggests that the links between regime type and regime macroeconomic performance are not limited to economic policies per se.

Environmental policy outcomes show a somewhat mixed picture, with the evidence for $CO_2$ emissions stronger than the evidence for sulfur emissions.

Education policy outcomes show policy divergence. Democratic stock is positively associated with educational attainment at some levels but not for primary and secondary schooling. One might speculate that mechanisms of accountability operate differently for different levels of schooling. (Alternatively, there may be systematic measurement error.)

Public health, proxied by infant mortality rates, is strongly and robustly associated with democratic stock.

Gender equality shows a fairly consistent picture. With one exception— the schooling gap—democratic stock is positively associated with the prodevelopment outcome, at conventional statistical levels of significance.

## Conclusions

This chapter has presented arguments and evidence drawn from a project in progress, indicating that that the effect of regime type on development is mediated by a country's history. Specifically, the length of a country's democratic experience—its democracy stock—explains its current level of policy performance on various dimensions of good governance related to domestic policy. This claim stands in sharp contrast to the conventional wisdom that there is no consistent relationship between democracy and development—or perhaps even a negative relationship.

In short, regime type is an important factor in a range of policies and policy outcomes generally recognized as positive for development. However, the full benefits of democracy are realized only if a regime accumulates considerable stock. A transition that is consolidated (and thus maintained over a long period of time) is likely to bring manifold benefits—economic, infrastructural, environmental, educational, public health, and gender based. If the findings of this study are correct, one may be optimistic that democratic regimes, over the long haul, will provide better governance than authoritarian regimes.

The policy prescription is clear. Democratic transitions are meaningless if they cannot be sustained. Thus, policy makers ought to focus on democratic consolidation as well on democratization.

Fortuitously, policy makers often have greater influence over long-term patterns of consolidation than over the highly unpredictable event of regime transformation. Indeed, there may be little policy makers can do to create the conditions for regime change, short of military conquest. But there are many things policy makers can probably do to enhance the quality of democracy and the endurance of democracy wherever a minimal level of political competition is already present, that is, in semidemocracies. One presumes that in such polities there is a substantial constituency for democracy, even if there remain bastions of opposition. In these cases, there are allies "on the ground" and civil society groups to work with. Here, programs focused on democracy and good governance may serve a vital supporting role.

NOTES

1. Granted, development may also condition the arrival and persistence of democracy. See Carles Boix and Susan C. Stokes, "Endogenous Democratization," *World Politics* 55, no. 4 (July 2003): 517–49. The relationship is, quite possibly, reciprocal. However, the causes of democracy are not our concern in this study. For this, see Barbara Geddes, "What Do We Know about Democratization after Twenty Years?" *Annual Review of Political Science* 2 (1999): 115–44; Boix and Stokes, "Endogenous Democratization"; and Laurence Whitehead, *Democratization: Theory and Experience* (Oxford: Oxford University Press, 2002). Naturally, we shall have to take some account of these factors in our analysis of democracy's causal effects.

2. Alice H. Amsden, *Asia's Next Giant: South Korea and Late Industrialization* (Oxford: Oxford University Press, 1989); Sylvia Chan, *Liberalism, Democracy and Development* (Cambridge: Cambridge University Press, 2002); Stephan Haggard, *Pathways from the Periphery: The Politics of Growth in the Newly Industrializing Countries* (Ithaca: Cornell University Press, 1990); Atul Kohli, *State-Directed Development: Political Power and Industrialization in the Global Periphery* (Cambridge: Cambridge University Press, 2004); T. J. Pempel, "Labor Exclusion and Privatized Welfare: Two Keys to Asian Capitalist Development," in Evelyne Huber, ed., *Models of Capitalism: Two Keys to Asian Capitalist Development* (University Park: Pennsylvania State University Press, 2002), pp. 277–300; Meredith Woo-Cumings, ed., *The Developmental State* (Ithaca: Cornell University Press, 1999).

3. Mancur Olson, *The Rise and Decline of Nations* (New Haven: Yale University Press, 1982).

4. Michael Lipton, *Why Poor People Stay Poor: Urban Bias in World Development* (Cambridge, MA: Harvard University Press, 1977).

5. James M. Buchanan, Robert Tollison, and Gordon Tullock, eds., *Toward a Theory of the Rent-Seeking Society* (College Station: Texas A&M University Press, 1980).

6. Jack L. Snyder, *From Voting to Violence: Democratization and Nationalist Conflict* (New York: W. W. Norton, 2000).

7. Jochen Hippler, ed., *The Democratization of Disempowerment: The Problem of Democracy in the Third World* (London: Pluto Press, 1995); Adrian Leftwich, ed., *Democracy and Development* (Cambridge: Polity Press, 1996); and Adrian Leftwich, "Democracy and Development: Is There Institutional Incompatibility?" *Democratization* 12, no. 5 (December 2005): 686–703.

8. See, for example, Chan, *Liberalism, Democracy and Development,* and Woo-Cumings, *The Developmental State.*

9. For example, Yi Feng, *Democracy, Governance, and Economic Performance: Theory and Evidence* (Cambridge, MA: MIT Press, 2003); Jonathan Krieckhaus, "The Regime Debate Revisited: A Sensitivity Analysis of Democracy's Effects," *British Journal of Political Science* 34, no. 4 (October 2004): 635–55; Charles K. Kurzman, Regina W. Werum, and Ross E. Burkhart, "Democracy's Effect on Economic Growth: A Pooled Time-Series Analysis, 1951–1980," *Studies in Comparative International Development* 37, no. 1 (2002): 3–33.

10. Deon Filmer and Lant Pritchett, "The Impact of Public Spending on Health: Does Money Matter?" *Social Science and Medicine* 49, no. 10 (November 1999): 1309–23; Michael L. Ross, "Is Democracy Good for the Poor?" *American Journal of Political Science* 50, no. 4 (October 2006): 860–74.

11. Jean Dreze and Amartya Sen, *Hunger and Public Action* (Oxford: Clarendon Press, 1989).

12. For a general review of democracy's effect across a host of public policies, see Casey Mulligan, Ricard Gil, and Xavier Sala-i-Martin, "Do Democracies Have Different Public Policies than Nondemocracies?" *Journal of Economic Perspectives* 18, no. 1 (Winter 2004): 51–74. It should be noted that some studies of a more popular (nonacademic) vein have presented a more optimistic view of democracy. For example, see Morton H. Halperin, Joseph T. Siegle, and Michael M. Weinstein, *The Democracy Advantage: How Democracies Promote Prosperity and Peace* (New York: Routledge, 2004). However, because the evidence seems thin, these studies have not had much impact on academic thinking.

13. Bruno S. Frey and Alois Stutzer, "Happiness, Economy, and Institutions," *Economic Journal* 110 (October 2000): 110, 466, 918–38 ; Bruno S. Frey and Alois Stutzer, *Happiness and Economics: How the Economy and Institutions Affect Human Well-Being* (Princeton: Princeton University Press, 2001).

14. United Nations Development Programme (UNDP), "Overview," in *Democracy in Latin America: Towards a Citizens' Democracy* (New York: United Nations Development Programme, 2004), www.undp.org/democracy_report_latin_america/, accessed May 16, 2004.

15. Richard J. Arneson, "Democracy Is Not Intrinsically Just," in Keith Dowding, Robert E. Goodin, and Carole Pateman, eds., *Justice and Democracy* (Cambridge: Cambridge University Press, 2004), pp. 40–58; William N. Nelson, *On Justifying Democracy* (London: Routledge & Kegan Paul, 1980). Nelson's well-thought-out justification for democracy rests on its propensity (he claims) to reach just decisions, thus identifying the virtue of democracy with the larger virtue of justice.

16. See Lee Kuan Yew, quoted in the *Economist*, August 27, 1994, p. 15.

17. For a full report of these findings, see John Gerring and Strom Thacker, *Democracy and Development: A Historical Perspective* (forthcoming).

18. Among extant studies, we have found only a few that approach the concept of democracy over time (e.g., Erich Weede, "Legitimacy, Democracy, and Comparative Economic Growth Reconsidered," *European Sociological Review* 12 [1996]: 217–25) and none that stretches back over the course of the twentieth century.

19. Ruth Berins Collier and David Collier, *Shaping the Political Arena: Critical Junctures, the Labor Movement, and Regime Dynamics in Latin America* (Princeton: Princeton University Press, 1991); Katherine Hite and Paola Cesarini, eds., *Authoritarian Legacies and Democracy in Latin America and Southern Europe* (Notre Dame: University of Notre Dame Press, 2004); Juan J. Linz and Alfred Stepan, *Problems of Democratic Transition and Consolidation: Southern Europe, South America, and Post-Communist Europe* (Baltimore: Johns Hopkins University Press, 1996); James Mahoney, *The Legacies of Liberalism: Path Dependence and Political Regimes in Central America* (Baltimore: Johns Hopkins University Press, 2002).

20. Marc Morjé Howard, *The Weakness of Civil Society in Post-Communist Europe* (Cambridge: Cambridge University Press, 2003).

21. Catherine Boone and Jake Batsell, "Politics and AIDS in Africa: Research Agendas in Political Science and International Relations," *Africa Today* 48, no. 2 (2001): 3–33; Richard Parker, "Policy, Activism, and AIDS in Brazil," in D. A. Feldman, ed., *Global AIDS Policy* (Westport, CT: Bergin & Garvey, 1994); Douglass Webb, "Legitimate Actors? The Future Roles for NGOs against HIV/AIDS in Sub-Saharan Africa," in Nana Poku and Alan Whiteside, eds., *The Political Economy of AIDS in Africa, Global Health* (Burlington, VT: Ashgate, 2004).

22. For helpful discussions of the meaning of accountability, see James D. Fearon, "Electoral Accountability and the Control of Politicians: Selecting Good Types versus Sanctioning Poor Performance," in Adam Przeworski, Susan Stokes, and Bernard Manin, eds., *Democracy, Accountability, and Representation* (Cambridge: Cambridge University Press, 1999), and Andreas Schedler, "Conceptualizing Accountability," in Andreas Schedler, Larry Diamond, and Marc F. Plattner, eds., *The Self-Restraining State: Power and Accountability in New Democracies* (Boulder, CO: Lynne Rienner, 1999), 13–28.

23. Guillermo A. O'Donnell, "Horizontal Accountability in New Democracies," *Journal of Democracy* 9, no. 3 (July 1998): 112–26.

24. David J. Samuels, "Presidentialism and Accountability for the Economy in Comparative Perspective," *American Political Science Review* 98, no. 3 (August 2004): 1–12.

25. Michael Lewis-Beck and Mary Stegmaier, "Economic Determinants of Electoral Outcomes," *Annual Review of Political Science* 3 (June 2000): 183–219.

26. Rudiger Dornbusch and Sebastian Edwards, eds., *The Macroeconomics of Populism in Latin America* (Chicago: University of Chicago Press, 1991).

27. Kurt Weyland, *The Politics of Market Reform in Fragile Democracies: Argentina, Brazil, Peru, and Venezuela* (Princeton: Princeton University Press, 2002).

28. Leslie Anderson and Lawrence C. Dodd, *Learning Democracy: Citizen Engagement and Electoral Choice in Nicaragua, 1990–2001* (Chicago: University of Chicago Press, 2005); Raymond M. Duch, "A Developmental Model of Heterogeneous Economic Voting in New Democracies," *American Political Science Review* 95, no. 4 (December 2001): 895–910.

29. Susan Carol Stokes, *Markets, Mandates, and Democracy: Neoliberalism by Surprise in Latin America* (Cambridge: Cambridge University Press, 2001); Susan Carol Stokes, ed., *Public Support for Market Reforms in New Democracies* (Cambridge: Cambridge University Press, 2002).

30. Peter A. Hall, "Policy Paradigms, Social Learning, and the State," *Comparative Politics* 25 (April 1993): 275–96; Hugh Heclo, *Modern Social Policies in Britain and Sweden: From Relief to Income Maintenance* (New Haven: Yale University Press, 1974); C. Mantzavinos, Douglass C. North, and Syed Shariq, "Learning, Institutions, and Economic Performance," *Perspectives on Politics* 2, no. 1 (2004): 75–84; Ulrich K. Preuss, "The Significance of Cognitive and Moral Learning for Democratic Institutions," in Ian Shapiro, Stephen Skowronek, and Galvin Daniel, eds., *Rethinking Political Institutions: The Art of the State* (New York: New York University Press, 2006), pp. 303–21; Kurt Weyland, ed., *Learning from Foreign Models in Latin American Policy Reform* (Washington, DC: Woodrow Wilson Center Press, 2004).

31. In Weberian terms, learning involves instrumental rationality, whereas deliberation involves more basic substantive rationality, where the goals themselves are called into question. The concept of *deliberation* covers both aspects of cognitive development. It is of course quite possible that democracies encourage not only learning but also deliberation over matters of substantive rationality. However, this claim is perhaps harder to sustain and is unnecessary, I think, to the broader argument.

32. Bruce Bueno de Mesquita, Alastair Smith, Randolph M. Siverson, and James D. Morrow, *The Logic of Political Survival* (Cambridge, MA: MIT Press, 2003).

33. The sheer number of decision makers may, by itself, enhance the quality of decision making, as suggested by recent research in social psychology; James Surowiecki, *The Wisdom of Crowds: Why the Many Are Smarter Than the Few and How Collective Wisdom Shapes Business, Economies, Societies, and Nations* (New York: Doubleday, 2004). As yet, there have been only a few attempts to test the "wisdom of crowds" in political settings. See Alan S. Blinder and John Morgan, "Are Two Heads Better Than One?: Monetary Policy by Committee," *Journal of Money, Credit and Banking* 37, no. 5 (2005): 789–812; Clare Lombardelli, James Proudman, and James Talbot, "Committees versus Individuals: An Experimental Analysis of Monetary Policy Decision Making," *International Journal of Central Banking* 1, no. 1 (May 2005): 181–205.

34. See John Gerring, Peter Kinstone, Matthew Lange, and Aseema Sinha, "Democracy and Economic Policy: A Historical Perspective," unpublished manuscript, Department of Political Science, Boston University, 2009.

35. Giovanni Sartori, *The Theory of Democracy Revisited* (Chatham, NJ: Chatham House, 1987), p. 152. In Sartori's words: "Elected officials seeking reelection (in a competitive setting) are conditioned, in their deciding, by the anticipation (expectation) of how electorates will react to what they decide. The rule of anticipated reactions thus provides the linkage between input and output, between the procedure . . . and its consequences." Sartori refers to this as a "feedback theory of democracy."

36. E. E. Schattschneider, *The Semi-sovereign People* (New York: Holt, Rinehart, and Winston, 1960), p. 12.

37. Charles R. Beitz, *Political Equality* (Princeton: Princeton University Press, 1989); Alexis de Tocqueville, *Democracy in America*, 2 vols. (New York: Alfred A. Knopf, 1945).

38. E. P. Thompson, *The Making of the English Working Class* (New York: Vintage Books, 1963); Sean Wilentz, *Chants Democratic* (New York: Oxford University Press, 1984).

39. Sonia E. Alvarez, Evelina Dagnino, and Arturo Escobar, "Introduction: The Cultural and the Political in Latin American Social Movements," in Sonia E. Alvarez, Evelina Dagnino, and Arturo Escobar, eds., *Cultures of Politics, Politics of Cultures* (Boulder, CO: Westview Press, 1998), p. 17; Leslie Elliott Armijo and Christine A. Kearney, "Does Democratization Alter the Polity Process? Trade Policymaking in Brazil," *Democratization* 15, no. 5 (December): 991–1017; Jorge I. Domingues, ed., *Social Movements in Latin America* (New York: Garland, 1994); Gunnar Myrdal, *An American Dilemma: The Negro Problem and Modern Democracy* (New York: Harper & Brothers, 1944); Charles Tilly, "Parliamentarization of Popular Contention in Great Britain, 1758–1834," *Theory and Society* 26 (1997): 245–73; Donna Lee Van Cott, "Building Inclusive Democracies: Indigenous Peoples and Ethnic Minorities in Latin America," *Democratization* 12, no. 5 (December 2005): 820–37; Deborah J. Yashar, *Contesting Citizenship in Latin America: The Rise of Indigenous Movements and the Postliberal Challenge* (Cambridge: Cambridge University Press, 2005).

40. I am cognizant of the various exceptions to the argument. Thus far, democracy has *not* worked toward the inclusion of out-groups in Sri Lanka (with respect to the Tamils) or in Thailand (with respect to the Muslim population in the south). Similarly, there are examples of authoritarian regimes (e.g., the Ottoman Empire) and semi-authoritarian regimes (e.g., Malaysia) that successfully deter, or at least defer, ethnic conflict. Nonetheless, it is notable that these regimes have not done so through processes of inclusion. Rather, they have practiced the art of ethnic separation.

41. It is important to keep in mind that social exclusion, while intrinsically bad, also has negative externalities. It reduces levels of trust across a society, removes large portions of society from active participation in higher education and in high-skilled sectors of the labor market, lowers the quality and reach of social service provision, and may also fuel ethnic conflict. Thus, I consider this a *general* mechanism leading to good governance rather than one with a restricted policy focus.

42. Robert A. Dahl, ed., *Political Oppositions in Western Democracies* (New Haven: Yale University Press, 1966); Harry Eckstein, *Division and Cohesion in Democracy: A Study of Norway* (Princeton: Princeton University Press, 1966); George J. Graham Jr., "Consensus," in Giovanni Sartori, ed., *Social Science Concepts: A Systematic Analysis* (Beverly Hills: Sage, 1984), pp. 89–104; Irving Louis Horowitz, "Consensus, Conflict, and Cooperation: A Sociological Inventory," *Social Forces* 41, no. 2 (December 1962): 177–88; Hans Keman, ed., *Politics of Problem-Solving in Postwar Democracies: Institutionalizing Conflict and Consensus* (Basingstoke: Macmillan, 1997); Arend Lijphart, *Patterns of Democracy: Government Forms and Performance in Thirty-six Countries* (New Haven: Yale University Press, 1999).

43. Francis Fukuyama, *The End of History and the Last Man* (New York: Avon Books, 1992).

44. Michael J. Crozier, Samuel P. Huntington, and Joji Watanuki, *The Crisis of Democracy* (New York: New York University Press, 1975).

45. Amy Chua, *World on Fire: How Exporting Free Market Democracy Breeds Ethnic Hatred and Global Instability* (New York: Random House, 2003); Helen Fein, "More Murder in the Middle: Life-Integrity Violations and Democracy in the World, 1987," *Human Rights Quarterly* 17, no. 1 (1995): 170–91; Demet Yalcin Mousseau, "Democratizing with Ethnic Divisions: A Source of Conflict?" *Journal of Peace Research* 38, no. 5 (2001): 547–67;

Elias Papaioannou and Gregorios Siourounis, "Democratization and Growth," *Economic Journal* 118 (October 2008): 1520–51; Snyder, *From Voting to Violence*.

46. Guillermo A. O'Donnell and Philippe Schmitter, *Transitions from Authoritarian Rule: Tentative Conclusions about Uncertain Democracies* (Baltimore: Johns Hopkins University Press, 1986).

47. Susan Eckstein, ed., *Power and Popular Protest: Latin American Social Movements* (Chapel Hill: University of North Carolina Press, 1989); Arturo Escobar and Sonia Alvarez, eds., *The Making of Social Movements in Latin America* (Boulder, CO: Westview Press, 1992); Alfred P. Stepan, *Democratizing Brazil: Problems of Transition and Consolidation* (Oxford: Oxford University Press, 1989); Sidney G. Tarrow, *Power in Movement: Social Movements and Contentious Politics* (Cambridge: Cambridge University Press, 1998).

48. Stephan Haggard and Robert R. Kaufman, *The Political Economy of Democratic Transitions* (Princeton: Princeton University Press, 1995), pp. 184–86.

49. Tilly, "Parliamentarization of Popular Contention in Great Britain, 1758–1834."

50. Douglass C. North, *Institutions, Institutional Change and Economic Performance* (Cambridge: Cambridge University Press, 1990), p. 6.

51. Russell Hardin, *Liberalism, Constitutionalism, and Democracy* (Oxford: Oxford University Press, 1999).

52. James G. March and Johan P. Olsen, *Democratic Governance* (New York: Free Press, 1995), pp. 99–100; Samuel P. Huntington, *Political Order in Changing Societies* (New Haven: Yale University Press, 1968); Steven Levitsky, "Institutionalization and Peronism: The Concept, the Case, and the Case for Unpacking the Concept," *Party Politics* 4, no. 1 (1998): 77–92; Nelson Polsby, "The Institutionalization of the U.S. House of Representatives," *American Political Science Review* 62, no. 1 (March 1968): 145.

53. Ignacio Sanchez-Cuenca, "Power, Rules, and Compliance," in José María Maravall and Adam Przeworski, eds., *Democracy and the Rule of Law* (Cambridge: Cambridge University Press, 2003), p. 68.

54. Harold G. Marcus, *A History of Ethiopia*, 2nd ed. (Berkeley: University of California Press, 2002).

55. There are a few notable exceptions to this general rule, for example, long-standing authoritarian states with highly institutionalized systems of rule such as China and Singapore, or long-standing democracies with poorly institutionalized public spheres such as Bangladesh and Papua New Guinea. But these exceptions do not gainsay the strong empirical trend.

56. Caroline Beer, "Democracy and Gender Equality," *Studies in Comparative International Development* 44 (2009): 212–27; David S. Brown, "Stock Concepts of Democracy and Human Capital," unpublished manuscript, Department of Political Science, University of Colorado at Boulder, 2010; Kevin P. Gallagher and Strom C. Thacker, "Democracy, Income, and Environmental Quality," unpublished manuscript, Department of International Relations, Boston University, 2010; John Gerring, Philip Bond, William Barndt, and Carola Moreno, "Democracy and Growth: A Historical Perspective," *World Politics* 57, no. 3 (April 2005): 323–64; John Gerring, Strom Thacker, and Rodrigo Alfaro, "Democracy and Human Development," unpublished manuscript, Department of Political Science, Boston University, 2010; Strom C. Thacker, "Does Democracy Promote Economic Openness?" unpublished manuscript, Department of International Relations, Boston University, 2010.

57. The Polity IV dataset is enlisted, despite its flaws, because it is the only global and historical dataset that measures democracy in a non-dichotomous fashion. For a description of its flaws, see Axel Hadenius and Jan Teorell, "Assessing Alternative Indices of Democracy," Working paper, Committee on Concepts and Methods, 2005; Gerardo L. Munck and Jay Verkuilen, "Measuring Democracy: Evaluating Alternative Indices," *Comparative Political Studies* 35, no. 1 (2002): 5–34; Shawn Treier and Simon Jackman, "Democracy as a Latent Variable," *American Journal of Political Science* 52, no. 1 (January 2008): 201–17.

58. The "Amelia" program is employed for imputing missing data. See James Honaker, Anne Joseph, Gary King, Kenneth Scheve, and Naunihal Singh, "AMELIA: A Program for Missing Data (Windows version)," Cambridge, MA, Harvard University, 2001, http://GKing.Harvard.edu/.

# Part III.  Does Democracy Diffuse?

## INTRODUCTION

Democratization involves changing the way a political system works. But is such change made more or less likely by the international environment in which a system operates? If so, can international actors take advantage of this and deliberately place their thumbs on the scales in any effective manner?

Talk of "waves" of democratization, of the emergence of democracy as an international norm, and of "promoting" democracy all implicitly assume a positive answer to these questions. Indeed, they suggest both that democratic practices can passively diffuse and that they can be actively and consciously spread. But if international effects are widely accepted, only recently have they been systematically investigated.

Perhaps unsurprisingly, those interested in making foreign policy have generally assumed their decisions matter. The Cold War itself might be seen as based in part on a view that a different sort of diffusion actually threatened democracy—that communist systems could supplant democratic ones through active efforts that might even use democratic tools for undemocratic ends.[1] Ironically, the American policy response that grew partly out of this view, sometimes dubbed "Cold War morality," was often held to result in the sacrifice of democratic and liberal values for short-term security interests (leading, for instance, to support of authoritarian dictatorships in southern Europe or undermining democratic regimes deemed unfriendly to American interests in Latin America). But, even more ironically, the Cold War ended when countries actually fell like dominoes in the opposite direction than had been feared. It was the communist countries that tumbled toward democracy rather than noncommunist ones falling to communism.

And it is that reverse domino effect—the "third wave" proclaimed by Samuel Huntington[2]—that has threatened to overwhelm theorizing since that time. There are so many cases to study, so many possible variables involved, so much enthusiasm generated, and so quick a rush to glib generalizations in some public discussions. The collapse of authoritarian and communist regimes led to a tremendous upsurge in interest by policy makers in democratization, peaking in the first years of the twenty-first century. But even though they were fascinated with the phenomenon of democratization themselves, scholars headed in the direction of considering international factors more slowly.

Earlier works on democratization, predating the third wave, had stressed domestic factors such as long-term historical trends, political economy, elite consensus, political culture, and institutional design. While fascinated by the collapse of authoritarian rule in southern Europe and Latin America as well as the collapse of communism, few specialists in comparative politics reached for international factors to explain developments. Unsurprisingly, it was therefore scholars of international relations (with their interest in the "democratic peace"—the view that established democracies rarely if ever fight wars) whose insights were echoed in policy debates.

Gradually in the 1990s, however, the issue of diffusion became more important as specialists in comparative politics began to incorporate the insight that democratization tends to emerge globally in waves; transitions to democracy were clustered, rather than distributed randomly across time. Quantitative studies confirmed that there were both global and regional demonstration effects.[3] It was hypothesized that international linkages and various forms of interdependence (e.g., military and economic) helped determine those states that would be most susceptible to diffusion.

Scholars investigated the variety of ways in which external forces shape the incentives and opportunities for the adoption of democratic forms of government. They viewed the oil shocks of the 1970s and the U.S. government's focus on human rights as important factors undermining authoritarian regimes in Latin America; the collapse of communism and lessons learned from previous transitions in southern Europe and Latin America emboldened prodemocracy activists in eastern Europe; and the international financial community pressured African leaders to reform through aid conditionality. The diffusion of democratic norms was also routinely credited for taking some of the edge off authoritarianism. Authoritarian regimes felt compelled to make a pretense of pursuing democratic reforms in order to be considered fully legitimate members of the international community. In the late 1990s there was a rise in research in how these norms were promoted and spread through transnational activist networks.[4]

But until the first decade of the current century, such interest in diffusion generally arose on the margins of the research agenda. Scholars had difficulty incorporating diffusion into general theories of democratization because diffusion seems to operate so unevenly. International effects seem to be stronger in central Europe and Latin America than in Africa, East Asia, or the former Soviet Union.[5] It seems to operate more powerfully at some times than others.

Part of the problem is that international pressures are filtered through domestic structures and institutions and that countries are linked very differently within the international system.[6] Thus, it should not be surprising that interest in international factors grew precisely as scholars became more comfortable with understanding the complexities of democratization and more sensitive to nuance and variation. The initial very general interest in the breakdown of authoritarian and communist regimes—one that only began to explore the distinctions among regime breakdown, democratization, consolidation—gave way to a far more sophisticated set of analytical distinctions and conceptual tools. And with that widening focus came far more friendliness to incorporating new international factors in the study of democratization.

Another problem is that we may be dealing not with a single (if highly varied) phenomenon but with a family of different ways in which international factors can matter—by promoting general conditions, by providing models and suggesting strategies, and by active attempts at promotion.

Indeed, we may be interested in two phenomena that might often be distinct: passive diffusion and active transport of democracy. The distinction may have been obscured because many of those most interested in diffusion were indeed precisely those who had a normative or policy commitment to spreading democratization.

Thus, in the 2000s academic interest in international dimensions of democratization increased in large part as democracy promotion became a central component of the foreign policy of the main Western powers.[7] The profile of democracy promotion was raised considerably when policy makers explicitly made democratization a national security issue in the wake of the

September 11, 2001, terrorist attacks. Interestingly, policy makers sometimes justified their focus (even before 2001) in terms that drew on scholarly debates (especially the democratic peace and the interest in civil society).

Because democracy has come to be imbued with such strong, positive, normative connotations, it sometimes seems to become quite literally a panacea. It is associated with security, economic growth, freedom, human rights, and in general a higher quality of life. As a result, interest in promoting democracy remained strong, along with a desire to understand how one can promote it more effectively. This has driven both policy and academic research.

In this volume, we seek to summarize the state of knowledge and advance debates with three contributions. First, Gregg Brazinsky reminds us that democracy promotion is a hoarier phenomenon than we often realize. And in fact, he finds a recurring pattern. In a time of flux and transition—the eras after both world wars and in the aftermath of the Cold War—a group of intellectuals and policy makers coalesced around an ambitious agenda of democracy promotion. In all three cases, both sides were eventually disenchanted with the experience—intellectuals felt their ideas were abandoned and policy makers felt they had been led into mistakes—producing a backlash against the idea of promoting American security through spreading democracy. But while all three efforts seem quixotic in retrospect, Brazinsky also notes that "the United States' continuing sense of its own exceptionalism is likely to lead to future efforts to spread democratic institutions and values to new parts of the world. When it does, intellectuals who can come up with meaningful visions for how and why the United States should promote democracy are likely to figure prominently."

Susan Hyde turns away from the messianic spirit of democracy promotion and the focus on the motives and record of the would-be exporters. Instead, she focuses on developments within societies, the empirical record of elections and electoral administration, and how international institutions and norms affect that record. She argues that an international norm has led not only to more elections—especially in authoritarian systems—but also to an increasingly sophisticated set of monitoring standards and institutions. The result has been a move toward homogenization of procedures—elections in various countries increasingly resemble each other. But the homogenization of form has not led to more predictable results—just the opposite. As opposed to Brazinsky's hubristic policy makers and intellectuals seeking to remake the world, Hyde's election monitors have effected slow but definite changes.

Finally, Valerie Bunce and Sharon Wolchik work to tackle the full complexities of diffusion (and of what we earlier termed "active transport" to refer to self-conscious efforts to spread democracy across borders). They explore concrete mechanisms, their limitations, how they change over time—and the learning that takes place not only among democracy's enthusiasts but also among its opponents. Like Hyde, they focus primarily on the would-be democratizing countries far more than the would-be exporters. And they find important changes over time and region on how democracy spreads. Perhaps most significantly, they find increasing agency on the part of veteran democracy activists (and also their opponents)—a sign that various actors involved in the struggle may have been quicker to learn than scholars studying the same processes.

At first glance, Brazinsky's analysis seems to pull in a different direction from the other two articles. While Brazinsky portrays American overreach, Hyde and Bunce and Wolchik show that international effects are real and how they operate. If Western democracy promoters are to take any lesson from this, it should not be that their efforts are bound to fail but that they may succeed in ways that are slow and subtle. The problem with conscious efforts to promote democracy has been its boom and bust, manic nature— the slow, complex, uneven, regionalized, and unpredictable way democracy spreads fits few grand visions.

## NOTES

1. Harvey Starr, "Democratic Dominoes: Diffusion Approaches to the Spread of Democracy in the International System," *Journal of Conflict Resolution* 35, no. 2 (June 1991): 356–81.

2. Samuel P. Huntington, *The Third Wave: Democratization in the Late Twentieth Century* (Norman: University of Oklahoma Press, 1991).

3. Starr, "Democratic Dominoes."

4. Margaret E. Keck and Kathryn Sikkink, *Activists beyond Borders* (Ithaca: Cornell University Press, 1998).

5. Steven Levitsky and Lucan A. Way, "Linkage versus Leverage: Rethinking the International Dimension of Regime Change," *Comparative Politics* 38 (July 2006): 379–99.

6. See Sylvia Sum-yee Chan, *Liberalism, Democracy, and Development* (New York: Cambridge University Press, 2002), p. 88, and Levitsky and Way, "Linkage versus Leverage."

7. For a discussion of the forces spurring democracy promotion in the 2000s, see Julia Buxton, "Securing Democracy in Complex Environments," *Democratization* 13, no. 5 (December 2006): 709–23.

# CHAPTER 9

# Policy Makers, Intellectuals, and Democracy Promotion in Twentieth-Century American Foreign Policy

*Gregg A. Brazinsky*

Democracy promotion has been a critical component of United States foreign policy during the twentieth century. Americans have long believed that they have a special and even divine mission to spread their institutions and ideals to other regions of the globe.[1] Since World War I and the advent of Wilsonianism, this long-standing faith in the universality of American political institutions has manifested itself in specific policies geared at spreading democracy abroad. The intellectual community has played a multifaceted role in this enterprise. Throughout the twentieth century, leading scholars and journalist have put forward ideas providing both justifications and methods for U.S. efforts to expand democracy. In critical junctures in American history, political leaders have drawn on some of these ideas to shape their policies. Inevitably, however, the task of spreading democracy in a complex, constantly shifting international system has proved more difficult than intellectuals anticipated. Other societies have held aspirations and embraced ideals that have defied the expectations of policy makers and scholars alike. As a result, the most significant American efforts to promote sweeping democratic change around the world have ultimately resulted in great disillusionment both in Washington and among the intellectuals who helped to shape U.S. policy.

While this chapter cannot exhaustively cover the interchange that has occurred between scholars and government officials on the question of democracy promotion, by examining and comparing the influence of several key groups of intellectuals, it seeks to demonstrate how academics have encouraged and constrained policy making in this area. In particular, it examines the progressive movement during the early twentieth century, modernization theory during the 1950s and 1960s, and neoconservatism during the past three decades. The specific nature of the interactions between intellectuals and policy makers differed greatly in each of these cases. Nevertheless, taken together they do point to some general conditions under which the intellectual community is most likely to exert a significant impact on political leaders. In particular, they suggest that when a president seeks to move policy in a new direction and scholars and journalists have coalesced around a common theory or framework, intellectual influence over policy is greatest.

## Progressivism

The influence of the progressive movement on nearly all aspects of American life during the early years of the twentieth century was immense. Although progressivism initially focused on resolving domestic social and economic problems, several major progressive thinkers eventually came to play a pioneering role in extending the influence of American intellectuals on foreign policy making in general and the task of promoting democracy abroad more specifically. The turmoil that swept over much of the world once the Great War began in 1914 led some of the movement's leaders to focus their attention on America's role in international affairs. They often sought to apply the same set of reformist principles that guided their efforts to improve democracy at home to the global arena. Although progressives did not really have a theory of democratization along the lines of those developed by scholars in the latter half of the twentieth century, their influence on American democracy promotion helped to set a precedent for interaction between the government and intellectuals. Ultimately, their ideas about how the United States could transform the world would exert a significant impact on American diplomacy for several decades.

Progressivism itself was a very broad reform movement that emerged as a response to the rapid changes brought about by industrialization and urbanization during the last thirty years of the nineteenth century. In the domestic context, progressives pursued objectives that included the regulation of big businesses, the improvement of conditions for workers, the creation of a more responsive federal government through measures such as the direct election of senators, and the expansion of women's political rights. During the early years of the twentieth century, a very wide range of politicians, social reformers, artists, and intellectuals all considered themselves "progressives."[2]

As the progressive movement started to gain in strength and popularity during the early years of the twentieth century, many of its leaders turned their attention to America's role in the world. There was not any single uniform "progressive" view of international affairs at the time. In fact, progressives were deeply split over how to see issues such as imperialism. Some supported American empire building in the Philippines and Cuba as a way of promoting social uplift at the international level and spreading the civilization of the United States. But other progressives strove to build an international peace movement and criticized American interventionism abroad, which had been on the upswing during the years before World War I.[3]

Although progressive intellectuals wrote prolifically about American foreign policy, their influence on Washington was, for the most part, indirect before the outbreak of World War I. The Great War, as it was called at the time, changed this, creating much more direct opportunities for intellectuals to participate in policy making. The combination of the war and the stunning triumph of Bolshevism in Russia in 1917 presented a major challenge to the president, Woodrow Wilson. Wilson responded to these challenges by forging a new vision of America's role in the world. This vision laid the basis for twentieth-century American foreign policy and for many subsequent U.S. efforts to project democratic institutions and ideals into other countries. In articulating and seeking to implement this vision, Wilson not only drew on the ideas of leading intellectuals but also sought to incorporate some of his strongest allies in the intellectual community directly into the policy-making process.

The Wilsonian vision of a new world order encompassed several key principles. It called for national self-determination, which included both national sovereignty and democratic self-government. Wilson also foresaw a global economy that was governed by the principles of free trade and freedom of the seas. Finally, the president wanted to create a system of collective security that would arbitrate international disputes and enforce international law. The ultimate objective of Wilsonianism was to create a peaceful, liberal world order that would be free from both imperialism and the kind of radicalism that had reared its head in Russia, and in which democracy would prevail.[4]

Wilson's vision of a new world order was likely derived from both the ideas that Wilson himself had articulated during his long, distinguished academic career and those of progressive intellectuals such as Herbert Croly and Walter Lippmann. Wilson had spent more time in academia than any other U.S. president. After earning a Ph.D. from Johns Hopkins in 1886 he taught politics at Wesleyan University, Bryn Mawr College, and Princeton University before becoming the president of Princeton in 1902.[5] During these years, Wilson's thinking was generally in line with that of some of the other leading progressive thinkers of his era. He subscribed to a somewhat elitist notion of democracy. He believed that the government needed to be responsible to the people but thought that political leaders needed to play a strong role in shaping values and managing society. Most of his scholarship did not deal with world affairs, but his later ambitions to reform the international community through providing strong leadership echoed his views of domestic politics.[6]

Other influential works written by progressive intellectuals during the first decade of the twentieth century, such as Herbert Croly's, *The Promise of American Life*, also paved the way for the emergence of Wilsonianism during World War I. Croly was a strong advocate of greater American internationalism: "The American nation just in so far as it believes in its nationality and is ready to become more of a nation, must assume a more definite and a more responsible place in the international system." Croly thought that changing circumstances would demand a greater willingness on the part of the United States to intervene in the affairs of Europe and Asia in order to preserve peace. Anticipating American involvement in World War I several years before the war had even started, Croly explained that in the future the United States might have "the obligation of interfering under certain possible circumstances in what may at first appear to be a purely European complication." Such an intervention, he contended, would be the result of "the general obligation of a democratic nation to make its foreign policy serve the cause of international peace."[7] Croly's argument that intervention in the affairs of Europe was legitimate and even desirable if it served peaceful democratic purposes helped in many ways to lay the intellectual groundwork for Wilson's later efforts to promote democracy.

But it was Walter Lippmann, Croly's close associate, who contributed most directly to the shaping of Wilson's outlook and policy. An editor of the influential journal the *New Republic*, Lippmann is widely recognized as one of the intellectual giants of his era. Although still in his twenties during most of the Wilson presidency, he had already risen to prominence through his writing. During the years between 1914 and 1917, as the United States moved closer and closer to a kind of military intervention in Europe that would have been unimaginable twenty years earlier, Lippmann played a key role in convincing the president that America's military power and moral authority could be used to build a new world order out of the havoc created by the Great War.

Like Croly's, Lippmann's wartime writings offered an impassioned plea for the United States to become more involved in world affairs. In 1915 he published a book entitled the *Stakes of Diplomacy*, which argued that "isolation must be abandoned if we are to do anything effective for internationalism." Moreover, Lippmann believed that American internationalism should serve a purpose. The "supreme task of world politics," he wrote, was "the satisfactory organization of mankind."[8] Lippmann was somewhat vague on the issue of what exactly constituted "the satisfactory organization of mankind," but his work helped to spread the idea that diplomacy and internationalism could have a transformative effect on people throughout the world.

Over the course of the next two years, Lippmann increasingly sought to directly influence the Wilson administration. In 1916 he published one editorial pointedly entitled "An Appeal to the President" that explained how American power could be used to serve moral ends. He also began making frequent visits to Washington, where, as a leading intellectual, he was granted audiences with key government officials. Seeking to attract the votes of progressives in the 1916 presidential election, Wilson proved amenable to Lippmann's influence. During the 1916 campaign, Lippmann worked hard to help get Wilson reelected. Editorial policy at the *New Republic* came to strongly favor Wilson, and Lippmann began writing campaign speeches for the president. Ultimately, Wilson won the election by a narrow margin over his Republican opponent Charles Evans Hughes. The impact of progressive voters persuaded to vote Democratic by Lippmann's articles left the president somewhat beholden to the young scholar. After the election, Lippmann received an invitation to the White House, and his influence in Washington circles continued to grow.[9]

It was really after the United States entered World War I in April, 1917 under Wilson's pledge to make the world "safe for democracy" that both the president and progressive intellectuals really began to focus on democracy promotion. Both politicians and intellectuals who supported the decision felt a need to find a moral cause to justify America's move away from its tradition of noninvolvement in European politics. The possibility of using the war and American participation in postwar peace negotiations to build a new, liberal democratic world order provided one. In the months after Wilson's declaration of war, intellectuals often felt inspired by the president's grandiose vision of using American power to transform the world, while the president increasingly drew on the ideas of the intellectual community.

In October 1917 Wilson's closest aide, Colonel Edward House, set up a top-secret commission consisting mostly of intellectuals that came to be known as the Inquiry. The directory of this secret committee included not only Lippmann but also other prominent intellectuals such as Columbia University historian James T. Shotwell and Isaiah Bowman, the director of the American Geographical Society. Working under the directorate was a staff of highly talented scholars that eventually grew to more than 126 members. Its ranks were filled with academics from a wide range of disciplines, including economics, geography, history, and political science. The Inquiry's chief purpose was to help provide the administration with information and plans that could be used in a peace conference when the war ended. Its members studied Europe carefully, seeking to find ways to assure national self-determination for the ethnic groups that sought it without creating new rivalries. Through proposing what it deemed just and fair solutions to the thorny problems of European politics, the Inquiry ultimately aimed to lay the basis for a more liberal democratic postwar order in Europe.[10]

Wilson studied the recommendations of the Inquiry carefully and integrated many of them quite directly into his famous Fourteen Points speech, which he delivered in Congress on January 8, 1918. Although the first five points and the fourteenth point, which dealt with general principles, were drawn up by Wilson, the other points, which sought to apply these general principles to specific territorial issues, reflected the work of the Inquiry.[11] The Wilson administration's use of this ad hoc committee was a significant innovation in bringing the expertise of intellectuals into the policy-making process. Although previous presidents had drawn informally on the advice of select thinkers, none had ever attempted to mobilize the intellectual community on such a large scale.

The collaborative ties formed between the Wilson administration and leading intellectuals during the war unraveled swiftly during the Paris Peace Treaty negotiations, however. Wilson had overestimated the capacity of both American power and his own personal influence to compel the allies to abandon secret agreements made during the war. Faced with persistent opposition from Britain and France on issues such as war reparations, the fate of Germany's colonies, and the territorial boundaries of eastern and central Europe, Wilson was forced to make concessions on many of the Fourteen Points. The president's inability to redeem the war through a just, durable peace swiftly alienated many of his erstwhile supporters in the intellectual community and bred disillusionment among progressives who had dreamed of changing the world. Journals such as the *New Republic*, which had spent much of the previous two years championing Wilson's cause, became fiercely critical of the administration when the terms of the Paris Peace Treaty were published in May 1919. Unwilling to accept the possibility that it was the stark realities of international politics that made progressive foreign policy objectives unattainable, writers such as Lippmann frequently blamed Wilson for not negotiating firmly enough.

In the end, progressive intellectuals, many of whom had strongly supported America's entry into World War I, joined with isolationists to urge the Senate not to ratify the Paris Peace Treaty. The Senate's rejection of the treaty marked the end of America's first major campaign to promote democracy abroad. The campaign ended in bitter disappointment for both intellectual and political leaders. From the vantage point of the twenty-first century, it may seem difficult to see how progressives could have believed that, simply by entering the war and participating in subsequent peace talks, the United States would be able to persuade the European powers to end centuries-old rivalries and put aside long-held ambitions for territorial aggrandizement. Yet the influence of progressives persisted. Aspects of progressive thinking informed subsequent efforts by American intellectuals to contribute to the spread of democracy abroad. In the aftermath of World War II, progressive ideals—now tempered by a measure of realism—were reflected in U.S. efforts to democratize Germany and Japan and to build new institutions, such as the United Nations and the World Bank, that were geared at preserving global peace and stability. Moreover, the work of modernization theorists, who I discuss next, was, in many ways, a social scientific codification of the progressive faith in America's capacity to transform the world.

## Modernization Theory and American Foreign Policy

The Cold War sparked a level of American involvement in world affairs that was far more durable and extensive than anything that had existed before World War II. The United States directly confronted new rivals, most notably the Soviet Union and the People's Republic of China, in a struggle for global influence. For American policy makers, assuming the burden of containing communism often went hand in hand with the goal of promoting democracy abroad. They believed that stable, prosperous, and democratic governments offered the best hope of undercutting the appeal of radicalism. During the late 1940s and early 1950s, Cold War hostilities most often focused on Europe, but by the late 1950s both the Free World and communist camps were paying greater attention to the dozens of newly independent states that were emerging in Asia and Africa. Promoting economic development and democracy in the Afro-Asian bloc and in Latin America, which was also considered vulnerable to radical subversion, became one of the top priorities of American policy makers.

Ties between the academic community and foreign policy makers had increased rapidly during the early years of the Cold War. As the United States became deeply involved in parts of the world that American officials knew little about, government agencies and philanthropic foundations with ties to the government, such as the Ford Foundation, had invested millions of dollars to encourage the study of Asia, the Soviet Union, Africa, and Latin America at leading American universities. Soon, a new generation of scholars that was willing and eager to share its expertise with the U.S. government emerged. Leading scholars helped to build new institutions with government funding such as the Center for International Studies (CENIS) at the Massachusetts Institute of Technology. The institution's founder, Walt Whitman Rostow, hoped quite specifically that CENIS would help to bridge the interests of American social scientists with the needs of the United States government.[12]

Many of the scholars who became active in CENIS and similar institutions touted modernization theory as the solution to the enormous difficulties face by developing nations. The basic premise behind modernization theory was that "traditional" or underdeveloped societies could be brought toward "modernity" through the assistance and tutelage of the advanced, industrialized nations of the West. By providing the right kind of assistance and advice, modernization theorists believed policy makers could manipulate the development process, thus spurring rapid economic growth and creating the vital preconditions for democracy. Modernization theory had much in common with the "elite theory of democracy," which was popular during the 1950s and 1960s. The latter theory argued that democracy required some level of consensus among societal elites who shared a common set of goals.[13] Modernization theorists tried to cultivate such elites in developing societies in the hopes that they could stimulate change.

Modernization theory employed a far more scientific outlook than progressivism did. Its advocates studied developing societies carefully and tried to identify specific methods of promoting change. At the same time, it shared with progressivism a tendency to view both mankind and international politics as objects that could be managed and transformed by American involvement. Leading proponents of the theory often combined social scientific language with calls for a more robust American globalism that were similar to those of the progressives.

Walt Rostow, perhaps the best-known proponent of modernization theory, exemplified this aspect of the theory. His book, *The Stages of Economic Growth: A Non-Communist Manifesto* (1960) captured the imagination of both social scientists and policy makers throughout the country because it offered an accessible explanation of how modernization occurred. Rostow delineated several stages that developing societies needed to pass through on the way to modernity. These included the "traditional society," the "the take-off" stage in which rapid economic growth occurred, and the era of high mass consumption, which Rostow believed the United States had entered. He also pointed to economic indicators that determined which stage particular societies were in. The influence of Rostow's works spread far beyond the field of development economics. Political scientists, sociologists, and historians focusing on particular regions of the world frequently deployed Rostow's theories to study social conditions. They frequently produced much more detailed studies of the obstacles to modernization in areas such as Latin America, Southeast Asia, and the Middle East and made recommendations for how the newly emerging nation-states in these regions could be transformed into prosperous democracies.

Links between economists and social scientists interested in modernization theory started to develop during the late 1950s but they reached their height during the Kennedy administration. By 1958, John F. Kennedy had emerged as a strong advocate of greater aid to developing countries in the Senate, and Rostow was already writing speeches for the young senator. JFK had been critical of the Eisenhower administration's failure to engage peoples in the Third World and was determined to find a new approach to the region. Modernization provided him with a meaningful framework for doing so. When Kennedy was elected president, Rostow and other leading modernization theorists ascended to prominent positions in the administration and played a critical role in shaping its policy toward Asia, Africa, and Latin America. Rostow himself was appointed deputy special assistant to the president for national security affairs. Other experts on development were sent as

ambassadors to specific regions. For instance, leading development economists John Kenneth Galbraith and Lincoln Gordon were dispatched as ambassadors to India and Brazil, respectively. Moreover, once the United States
Agency for International Development was created in 1961 its missions, filled
with economists who were schooled in modernization theory, were deployed
in developing countries throughout the world.

The ideas of modernization theorists contributed very directly to the
agenda of the Kennedy administration. Kennedy incorporated a memoran-
dum written by Rostow, which called for a "Decade of Development," into a
speech he gave to Congress in March 1961, requesting a significant increase
in American aid toward developing countries. Like Rostow, Kennedy emphasized that by infusing specific countries with developmental assistance, the
United States could foster self-sustaining economic growth and win new allies. The speech proved critical not only in convincing the House and Senate
to set aside new funds for economic development but also for providing the
world with a vision of what the new administration aimed to accomplish. Ultimately, Kennedy and Rostow convinced Congress to set aside new funds for
economic development and to fund new agencies and institutions that would
be responsible for designing and implementing modernization programs
for different regions of the world.[14]

The Alliance for Progress offers perhaps the most clear-cut example of how
intellectuals and Kennedy administration officials worked together to design
programs that linked economic and political reform. The alliance itself was a
broad, ambitious ten-year plan to advance major changes in Latin America.
Officials in the Kennedy administration feared that, in the wake of the Cuban
Revolution, Fidel Castro would seek to expand his influence to other parts of
Latin America. They believed that economic prosperity and free political institutions offered the best hope of undercutting the appeal of Castro's brand
of revolutionary nationalism. The alliance's charter was formally approved at
an inter-American conference held in Uruguay in 1961. It called for, among
other things, a minimum annual increase of 2.5 percent in per capita income,
the establishment of democratic governments, and more economic and social
planning. The alliance's basic principle was that "free men working through
the institutions of representative democracy can best satisfy man's aspirations
including those for work, home and land, health and schools."[15] More than
almost any of the other grand initiatives launched by the Kennedy administration, the Alliance for Progress reflected a faith that the economic modern-

ization and democratization of developing countries were deeply interconnected phenomena that needed to be pursued simultaneously.

Rostow played an active role in planning, advocating, and implementing the Alliance for Progress. Rostow worked together closely with Richard Goodwin, the deputy assistant secretary of state for inter-American affairs, in drafting the alliance's charter. During the mid-1960s, as the U.S. Agency for International Development (USAID) showed signs of frustration in dealing with national governments in Latin America, Rostow helped to devise what he hoped would be the solution. He called for the United States to focus its policies on regions within nations rather than at the national level, hoping to bypass the problems created by the more obdurate governments.[16]

Ultimately, however, implementing modernization programs proved much harder than devising them. For a variety of reasons, these programs often (but not always) failed to accelerate economic and political reform as the Kennedy administration had hoped. In some instances, people in the developing world clung to "traditional" mores and ideas that modernization theorists had argued could be swept away. In other places indigenous elites proved unwilling to serve as agents of the kind of reform that the United States encouraged. Finally, although Americans generally saw the modernization of the developing world as crucial to U.S. security, U.S. officials sometimes felt the need to support conservative autocrats who resisted communism even if they were not interested in development.

This combination of problems hampered American efforts to promote development and democracy through modernization in many different regions. JFK had initially hoped that a modernization program emphasizing economic and political reform might help to stabilize South Vietnam. His administration backed the Strategic Hamlet Program, an ambitious effort to move the civilian population to new areas where they could simultaneously be protected from communist influence and gain a new sense of identity as citizens of a modern nation-state. In the hamlets, Vietnamese peasants would learn to shed their traditional attitudes and come to desire economic development and modernization. Yet there is little evidence that the hamlets produced the intended effects on South Vietnamese peasants. In the meantime, the corruption of the Ngo Dinh Diem government in South Vietnam made it difficult to assure that the resources allocated for the program were used as intended.[17] The Alliance for Progress suffered from similar problems. Latin American leaders often refused to carry out the measures called for by the alliance. They were particularly resistant to carrying out land reforms, a measure that had been crucial to establishing greater social stability in East Asian countries such as Japan, Taiwan, and South Korea but which Latin American oligarchs viewed as deeply threatening. Moreover, when democratic governments gained power in Latin America, they often proved no better at managing the complex socioeconomic problems faced in their countries than their autocratic predecessors. As a result, the United States came first to tolerate and ultimately to endorse military governments that were devoted anticommunists.[18]

As efforts to carry out modernization in the developing world stumbled, frictions developed both among scholars and between scholars and policy makers. For instance, Rostow became increasingly convinced that modernization in South Vietnam needed to be backed by large-scale military efforts to suppress communist insurgents. Kennedy, however, continued to hope that a well-thought-out program of modernization could eliminate the need for greater military involvement. As a result, Rostow's influence over Kennedy's policy declined, and he was eventually moved from the White House to the State Department.[19] At the same time, criticisms of modernization theory emerged from scholars on both the right and the left as development programs repeatedly failed to produce their intended outcomes. Leftist development experts emphasized "dependency theory," which claimed that many postcolonial societies were poor not because they lacked the prerequisites for an economic takeoff but because they were being exploited by more wealthy and powerful countries. Conservatives, on the other hand, drew links between the failure of development aid abroad and the failure of LBJ's Great Society programs at home.

The influence of modernization theory on American foreign policy declined significantly with the ascension of Richard Nixon to the presidency in 1969. Nixon's foreign policy embraced realism, while deemphasizing the neoliberal viewpoints that had guided American development policy during the 1960s. Rather than trying to promote democracy, Nixon was generally willing to deal with autocratic governments in an effort to mold an international balance of power favorable to the United States. Modernization theory itself increasingly fell out of fashion among academics during the 1970s. But Nixon managed to limit American efforts to promote democracy abroad for a brief period of time. By the 1980s Washington was once again seeking to transform the world and a new group of intellectuals with yet another set of ideas about how best to do so had emerged.

## Neoconservatives and American Foreign Policy

The years between 1945 and 1968 had been marked by a broad liberal consensus in the United States. This was especially true in the realm of foreign policy where most intellectuals and political leaders had agreed on the need to contain communism and supported America's Cold War policies. This consensus broke down in the late 1960s and 1970s, however, as a result of both divisions over the U.S. role in Vietnam and the future of domestic social programs. One result of this sudden fracturing of the liberal consensus was the radicalization of the American Left, which often linked protests against the Vietnam War with a much broader critique of U.S. foreign policy toward the developing world. But the manifestation of a "New Left" was not the only political consequence of the social turbulence that prevailed during the late 1960s and 1970s. Many who had once considered themselves liberals began to fear that the Left was leading the United States in a direction that would destroy its culture and undermine its interests abroad. Eventually, a significant number of those who thought in this vain came to identify themselves as "neoconservatives."

Neoconservatism is the most open-ended of the three frameworks discussed in this essay. The label has been used to describe a relatively broad spectrum of intellectuals. Despite its name, neoconservatism draws on the same kind of liberal universalism that guided progressives and advocates of modernization theory. It, too, is based on the idea that democracy can be exported to other societies regardless of whether they have socioeconomic institutions resembling those of Europe and the United States. At the same time, its proponents have placed a much stronger emphasis on the use of American power—especially military power—to spread democracy. They have tended to emphasize that America's enemies needed to be humbled or defeated for democracy to prevail.

The most prominent neoconservatives included politicians, academics, journalists, and literary and cultural critics. Among the intellectual stars of the new movement were Irving Kristol and Norman Podhoretz, Daniel Patrick Moynihan, and Nathan Glazer. Often they had originally been members of the Democratic Party who were committed to reform at home and anticommunism abroad. But they felt alienated by the party's drift to the left in general and its choice of the dovish George McGovern as the nominee in 1972 in particular. Yet they could not fully embrace Richard Nixon either, because they viewed his emphasis on realpolitik and willingness to negotiate with the PRC and the Soviet Union as amoral. Using the pages of the influential journals *Commentary* and the *Public Interest*, this new political coalition called for the United States to stand up more firmly for liberal democratic values in the international arena.[20]

Unsurprisingly, leading neoconservatives moved away from the Democratic Party during the 1970s and gravitated to the Republicans, who called for the restoration of American strength. In the election of 1976 many neoconservatives initially stayed within the Democratic Party's folds, vesting their hopes in Senator Henry M. "Scoop" Jackson, a conservative Democrat from Washington. But they could never bring themselves to fully support the party's eventual nominee, Jimmy Carter, and would only become more critical of Carter's policies after he became president. Ronald Reagan, on the other hand, who had argued that the United States needed to staunchly resist Soviet expansionism and counter radicalism in the Third World, embraced at least some of the neoconservatives' key priorities.[21]

After the 1980 presidential election, neoconservatives began looking for ways to exert their influence on the Reagan administration. They recognized that Reagan himself was looking to change the content and tone of American diplomacy after Americans had come to despair of their country's apparent weakness during the Carter administration. Seeking to take advantage of the new president's desire for a new kind of foreign policy, the journalist Midge Dechter announced the formation of the Committee for the Free World in February 1981. In the words of its charter, the committee consisted of "writers, artists, editors, scholars . . . and publishers" whose goal was to "preserve [the free world] against the rising menace of totalitarianism." Funded by conservative foundations and corporations, the committee swiftly gained access to high-ranking officials in the administration. Dechter was a guest at the White House on several occasions, and other members of the Reagan administration started participating in the committee's programs.[22]

The role of the neoconservatives in U.S. democracy promotion during the Reagan era was a somewhat complicated one. Although they were in broad agreement on the need to firmly resist Communist influence, the neocons did not have a uniform position on the issue. Younger members of the movement such as Elliot Abrams and Joshua Muravchik tended to favor active efforts to spread democratic institutions more than some of its more long-standing stalwarts did. But the most prominent neoconservatives who were appointed to positions in the Reagan administration did have definite ideas about how the United States could promote democracy and exerted a clear influence on American policy.

Perhaps the best-known neoconservative intellectual to serve in the Reagan administration was Jeanne Kirkpatrick. A professor of politics at Georgetown University, Kirkpatrick served as a foreign policy adviser to Reagan during the 1980 campaign before being appointed the U.S. ambassador to the United Nations. She rose to national prominence through an article that she wrote for the November 1979 issue of *Commentary* entitled "Dictatorships and Double Standards." In the piece, Kirkpatrick excoriated the Carter administration for abandoning America's allies and creating conditions favorable to Soviet expansionism in the Third World. She drew a distinction between the conservative authoritarian states such as South Korea and Argentina that the United States had generally supported during the Cold War and leftist totalitarian states that were allegedly the products of Soviet or Chinese influence. According to Kirkpatrick, the former had a much greater chance of evolving into democracies than the latter. The Carter administration, she contended, had been undercutting the national interest by pressuring America's allies to improve their human rights records when they were under pressure from leftist insurgencies, because the policy had the potential to lead to far more systematic and repressive dictatorships.[23]

At first blush, Kirkpatrick's arguments did not seem to offer any sort of program for democracy promotion whatsoever. Both Kirkpatrick's rivals within the Reagan administration and her critics in the academic community often claimed that, quite to the contrary, she was simply providing a justification of American support for right-wing autocrats. But, in fact, she did have some definite ideas about how to encourage democratization that she pushed with some success during her tenure at the UN. Kirkpatrick believed first and foremost that democracies almost never took shape overnight. Instead, they "came into being slowly, after extended prior experience with more limited forms of political participation." The United States should still seek to encourage democratization, she argued, but it needed to do so cautiously and deliberately if it wanted to be successful. According to Kirkpatrick, America's role should be to "encourage . . . liberalization and democratization, provided that the effort is not made at a time when the incumbent government is fighting for its life against violent adversaries, and that proposed reforms are aimed at producing gradual change rather than perfect democracy overnight."[24] In short, the United States needed to be careful that efforts to promote democracy did not inadvertently replace right-wing dictatorships with communist totalitarianism.

The broad outlines of Reagan's policy toward the autocratic regimes of the Philippines, South Korea, Taiwan, and South Africa did seem to reflect some of Kirkpatrick's ideas. In the early 1980s when Cold War frictions remained prevalent, the Reagan administration was far less strident in encouraging these regimes to democratize than its predecessor had been. Instead, Reagan tended to rely on "quiet diplomacy" to protect dissidents, encourage economic liberalization, and restrain allied governments from carrying out the sorts of flagrant human rights abuses that would provoke international criticism. After 1985, as tensions with the Soviet Union began to wind down, the Reagan administration more openly encouraged some of its closest "friends" to surrender power to democratic elements.

Elliott Abrams was another neoconservative intellectual who gained a significant measure of influence on policy during the Reagan era. Although Abrams spent much of his early career as a congressional staffer rather than in academia or journalism, he had developed a close relationship with Nathan Glazer as a student at Harvard College and Harvard Law School. Abrams served as assistant secretary of state for human rights and humanitarian affairs, and later as assistant secretary for inter-American affairs.[25] Abrams assumed responsibility for the Reagan administration's human rights policy during the early 1980s and strove to make it an important part of the president's agenda. Abrams was in many ways similar to Kirkpatrick in his outlook. He too thought that democracy needed to expand gradually and could not be imposed over night. Thus, when many critics of the administration demanded that it do more to curtail human rights abuses in El Salvador, where the United States was supporting a right-wing military government under attack from insurgents, Abrams argued that the regime needed to be supported. But he believed that more subtle efforts could yield more stable democracies. During Reagan's second term, Abrams took the lead in implementing a "quiet diplomacy" approach toward Augusto Pinochet's government in Chile. Although Chile remained an ally of the United States during this period, the State Department continuously tried to push it toward greater democratization.

Through the rise of figures such as Jeane Kirkpatrick and Elliott Abrams, neoconservatives were able to exert a clear influence on Reagan administration efforts to promote democracy. Their influence in Washington declined during the 1990s, however. While the influence of the progressives and modernization theorists faded because it became clear that it would be impossible to turn their ideas into reality, the influence of the neocons seemed to wane in part because of their apparent success. With the collapse of the Soviet Union and optimistic claims by scholars such as Frances Fukuyama that liberal democracy would inevitably triumph around the world, neoconservatives had greater difficulty in defining their agenda and maintaining a sense of purpose. New divisions arose among neoconservatives on foreign policy issues as well, with some arguing for a realist approach and some advocating continued American efforts to promote democracy. The result was a more than decade long eclipse of neoconservative influence and power in Washington.[26]

The resurgence of neoconservative influence after 9/11 has been subject to a great deal of scrutiny and criticism among academics and journalists.[27] Initially, George W. Bush did not seem likely to follow the neoconservative agenda. When he campaigned for the presidency, Bush steered clear of the missionary zealotry that had come to characterize the thought of many neoconservative intellectuals and hewed toward more traditional conservatism. In the 2000 presidential debate, he declared that he would consider the use of force only to defend a vital national interest and vowed not to use the American military in nation-building missions. Moreover, few of the highest posts in the Bush's foreign policy apparatus were filled by known neocons. Condoleezza Rice, Colin Powell, and Donald Rumsfeld were more known for their pragmatism than their ideological fervor. Nevertheless, a few neoconservatives, some of whom had served under Reagan, did lobby for and gain appointments in the new administration, albeit not the most coveted ones. Perhaps the most notable of these was the new assistant secretary of defense Paul Wolfowitz, who had earned a Ph.D. in political science and taught briefly at Yale before serving in the Nixon and Reagan administrations.[28]

The terrorist attacks of September 11 played a pivotal role in strengthening the influence of neoconservatives in the Bush administration. Since the end of the Cold War, many of them had been warning about the threat posed by Islamic fundamentalism, and the attacks seemed to vindicate their arguments. In the dark days after this unprecedented national tragedy, the neoconservatives, with their firm ideological convictions, seemed a logical place for a president whose foreign policy had previously lacked a clear objective to turn to.[29] In subsequent months, the imprint of neoconservative thinking on Bush's foreign policy would become increasingly evident.

President Bush's 2002 State of the Union address was striking for both its bold rhetorical tone and the extent to which it reflected neoconservative influence. Much of the address had been written by David Frum, a writer and journalist who had loose ties to the neoconservative movement.[30] During the speech, Bush famously claimed that Iran, Iraq, and North Korea constituted an "axis of evil" that could threaten the United States and its allies. The president's use of stark language to divide the world between good and evil nations that were either "for" or "against" the United States helped to set the stage for future American efforts to force regime change in Iraq.

The influence of neoconservatives on the Bush administration reached its apex in 2003 with the decision to invade Iraq and topple Saddam Hussein. More than any other foreign policy decision made by Bush, the Iraq War was a product of neoconservative influence. Neoconservative writers, journalists, and think tanks joined in lobbying for the war and finding ways to justify it to the American public. Typical was the think tank, the Project for the New American Century, which sent a letter to the president signed by forty leading neoconservatives arguing that the failure to overthrow Saddam Hussein would be considered a sign of surrender in the war against terror.[31] The project would continue to exert a strong influence on high-level officials in the Bush administration. In the meantime, neoconservatives within the administration, such as Wolfowitz, emerged as the key architects for the war.

With the invasion of Iraq and subsequent American efforts to create a democracy there, the influence of neoconservatism on U.S. foreign policy reached its apex. But the neoconservatives would soon suffer from setbacks that were not altogether dissimilar to those suffered by progressives during the years after World War I and modernization theorists during the late 1960s. Transforming the world through the creation of new democracies proved much harder to accomplish in practice than intellectual advocates of democratizing crusades had anticipated. As it had in the aftermath of World War I and during the years after the Vietnam War, the public grew increasingly frustrated with the costs of expanding democracy. Yet the idea that the United States has a special world historical mission to extend freedom has long been a critical component of how Americans view their relationship with the rest of the world. It is unlikely to be eclipsed forever. And when it reemerges, intellectuals may very well take the lead once again in proposing new ideas and strategies for promoting democracy.

# Conclusion

What lessons can be drawn from the campaigns waged by progressives, modernization theorists, and neoconservatives to shape American democracy promotion? Perhaps most significantly, the interactions between these very different groups of thinkers and policy makers point to some of the circumstances under which intellectuals are most likely to exert some influence on American strategies for spreading democracy. First, their influence seems greatest when the president has a strong motive to move American diplomacy in a new direction. Wilson, Kennedy, and Reagan all drew on the ideas of scholars because they wanted to make a significant departure from the policies of their predecessors. Wilson had to overcome an enduring American reluctance to intervene in European affairs, and progressives helped to provide him with a moral basis for doing so. During the fifties, Kennedy had grown frustrated with the failings of the Eisenhower administration to promote economic development and democracy in the Third World. Modernization theorists offered a new, more promising approach that was rooted in the most sophisticated social science scholarship of the era. Finally, Reagan believed that American diplomacy needed to break out of the defeatist tendencies that had plagued it since the end of the Vietnam War. Neoconservative ideology helped to provide intellectual grounding for renewed confrontation with the Soviet Union and more assertive efforts to stand up for democracy abroad.

Second, the intellectual community has tended to be most influential when large numbers of scholars have coalesced around particular epistemological viewpoints that were relevant to the major international challenges faced in their era. Progressivism, modernization theory, and neoconservatism all informed the work of a wide range of scholars and writers both inside and outside the university. Of course, the nature of the university, its impact on public life, and the broader role of intellectuals in society have all evolved over the course of the twentieth century. Yet despite these changing circumstances, presidents have generally found it easiest to include intellectuals in policymaking decisions when they have been able to draw on the assistance of a range of scholars with similar ideas about how to promote democracy.

America's determination to spread democracy abroad has waxed and waned over the twentieth century and will, in all likelihood, continue to do so in the future. The United States' continuing sense of its own exceptionalism is likely to lead to future efforts to spread democratic institutions and values to new parts of the world. When it does, intellectuals who can come up with meaningful visions for how and why the United States should promote democracy are likely to figure prominently.

## NOTES

1. Tony Smith, *America's Mission: The U.S. and the Global Struggle for Democracy in the 20th Century* (Princeton: Princeton University Press, 1994), most explicitly addresses the role of the U.S. in democracy promotion abroad.

2. For a more detailed description of the progressives and their aims, see Michael McGerr, *A Fierce Discontent: The Rise and Fall of the Progressive Movement in America, 1870–1920* (New York: Free Press, 2003).

3. Alan Dawley, *Changing the World: American Progressives in War and Revolution* (Princeton: Princeton University Press, 2003), pp. 76–83, 92–96.

4. Lloyd Ambrosius, *Wilsonianism: Woodrow Wilson and His Legacy in American Foreign Relations* (New York: Palgrave, 2002), pp. 1–2.

5. Arthur Walworth, *Woodrow Wilson*, 3rd ed. (New York: Norton, 1978), p. 1978.

6. Ambrosius, *Wilsonianism*, pp. 27–29.

7. Herbert Croly, *The Promise of American Life* (New York: Filquarian, 2007), pp. 317–18, 341.

8. Ronald Steel, *Walter Lippmann and the American Century* (New Brunswick: Transaction Publishers, 1999), p. 92.

9. Ibid., pp. 101–15.

10. Ibid., pp. 128–40.

11. Ibid.

12. Mark Haefele, "Walt Rostow's Stages of Economic Growth," in David Engerman et al., eds., *Staging Growth: Modernization, Development and the Global Cold War* (Amherst: University of Massachusetts Press, 2003), p. 83.

13. Nils Gilman, "Modernization Theory: The Highest Stage in American Intellectual History," in Engerman et al., *Staging Growth: Modernization*, p. 59.

14. Ibid., pp. 94–95.

15. Cited in Smith, *America's Mission*, p. 217. The charter itself was reprinted in *State Department Bulletin* 45, no. 1159 (September 11, 1961).

16. Kimber Charles Pearce, *Rostow, Kennedy and the Rhetoric of Foreign Aid* (Lansing: Michigan State University Press, 2001), pp. 103–16.

17. On the Strategic Hamlet Program, see Phillip E. Catton, *Diem's Final Failure: Prelude to America's War in Vietnam* (Lawrence: University Press of Kansas, 2003).

18. Smith, *America's Mission*, pp. 223–28.

19. Haefele, "Walt Rostow's Stages of Economic Growth," pp. 95–96.

20. John Ehrman, *The Rise of Neoconservatism* (New Haven: Yale University Press, 1995), pp. 35–36.

21. Ibid., pp. 137–39.

22. Ibid., pp. 140–41.

23. Jeanne Kirkpatrick, "Dictatorships and Double Standards," *Commentary*, November 1979, pp. 34–45.

24. Cited in Ehrman, *The Rise of Neoconservatism*, pp. 120–21.

25. Jacob Heilbrunn, *They Knew They Were Right: The Rise of the Neocons* (New York: Doubleday, 2008), pp. 174–83.

26. Ira Chernus, *Monsters to Destroy: The Neoconservative War on Terror and Sin* (Boulder, CO: Paradigm, 2006), pp. 39–43.

27. See, for instance, Chernus, *Monsters to Destroy*; Patrick J. Buchanan, *Where the Right Went Wrong: How Neoconservative Subverted the Reagan Revolution and Hijacked the Bush Presidency* (New York: St. Martin's 2005); Stefan Halper, *America Alone: The Neoconservatives and the Global Order* (Cambridge: Cambridge University Press, 2005).

28. Heilbrunn, *They Knew They Were Right*, pp. 228–32.

29. Ibid., p. 227; Chernus, *Monsters to Destroy*, pp. 115–18.

30. Frum talks about his role in writing the speech in David Frum, *The Right Man: An Inside Account of the Bush White House* (New York: Random House, 2005), pp. 224–46.

31. Heilbrunn, *They Knew They Were Right*, pp. 250–51.

CHAPTER 10

# International Dimensions of Elections

## Susan D. Hyde

Out of all independent states in the world, only a handful do not yet hold some form of regular national elections. These elections, however, vary widely in their relationship to democracy, with some countries holding entirely undemocratic elections. North Korea, for example, held national assembly elections in 2003 in which virtually no competition was allowed. Nevertheless, the government went to some effort to publicize the elections, reporting an incredible 100 percent turnout and explaining in a press release that "those electors who are not able to go to the polls due to old age and diseases cast their ballots into . . . mobile ballot boxes."[1] In 1995 Saddam Hussein's government held presidential elections in which he was the only candidate on the ballot and voters were presented with two options: yes or no. Voting no was perceived to be a sure path to persecution. Somewhat surprisingly, the Iraqi government sought international media attention in advance of the elections by announcing that they were welcoming ten thousand foreign observers (although none reportedly accepted the invitation).[2]

National-level elections have spread globally, to all but a few of the least democratic countries in the world. Of the 172 independent states in existence between 2000 and 2006,[3] only 11 states failed to have some form of direct election for national office: Angola, Bhutan, China, Eritrea, Libya, Myanmar (Burma), Nepal, Qatar, Saudi Arabia, Somalia, and the United Arab Emirates. Four of these states—Angola, Bhutan, Myanmar, and Nepal—held elections in 2007 or 2008, including a 2008 referendum in Myanmar. Why have elections become so widespread? Why do even the most autocratic leaders bother to hold elections, even when they are quite obviously shams? Throughout the developing world, how do international actors affect elections? More importantly, what are the consequences of these global trends for the quality of elections and for democratization?

The primary goal of this chapter is to explore the international dimension of elections, and to highlight consequences of international pressure for elections and democracy. I do not argue that elections are inevitably good, or that they are never corrupted, rigged, stolen, or exploited by leaders for purposes unrelated to democracy (for more on "semi-authoritarianism," see Nathan Brown's and Henry Hale's contributions to this volume). Rather, I focus on the combined effect of several international-level variables that together generate greater constraints on autocratic leaders. Because of international pressure, governments are more likely than ever before to hold elections, invite international election monitors, and comply with widely accepted electoral practices. Although some leaders successfully evade these international pressures, rig elections for their own purposes, or strategically evade a negative report from international election observers, I argue that, on average, international pressure for democracy and international expectations about the appropriate behavior of election-holding governments have increased constraints on autocratic leaders.

Various explanations exist for elections in autocratic regimes, most of which focus on domestic variables. Existing work argues that elections help dictators allocate resources among politicians within the party or among voters; are tools to keep the political opposition divided or to demonstrate the strength of hegemonic parties, thereby discouraging defection from within the party; or reduce the risk that autocrats will be removed from office violently.[4] I do not dispute these theories or the idea that domestic factors are the primary determinants of when and why leaders choose to hold elections. Rather, I argue that international-level variables are also important in explaining and understanding the global spread of elections. By increasing the associated benefits, international pressure for elections and democracy make elections more likely in countries whose leaders would otherwise prefer to avoid them. Similarly, external pressure, combined in many cases with direct democracy assistance, causes changes in the form these elections take, in some cases improving the quality of elections.

That the spread of elections and democracy has something to do with international politics is increasingly accepted, and it is no longer particularly controversial to argue that some leaders hold elections and agree to some political liberalization in part to please international audiences.[5] Less widely discussed are the consequences of the increase in elections resulting from international pressure for democracy. In this chapter, I present several related trends in order to explore the international dimensions of elections. Drawing on recent findings in the literature, I argue that international variables play an important and sometimes unanticipated role and make three general points about the international dimensions of elections.

First, international pressure is in part responsible for the global spread of elections, particularly to the most undemocratic regimes. Even for dictators who allow little competition, antidemocratic elections are more risky than banning elections entirely. Therefore, compared to a world without international pressure for elections, the increase in authoritarian elections should mean that transitions are more likely.[6]

Second, international election monitoring has become an international norm, reinforcing the expectation that leaders of democratizing countries will invite international observers if they are to hold credible elections. This development further constrains would-be cheaters by deterring fraud directly and by making it less likely that they will go unpunished for overt election fraud by international and domestic audiences.[7]

Third, international pressure for democracy, including direct democracy assistance, also constrains leaders (and perhaps improves the quality of elections) by causing the spread of election-related characteristics, making electoral processes more uniform, and eliminating several of the easiest methods of stealing elections. Throughout the world, direct democracy assistance has made many features of elections widespread, including independent election commissions, uniform national ballots, transparent and secure ballot boxes, participation of political party witnesses, domestic nonpartisan election monitoring, and the public release of disaggregated election results. All of these relatively uninteresting procedural changes combine to make it more difficult for election fraud to go uncovered.

I argue that, taken together, these trends result in autocratic leaders who are constrained on many fronts and face difficult trade-offs that would not exist in the absence of international pressure for democracy. Before elaborating on these points, it is first necessary to address several common misperceptions that tend to surface in debate over the international dimensions of elections and democratization.

## Common Misperceptions about Democracy Promotion

There remains well-rooted suspicion within some circles of comparative politics and international relations about the international dimensions of elections, as well as external influences on democratization more generally. This is due in part to a tendency for scholars to talk past each other on several important issues. First, numerous articles, including Terry Karl's influential 1986 piece on "the fallacy of electoralism," forcefully argue against the idea that holding elections necessarily causes democracy.[8] Yet, as far as I can tell, no one makes this argument in print. As Thomas Carothers points out, it is also incorrect that practitioners of democracy promotion are under the impression that internationally imposed elections will automatically cause stable, long-term democracy.[9] The closest argument is made by proponents of procedural democracy, beginning with Schumpeter, and including Robert Dahl, Samuel Huntington, and Adam Przeworski, but even these scholars emphasize the competitiveness of elections as fundamental, which, they argue, cannot occur in the absence of a variety of political and civil rights.[10] At least within the academic community, the idea that elections equal democracy is a straw man of an argument, and scholars widely endorse the idea that elections are a necessary but not sufficient condition to bring about democratization.

To be fair, those individuals arguing against "electoral fetishism" frequently have their sights set on the policy community, with writers such as Fareed Zakaria arguing that the emphasis on spreading multiparty elections is a poor or even dangerous substitute for what he argues should be a focus on promoting constitutional liberalism.[11] However, criticism that practitioners assume elections are equal to democracy is also overstated. Advocates of democracy promotion tend to subscribe to a more nuanced view of the relationship between elections and democracy: in many situations in which governance is difficult, such as following violent conflict, economic collapse, the fall of a dictator, a military coup, or new statehood, elections are known to be a risky proposition, but they are thought to be better than the available alternatives. Most scholars of democratization can name at least a dozen cases in which elections held in part because of international pressure were followed almost immediately by extreme instability, resumption of civil conflict, collapse of the economy, or other disastrous consequences. This sequence of events, of course, does not demonstrate that holding elections caused the disastrous consequences. If these cases are instead viewed as the most difficult of circumstances, in which no legitimate governing authority exists and peace is nonexistent or unstable, it is not clear which other options might be more likely to bring about stable governance. Elections, in these cases, can be the last-best option, and it is not surprising that under these conditions they are occasionally followed by spectacular failures.[12]

Of course, there may also be real risks to holding elections too early or under certain conditions, as Henry Hale discusses at greater length in this volume, and as other scholars have highlighted.[13] My point is simply that it is difficult to know what would have happened in the most extreme cases if elections had not been held, as the counterfactual is inherently unobservable, and there are measurement-based challenges to studying the relationship between democratization and violence using traditional measures of democracy.[14] To phrase the issue a bit differently and more directly sum up the challenges faced within the democracy promotion policy community, we might ask, in the absence of elections and any recognized leadership in a country, how else might effective governance be established. The other options range from the very difficult to the irresponsible and somewhat ridiculous, such as the creation of long-standing international protectorates that rely on UN peacekeeping forces, the imposition of a dictator (an option currently out of fashion but occasionally suggested), encouragement of a civil war until one side achieves overwhelming victory, or imposition of a monarch with widely recognized divine authority. Compared to these more extreme options, holding national elections, even if they must take place under less than ideal circumstances, becomes a more reasonable option.[15] Even among practitioners within the democracy promotion community, elections are seldom viewed naively.

Finally, another rarely argued but frequently argued-against point is that advocates of democracy promotion believe that democracy can and should be forcefully imposed. As Gregg Brazinsky details in this volume, this perception has become closely tied to the U.S. war in Iraq, which has caused a sea change in the perception of democracy promotion, both in the United States and in countries subject to democracy assistance.[16] Without a doubt, the case of Iraq is important, but it is very unique in the field of democracy promotion. Bracketing the case of Iraq and all of the controversy that accompanies it, the more common perception among democracy promoters and scholars of democracy promotion is that international actors can help facilitate democracy in places where citizens demand it.[17] This effect sometimes takes place on the margins, as Philippe Schmitter has argued.[18] However, even marginal effects can be instrumental in triggering democratic transitions, a fact that has been reflected in the foreign policies of many governments, most prominently the United States (Brazinsky, in this volume).

Similarly, a favorite piece of rhetoric among skeptics is that democracy promotion cannot be effective or genuine because there are cases in which democracy-promoting states and countries have failed to promote democracy consistently, such as the U.S. support for anticommunist dictators during the Cold War. It is not strictly necessary for democracy promotion to be consistent in order for it to work. Increasing consistency might improve the efficacy of democracy promotion (itself an empirical question), but it is not true that inconsistent application of a policy at the global level invalidates the entire enterprise of democracy promotion. It remains highly unlikely that democracy promotion will ever outweigh all other foreign policy goals, nor should it. Democracy-promoting states will always care disproportionately more about their own territorial integrity, the safety of their population, and economic strength. Even given this, however, it is still possible that leaders of not-yet democratic states have reason to believe they will be better off if they appear to move toward democracy than if they do not. It is true that Egypt, because of its strategic importance to the United States, will continue to receive high levels of foreign aid even if Hosni Mubarak suspends elections entirely and creates a system of formal hereditary succession. It may also be true, however, that if Mubarak led his country toward further political liberalization, he would receive even more international benefits from democracy-promoting states. In Mubarak's case, the risks associated with fully competitive elections clearly outweigh the international benefits of political liberalization, but it is likely not true for dozens of other leaders who are motivated to risk somewhat democratic elections in order to appear to be democratizing leaders.

Within this somewhat more pragmatic view of the role of elections and democracy promotion, I now turn to a discussion of the three trends that I outlined in the introduction: the global spread of elections, the international norm of international election monitoring, and the homogenization of electoral practices.

## Trend 1: The Global Spread of Elections

International pressure is in part responsible for the global spread of elections, as well as the global spread of manipulated elections.[19] This trend can be most starkly seen in Africa, where geopolitical concerns during the Cold War meant that many leaders felt immune from pressures to democratize. After the end of the Cold War, domestic and international pressure for democracy combined and resulted in an enormous increase in the number of elections, nearly doubling the average number held in the region each year. Many of these elections are so rigged that any form of meaningful competition is impossible, and many scholars choose to ignore them. Recent work, however, has highlighted two ways in which antidemocratic elections are more risky than having no elections at all.[20]

First, fraudulent elections can serve as a focal point for citizens who are unhappy with the status quo to revolt against the regime.[21] Coordination among citizens is difficult, plagued by the problems of collective action. Elections are a nationally recognized moment of citizen expression and, even when such expression is limited or repressed, the fact that elections occur can give a group of individuals the motivation, opportunity, and information necessary for coordinated action against the regime. Compared to a regime holding no elections, even spectacularly flawed elections can increase the probability of an electoral revolution.[22]

Second, as highlighted by Samuel Huntington in his discussion of democratic transition through "stunning elections," autocrats are not always able to accurately judge their own popularity, and some seem to dramatically overestimate their ability to win genuine elections.[23] The ease of stealing an election may be overestimated, and some autocrats have held elections, attempted to win through fraud, but lost anyway. For electoral autocrats, knowing one's own popularity and stealing elections when needed may be harder than it looks. After experiencing a "stunning" defeat, leaders can attempt to repress the release of election results, but as Noriega learned after the 1989 Panamanian elections, and as Mugabe learned in Zimbabwe in 2008, postelection fabrication of the election results is rarely convincing, and can also trigger postelection protests, widespread violence, international condemnation, or other reactions that weaken their hold on power.

Thus, in comparison to a world absent international pressure for elections, the increase in elections should mean that alterations in power are more likely.[24] Figure 10.1 illustrates the trend in elections over time, excluding elections in long-term developed democracies. The dramatic increase in the number of elections held after 1990 was caused partly by elections in newly inde-

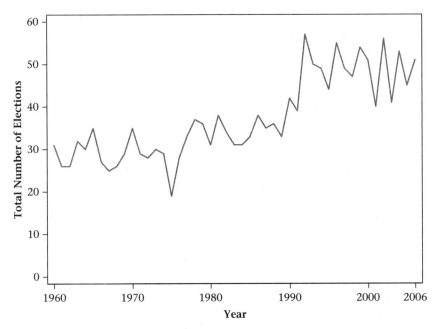

*Figure 10.1.* Total Number of Elections Held Each Year. *Source:* Data on elections from the National Elections across Democracy and Autocracy data. Susan D. Hyde and Nikolay Marinov, "National Elections across Democracy and Autocracy," unpublished manuscript, Yale University, 2009.

pendent states, but the trend looks similar when presented as the annual percent of countries in the world holding elections.

Some scholars question whether anyone is fooled by sham elections, including Nathan Brown in this volume, as well as Jennifer Gandhi and Ellen Lust-Okar, who argue that there must be some other purpose to holding blatantly rigged elections.[25] Domestic audiences are not persuaded by fraudulent elections, as it is relatively easy even for individual voters to distinguish between an election in which opposition is allowed to compete freely and an election in which the opposition is banned. Even willfully naive international actors were not persuaded that recent elections in Cuba, Laos, Vietnam, North Korea, or Turkmenistan resembled democratic elections. National elections are clearly observable: either governments hold national elections or they do not. Judging the quality of election is much more subjective, and my argument is simply that refusing elections entirely sends a different message to domestic and international actors than not holding elections at all. At the risk of stating the obvious, the global spread of elections means that the types of regimes holding elections are diverse, but the types of governments refusing elections are not. After 2000, refusing national elections entirely would put a regime in the same category with China, Libya, Qatar, Saudi Arabia, and Somalia. To be sure, these governments differ in important ways, but they are disproportionately anti-Western and isolationist. And even the Chinese government argues that the country is moving toward democratization (see Bruce Dickson, in this volume). For countries less powerful than China, less wealthy than Saudi Arabia or Qatar, and with more of a functioning government than Somalia, holding elections allows them to make the argument (however implausible) that they are engaging in political liberalization.

## Trend 2: International Election Monitoring Is Nearly Universal

Today, merely holding elections is not enough. In order to meet international expectations, leaders today must do much more than merely hold rigged elections. Particularly since the end of the Cold War, international norms have changed such that leaders are also expected to hold elections and seek international scrutiny of their elections by inviting foreign election monitors.[26] International election monitoring, now widely referred to as an international norm, arguably further constrains leaders in their ability to steal elections.

International monitors are nearly always invited by the incumbent government and are prohibited from interfering in the electoral process in any way. Nevertheless, their increasing ability to detect election fraud, their status as impartial third-party judges of election quality, and their willingness to call out serious election manipulation make them willing and able to expose leaders who try to steal elections. One might therefore expect that leaders are strategic in choosing when to invite international observers. This was undoubtedly the case when election monitoring was initiated. However, because election monitoring has become an international norm, the refusal to invite observers has itself become a reason to impose costs on governments.[27]

Huntington neatly sums up the dilemma facing leaders: "Foreign observers made it difficult if not impossible for governments quietly and secretly to steal an election. Blatant theft, as in the Philippines and Panama, however, defeated the purpose of having the election, which was to enhance the domestic and international legitimacy of the rulers. If, on the other hand, the govern-

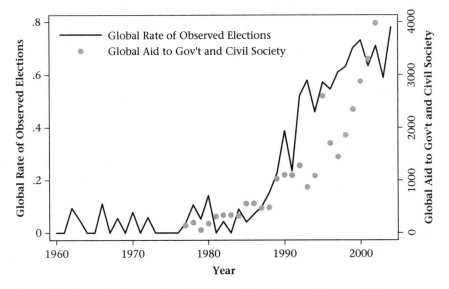

*Figure 10.2.* Trends in Internationally Observed Elections and Foreign Aid to Government and Civil Society. *Source:* Data on election observation collected by author. Data on aid to Government and Civil Society from the OECD Development Cooperation Directorate, www.oecd.org/dac.

ment refused to allow 'impartial' external observers to witness the vote, that in itself now became proof that it was rigging the election."[28] As shown in Figure 10.2, excluding those elections that take place outside of the long-term consolidated democracies, international election observers are now invited to more than four out of every five national elections.

Other research suggests several ways in which election monitors constrain autocrats who hold elections or invite observers in response to international pressure. Foreign observers can reduce election day fraud directly by visiting hundreds or even thousands of polling stations on election day, thus making it more costly for leaders to steal elections outright.[29] International observers also give opposition parties an audience and may make preelection boycotts of the electoral process more likely.[30] Alternatively, it is also possible that observers provide cover for autocrats and help legitimate stolen elections, an outcome that caused many to criticize international election monitors.[31] In response to criticism of their methods, observers have dramatically expanded the scope of their observation, and reputable observers increasingly criticize elections. Even given this potential for observers to sometimes validate poor elections, this observer error may be a necessary part of the trend, as the possibility that observers will validate stolen elections may be one reason why pseudodemocrats risk inviting them in the first place.[32]

## Trend 3: Homogenization of Elections Driven by Democracy Assistance

A third trend associated with the global spread of elections pertains to the way that elections are conducted. Universal adult suffrage and protections for the secret ballot, as outlined in the Universal Declaration of Human Rights, are virtually the only formally and universally recognized international standards for democratic elections.[33] And yet many elections held throughout the developing world are now administered in remarkably similar ways, including the use of uniform national ballots, standardized processes for voter registration and maintenance of the voter register, the establishment of nominally independent election commissions, public posting of election results at polling stations, the use of translucent ballot boxes, regulations mandating official political party witnesses inside polling stations, transparent procedures for vote tabulation and aggregation, and the now iconic use of indelible ink on voters' fingers to prevent multiple voting. This list is incomplete, and some practices are regional rather than global, or not adopted for other reasons, but given that the choice of electoral institutions is made by individual governments, there has been a remarkable diffusion of practices intended to make elections more transparent, observable, and free of election manipulation.

This coincidence in practice results in part from the fact that election-holding leaders are courting domestic and international audiences, but it is also due to a more overt form of international involvement via democracy assistance. Democracy assistance consists of support from international organizations such as the UN in funding or organizing parts of the electoral process and providing extensive technical assistance on the conduct of elections.[34] Democracy assistance frequently brings about relatively small changes in practice. Any one of these small changes in the administration of elections is unlikely to bring about democratic elections in places that are not already predisposed to have them. However, when these trends are numerous and permeate the electoral process, their combined effect may be to make genuine electoral competition more likely. Or, like the effects of election monitoring, these changes can make fraudulent elections more likely to be exposed and punished.

Even election-holding autocrats are vulnerable to these trends. Robert Mugabe's government, in the first round of the 2008 presidential elections, agreed to post initial vote tallies outside of polling stations. It is unclear why this change in practice took place, but releasing election results at the local level allowed domestic groups and opposition parties to document Mugabe's loss in first round of the election and demonstrate that Morgan Tsvangirai nearly won the first round outright. Why did Mugabe's government allow the local-level posting of election results? Similarly, why have so many governments allowed quick counts to be carried out by domestic and international observers? Why do governments—even those planning to commit election fraud—voluntarily adopt practices that make fraud more difficult, such as independent election commissions, secure ballot boxes, verifiable vote counting systems, audits of their voter register, uniform voting booths to protect voter secrecy, and protections against multiple voting? As these features of elections become more widespread among democratizing countries, my argument is that it is harder for governments to avoid these changes without increasing suspicion about their commitment to democracy and the quality of their elections. Additionally, by adopting practices that are recommended by international organizations and donors, governments attract increased international funding to pay for their elections.

## Internationally Constrained Leaders and the Incentive to Fake Democracy

Taken together, recent research paints a picture of domestic elections held under international constraints. For leaders of countries that are not already considered democratic, international pressure for democracy and its associated trends mean that they face more constrained and therefore more difficult choices about their domestic political institutions. Leaders today are more likely to hold elections and less likely to get away with election manipulation. Given the increased probability of negative outcomes following fraudulent elections, one might expect that the number of leaders choosing to hold elections would decrease. On the contrary, the evidence points to the majority of autocrats choosing the risks of elections over the expected penalties for not having them at all. As Andreas Schedler sums up this balancing act,

> Electoral authoritarian regimes neither practice democracy nor resort regularly
> to naked repression. By organizing periodic elections they try to obtain at least
> a semblance of democratic legitimacy, hoping to satisfy external as well as inter-
> nal actors. At the same time, by placing those elections under tight authoritarian
> controls they try to cement their continued hold on power. Their dream is to
> reap the fruits of electoral legitimacy without running the risks of democratic
> uncertainty. Balancing between electoral control and electoral credibility, they
> situate themselves in a nebulous zone of structural ambivalence.[35]

Many "electoral autocrats" simultaneously face domestic and international
pressure to hold elections and are under ever-increasing scrutiny of the quality of those elections. Combined, these trends give a subset of leaders in the
international system the incentive to attempt to fake democracy. Leaders who
are not sufficiently skilled at holding elections that are "democratic enough"
while minimizing electoral uncertainty are unable to maintain the charade,
resulting in a greater likelihood of democratic transitions than would be the
case in the absence of international pressure.

It is an open question whether the form of democracy that results from
international pressure is the same or different from the type of democracy
that grows out of changes in domestic politics over decades and appears to
be irreversible once a country has also achieved a certain level of wealth.[36]
Experience with pseudodemocracy—by both citizens and leaders—may have
long-term deleterious consequences on the probability of democratic consolidation. On the other hand, evidence from Latin America suggests that
the demand for democracy among citizens appears surprisingly resilient,
even in countries with extended experiences with the low-grade democratic
governance.

Yet there are also countervailing trends. The adoption of electronic voting
has been used successfully in some countries, but in other cases, such as Venezuela, it appears that electronic voting has played a part in seriously undermining voter confidence and the belief among some sections of the population that their vote is secret. New technologies have also had enormous
influences on voter access to information and the ability of opposition movements to communicate with their supporters abroad, but, as the 2009 elections in Iran showed, such technologies can also be used by autocratic governments to control citizen access to information, persecute opposition leaders,
and generate the appearance of mass support for the government. It is not yet

clear how the use of such tactics by electoral autocrats will spread, nor how they will affect the international dimensions of elections outlined in this chapter.

## Conclusion

Although it is difficult to prove conclusively, anecdotal and cross-national evidence suggests that international pressure is one factor explaining the global spread of elections. Holding elections has become an international norm, illustrated in part by the fact that every single newly independent state since the end of the Cold War has held national elections. Once countries begin holding elections, they are very likely to continue to hold elections (Brown, in this volume). Election-holding regimes that are not already widely classified as consolidated democracies are expected to invite international election monitors and to comply with other trends in the way elections are held, a change that I argue makes it more difficult for leaders to hold elections and get away with manipulation.

This does not mean that the world is moving inevitably toward a world free of autocrats or fraudulent elections, as Henry Hale explores more thoroughly. The same forces that I have described are also likely to cause some leaders to become further entrenched by motivating the development of more creative and potentially more destructive ways of staying in power. Leaders with sufficient motivation to stay in power tend to find ways to do so, even if they hold elections and respond to international pressures. Nevertheless, increasing international constraints on leaders should increase risks for autocrats and lead to greater probability of political liberalization across a number of countries.

NOTES

I am grateful for helpful comments from Nathan Brown, Sherri Berman, Cynthia McClintock, Ellen Lust, Nikolay Marinov, and the other authors who contributed to this project.
1. North Korean News Agency, "North Korea Reports All Voters Participated in Assembly Elections," *BBC Summary of World Broadcasts* (Pyongyang, August 3, 2003).
2. See also Nathan Brown's discussion of elections in the Middle East (chapter 2 in this volume).
3. This number excludes states with population less than 250,000.

    4. Beatriz Magaloni, *Voting for Autocracy: Hegemonic Party Survival and Its Demise in Mexico*, (Cambridge: Cambridge University Press, 2006); Ellen Lust-Okar, "Divided They Rule: The Management and Manipulation of Political Opposition," *Comparative Politics* 36, no. 2 (2004): 159–79; Jason Brownlee, *Authoritarianism in an Age of Democratization* (Cambridge: Cambridge University Press, 2007); Alberto Simpser, "Making Votes Not Count: Strategic Incentives for Electoral Corruption" (Ph.D. dissertation, Stanford University, 2005); Gary Cox, "Authoritarian Elections and Leadership Succession, 1975–2000," unpublished manuscript, University of California, San Diego, 2008; Barbara Geddes, "What Do We Know about Democratization after Twenty Years?" *Annual Review of Political Science* 2 (1999): 115–44; Hein E. Goemans, Kristian Skrede Gleditsch, and Giacomo Chiozza, "Introducing Archigos: A Data Set of Political Leaders," *Journal of Peace Research* 46, no. 2 (2009): 269–83; Hein E. Goemans, "Which Way Out? The Manner and Consequences of Losing Office," *Journal of Conflict Resolution* 52, no. 6 (August 27, 2008): 771–94.

    5. Paul W. Drake, "The International Causes of Democratization, 1974–1990," in Paul W. Drake and Mathew D. McCubbins, eds., *The Origins of Liberty: Political and Economic Liberalization in the Modern World* (Princeton: Princeton University Press, 1998); Kristian Skrede Gleditsch and Michael D. Ward, "Diffusion and the International Context of Democratization," *International Organization* 60, no. 4 (2006): 911–33; Susan D. Hyde, *The Pseudo-Democrat's Dilemma: Why Election Monitoring Became an International Norm* (Ithaca: Cornell University Press, forthcoming); Steven Levitsky and Lucan Way, "International Linkage and Democratization," *Journal of Democracy* 16, no. 3 (2005): 20–34; Jon C. Pevehouse, *Democracy from Above: Regional Organizations and Democratization* (Cambridge: Cambridge University Press, 2005); Jon C. Pevehouse, "Democracy from the Outside-In? International Organizations and Democratization," *International Organization* 56, no. 3 (2003): 515–49; Beth A. Simmons, Frank Dobbin, and Geoffrey Garrett, *The Global Diffusion of Markets and Democracy* (Cambridge: Cambridge University Press, 2008); Laurence Whitehead, ed., *The International Dimensions of Democratization: Europe and the Americas* (Oxford: Oxford University Press, 1996).

    6. Nikolay Marinov, "Is the Globalization of Elections Good for Democracy?" paper presented at the annual meeting of the International Studies Association, San Diego, 2006.

    7. Susan Hyde, "The Observer Effect in International Politics: Evidence from a Natural Experiment," *World Politics* 60, no. 1 (2007): 37–63; Susan Hyde and Nikolay Marinov, "Does Information Facilitate Self-Enforcing Democracy? The Role of International Election Monitoring," 2008, http://papers.ssrn.com/sol3/papers.cfm?abstract_id=1266678.

    8. Terry Lynn Karl, "Imposing Consent? Electoralism vs. Democratization in El Salvador," in Paul W. Drake and Eduardo Silva, eds., *Elections and Democratization in Latin America* (San Diego: Center for Iberian and Latin American Studies, University of California, 1986), pp. 9–36; Fareed Zakaria, "The Rise of Illiberal Democracy," *Foreign Affairs* 76, no. 6 (1997): 22–43.

    9. Thomas Carothers, "The Observers Observed," *Journal of Democracy* 8, no. 3 (1997) 17–31.

    10. Joseph A. Schumpeter, *Capitalism, Socialism, and Democracy*, 3rd ed. (New York: Harper Perennial, 1962); Robert Dahl, *Polyarchy: Participation and Opposition* (New

Haven: Yale University Press, 1971); Samuel P. Huntington, *The Third Wave: Democratization in the Late Twentieth Century* (Norman: University of Oklahoma Press, 1991); Adam Przeworski, *Democracy and the Market: Political and Economic Reforms in Eastern Europe and Latin America* (Cambridge: Cambridge University Press, 1991); Adam Przeworski, Michael E. Alvarez, José Antonio Cheibub, and Fernando Limongi, *Democracy and Development: Political Institutions and Well-Being in the World, 1950–1990* (Cambridge: Cambridge University Press, 2000). Note also the related arguments about whether the repetition of even bad elections is good for democracy. See Staffan I. Lindberg, *Democracy and Elections in Africa* (Baltimore: Johns Hopkins University Press, 2006).

11. Zakaria, "The Rise of Illiberal Democracy."

12. Virginia Page Fortna, "Peacekeeping and Democratization," in Anna Jarstad and Timothy Sisk, eds., *From War to Democracy: Dilemmas of Peacebuilding* (Cambridge: Cambridge University Press, 2008).

13. Thomas Edward Flores and Irfan Nooruddin, "Democracy under the Gun: Understanding Postconflict Economic Recovery," *Journal of Conflict Resolution* 53, no. 1 (February 1, 2009): 3–29; Edward D. Mansfield and Jack L. Snyder, *Electing to Fight: Why Emerging Democracies Go to War* (Cambridge, MA: MIT Press, 2005); Irfan Nooruddin, "Voting for Peace: International Donors and Pressures for Democracy in Post-Conflict Societies," unpublished manuscript, Ohio State, 2008; Jack L. Snyder, *From Voting to Violence* (New York: Norton: 2000).

14. James Raymond Vreeland, "The Effect of Political Regime on Civil War: Unpacking Anocracy," *Journal of Conflict Resolution* 52, no. 3 (June 1, 2008): 401–25.

15. Although election-holding hybrid regimes have been associated with a number of other undesirable characteristics, as underscored in Henry Hale's contribution to this volume in chapter 1.

16. Thomas Carothers, "The Backlash against Democracy Promotion," *Foreign Affairs* 85, no. 2 (2006): 55.

17. Thomas Carothers, *Aiding Democracy Abroad: The Learning Curve* (Washington, DC: Carnegie Endowment for International Peace, 1999).

18. Philippe C. Schmitter, "An Introduction to Southern European Transitions from Authoritarian Rule: Italy, Greece, Portugal, Spain, and Turkey," in Guillermo O'Donnell and Philippe C. Schmitter, eds., *Transitions from Authoritarian Rule* (Baltimore: Johns Hopkins University Press, 1986), pp. 3–10.

19. Andreas Schedler, "The Nested Game of Democratization by Elections," *International Political Science Review* 23, no. 1 (January 1, 2002): 103–22.

20. Daron Acemoglu and James A. Robinson, *Economic Origins of Dictatorship and Democracy* (Cambridge: Cambridge University Press, 2005); Cox, "Authoritarian Elections and Leadership Succession, 1975–2000"; James Fearon, "Self-Enforcing Democracy," paper presented at the annual meeting of the American Political Science Association, Philadelphia, 2006; Marinov, "Is the Globalization of Elections Good for Democracy?"

21. Timur Kuran, *Private Truths, Public Lies: The Social Consequences of Preference Falsification* (Cambridge, MA: Harvard University Press, 1995); Susanne Lohmann, "The Dynamics of Informational Cascades: The Monday Demonstrations in Leipzig, East Germany, 1989–91," *World Politics* 47, no. 1 (October 1994): 42–101.

22. Valerie J. Bunce and Sharon L. Wolchik, "International Diffusion and Postcommunist Electoral Revolutions," *Communist and Post-Communist Studies* 39, no. 3 (September 2006): 283–304; Marinov, "Is the Globalization of Elections Good for Democracy?"; Joshua Tucker, "Enough! Electoral Fraud, Collective Action Problems, and Post-Communist Colored Revolutions," *Perspectives on Politics* 5, no. 3 (2007): 535–51.

23. Huntington, *The Third Wave.*

24. Marinov, "Is the Globalization of Elections Good for Democracy?"

25. Jennifer Gandhi and Ellen Lust-Okar, "Elections under Authoritarianism," *Annual Review of Political Science* 12 (2009): 403–22.

26. Eric Bjornlund, *Beyond Free and Fair: Monitoring Elections and Building Democracy* (Washington, DC: Woodrow Wilson Center Press, 2004); Hyde, *The Pseudo-Democrat's Dilemma*; Judith Kelley, "Assessing the Complex Evolution of Norms: The Rise of International Election Monitoring," *International Organization* 62, no. 2 (2008): 221–55; Roland Rich, "Bringing Democracy into International Law," *Journal of Democracy* 12, no. 3 (2001): 20–34.

27. Susan D. Hyde, "Catch Us if You Can: Election Monitoring and International Norm Creation," unpublished manuscript, Yale University, 2010.

28. Huntington, *The Third Wave,* p. 184.

29. Hyde, "The Observer Effect in International Politics."

30. Emily Beaulieu and Susan D. Hyde, "In the Shadow of Democracy Promotion: Strategic Manipulation, International Observers, and Election Boycotts," *Comparative Political Studies* 42, no. 3 (2009): 392–415.

31. Carothers, "The Observers Observed"; Gisela Geisler, "Fair? What Has Fairness Got to Do with It? Vagaries of Election Observations and Democratic Standards," *Journal of Modern African Studies* 31, no. 4 (December 1993): 613–37; Judith Kelley, "D-Minus Elections: The Politics and Norms of International Election Observation," *International Organization* 63 (2009): 765–87.

32. Hyde, *The Pseudo-Democrat's Dilemma.*

33. See Michael Boda, ed., *Revisiting Free and Fair Elections: An International Round Table on Election Standards* (Geneva: Inter-Parliamentary Union, 2005), and Guy S. Goodwin-Gill, *Free and Fair Elections: International Law and Practice* (Geneva: Inter-Parliamentary Union, 2006), for an alternative view, including customary international law as universal standards for democratic elections.

34. Peter J. Burnell, *Democracy Assistance: International Co-operation for Democratization,* Democratization Studies (London: F. Cass, 2000); Peter J. Burnell, "From Evaluating Democracy Assistance to Appraising Democracy Promotion," *Political Studies* 56, no. 2 (2008): 414–34.

35. Andreas Schedler, "The Menu of Manipulation," *Journal of Democracy* 13, no. 2 (2002): 35–36.

36. Przeworski et al., *Democracy and Development.*

# CHAPTER 11

# International Diffusion and Democratic Change

## *Valerie J. Bunce and Sharon L. Wolchik*

Is democracy contagious? Various scholars who have analyzed cross-national patterns of democratic change over time have argued that democracy does indeed seem to spread among states.[1] As evidence in support of this conclusion, analysts have pointed, first, to the pronounced tendency of transitions to democracy to occur in "bunches," whether these transitions took place after the First or Second World Wars or, since the mid-1970s, during what has been termed the third wave of democratization. Second, the global reach of democratic change, which has been characteristic of the third wave in particular, is hard to explain without reference to contagion effects. Here, what is notable is not just the redemocratization of virtually all of Latin America during the 1970s and 1980s, but also soon thereafter the far more surprising rise of democracy in two parts of the world which in most cases had no democratic past to recycle, that is, sub-Saharan Africa and the Soviet bloc. Finally, as these examples suggest, patterns of democratic change seem to follow a regional logic. Thus, democratic developments in one state have often been followed in relatively short order by similar changes in neighboring states. The "virus" of democracy, in short, seems to thrive in close quarters.

The wavelike character of democratization, therefore, seems to reflect not so much the cumulative effects of similar and separate political dynamics taking place within a large number of countries as the impact of similar and *related* efforts supporting democratic change. In this sense, the spread of democracy suggests a strong role for international diffusion, which has been succinctly summarized as a dynamic wherein "past events make future events more likely."[2]

While persuasive, however, the case for the cross-national diffusion of democracy leaves some important questions unanswered—questions that need to be addressed before we can be convinced that diffusion dynamics are in play in the spread of democratic change. First, why and how does democracy spread across countries? Is the underlying dynamic an accidental one—for instance, ease of emulation as a consequence of similarities among states? Or is it a more purposive one—for example, conscious and orchestrated actions by actors intent on copying attractive precedents set in other states? Second, what exactly is traveling: the idea and ideal of democracy, democratic institutions, or effective strategies for either replacing authoritarian with democratic political leaders or building democratic systems? The problem here is not just that diffusion refers to the movement of a specific innovation but also that "democracy" is too complex a development and likely too much a result of a host of prior innovations, rather than the innovation itself, to serve as the focus of the cross-national transfer of political change. Finally, there are always geographic limits to diffusion, and the cross-national spread of democracy is no exception to this rule. Thus, despite the global reach of democratization, the world is nonetheless populated by quite durable authoritarian regimes, with the Middle East (minus Israel) and China cases in point. This introduces a final question: why are some countries more susceptible to the democratic contagion than others?

The purpose of this chapter is to provide some answers to these questions about the cross-national diffusion of democratic change. We begin our discussion by defining diffusion and highlighting some of its key characteristics. We then carry out a case study of one recent cross-national wave of democratic change that took place from 1996 to 2005 in the postcommunist region.[3] Over the course of this wave, eight national elections were held that led to the similar and surprising outcome of replacing semi-authoritarian or illiberal leaders with leaders of the democratic opposition. What makes this run of electoral turnovers so illuminating for our purposes is that it affords us an opportunity to analyze in an unusually rigorous way the diffusion of democratic change. This is, first, because we have a large number of similar and innovative developments—that is, electoral turnovers in regimes dominated by authoritarian leaders—that took place in the same region within a limited span of time. Second, in contrast to the "sprawl" of democracy, elections are finite events with clear beginnings and endings. Finally, from both a definitional standpoint and the perspectives of citizens, elections are closely associated with democracy.[4] In addition, the removal of authoritarians from office usually constitutes the first step in democratic change—albeit one that is far from sufficient for the formation of a full-scale and durable democratic system. The point here is that elections, when democratic oppositions are empowered, provide a democratic opening. Indeed, this is a finding of several recent studies that analyze transitions to democracy around the world.[5]

This case study is also useful because we are able to analyze this wave of electoral change not from a distance, which is the case in most diffusion studies because of their reliance on aggregated statistics, but rather from the ground up. Thus, we bring to this discussion the results of more than two hundred interviews we conducted with domestic and international participants in the electoral breakthroughs that took place in seven of these eight countries, as well as of interviews conducted on our behalf in Kyrgyzstan. It is this information that is vital to documenting the conclusions we draw— namely, that diffusion was in fact in play in the cross-national spread of these electoral breakthroughs; that the key innovation was an ensemble of new electoral strategies that oppositions and their allies deployed; and that this ensemble of activities spread across the region because of its success in defeating authoritarians, the transportability of these strategies, similarities among states that were widely perceived by key players, the widespread opportunities for change provided by the holding of regular elections, and the hard and creative work of transnational networks that brought together Western, regional, and local democratic activists in a common political project.

In the second half of the chapter, we introduce some new cases that help us extend and refine our explanation of the diffusion of democratic change. Thus, we add to our original cases six elections that took place in the postcommunist region that, while sharing similarities with the original group, had the contrasting outcome of returning authoritarians to power. Once again, we draw upon a wide range of data, including interviews that we conducted with domestic and international participants in four of these failed attempts at unseating authoritarian rulers (in Armenia and Azerbaijan). Here, we discover that three factors distinguish between successful and failed attempts to remove authoritarians from office—variations in regime repression and economic performance; responses to challenges by the opposition and NGO communities before, during, and after the election; and, most importantly, differences in whether some or all of the electoral strategies for winning power that succeeded in our first group of cases were transferred to these countries.

Finally, we close our discussion by assessing whether our explanation of the diffusion of electoral innovations travels well to other contexts that also exhibit wavelike patterns of democratic change. Here, we compare our electoral dynamic with an earlier wave of change in the same region that shared the focus on popular challenges to authoritarian rule but that took a somewhat different form: the cross-national spread of popular protests that brought down communist regimes in the Soviet Union and in central and eastern Europe from 1987 to 1990. This comparison suggests that, while this earlier round of democratic change was also a product of cross-national diffusion, the spread of political protests was influenced in fact by somewhat different processes. As a result, the differences of opinion among analysts regarding the drivers of diffusion exist for a good reason. Innovations travel for different reasons and in different ways.

## Defining Diffusion

What does diffusion mean? Diffusion has been defined as a process wherein new ideas, institutions, policies, models, or repertoires of behavior spread geographically from a core site to new sites, sites that include not just states but also businesses, organizations, or local governments.[6] Thus, a convincing claim that diffusion is taking place rests upon meeting several conditions—that something is created that represents a significant departure from previous practices or thinking, that this innovation moves to new places within a limited span of time, and that there are international processes involved that encourage the spread of these similar developments.

But what are the underlying dynamics that facilitate cross-national transfer? Scholars have generated a number of competing explanations that vary from one another with respect to whether they see the process as deliberate or accidental and whether the key influences are seen as being largely structural in nature, such as similarities in political, economic, and social contexts, or more agency-oriented, including deliberate actions taken by entrepreneurs located outside and within the "sending" and the "receiving" countries. However, we can prune back this thicket of debates to reveal three key drivers of diffusion. First, diffusion can occur because the model itself is unusually amenable to cross-national transplantation—because it is easily packaged and consists of a clear set of actions, targets widely available opportunities for change, has a record of success with few costs, and has easy resonance with the interests of key players. The second explanation for diffusion is the presence of similar local conditions in both the "sending" and the "receiving" sites. These can include objective similarities in areas such as regime type, needs, and barriers to and opportunities for mobilizing citizens and, perhaps more important, perceived similarities, that is, the belief on the part of players in both sites that the issues faced were common enough that the solution used in one country would be useful in another. Finally, the diffusion of innovation can take place because of the existence of transnational networks committed to the spread of the model from one site to others. Such networks typically support coalition formation between local and international actors around a common project.

We can close this brief discussion of diffusion by highlighting some patterns typical of diffusion dynamics. One is that innovations change in terms of their forms and their consequences as they make their cross-national journey. This is in part because of the influence of local circumstances and in part because the growing distance in time and space from the original site of change leaves room for variable interpretations and actions. There is also a predictable cycle in diffusion. Thus, innovations first take shape in contexts that are unusually amenable to change, and they then move to increasingly challenging environments. At the same time, just as supporters of change learn from precedents in the neighborhood, so do opponents, who are also advantaged by the tendency over the course of the diffusion dynamic for adopters to become too optimistic about the prospects for change and thus less willing to devote the time or the attention to the details that the change requires. Indeed, it is for many of the same reasons that, just as innovations at the end of the cycle tend to be ever-more-pale reflections of the original innovation, so the wave of change eventually exhausts itself and comes to an end.

## The Electoral Wave

The wave of electoral defeat of dictators, or democratizing elections, in the postcommunist world began with four interconnected political struggles that took place in Serbia, Bulgaria, Romania, and Slovakia from 1996 to 1998.[7] The first was the massive three-month-long protest that occurred in Serbia from 1996 to 1997—protests that were motivated by Milosevic's attempt to deny the opposition its significant victories in many of the local elections that took place in 1996.[8] These protests (as in the cases that followed) built upon previous rounds of antiregime mobilizations—in the Serbian case going back to the early 1980s and in Romania, Slovakia, and Bulgaria to 1989 (and even during the communist period, as in the miners' strikes in Romania during the 1980s). Although the Serbian protests failed in the short term, they contributed in important ways to a subsequent round of election-based protests in the fall of 2000 that succeeded in bringing down Slobodan Milosevic. Milosevic's decision after these protests to crack down on the autonomy of universities, local governments, and the media was also helpful in producing a new generation of protesters and expanding the geography of anti-Milosevic sentiment.[9]

These events were followed by developments in Romania, where the liberal opposition finally came together and ran a political campaign that, together with support from nongovernmental organizations (NGOs), succeeded in replacing the incumbent president, a former communist official, with a candidate with far stronger liberal credentials and commitments as well as securing an opposition victory in parliamentary elections. The third set of struggles occurred in Bulgaria at roughly the same time. In Bulgaria, Serbian protests had been very influential in motivating the unions, which were eventually joined by intellectuals and leaders of the opposition, to carry out large-scale protests that brought down the government headed by former communists and that led to a new election which a united liberal opposition won.[10] The process then moved to Slovakia. In a pivotal meeting that took place in the Vienna airport at the end of 1997, leaders of the Slovak NGO community, the U.S. ambassadors to Slovakia and the Czech Republic, political activists from Romania and Bulgaria, and international democracy promoters and funders (including the International Republican Institute, the National Democratic Institute, Freedom House, the National Endowment for Democracy, and the Foundation for a Civil Society as well as a number of European organizations) came together to devise a strategy for unseating Vladimir Meciar, the illiberal Slovak prime minister, in the upcoming parliamentary elections. This meeting led to the OK98 campaign, which, with the formation of a cohesive political opposition, brought together all the components of a sophisticated strategy for winning elections—ambitious campaigns to register voters, to advertise the costs of the Meciar regime, and to get out the vote; the deployment of both domestic and international election monitoring; and the conducting of exit polls. As a result of these efforts and especially because of the turnout of first-time voters, Meciar left office and a coalition of opposition parties formed a new government that ended the period of de-democratization that occurred under Meciar.[11]

The next application of this electoral tool kit was in Croatia in 2000, where the death of the long-serving dictator Franjo Tudjman in 1999 had weakened the governing party and provided an opportunity for the opposition to win power.[12] The Croatian NGO community and opposition then applied the "Slovak model" to their own situation. In this case, Slovak activists and European and especially American democracy promoters provided money, strategic advice, and even election playbooks. In all of these cases, the mobilization of voters in the context of election campaigns, coupled, in the Bulgarian case, with popular protests to force the government to call elections, were sufficient to bring about the ouster of semi-authoritarian leaders and their replacement by opposition leaders more firmly committed to democracy and, as in the Bulgarian case, the creation of a market economy.

Serbia also experienced an electoral breakthrough later in 2000. Here, there were several key differences—as is typical of innovations originating abroad that are then imported. In contrast to the preceding cases, the struggle against Milosevic was severely constrained by the heavy authoritarian hand of the regime. Thus, there were no external election monitors in Serbia in the fall 2000 elections, and the media were closely controlled by Milosevic. The opposition faced continual threats, and the assistance provided by the international community was important but located, in the case of the U.S. and western European countries, necessarily outside the borders of the state, as a result of the NATO-led bombing of Serbia in 1999 and the closure of the embassies (though the Canadian Embassy substituted for the U.S. Embassy effectively). A student group, Otpor, played the central role in the struggle against Milosevic, and the size, dedication, and geographic spread of this movement are what, arguably, proved to be politically decisive. Finally, the victory of the opposition, which included eighteen parties that supported the candidacy of a moderate nationalist, Vojislav Kostunica, was delayed by Milosevic's refusal to cede power. In contrast to the previous cases discussed, where authoritarian leaders immediately left office, Milosevic stepped down only after the opposition mounted massive countrywide protests.[13]

The Georgian opposition then followed suit in the 2003 parliamentary elections—though this produced, it is important to recognize, a coup d'etat by the opposition, because the long-serving president, Eduard Shevardnadze, resigned but was not in fact up for reelection.[14] In Georgia, the political context was less constraining than in Serbia, especially given the lackluster campaign run by Shevardnadze's allies, the defection of so many key players from the ruling group to the opposition (such as Mikheil Saakashvili, who became president), and the relative openness of the Georgian media. However, the playbook was nonetheless remarkably similar and included the formation of both a united opposition and a youth group in support of political change (Kmara); the generation of opposition versus regime vote totals that exposed regime fraud; close collaboration between the opposition and the third sector; and, finally, an extraordinarily ambitious campaign by Mikheil Saakashvili that brought him to virtually every village in Georgia.

The next successful electoral breakthrough occurred in Ukraine a year later.[15] As in the Georgian case, a single charismatic politician—in this case, Viktor Yushchenko—played a critical role. As in both the Georgian and Serbian cases, the successful political breakthrough exploited the record of a leadership that had grown increasingly corrupt, careless, and violent; benefited from defections from the ruling circles; built upon earlier rounds of protests and recent successes in local elections; and reached out to diverse groups, including young people whose role was nearly as important as that of Otpor's in Serbia. As in Serbia and Georgia, political protests after the election (which were larger and of longer duration than those in Serbia) were again necessary to force the authoritarian challenger to admit defeat.

The wave of electoral change then moved to Kyrgyzstan, where it succeeded, as in Georgia, in deposing the long-serving president, despite the fact that these elections were also parliamentary, not presidential.[16] There is less evidence in this case than in those we have discussed previously of a well-orchestrated electoral challenge being mounted. Instead, dissatisfaction with electoral outcomes in the south of the country, which undermined existing patronage networks linked to the Akayev regime, produced protests that then spread to the north, where the capital, Bishkek, is located. The result in very short order was that the president of Kyrgyzstan, Askar Akayev, panicked and abdicated, fleeing to Moscow—despite the fact that the protests were hardly at a level forcing such a response. Although youth activists in Kel Kel participated in the events once they reached Bishkek, they were few in number and played a limited role in the outcome, in contrast to the role of youth in Slovakia, Serbia, and Ukraine.

## Diffusion and Democracy

We can now step back from these events and ask the following question. Is this wave of electoral change best understood, as many analysts have suggested, as a cluster of similar but independent developments, in which liberal oppositions in each of the eight countries were able to successfully exploit domestic opportunities for democratic change through elections in vulnerable regimes?[17] Or, as the depiction of these events as a wave implies, did these electoral breakthroughs occur as the result of a process of cross-national diffusion?[18]

We would argue in favor of the second interpretation, given not just the otherwise quite improbable clustering of so many similar electoral outcomes over time and space and in the context of regimes that varied substantially in their mixture of authoritarian and democratic elements, but also the presence in each case (though least so in Kyrgyzstan) of a similar and distinctive approach to defeating dictators.[19] It is the latter which is of particular interest with respect to the claim of diffusion, because it focuses our attention on the innovation itself rather than its consequences. As our brief overview of the democratizing elections under study highlighted, all the familiar components of a dynamic of diffusion were in fact present. The breakthrough elections took place in lagged fashion across a large group of countries located within the postcommunist region. Moreover, the contexts within which these elections took place were roughly similar. While varying in their extent of both levels of repression and democratic "decorations," all of these regimes nonetheless fell into that large space between full-scale democracies and full-scale dictatorships. Thus, as mixed regimes, they combined democratic institutions, such as parliaments, courts, a sprinkling of civil liberties, and at least semicompetitive elections with authoritarian incumbents and political practices.[20] Perhaps the most important indicator of diffusion, however, is that these elections marked a similar and sharp departure from the past in two ways. One is that actors in each case used elections to accomplish the same end, the defeat of dictators, and the other is that opposition movements used new and similar strategies to win power. This ensemble of strategies, moreover, was not deployed in earlier elections when, as in all the cases except Slovakia and Bulgaria, the opposition had invariably failed to win office.

What were the strategies that were used?[21] While familiar to most citizens, political activists, and political scientists in established democracies, the tasks associated with this model of winning elections were new to this region and very difficult—and often dangerous—to carry out for the simple reason that authoritarian leaders had considerable resources at their disposal to maintain power. For example, they controlled large-scale patronage networks in these very corrupt systems, along with the media, and electoral procedures, including the tabulation of the vote. Moreover, these leaders engaged in significant harassment of the opposition and civil society groups and, in Serbia and Ukraine in particular, had become increasingly prone to use violence against their opponents. At the same time, ordinary citizens saw these regimes as impregnable, and they had grown increasingly pessimistic not just about the prospects for political change, but also about the very value of an opposition victory as a result of the opposition's long and sorry record of internal divisions, incompetent politics, and in some cases collaboration with the regime.

The very purpose of the new electoral strategies that moved throughout the postcommunist region was to counteract these formidable constraints on the defeat of authoritarian leaders. Thus, the tasks involved included exerting considerable pressures on the regime (in alliance with their international allies) to reform electoral procedures; organizing large-scale voter registration and turnout drives; forming a united opposition; carrying out unusually ambitious political campaigns that forced opposition candidates for the first time to go outside the major cities; and conducting (where politically tolerated) sophisticated public opinion polls, parallel tabulation of votes, and exit polls.[22] All these features were critical because, just as they made it harder for authoritarians to win elections and to stay in power, so they gave the opposition and its allies the tools, the political support, and the feeling of optimism they needed to prevail. They also helped citizens have more confidence in the opposition and its ability to triumph.

In fact, these strategies often made all the difference. Electoral turnout had declined over time in many of these countries because citizens had become dispirited, divided, and demobilized, as well as increasingly skeptical about the ability of the opposition to win and, for that matter, to be worthy of their support.[23] It is telling, for example, that electoral turnout was unusually high in many of these elections (especially in Slovakia, Croatia, and Serbia) and that most of these elections were in fact very close (especially in Bulgaria, Slovakia, Serbia, and Ukraine). The 2000 Serbian election is revealing in this respect. With two hours left before the polls closed, activists at CeSID (the

Center for Elections and Democracy), a nongovernmental organization involved in getting out the vote, voter registration, and parallel vote tabulation, realized that turnout in key areas was too low to guarantee a victory for the opposition. As a result, they mobilized an ambitious and targeted get-out-the-vote campaign at the last minute that delivered a narrow victory to Vojislav Kostunica, the opposition presidential candidate.

In addition to these core features of the electoral model outlined here, there were other similarities across these electoral episodes in strategies deployed and the distinctiveness of those strategies in comparison with previous elections. For example, in many of these democratizing elections the opposition and NGO communities made extensive use of rock concerts, street theater, marches, and unusually widespread distribution of posters, stickers, and t-shirts in order to expand interest in the election and voter turnout. In addition, new organizations formed to monitor elections, get out the vote, tabulate the vote, and engage young people. Close ties were forged for the first time between civil society groups and the opposition, and, in the more repressive polities, such as Serbia, Georgia, and Ukraine, protests were organized to force recalcitrant dictators to admit defeat and leave office. Central to the success of these protests, moreover, were conversations during the campaign between opposition leaders and members of the security apparatus.

There are also other patterns in this wave of electoral change that are typical of diffusion dynamics. One is the fact that, while maintaining a core set of tasks, the model was nonetheless amended as it made its cross-national journey—for instance, the use of parliamentary elections to oust presidents, the elaborate coordination of food and shelter for protesters in Kyiv and other major cities in Ukraine, and the addition of massive public protests in more authoritarian political contexts. At the same time, we see a familiar cycle, wherein the "early risers" tended to combine more supportive contexts for change, more planning, and a more-faithful application of the model than "late risers," where domestic conditions were less supportive and where the power of attractive precedents outran careful preparations.[24] The learning that took place on the part of those defending the status quo was also important. Two concrete examples show how political opportunities for change varied over the course of the wave: just as the earlier breakthrough elections took place in more democratic contexts than the electoral confrontations that occurred at the end of the wave, so oppositions in Bulgaria, Romania, and Slovakia—that is, in the earliest breakthrough cases—benefited from having accumulated far more governmental experience before the breakthrough elections than was the case for their counterparts in Croatia, Serbia, Georgia, Ukraine, and Kyrgyzstan.

A strong case for diffusion, however, depends on demonstrating as well why and how innovations—that is, these new electoral strategies—moved from country to country. Here, we find that all three mechanisms described earlier played a role in the spread of these electoral strategies. Thus, the electoral model, with its clear set of tasks and focus on elections that have an evident objective and take place within a limited time frame, was a particularly attractive approach for domestic actors and international organizations seeking democratic change in semi-authoritarian regimes in the region. This was particularly true once it took full shape and succeeded in Slovakia. The diffusion of the model was also aided by the similar conditions that existed in the countries where it succeeded and other semi-authoritarian contexts and by the perception of these similarities on the part of activists within and outside these countries. These included economic and political problems common to postcommunist states due to the legacy of communism and similarities in institutional structure, policies, and the resources available to leaders and citizens; national divisions and conflicts over state boundaries that arose from the problems associated with diverse populations and (except in Bulgaria and Romania) the formation of new states; and the limitations on opposition to the government posed by the semi-autocratic nature of their current regimes in all but Bulgaria, where elections were generally free and fair, but movement toward a market economy to underpin democracy was stymied by the government in power, leading to a near economic collapse. The diffusion of this model was also facilitated by the formation and spread of transnational democracy promotion networks that brought together three sets of players: Western-based democracy promoters, local opposition and civil society groups, and "graduates" of earlier and successful electoral struggles who were able and eager to share their experiences. It was this large and expanding network that developed, applied, and transferred the electoral model. Indeed, the story of this network goes further back in time, with many of the Western players in these elections influenced by electoral confrontations with authoritarian rule in the Philippines in 1986 and in Chile in 1988.

We have analyzed elsewhere how this transnational network took shape and its role in each of our eight countries.[25] As we have argued, the success of efforts to use elections to oust dictators depended on the courage, persistence, determination, and willingness to take risks, as well as self-interest of leaders and citizens within particular countries. However, outside actors, including Western, and particularly American, democracy promoters and participants in earlier successful uses of the electoral model also played important roles. These included encouraging the opposition to unite and convincing nongovernmental organizations that their role could legitimately include involvement in (nonpartisan) political activities such as getting out the vote, educating citizens about their rights in an election and the positions of various political parties and candidates on the issues, and holding the government accountable for its record. Western participants, particularly such groups as the Open Society Foundation and Freedom House, facilitated contact between "graduates" of earlier successful democratizing elections and activists wishing to benefit from their example. They also provided considerable financial assistance for the long-term development of civil society and, in most cases, the activities NGOs undertook during the campaigns. Finally, Western diplomats and governments also were active, more so in some cases than in others, in signaling their interest in free and fair elections. Often signs were present that indicated Western interest in regime change and urged defeated leaders to leave office peacefully.

"Graduates," or participants in earlier rounds of democratizing elections, were instrumental in the cross-national diffusion of this ensemble of distinctive and highly effective electoral strategies. Thus, Slovak NGO leaders and activists were inspired by Bulgarian and Romanian NGO leaders and, in turn, served as both inspiration and models for Croatian and Serbian activists. Activists from all of these cases were then involved in sharing their experiences and, in some cases, providing concrete advice concerning strategy as well as training in nonviolent methods of resistance, civic organizing, and election and media monitoring in Georgia and Ukraine. It is not "accidental," as communist leaders commonly claimed in discussing the misdeeds of their colleagues or negative events they would go on to attribute to capitalist machinations, that the Georgian youth organization used Otpor's raised fist as its symbol or that opposition campaigns and even the very names given to youth groups built upon the slogans, such as "enough" and "it's time (for a change)," that figured prominently in the Serbian campaign against Milosevic. Because they were presumed to have faced similar problems and dangers, and also had to live with the consequences of their actions, "graduates" had more credibility in many cases than Western members of the transnational networks involved in the diffusion of these electoral strategies. This was true even in the case of Kyrgyzstan, where the activities of both Western democracy promoters, apart from aid for civil society development, and "graduates" were quite limited before 2005. In this case, in which there was very little direct transmission of the electoral model, certain actors, such as the youth organized in Kel Kel, drew their inspiration from the experiences of those who had been successful elsewhere. Indeed, they even drew upon the ideas and precedents of earlier confrontations with communism, which reflected in part the engagement of some Polish activists in civil society development in Kyrgyzstan. Moreover, in the 2005 election in that country, the United States went much further than in the past in pressing for electoral reforms.

## Incomplete Diffusion

Thus far, we have focused exclusively on the successful cross-national diffusion of democratizing elections, with success indicated by both the adoption of innovative electoral strategies and the ability of oppositions to win power through elections. However, there are always limits to diffusion, particularly in cases in which, as with democratizing elections, the innovation being analyzed threatens in a profound way the prevailing distribution of political and economic power. In these circumstances, incumbent elites and their domestic and international allies stand as unusually resolute guardians of the status quo.

The barriers to the diffusion of democratic change can be identified by carrying out a controlled comparison between a subset of our successful cases where authoritarians were removed from office—that is, Croatia, Georgia, Serbia, Slovakia, and Ukraine—and a group of elections in other countries in the region that failed to achieve the same outcome—that is, national elections that were held in Belarus in 2006, Armenia in 2003 and 2008, and Azerbaijan in 2003 and 2005. What makes this comparison so instructive for our purposes is not just the contrast between electoral outcomes and our ability to hold region constant, but also some key commonalities that cross the divide between these two sets of cases. In particular, all of these elections took place in roughly similar regime contexts that combined authoritarian politics with a modicum of democratic institutions and processes, and they shared at the same time two other features that in theory should have led to identical political results and, what is more, results favorable to the opposition: widespread public perceptions that the elections were fraudulent, which were expressed in large-scale popular protests following tabulation of the vote, and oppositions that, in contrast to their usual behavior, succeeded in forming alliances in order to compete more effectively for votes. Put simply, what we find in Armenia, Azerbaijan, and Belarus at the time of these elections were some important elements of the very electoral strategies that we outlined earlier as critical to the successful defeat of authoritarians.[26]

What, then, explains the contrasting electoral outcomes? Three obstacles to electoral change stand out as particularly important. One was the fact that the regimes in Armenia, Azerbaijan, and Belarus were on the whole more repressive than the regimes where electoral turnover took place—though it is important to recognize that the regimes in both Serbia and Kyrgyzstan were also quite harsh, and that Georgia and especially Ukraine in the last years of Kuchma were not that far behind. It is important to keep in mind that repression had in fact increased in virtually all of these countries in the years leading up to the elections, whether authoritarians were defeated or not (with Azerbaijan in 2003 the only exception), and, moreover, that, while this trend deepened in all the countries where challenges to authoritarian rule failed, despite significant popular protests, authoritarianism declined in all of the countries where electoral change took place (though trends in Georgia more closely resembled the first group). This pattern suggests that, just as growing authoritarianism does not predict electoral outcomes, so there is evidence that the very term *democratizing elections* is an accurate summary of the important role these electoral shifts played in moving politics in a more democratic direction.

Second, there was a clear contrast in economic performance between our two sets of cases. However, this explanation is less compelling once we recognize that the breakthrough elections in Serbia, Ukraine, and Georgia in particular took place when the economies were performing better than they had in many years. At the same time, earlier elections in these countries that took place during very difficult economic times had produced victories, not defeats, for authoritarians. Economic vulnerability, therefore, does not seem to explain very well the uneven geography of the diffusion of new electoral strategies.

Finally, the clearest contrast between our two sets of elections takes us back to our earlier discussion of the general patterns associated with the diffusion of innovation. In the three countries where electoral challenges to authoritarian rule failed (Armenia, Azerbaijan, and Belarus), we find clear evidence of only a partial implementation of the new electoral strategies. For example, the opposition did not run ambitious campaigns in any of these cases; parallel vote tabulation was not used, and exit polls, if used, were of uneven quality; youth movements were either nonexistent or very small; and ties between opposition parties and civil society groups were limited. Moreover, we do not find a key role in these elections and the politics leading up to them for the graduates of successful electoral challenges to authoritarian rule. Diffusion, in short, was uneven, and it was the absence of full deployment of the electoral tool kit that accounts for the contrast between our two sets of elections.

It could be countered, of course, that what we have discovered is simply the power of repressive local politics in blocking democratic change through elections. However, while there are some reasons to give this factor some explanatory power, there are also reasons to construct a more complex story that takes into account the logic of diffusion itself. First, as already noted, electoral breakthroughs took place in fact in some relatively authoritarian regimes, along with some relatively democratic polities, especially early in the wave, as in the cases of Bulgaria and Romania. Second, the elections that failed to unseat authoritarians took place toward the end of the diffusion cycle, when authoritarian elites had been able to learn from dangerous precedents in their midst; when opposition and civil society groups were less willing, as well as able, to carry out the arduous tasks necessary for victory; and, more generally, when innovations and transnational networks were further and further removed from the origin of the diffusion dynamic. What we are suggesting, therefore, is that, while there were structural impediments to electoral change that were purely domestic in nature, there were also other constraints that grew out of both the role of agency in these processes—that is, actions by oppositions and their allies, as well as preemptive strikes by authoritarian incumbents—and the very logic of diffusion itself, especially as the impulse for change, the strategies attached to that impulse, and the transnational networks that supported its transplantation to new places all "thin out" over the course of the cross-national journey of the innovation. Moreover, when all is said and done, the fact is that, especially in more authoritarian settings, as was the case in Croatia, Serbia, Georgia, and Ukraine in particular, faithful deployment of the full ensemble of electoral innovations was critical to the electoral success of the opposition. When that did not happen, authoritarian rulers prevailed.

## Diffusion in 1987 to 1990

We now turn to a final test of our arguments about the cross-national diffusion of democratizing elections—whether our explanation of why and how electoral innovations traveled can itself travel to other waves of democratic change. Here, we extend our analysis back in time within the same region to the dramatic events of 1989–91, which saw the end of communism in the Soviet Union and eastern Europe.[27] Our analysis focuses on two main questions: first, were the two waves of diffusion separate or part of the same process and, second, was the process the same in the two sets of cases? Comparing these two waves of democratic change is particularly illuminating because it allows us to hold the region constant. In fact, many of the democratizing elections we analyzed in the first part of this chapter occurred in countries that also saw significant popular protests at the end of the communist era—Croatia, Georgia, Serbia, Slovakia, and Ukraine, as well as those countries in which some though not all elements of the model were evident, Bulgaria and Romania.

As the demise of communism in the region has been well chronicled by numerous scholars as well as participants, we set out only the briefest outline of the most important events in this process here.[28] After decades in which outside analysts of the Soviet economy predicted that it could not last and shelves of books that all included the words *crisis* or *the abyss* in their titles were written about Poland, the unthinkable happened: elite pacts and mass protests, sometimes coupled and more often not, brought about not only the end of communism in central and eastern Europe but its demise in the Soviet Union as well. These events were followed shortly afterward by the breakup of the three federal communist states, the Soviet Union, Yugoslavia, and Czechoslovakia. The underlying causes for the demise of communism have been traced to a variety of sources, ranging from the costs associated with the fusion of economic and political power in these systems and the growing costs for the Soviet Union of control over eastern Europe to the lack of legitimacy of most of the communist regimes in eastern Europe and the role of intellectuals or dissidents in undermining the system and the decisions of crucial decision makers at critical junctures.

However, most agree that there was a series of more proximate events that set this process in motion in both the Soviet Union and central and eastern Europe. In the USSR, these events involved a sea change in the policies and

formula of rule at the center as articulated by Mikhail Gorbachev after his rise
to power in 1985. With his policies of perestroika and glasnost, Gorbachev
emulated and extended some of the arguments made in fact by the reform
leadership of Alexander Dubcek in the Prague Spring. These included, among
other things, the plan to base the party's rule on greater participation by ordinary citizens (under party leadership, of course, and without the development of a true opposition political party), that is, to shift the basis of rule from
one that relied on the provision of material benefits and selective use of coercion against those who forcefully challenged the limits, primarily intellectuals, to one based on genuine legitimacy. The weakening of the center (whether
defined as the Soviet Union within the bloc or the governing communist parties within each state), greater openness of the political system, and the economic chaos that resulted from uncoordinated and incomplete economic reforms in turn created space for the development of a multitude of independent
groups, a dynamic that created competition not just between democrats and
authoritarians over the regime but also among nationalist leaders over the
sovereignty of existing states (especially in the "external" empire in eastern
Europe) and, within the Soviet, Yugoslav, and Czechoslovak ethnofederations,
over the very boundaries of the state itself. After 1987, Gorbachev's frustration
with the lack of progress in economic reform led him to set in motion another
group of actors whose activities would soon go beyond what he envisioned,
popular fronts in the constituent republics. Mass protests and calls for greater
autonomy and eventually independence soon followed not only in the Baltic
countries but also in the Caucasus, where nationalist sentiments had been
the basis for earlier mass mobilizations.

At the same time, developments in central and eastern Europe began that
would eventually lead to the end of communism in that region. These included, first of all, the development of a rift in Yugoslavia (which had its own
model of socialism and allowed far more room for debate than the Soviet
model) between Slovenia and Serbia and the growth of nationalist mobilization in both Croatia and Serbia. Eventually, these conflicts would lead to the
development of a mass movement in Slovenia, led by communist leaders that
wanted to see change in a more democratic direction, and, in 1991, as nationalism became the ever more important focus of Milosevic and the Serbian
elites around him, the dissolution of the country. Events in Poland also came
to a head in the late 1980s, when the deterioration of the economic situation,
coupled with widespread corruption, led to the resumption of mass protests

by Solidarity activists and eventually to the roundtable talks between the regime and Solidarity that would be followed by Solidarity's surprise victory in the June 1989 semifree elections and the eventual formation of a Solidarity-led government. The "negotiated revolution" taking place in Hungary in a similar roundtable, but without mass participation as in Poland, was the second of the transitions in the region that resembled the pacted transitions in Latin America and southern Europe. Meanwhile, peaceful mass protests in Germany, which had their roots in demonstrations organized by Protestant activists in the last years of the 1980s, grew and eventually led to the fall of the Berlin Wall in November 9, 1989. The fall of the Wall and, with it, the hard-line Honecker regime in East Germany, in turn were followed in short order by massive protests in Czechoslovakia, which were followed by large protests in Bulgaria, Romania, and then Albania.

As with many of the domestic changes that had begun to occur in some of these countries after Gorbachev came to power, the end of communism in central and eastern Europe also reflected the impact of change in Soviet policy toward the region. In addition to encouraging reforms similar to those he was attempting in the Soviet Union, Gorbachev also made it clear in a number of speeches as well as in more private communications with central and eastern European leaders from 1987 to 1989 that the Soviet Union was prepared to allow the citizens and leaders of the region to make their own decisions about the kind of economic and political systems they wanted. Perhaps as important as these changes, he also made it clear that the Soviet Union was not going to intervene to put down "counterrevolution" as in Hungary in 1956 or "save socialism" as it allegedly had in Czechoslovakia in 1968 or, in fact, save communist leaders in the region from the actions of their citizens.

As this brief rehearsal of the events of 1989–90 demonstrates, there was a clear diffusion dynamic at work in the region during this time. Like all diffusion processes, including the later wave of democratizing elections, however, the protests that began in 1987 eventually came to an end—as both social movement theorists and analysts of diffusion would predict.[29] As in the set of democratizing elections that we have analyzed, the impact of these protests also changed as they moved from one country to another. Dramatic and thoroughgoing democratic breakthroughs took place in the "early riser" (to borrow again from Mark Beissinger) countries of Poland, Hungary, Czechoslovakia, and East Germany, testifying to the size, popularity, experience and cohesion of their oppositions and the presence in these countries of either very vulnerable communists or communists ready to collaborate with the opposition. The political outcomes of the confrontations between regimes and oppositions in the streets and at roundtables that took place later in the wave were different. In Bulgaria and especially Romania and Albania, where smaller, more divided, and less experienced oppositions faced communists who were better positioned to defend themselves (in part because they were eager students of what had transpired in East Germany and Czechoslovakia in particular), the transition produced mixed regimes with a rough balance between the former communists and the opposition.[30] Subsequently, two of these cases (Bulgaria and Romania) were sites where elements of what would become the electoral tool kit used for opposition victories were first elaborated and tested.

There are similarities between these events and those that occurred in the diffusion of the electoral model in the democratizing elections that took place between 1996 and 2005. These include a common focus on removing authoritarian leaders from power; a dramatic upsurge in innovative antiregime actions taken, often in close collaboration with one another, by oppositions, civil society groups, and ordinary citizens; and similar constellations of challenges to authoritarian rule repeated in multiple countries. Moreover, the outcomes of these two waves resembled one another. Each wave moved from more to less supportive conditions for democratic change, and the political consequences of the breakthroughs in the two cases duly registered that fact.

However, the two sets of challenges to authoritarian rule were nonetheless both different from one another and separate processes, although the first influenced the second in important ways. Thus, there were different players involved, and the sites and techniques of confrontation also differed. This fact is not surprising, given a radically altered domestic and international context, a new ensemble of domestic and international actors, and the availability by the 1990s of new models for challenging dictatorial rule. Although the same three sets of factors promoted diffusion in both instances, the relative weights attached to each were in fact very different in the two diffusion processes. In the case of democratizing elections, the roles that the nature of the innovation being diffused (the electoral model), cross-national opportunities for change due to similar conditions, and transnational networks played were all important, but it was the final one that played the most critical role in developing, implementing, and transferring the electoral tool kit. By contrast, in the earlier wave of mobilizations against dictatorship, it was the middle factor—that is, expanded opportunities across the region for democratic change as the result of both domestic crisis and changes in Soviet policies—that was the most central to the diffusion dynamic.

Thus, in 1989 there was no clear model for successfully getting rid of communist rule. Roundtables that led to elite pacts were used in some cases, while in others such negotiations largely formalized results that had already been achieved by protests in the streets. The impact of success in one country, such as Solidarity's unanticipated victory in the June 1989 parliamentary elections in Poland and the fall of the Berlin Wall, was far-reaching, but its impact was felt more as the result of demonstration effects than conscious sharing or transfer of experiences. The two waves also differed from one another in another significant way. With the possible exception of the Hungarian case, the victories of 1989 were for the most part not anticipated or planned far in advance. Nor did they come about as the result of a coherent, carefully articulated strategy for getting rid of communist rule. This was particularly true in those cases, such as East Germany, Czechoslovakia, and Romania, where mass demonstrations, which were led by intellectuals and dissidents only after they had begun, very quickly brought about the fall of hard-line repressive regimes.

Conditions also were not nearly as favorable for the development of transnational networks to promote democracy during this period as during the later wave of democratizing elections in the region. Outside actors, such as the United States and other Western governments, were involved to some extent in some countries in supporting human rights groups and, in the case of Poland, Solidarity, through mechanisms such as the SEED (Support for East European Democracies) Act. However, it was after communism that the West shifted its foreign policy in a consistent way in the direction of supporting democratic change throughout the world. There was also some contact among dissident communities that emerged in the late communist period, particularly among Polish, Czech, and Hungarian dissidents. The opportunities for the West to be active in these societies and for dissidents to meet were nonetheless negligible, and dissident cultures under communism, reflecting different domestic constraints and opportunities, produced different strategies that erected, as a result, some barriers to cross-national collaboration and action. Given the strictures on political opposition and limits on independent organizing, even in the last years in the more liberal countries, under communism and the government's control of the media, there were relatively few domestic partners for such outside actors in any event.

The conditions that facilitated diffusion, then, differed significantly in the two waves. As a result, the process of diffusion also differed. Instead of the purposive diffusion of strategies and tactics used in successful cases, as occurred in the second round, diffusion occurred largely by demonstration effects in the first. Developments in one country clearly had an impact on the behavior of the regime, opposition leaders, and citizens in others, and learning what others had done elsewhere inspired emulation. But the coordination and conscious decision to use and adapt strategies used elsewhere was largely absent. In part, this reflected the different conditions in communist and semi-authoritarian regimes; it also reflected the much smaller presence and far more restricted range of activities possible for the outside actors who would come to play such a critical role in diffusion in the second round during communism. Finally, while electoral breakthroughs in one country influenced the goals and strategies of players in other countries in the postcommunist region, this dynamic was less "automatic" than was the case during communism when regimes were not just more similar to one another as a result of the influence of the Soviet model but also closely tied to each other through the very structure of the Soviet bloc.

## Conclusions

The evidence in this chapter provides strong support for the argument that diffusion has played an important role in bringing about democratic change in the postcommunist region. This role has been particularly evident in the wave of electoral defeats of authoritarian leaders that took place from 1996 to 2005 in postcommunist Europe and Eurasia. In this wave of electoral change, the nature of the innovation being diffused, as well as similar conditions, and the role in particular of transnational networks of outside democracy promoters, domestic actors, and "graduates" of successful cases all were important in fostering diffusion. As the "failed cases" we examined remind us, however, diffusion does not always succeed, especially when regimes are more repressive and economically successful; when authoritarian leaders benefit from seeing why and how their counterparts elsewhere in the region lost power and very actively take measures to defend their rule and prevent diffusion from occurring; and, most importantly, when the transfer of innovative electoral strategies to oppositions and their allies is incomplete. Finally, comparison of the wave of democratizing elections in the postcommunist world and the fall of communism in the region in 1989–91 illustrates a further important point about diffusion and democratization. Different domestic and international contexts mean that diffusion will occur in different ways.

We can now step back from these conclusions and highlight three lessons that policy makers and academics can draw about the diffusion of democratic change. First and most obviously, democratization must be understood as not just a domestic process but also an international one. It is a mistake, as a result, to assume, as many analysts of democratic transitions have done, whether focusing on the earliest transitions to democracy in the world or more recent ones, that the international system is irrelevant to local struggles for democratic change. Just as the international system can provide ideas and precedents and thereby alter goals and redistribute resources between the defenders of and the challengers to the political status quo, so it can furnish needed allies and vital resources that can help tip the political balance in the favor of democratic progress. However, international influences are influential only insofar as they resonate with a receptive local environment. For example, international democracy promoters will make a positive difference only if local conditions are receptive and, in a more concrete sense, if they are able to strike close alliances with local supporters of political change. In addition, international influences are always Janus-faced. Just as democrats can learn and be empowered because of important changes that take place in their neighborhood, so authoritarians can draw important lessons from these developments as well.

Second, to argue in support of the international diffusion of democracy is to take on a substantial burden of proof. Democracy is too complex, too much shaped by local conditions, and too much the product of multiple influences to move in some magical and holistic way from one country to others. It is advisable, therefore, to focus on the diffusion of specific innovations that create democratic openings or that contribute in some concrete way to democratic development. At the same time, diffusion is a very complex process. It can occur because of the amenability of the innovation to transplantation, appealing precedents, similar local conditions and opportunities for change, and/or the formation of creative and hardworking transnational networks. However, in the absence of identifying these influences and tracing their effects, diffusion can be in fact an illusion, created, for example, by similar internal developments in a group of countries or similar changes orchestrated by powerful actors in the international system.[31]

Finally, in contrast to many analysts of diffusion, we would argue that human beings—their goals, their values and interests, their knowledge about events outside their borders, their resources, and their political strategies—lie at the heart of the diffusion of democratic change. While the portability of the model itself matters, as do similarities among countries and attractive precedents set in the neighborhood, it is local, regional, and Western democratic activists, opposition parties and candidates, and ordinary citizens who, in the final analysis, do the tedious and sometimes dangerous tasks of crafting the model, applying it, carrying it to new places, and amending it in keeping with local circumstances. In this sense, diffusion is never purely accidental; it is always purposive. This generalization, moreover, is particularly apt in situations where the innovation is subversive and therefore heavily dependent necessarily on both political struggle and detailed planning.

NOTES

1. Daniel Brinks and Michael Coppedge, "Diffusion Is No Illusion: Neighbor Emulation in the Third Wave of Democracy," *Comparative Political Studies* 39, no. 4 (May 2006): 463–89; S. Gleditsch and Michael Shin, "The Diffusion of Democracy, 1946–1994," *Annals of the Association of American Geographers* 88, no. 4 (2006): 545–74.

2. Pamela E. Oliver and Daniel J. Meyers, "Networks, Diffusion, and Collective Cycles of Action," in Mario Diani and Doug McAdam, eds., *Social Movements and Networks: Relational Approaches to Collective Action* (Oxford: Oxford University Press, 2003), p. 174.

3. This wave of electoral change is the subject of our book, *Defeating Authoritarian Leaders in Postcommunist Countries* (Cambridge: Cambridge University Press, 2011).

4. Russell J. Dalton, Doh L. Shin, and Willy Jou, "Popular Conceptions of the Meaning of Democracy: Democratic Understanding in Unlikely Places," Center for the Study of Democracy, Paper 07-03, May 18, 2007, http://repositories.cdlib.org/csd/07-03.

5. Philip G. Roessler and Marc M. Howard, "Post-Cold-War Political Regimes: When Do Elections Matter?" 101–27; Andreas Schedler, "Sources of Competition under Electoral Authoritarianism," 179–201; Andreas Schedler, "The Contingent Power of Elections," 291–313; and Jan Teorell and Axel Hadenius, "Elections as Levers of Democracy? A Global Inquiry," 77–100; all in Staffan Lindberg, ed., *Democratization by Elections: A New Mode of Transition?* (Baltimore: Johns Hopkins University Press, 2009).

6. See, for example, Everett M. Rogers, *Diffusion of Innovations* (New York: Free Press, 1995); David Strang and Sarah Soule, "Diffusion in Organizations and Social Movements: From Hybrid Corn to Poison Pills," *Annual Review of Sociology* 24 (1998): 265–90; Beth Simmons, Frank Dobbin, and Geoffrey Garrett, "Introduction: The International Diffusion of Liberalism," *International Organization* 60 (Fall 2006): 781–810.

7. For more detail and references to studies of these specific cases, Bunce and Wolchik, *Defeating Authoritarian Leaders in Postcommunist Countries,* chaps. 5–8.

8. See, especially, Mladen Lazi and Liljana Nikoli, *Protest in Belgrade: Winter of Discontent* (Budapest: Central European University Press, 1999).

9. Ognjen Pribicevic, "Serbia after Milosevic," *Journal of Southeast European & Black Sea Studies* 4, no. 1 (January 2004): 107–18; V. Goati, "The Nature of the Order and the October Overthrow in Serbia," in I. Spasic and M. Subotic, eds., *Revolution and Order: Serbia after October 2000* (Belgrade: Institute for Philosophy and Sociology, 2001), pp. 45–58; and Ivana Spasic and Milan Subotic, *R/Evolution and Order: Serbia after October 2000* (Belgrade: University of Belgrade, Institute for Philosophy and Social Theory, 2001).

10. Venelin I. Ganev, *Preying on the State: The Transformation of Bulgaria after 1989* (Ithaca: Cornell University Press, 2007), and Tsveta Petrova, "A Postcommunist Transition in Two Acts: The 1996–1997 Anti-government Struggle in Bulgaria as a Bridge between the First and Second Waves of Transition in Eastern Europe," in Valerie Bunce, Michael McFaul, and Kathryn Stoner-Weiss, eds., *Democracy and Authoritarianism in the Postcommunist World* (Cambridge: Cambridge University Press, 2009).

11. Valerie Bunce and Sharon Wolchik, "Defining and Domesticating the Electoral Model: A Comparison of Slovakia and Serbia," in Bunce, McFaul, and Stoner-Weiss, *Democracy and Authoritarianism in the Postcommunist World*, 134–54. See also Martin Butora, Grigorij Meseznikov, and Zora Butorova, eds., *Kto? Preco? Ako? Slovenske vol'by '98* (Bratislava: Institut pre verejne otazky, 1999), and Sharon Fisher, *Political Change in Post-Communist Slovakia and Croatia: From Nationalist to Europeanist* (London: Palgrave Macmillan, 2006).

12. See Fisher, *Political Change in Post-Communist Slovakia*; Jill Irvine, "Women's Organizations and Critical Elections in Croatia," *Politics and Gender* 3, no. 1 (March 2007): 7–32; and Sharon Fisher and Biljana Bijelic, "Glas 99: Civil Society Preparing the Ground for Post-Tudjman Croatia," in Joerg Forbrig and Pavol Demes, eds., *Reclaiming Democracy: Civil Society and Electoral Change in Central and Eastern Europe* (Washington, DC: German Marshall Fund, 2007), pp. 53–77.

13. On the Serbian case, see, for example, Bunce and Wolchik, "Defining and Domesticating the Electoral Model"; Sarah Birch, "The 2000 Elections in Yugoslavia: The 'Bulldozer Revolution,'" *Electoral Studies* 21, no. 3 (September 2002): 499–511; and Florian Bieber, "The Serbian Transition and Civil Society: Roots of the Delayed Transition in Serbia," *International Journal of Politics, Culture, and Society* 17, no. 1 (Fall 2003): 73–90.

14. See, for instance, Giorgi Kandelaki, *Georgia's Rose Revolution: A Participant's Perspective*, Special Report, vol. 167 (Washington, DC: United States Institute of Peace, 2006); Cory Welt, "Regime Weakness and Electoral Breakthrough in Georgia," in Bunce, McFaul, and Stoner-Weiss, *Democracy and Authoritarianism in the Postcommunist World*, 155–88; and Jonathan Wheatley, *Georgia from National Awakening to Rose Revolution: Delayed Transition in the Former Soviet Union* (Burlington, VT: Ashgate, 2005).

15. See Anders Åslund and Michael McFaul, *Revolution in Orange: The Origins of Ukraine's Democratic Breakthrough* (Washington, DC: Carnegie Endowment for International Peace, 2006); Anika Locke Binnendijk and Ivan Marovic, "Power and Persuasion: Nonviolent Strategies to Influence State Security Forces in Serbia (2000) and Ukraine (2004)," *Communist and Post-Communist Studies* 39, no. 3 (September 2006): 422–25; and Taras Kuzio, "From Kuchma to Yushchenko: Ukraine's 2004 Presidential Elections

308    *V. J. Bunce and S. L. Wolchik*

and the Orange Revolution," *Problems of Post-Communism* 52, no. 2 (March–April 2005): 29–44.

16. See Matthew Fuhrmann, "A Tale of Two Social Capitals: Revolutionary Collective Action in Kyrgyzstan," *Problems of Postcommunism* 53, no. 6 (November–December 2006): 16–29, and Scott Radnitz, "A Horse of a Different Color: Revolution and Regression in Kyrgyzstan," in Bunce, McFaul, and Stoner-Weiss, *Democracy and Authoritarianism in the Postcommunist World*, 300–324.

17. Lucan A. Way, "Authoritarian State Building and the Sources of Regime Competitiveness in the Fourth Wave: The Cases of Belarus, Moldova, Russia, and Ukraine," *World Politics* 57, no. 2 (January 2005): 231–61, and Henry Hale, "Democracy or Autocracy on the March? The Colored Revolutions as Normal Dynamics of Patronal Presidentialism," *Communist and Postcommunist Studies* 39 (2006): 305–29.

18. See, especially, the debate about the role of structural factors, short-term influences, and diffusion in this wave of electoral change that took place in these issues of the *Journal of Democracy*: Lucan Way, "The Real Causes of the Color Revolutions," 19, no. 3 (July 2008): 55–69; Valerie Bunce and Sharon Wolchik, "Getting Real about Real Causes," 20, no. 1 (January 2009): 69–73; and Mark Beissinger, "An Interrelated Wave," 20, no. 1 (January 2009): 74–77.

19. See Bunce and Wolchik, *Defeating Authoritarian Leaders in Postcommunist Countries,* chap. 9.

20. See Andreas Schedler, ed., *Electoral Authoritarianism: The Dynamics of Unfree Competition* (Boulder, CO: Lynne Rienner, 2006); Larry Diamond, "Thinking about Hybrid Regimes," *Journal of Democracy* 13 (April 2002): 21–35; Philip G. Roessler and Marc M. Howard, "Post-Cold-War Political Regimes: When Do Elections Matter?" 101–27, and Andreas Schedler, "Sources of Competition under Electoral Authoritarianism," 179–201, both in Lindberg, *Democratization by Elections.*

21. Bunce and Wolchik, *Defeating Authoritarian Leaders in Postcommunist Countries,* chap. 4.

22. On the issue of the role of opposition division and unity, see Vladimir Gelman, "Political Opposition in Russia: A Dying Species?" *Post-Soviet Affairs* 3 (2005): 226–46; Nicolas Van de Walle, "Tipping Games: When Do Opposition Parties Coalesce?" in Schedler, *Electoral Authoritarianism*, pp. 77–94; and Marc Morjé Howard and Philip G. Roessler, "Liberalizing Electoral Outcomes in Competitive Authoritarian Regimes," *American Journal of Political Science* 50, no. 2 (April 2006): 362–68. On parallel vote tabulation, see Larry Garber and Glenn Cowan, "The Virtues of Parallel Vote Tabulations," *Journal of Democracy* 4 (April 2003): 95–107.

23. For evidence on this point, see Jasna Milosevic-Djordjevic, "Cinioci izborne apstinencije u Srbiji," in Zoran Lutovac, ed., *Politicke stranke u Srbiji: Struktura and funkcionisanje* (Belgrade: Friedrich Ebert Stiftung/Institut drustvenih Nauka, 2005), and Bunce and Wolchik, "Getting Real."

24. We draw here on the terminology of Mark Beissinger, *Nationalist Mobilization and the Collapse of the Soviet State* (Cambridge: Cambridge University Press, 2002).

25. Bunce and Wolchik, *Defeating Authoritarian Leaders in Postcommunist Countries,* chaps. 5–9.

26. This comparison between successful and failed attempts to defeat authoritarian leaders is elaborated in Bunce and Wolchik, *Defeating Authoritarian Leaders in Postcom-*

*munist Countries,* chap. 11; Valerie J. Bunce and Sharon L. Wolchik, "Bringing Down Dictators: Successful Versus Failed Electoral Revolutions in Postcommunist Europe and Eurasia," in Lindberg, *Democratization by Elections,* 246–68; and Valerie J. Bunce and Sharon L. Wolchik, "Defeating Dictators: Electoral Change and Stability in Competitive Authoritarian Regimes," *World Politics* 62, no. 1 (January 2010): 43–86.

27. Bunce and Wolchik, *Defeating Authoritarian Leaders in Postcommunist Countries,* chap. 10, "A Regional Tradition."

28. See, for example, Gale Stokes, *The Walls Came Tumbling Down: The Collapse of Communism in Eastern Europe* (New York: Oxford University Press, 1993).

29. Albert Hirschman, *The Passions and the Interests: Political Arguments for Capitalism before Its Triumph* (Princeton: Princeton University Press, 1977); Dennis Chong, *Collective Action and the Civil Rights Movement* (Chicago: University of Chicago Press, 1991); and Sidney G. Tarrow, *The New Transnational Activism,* Cambridge Studies in Contentious Politics (Cambridge: Cambridge University Press, 2005).

30. Valerie Bunce, "The Political Economy of Postsocialism," *Slavic Review* 58, no. 4 (Winter 1999): 756–93, and Michael McFaul, "The Fourth Wave of Democracy and Dictatorship: Noncooperative Transitions in the Postcommunist World," *World Politics* 54, no. 2 (January 2002): 212–44.

31. Brinks and Coppedge, "Diffusion Is No Illusion."

# Conclusion

## Nathan J. Brown and Craig M. Kauffman

In this book, we have explored the ways in which democracy emerges, the record of its performance, and the possibilities of it being consciously promoted. We have learned that democratization cannot be understood without probing the nature of authoritarianism; that it seems to have some benefits; and that efforts to promote it can have some effects, but expectations should be specific and modest. And we have implicitly suggested that the attention of those interested in democratization is often best focused on decades rather than dramatic moments or long historical epochs.

To expand on these findings, we should return to the three questions that have motivated this book. But after exploring our answer to these questions, we will probe what we may still be missing.

### What Causes a Democracy to Emerge and Then Maintains It?

In the introduction, we claimed that this volume is perhaps most helpful in pointing where to look if we wish to find out how democracies emerge and are sustained. We can now be more specific, referring to temporal and economic aspects of the question as well as the way to select relevant cases. Having done so, we are able to see how most authors point to the necessity of linking understandings of democratization with far better understandings of authoritarianism.

First, in temporal terms, the authors largely focus on what might be called a medium-term perspective. They rarely reach back centuries; the articles here buck the determinism that characterized some of the older efforts at describing democracy's emergence in broad civilizational, historical, and cultural terms. But neither do they focus on the to-and-fro of the transition moment.

Indeed, the authors implicitly devalue the importance of such moments and rarely speak of them. It is not just that the process of democratization—and especially its consolidation—takes place over such a range of years. More subtly, a historical range is necessary to understand the trajectory of change: historical and institutional legacies loom large in many of the chapters included here. Democratization can bring dramatic change, but it does not create a wholly new political system. Sorting through the historical and institutional factors that are significant is a major concern for most of our authors. They find no single cause or path leading to the emergence of democracy but do show how the historical and institutional legacies that emerge over the medium term play a crucial role in shaping the democratization process and outcomes.

Second, in economic terms, we also have a shift in focus to the medium term, but this time looking forward more than backward. Those authors who have examined here the ways in which economic patterns affect democratization have helped redirect most of our attention from the birth of democracy to its stability. Cheibub and Vreeland in very broad ways and Lindberg and Meerow more narrowly lead us to concentrate on asking how economic development patterns affect the consolidation of democracy.

Third, in terms of case selection, this volume at first glance may seem to be based on two contrasting views. One emphasizes the regionally grounded nature of democratization (the chapters on Latin American, the former Soviet states, China, the Arab world, and Africa) and assumes that region is a conceptually relevant category, or at least a valuable tool for studying similar cases. Others (Cheibub and Vreeland, Fish, Hale, and Gerring) take a broadly global view, examining an enormous range of cases without attempting to situate them in a regional context. But this distinction is less than meets the eye, because no author insists that his or her approach negates the justification for any other (and, indeed, most of the contributors have presented work outside of this volume that is either much more or much less regionally grounded than the chapter contained here). The larger-scope studies are useful for showing general patterns and teasing out specific relationships; the more regionally centered ones can help us probe the complexity and multiplicity of patterns of change.

The real vision that unites more than divides the contributors is the interest in studying a wide variety of types of cases—authoritarian, unstable democracies, hybrid regimes, consolidated democracies, and so on—rather than simply those countries that have undergone something identifiable as a transition. Some chapters actually focus far more on varieties of authoritarianism than on democracy in their efforts to understand democratization and its absence.

And that leads us to a more general finding: a book about democratization cannot go more than a few pages without delving back into the subject of authoritarianism. The tendency of much work on democratization—to treat authoritarianism as a residual category for all regimes that are not democratic or that precede a democracy—serves us poorly in our efforts to understand democratization. We have alluded already to some ways in which our authors insist on a more nuanced understanding of nondemocratic systems in explorations of democratization—historical and institutional legacies matter and shape the myriad ways in which democracies develop and wither.

But there is another reason why the contributions here demonstrate how the study of democratization and authoritarianism must go hand in hand as well as how the study of democratization necessarily relies on more sophisticated understandings of the varieties of authoritarianism—many of the structures, institutions, and practices that we take to be fundamental to democratic life (elections, political parties, parliaments) are very much present in nondemocratic systems. Many of the chapters in this volume have been devoted to efforts at understanding precisely how those structures, institutions, and practices operate in ways that sustain and undermine authoritarianism and democracy.

## Does Democracy Make Things Better?

We claimed in the introduction that on balance and over the long term, democracy probably has some beneficial effects. It should now be clear why such a highly hedged statement is helpful—it directs us away from the impossibly big answers to the more helpful nuances. First, it is necessary to say "on balance" because there are many different things that we might want to measure—even restricting ourselves primarily to the economic sphere (as we have largely done here) still leaves many possible measures. Second, it is necessary to say "over the long term" because—as Gerring argues convincingly—any claimed benefits of democratic governance are likely to be felt most clearly not immediately but only over a period of many years. Finally, it is necessary to say "probably" because the topic is so complex, the ways of examining the relationship between economic performance and governance so many, and the results sometimes so mixed that it is important to remember that we are dealing with findings that will always need to be qualified and tentative.

It should also be noted that the contributors to this volume have worked carefully against conflation: finding some evidence of relationships between democratic governance and policy performance should not lead us to elide carelessly among all things we deem good (freedom, democracy, prosperity) but instead inspire us to tease out what are likely to be complex causal relationships.

## Can Democracy Be Promoted?

Yes, but democracy promotion is slow and uncertain work.

International conditions do affect the likelihood and course of democratization. But those conditions must work through domestic structures to have any effect. And stating that international conditions matter is not the same as saying that they can be consciously manipulated, as democracy promotion efforts aim to do. The essays in this volume that focus on international conditions do show that conscious efforts can have some effects, but if we take the three articles in the section on diffusion together, we would have to conclude that these effects are subtle, working sometimes at the margins of political dynamics, and that they vary over time and place. And (as with the other two questions) the most appropriate time horizon is measured in years or decades. And the efforts to affect the possibilities and nature of democratizing outcomes are not the monopoly of governments or even of those who promote democracy—prodemocracy activists and those seeking to counter their efforts have been very much at work in some cases.

## Is There Anything We Are Still Missing?

Finally, let us turn our attention to what we may still be missing in our study of democratization. And here we might best frame the question by comparing the tone of studies of democratization with those that focus on established democracies: what do those who study well-established democracies assume about how those systems work that those who are interested in the emergence of democracies pass over? The most striking difference between studies of democracy and those on democratization is one of tone. Whereas studies of democratization implicitly emphasize the benefits of democracy, studies of established democracies note their shortcomings, problems, and even crises. Three sorts of problems emerge in those writings.

First, policy performance of established democracies is often disappointing, particularly in meeting economic crisis. More fundamentally, perhaps, existing democracies often seem to be unable to address issues of inequality. In democracy's early days up to the second half of the twentieth century, it was seen as a form of government that would naturally produce policies favorable toward economic equality. The majority, if it ruled, would do so in its own benefit. But democracy today seems often to be predicated on the exclusion of basic questions of social and economic equality from the political realm.[1] Second, the quality of political discourse in established democracies has deeply troubled normative political theorists and led to a burgeoning interest in the possibilities for "deliberative democracy"—governance by public discussion, political argumentation based on public reason and persuasion rather than haggling and hectoring, and an almost didactic public life. Third, works on the United States and western Europe note a host of related problems of "governability" or sometimes of a "crisis of participation"—a focus among political leaders on the contest for political authority that makes that authority more difficult to use once it is won because of deepening partisanship, increasing political alienation and cynicism, and abandonment of political parties among the broader society.

Oddly, such writings on what might be called the quality of democracy have not shown growing influence over studies of democratization despite the greater interest in hybrid regimes, semiauthoritarianism, and other explorations of the resemblance between varieties of authoritarianism and varieties of democracy. To be sure, there has always been some crossover of analysis. As was mentioned in the introduction, the narrowing of the political field in democratic polities—the necessity to trade concerns for economic equality in the effort to build democracy—was an early (though largely forgotten) theme of the early literature on transitions from authoritarianism. And talk of a "crisis of representation" began soon after South American democracies were reestablished in the 1980s and 1990s.[2] But the influence of critiques of existing democracies on studies of democratization is still limited.

Most likely, the normative pull of democracy is still so strong on both activists and scholars that the problems afflicting established democracy have done little to inhibit the attractiveness of democracy or to color the scholarly agenda of those who study democratization. Focusing on the warts of existing democracies may spark suspicions that it will lead to minimizing its appeal. In this sense, the study of democracy is still inseparable from normative concerns. And perhaps that is as it should be. But one of this volume's central themes—that it is difficult to understand democracy and democratization without understanding authoritarianism—should lead us also to be alert to the ways in which democratizing and semiauthoritarian regimes can partake of some of the features of democratic ones—including, perhaps, some of their flaws. We might be able to learn far more about policy performance in democracies, the quality and nature of their deliberations and arguments, and the ways that they experience crises of governability and representation by exploring their origins (i.e., democratizing regimes) and their hybrid (i.e., semiauthoritarian) cousins.

If we may close with a message to those who might be most interested not in academic fashions but in practical results, we would emphasize that there are clear implications of this volume for the democracy-promotion industry. Messianism and manic mood swings should be avoided: democracy emerges slowly and is no panacea. Those expecting immediate democracy and a host of immediate benefits will likely be disappointed. Worse, their efforts may backfire by causing disillusionment.

And here there is an ironic lesson indeed: democracy promotion cannot be tied to the electoral cycle.

NOTES

1. See, for instance, Thomas Frank, *What's the Matter with Kansas* (New York: Metropolitan Books, 2004).
2. Jorge Dominguez, "Latin America's Crisis of Representation," *Foreign Affairs* 76, no. 1 (1997): 100–113.

# Contributors

*Gregg A. Brazinsky* is an associate professor of history and international affairs at the George Washington University. He is the author of *Nation Building in South Korea: Koreans, Americans and the Making of a Democracy* (2007).

*Nathan J. Brown* is professor of political science and international affairs at the George Washington University and nonresident senior associate at the Carnegie Endowment for International Peace. He is author of four books as well as the forthcoming *Participation Not Domination: Islamist Movements and Semiauthoritarian Politics in the Arab World* (2011).

*Kathleen Bruhn* is professor of political science at the University of California at Santa Barbara. Her work has focused on political parties and social movements in Latin America.

*Valerie J. Bunce* is professor of government and the Aaron Binenkorb Chair of International Studies at Cornell University. She is the coauthor (with Sharon Wolchik) of *Democratizing Elections, Diffusion, and Democracy Assistance* (2011).

*José Antonio Cheibub* is professor of political science at the University of Illinois at Urbana-Champaign where he also serves as Boeschenstein Professor of Political Economy and Public Policy. His most recent book is *Presidentialism, Parliamentarism, and Democracy* (2007).

*Bruce J. Dickson* is professor of political science and international affairs at the George Washington University. His research concentrates on political dynamics in China, particularly the adaptability of the Chinese Communist Party.

*M. Steven Fish* is professor of political science at the University of California at Berkeley. His most recent book is *Are Muslims Distinctive? A Comparative Analysis of Muslims and Non-Muslims in Social and Political Life* (2011).

*John Gerring* is professor of political science at Boston University, where he teaches courses on methodology and comparative politics. His books include *A Centripetal Theory of Democratic Governance* (2008), *Social Science Methodology: Tasks, Strategies, and Criteria* (2011), and *Democracy and Development: A Historical Perspective* (in preparation).

*Henry E. Hale* is associate professor of political science and international affairs at the George Washington University. He is the author of *The Foundations of Ethnic Politics* (2008), *Why Not Parties in Russia?* (2006), and a manuscript in progress under the working title *Great Expectations: The Politics of Regime Change in Eurasia*.

*Susan D. Hyde* is an assistant professor of political science and international affairs at Yale University. Her published research focuses on democracy promotion, elections, and international influences on the domestic politics of sovereign states.

*Craig M. Kauffman* is a Ph.D. candidate in political science at the George Washington University whose research interests include democratization, decentralization, and local governance. His dissertation examines the role of transnational actors in shaping local governance reforms in Ecuador and has been supported by the Inter-American Foundation, the Rotary Foundation, and the Facultad Latinoamericana de Ciencias Sociales Sede Ecuador.

*Staffan I. Lindberg* is associate professor in the Department of Political Science and the Center for African Studies at the University of Florida. He is also holds positions as research fellow for the World Values Survey, affiliated researcher at the Quality of Government Institute, and associate professor in the Department of Political Science at Gothenburg University (Sweden).

*Sara Meerow* is a student in the International Development Studies program at the University of Amsterdam.

*James Raymond Vreeland* is associate professor at the Edmund A. Walsh School of Foreign Service and the Department of Government, Georgetown University. He has also held teaching and research affiliations with universities on five continents including Bond University (Australia), ESADE (Spain), Georg-August-Universität Göttingen (Germany), the KOF Swiss Economic Institute at ETH Zürich, Korea University, University of California at Los Angeles, Universidad Nacional de San Martín (Argentina), University of São Paulo, and Yale University.

*Sharon L. Wolchik* is professor of political science and international affairs at George Washington University. She is currently doing research on the use of elections to remove semi-authoritarian leaders with Valerie J. Bunce and is coauthor with Valerie J. Bunce of *Democratizing Elections, Diffusion, and Democracy Assistance* (2011).

# Index

AARP, 217
Abrams, Elliot, 258, 260
accountability, 31, 71, 138, 215–16, 226;
  economic, 219; mechanisms for, 217–18
Acemoglu, Daron, 162, 170–73
ACLU, 217
activism, 3, 9, 53, 61, 100, 241–43, 285,
  288–89, 291
Afghanistan, 8
Africa, 25, 31, 64, 76; and constitutionalism,
  125; and legislatures, 126
Afrikaners, 23
Akayev, Askar, 290
Algeria, 55
Aliyev, Heydar, 135–36
Aliyev, Ilham, 135
All-China Federation of Trade Unions, 101
Alliance for Progress, 254–55
Alvarez, Mike, 156, 159–60, 162–67, 170
American Geographical Society, 250
American Left, 257
American Political Science Association, 12
Angola, 183, 189–90, 266
Apartheid, 35
Arabian Peninsula, 49
Arab nationalism, 55
Arafat, Yasser, 55
Arat, Zehra, 151
Arce, Moises, 73
Argentina, 3, 6, 66, 69, 74, 80, 154, 259
aristocracy, 153, 217
Aristotle, 4
Armenia, 285

asset specificity, 158–59
Aung San Suu Kyi, 101
Australia, 122
Austria, 163
authoritarianism, 1; adaptation of, 21; collapse
  of, 3, 6–9, 20, 148, 269, 284, 288, 290;
  economic development and, 11, 143, 145,
  147, 153, 157, 161, 169, 212; and elections,
  266; emergence of, 5–6; evolution of, 226;
  and institutional complexity, 150; nature of,
  13; and popular support for, 272; and power,
  226; and restriction, 222, 284; retrenchment
  of, 133, 185, 188, 197; and rule-of-law, 225;
  stability of, 11–13, 18, 21, 52, 94–114, 157,
  185–87, 198, 218, 292; transition from, 87,
  149, 173, 188, 214–19, 240–41, 284; varieties
  of, 17, 34, 214, 291; weakening of, 9–12,
  18–19
"axis of evil," 262
Azerbaijan, 135–36, 285

Bahrain, 50
bargaining, 9, 56, 224
Bates, Robert, 158
Beijing, 109–10
Belarus, 136
Belgium, 163
Belgrade, 110
Bellinger, Paul, 73
Benin, 127, 129, 137
Bhutan, 266
Bishkek, 290
blackmail, 37–38

Boix, Charles, 158–66, 170
Bolivia, 66, 73–75
Bolshevism, 247
Bongo, Omar, 134
Bosnia, 8
Botswana, 190
bourgeois democracy, 68
Bowman, Isaiah, 250
boycott, 54–56, 275
Bozizé, François, 135
Bratton, Michael, 183, 199
Brazil, 69, 74, 154, 174, 254
Britain, 250
British Parliament, 120
Bryn Mawr College, 247
Bueno de Mesquita, Bruce, 98
Bulgaria, 165, 287–89, 291
Burkina Faso, 127, 194
Bush, George W., 261–62
business confidence, 32, 40

Cameroon, 192
Canada, 122, 162
capitalism, 74, 84, 96, 106–7, 153, 155, 225
Carothers, Thomas, 25, 269
Carrefour, 110
Carter, Jimmy, 258–59
Castro, Fidel, 254
Catholicism, 157
censorship, 99
Center for International Studies (CENIS), 252
Central African Republic, 128, 135
Chad, 135
charitable organizations, 58
Chavez, Hugo, 74
Chen Liangyu, 97
Chen Xitong, 97
Children's Defense Fund, 217
Chile, 6, 66, 69, 74, 154, 260
China, 21, 284; and dissent, 101; and economic growth/reform, 93, 97, 103–4, 148; and elections, 266; and international relations, 93, 97, 251, 258–59; and modernization, 154; and pervasiveness of regime, 216; and political reform, 94, 273;

and regime stability, 94–95; and restriction of information access, 99–100, 113; and restriction of political freedoms, 98; and the World Trade Organization, 146
China Democratic Party, 100
Chinese Communist Party (CCP), 21; and capitalists, 97, 106; and economic reform, 107, 148; and equitable growth, 107–8; and higher education, 99; ideology of, 97; institutionalization of, 111–12; and labor, 101, 108; leaders of, 96; and the opposition, 95, 101; popular support for, 95, 104, 109–11, 114; and the public, 94; and reform, 94, 97, 104; and renunciation of class struggle, 96; and repression, 98–99, 103–4, 109; United Front Department of, 102
Christian parties, 58
citizenship, 222, 272
civil liberties, 60, 87, 190, 193–94, 201–13, 269, 291; and democracy, 227
civil rights movement (United States), 222
civil society: and accountability, 82, 217; and authoritarian regimes, 216; definition of, 216; and democratization, 7, 9, 119, 137, 213, 215–16, 226; and economic development, 151–52, 170; emergence of, 150, 217; and liberalization, 188; and mobilization, 183; and the regime, 102; strength of, 172, 216–17; types of, 102, 105; weakness of, 100–101
civil war, 32, 133, 174, 269–70
class structure, 151–52, 155, 165, 174, 218, 222–23
Clinton, Bill, 146
coalition governments, 76
coercion: and authoritarian rule, 94–96, 103, 109, 114, 150, 186, 221, 225; costs of, 100; decline in usage of, 97–98; and the "harmonious society" in China, 108–9
Cold War, 5, 69–84, 133, 146–54, 183–202, 239–42, 251–52, 259–60, 271–72, 274, 279
collective action, 13
collective goods, 212
Collier, Paul, 166
colonialism, 156, 171–72, 250, 256
Color Revolutions, the, 39